CW00536821

2 2 JUN 1992

ENGLISH BOOKS & READERS
1475 to 1557

By the same author

ENGLISH
BOOKS & READERS
1558 TO 1603

ENGLISH
BOOKS & READERS
1475 to 1557

BEING A STUDY IN
THE HISTORY OF THE BOOK TRADE FROM
CAXTON TO THE INCORPORATION OF
THE STATIONERS' COMPANY

BY

H. S. BENNETT

*Fellow of the British Academy and formerly Reader in English
in the University of Cambridge*

SECOND EDITION

CAMBRIDGE
AT THE UNIVERSITY PRESS
1970

Published by the Syndics of the Cambridge University Press
Bentley House, 200 Euston Road, London, N.W. 1
American Branch: 32 East 57th Street, New York, N.Y. 10022

This edition © Cambridge University Press 1969

ISBN 0 521 07609 9

First edition 1952
Second edition 1969
Reprinted 1970

First printed in Great Britain
at the University Printing House, Cambridge
Reprinted in Great Britain by
Lewis Reprints Limited, Port Talbot, Glamorgan

TO
J. B.
1921-1951

PREFACE

The writing of this book has been made possible largely by the work of others. First, there is the *Short-title Catalogue* edited by A. W. Pollard and G. R. Redgrave, and published by the Bibliographical Society in 1926. From this the titles of most books printed in the period 1475–1557 can be discovered, and the researcher would be like a semi-blind man without it. Secondly comes the rearrangement of the alphabetical items of the *Short-title Catalogue* in chronological sequence, making it possible for the student to see at once the names of all the books published in one year. This most valuable work we owe to the enterprise of Mr William A. Jackson, Director of the Houghton Library, Harvard University. Thirdly, while at the University of Chicago in 1948, I discovered that Dr Paul G. Morrison, Curator of Rare Books, had analysed the short-title entries under their respective printers, thus making it possible to see exactly what each printer had done.[1] Dr Morrison generously gave me access to this material, so that from these three sources I was able for the first time to compile a list of the books printed in this period, and to arrange them at will under their authors, their printers, or their dates of publication. It has thus become possible to ascertain more exactly a great many things about our earliest printed books and their printers that were formerly matters of hopeful guessing. It is upon such a groundwork that this study has been constructed.

The present work has a fourfold purpose. First it endeavours to establish what was the cultural situation when Caxton began to print. This involves a survey of fifteenth-century manuscript conditions, the ways in which authors obtained a hearing, and the size and nature of the reading public. From this it

---

[1] This work has since been published by the Bibliographical Society of the University of Virginia (1950), under the title of *Index of Printers, Publishers and Booksellers in 'A Short-title Catalogue...1475-1640.'*

goes on to consider Caxton's work as a bridge between the manuscript era and the age of print, and this in turn leads to a detailed study of the work of his immediate successors in stabilizing and developing the new craft.

Next an attempt is made to give a complete view of the output of the printers once they were reasonably well established by 1500. By the use of the aids mentioned above it has been possible to make an analysis of the 5000 books printed by 1557, listed in the *Short-title Catalogue*, so that now we can see how the various branches of knowledge and the everyday interests of men were served by the printers. Great use has been made of the introductory matter often found in the shape of a dedicatory letter or an address to the reader, for from these may be seen the reasons which have prompted the writing or printing of the book, and the hopes and fears of its progenitors. In short, my endeavour has been to get behind the printed word and the physical appearance of the book to the conditions which gave it significance and to the readers whose support was essential for its success.

The printed word and physical appearance of the book have not been neglected, however, for in the final chapters the making of a book from the reception of the manuscript to its appearance on the bookseller's stall is considered in detail. This has been made possible by the accumulation of a mass of information, most of it of seemingly slight importance, but which falls into its place as part of the total picture. The comparatively small change which appears to have taken place in printing-house practice throughout this period makes the production of this composite 'still' a reasonably true picture.

Apart from my reliance on a number of standard works by Gordon Duff and other bibliographers, a study of this kind owes much to the co-operation of scholars and librarians to whom I have so often turned. First I should mention the late Librarian of the Cambridge University Library (Mr A. F. Scholfield), and his successor (Mr H. R. Creswick), who gave me special facilities for consulting the early printed books in their custody, and by so doing greatly eased my labours. The University Library is particularly rich in books of this period, and it was of the greatest assistance to be able to use them so freely.

While the rules of the British Museum cannot be expected to allow such privileges to one of their many readers, Mr H. Sellers and the staff of the North Library were untiring in meeting my demands, which the nature of my inquiry made heavier than is normal. Not only this, but the help rendered so generously by officials of the Library when consulted on technical points made it a pleasure and an education to work there.

It would be ungenerous of me if I did not also mention the great help I obtained in what might well be thought one of the last places where the study of our early printed books could be pursued—the Library of the University of Chicago. Thanks to the enlightened policy of the authorities, the University has a large collection of microfilms of these books, and a wealth of equipment for their use. During my stay there as visiting Professor I made almost daily use of these facilities, and my work profited accordingly.

Finally, I have to thank the Leverhulme Trustees for the award of a Fellowship for 1947-9, which enabled me to prosecute my work more actively and rapidly than otherwise would have been possible.

In the many quotations I have made from the books of the period certain liberties have been taken. While the spelling of the original has been preserved, capitalization and punctuation have often been modified to suit the needs of the modern reader, and *i* and *u* have replaced *j* and *v* in accordance with modern usage, and occasionally an overlong paragraph has been broken up for ease of reading.

H. S. B.

DECEMBER, 1951

CONTENTS

PROLOGUE

On 20 August 1556 Sir William More of Loseley House in Surrey drew up an inventory of his household goods, in the course of which he gives a picture of a well-to-do country gentleman's library at that time.[1] On the walls hung maps of the world, of England, Scotland and France, a perpetual almanack and one small picture. A globe, a counter-board and cast of counters with which to make calculations and cast accounts, and a slate for memoranda stood about the room. Upon his desk were various accessories such as a pair of compasses, an inkstand of pewter, a pounce box, pens of bone and of steel, a penknife and other odds and ends. But the chief contents of the room were the books and manuscripts, which ran to about one hundred and forty in number, and were written in many languages—particularly English, French and Italian, although a few works in Latin were also to be seen. It is the English books, however, that principally concern us, and these numbered nearly one hundred. Among them were some of the best known chronicles of the time compiled by Hardyng, Fabian, Carion and Arnold; a number of translations from the classics; some religious works, amongst them the Bible, Hilton's *Scale of Perfection*, and a New Testament. In addition there were medical treatises on the use of leeches, or the treatment of the sweat, the well-known *Glass of Health* and a book on physic and one on surgery. Practical affairs were not ignored, for Sir William had volumes on surveying, geometry, cosmography, the treatment of horses and the names of those paying Knight's fees in Surrey. Then as a Justice of the Peace he had at hand a number of volumes containing the Statutes from the earliest times until his own day. He had also a stock of smaller treatises which set out such legal

[1] J. Evans, 'Extracts from the Private Account Book of Sir W. More', *Archaeologia*, vol. XXXVI (1855), pp. 284–92.

xiii

matters and formularies as would be likely to concern a country justice. For his recreation (apart from his French and Italian works) he could turn to his copy of Chaucer, to Gower's *Confessio Amantis*, to translations by Lydgate, and the more recent work of Barclay and Skelton. For lighter moments he had several little books of ballads, songs, proverbs or fables. One of his most recent purchases must have been John Heywood's *The spider and the flie*, 'a parable', printed by T. Powell in 1556.

His books in foreign languages may be more briefly described. Latin was represented by Caesar, Horace, Juvenal, Cicero, Suetonius and others; French by Froissart and minor works; Italian by Boccaccio, Petrarch and Machiavelli, and translations into Italian of the New Testament and Ovid.

Here then was the library of a man well enough off to indulge his tastes, and no doubt few of his Surrey neighbours could have displayed such a library. Indeed, it may well be that throughout the country there were not many private libraries better stocked with such a variety of books,[1] but Sir William's collection is an example of what could be done, given the means and the initiative.

How this state of affairs had been brought about by the middle of the sixteenth century will be the subject of the following chapters.

---

[1] Captain Cox's celebrated library of 1575 may usefully be compared with that of Sir William. Cox was a Coventry mason, and had a remarkable collection of English books—romances, tales, jest-books, plays, riddles, ballads, etc. See F. J. Furnivall, *Robert Laneham's Letters*, New Shakespeare Society, ser. 6, no. XIV (1890), pp. xii ff.

CHAPTER I

CAXTON AND HIS LITERARY HERITAGE

The profession of letters has always been a precarious one, and before the advent of printing the lot of the writer was even more unenviable than it was to become in subsequent centuries. We are so accustomed to the highly organized arrangements which exist nowadays in order to bring a writer's wares before the widest possible public that we are apt to forget how comparatively modern they are, and that the medieval author had little or no means of foreseeing what demand there would be for his work. An impenetrable fog of ignorance or, at best, of uncertainty left him without knowledge of the work of others. For example, during the fifteenth century, three separate translations were made of the travels of Sir John Mandeville, two of the translators not knowing that the work had already been done. Many other instances might be given to illustrate this difficulty, and on the whole writers were wise to go ahead, oblivious of the labours of others, for the circulation of medieval manuscripts was a fortuitous and patchy affair looked at from a modern point of view.

This patchiness was largely the result of dialect differences in various parts of the country, which made the reading of a work by a London author a matter of difficulty for a reader north of the Trent. Chaucer speaks of the 'gret diversite In Englissh and in writyng of oure tonge', while nearly a century later Caxton is vexed by the same difficulty, and after much thought and research decides that the best he can do is to use 'Englysshe not ouer rude, ne curyous, but in suche termes as shall be understanden by goddyes grace'. Most authors, therefore, found their circulation limited by peculiarities of dialect, and even more perhaps by the uncertain and wellnigh unpredictable nature of the demand for their works. This, it would seem, must have been largely a matter of personal recommendation or perhaps arose from the hearing of a work read in the house of others. The well-known illumination which serves as a frontispiece to the manuscript of *Troilus and Criseyde* in the library of Corpus Christi College, Cambridge, shows Chaucer reading to the Court, and the whole poem (in common with many medieval poems) is full of references to listeners. As a result of friendly comment and recommendation, the author could hope for a demand for copies of his work by those interested and able to afford the heavy expense entailed. How much this helped the author financially it is impossible to determine. If copies of his work were made by professional scriveners in the ordinary course of their business, we may imagine that the author got some recompense for the loan of his manuscript. On the other hand, it was not easy to prevent unauthorized reproduction. Once a copy of the original had left the author's hands it was impossible for him to control its recopying. That such a thing could happen we know from the complaints of Guillaume de Deguileville, who tells us in the preface to his *Pèlerinage de la vie humaine*, that

he first wrote down his dream in 1330, but intended to correct and revise it. It was stolen from him and published abroad throughout the world. The thief had little thought of the author's profit. Until the theft he had been free to cut out passages and add others as he wished; but this unauthorized publication has taken away this freedom. Now after 25 years he has made a thorough revision, which he will send forth to every country where the work has previously been against his will. It ought not to have travelled thus without his leave.[1]

Again, in the fifteenth century, Bishop Pecock complains that some of his books

ben runne abrood and copied aȝens my wil and myn entent, as y have openli prechid at Pauls, and that by uncurtesie and undiscre-

---

[1] Quoted from R. K. Root, 'Publication before Printing', *Publications of the Modern Language Association of America*, vol. XXVIII (1913), p. 428.

cioun of freendis, into whos singular siȝt y lousid the writingis to go, and forto not have go ferther into tyme thei were better examyned of me and approvid of my lordis and fadris of the Churche—Y wole to be as noon of myn: but in as moche as in me is, y wole thei be rendrid up aȝen, and bettir formes of the same be to hem delivered, whanne dewe deliveraunce thereof schal be made.[1]

These very important statements show how impotent an author was, once his work had passed out of his own hands, and how little he could rely on it as a source of income. The conclusion we are forced to is that it was wellnigh impossible, and wellnigh unknown, for an author in medieval times to make a living out of his writings. Granted that he was conscious that a potential need existed, he had first to compose his work, a matter requiring time, materials, privacy—all difficult things to come by—and then, his rough draft completed, he had to get it copied out fairly, and in such a state that it could be offered to someone willing to recompense him for his time and labour. Few writers were willing to struggle for a hearing under such conditions, and fewer could have afforded to do so. It would be difficult to point to any author of repute in the five centuries before Caxton who was primarily an author, and who depended on writing for his living. Most writers were ecclesiastics supported by the Church, or private retainers of some royal or aristocratic family, or men who practised writing only as a hobby or spare-time recreation. The number of writers who were ecclesiastics is overwhelming. In the fourteenth and fifteenth centuries alone we have Robert Mannyng of Brunne, Walter Hilton, Richard Rolle, John Wycliffe, William Langland, John Lydgate, Reginald Pecock, Stephen Hawes, John Capgrave and Osbern Bokenham—to name the most outstanding only. All of these had an assured income—not large, perhaps, but sufficient—and this enabled them to indulge their delight in writing. Those of them who were members of religious Orders may have written at the command

---

[1] *The Donet*, ed. E. V. Hitchcock, Early English Text Society, Ordinary Series, no. 156 (1921), p. 7.

1-2

of their superiors, or to meet known gaps in their own or other monastic libraries. For them, the quiet hours in the *scriptorium* passed by happily enough. Only the recitation of the daily offices and the routine of conventual life broke in upon their placid existence. Their daily bread was assured, their reputation as authors a matter of legitimate pride, both to them and to their brethren. The great chronicles of the monastic writers, such as William of Malmesbury or Matthew Paris, brought fame to them and to their monastery; while the outstanding poet of fifteenth-century England was John Lydgate, monk of the Benedictine Abbey of Bury St Edmunds. It was not without reason that Langland wrote of such a life as the height of worldly bliss:

> For if hevene be on this erthe . and ese to any soule,
> It is in cloistere or in scole . be many skilles I fynde:
> For in cloistere cometh no man . to chide ne to fi3te,
> But alle is buxumnesse there and bokes . to rede and to lerne.[1]

For those who had no such safe anchorage as this, things were precarious. Some, it is true, were attached to a lord, and did what they were told for the main part. Many romances undoubtedly were put into English at the express desire of a lord, as was *William of Palerne*, which was translated:

> For the hende Erl of Herford, sir Humphrey de Bowne,
> The King Edwardes newe, at Glouseter that ligges,
> For he of Frensche this fayre tayle first dyd translate,
> In ese of Englysh men, in Englysch speche,[2]

and this in an earlier stage had been translated from Latin into French by command of Yolande, daughter of Baldwin IV, Count of Hainault. These anonymous translators, like hundreds of their kind, existed to carry out the commands of their lords. Even so great a romance writer as Chrétien de Troyes, and so

---

[1] *skilles*, reasons; *buxumnesse*, obedience, courtesy.
[2] For the fair Earl of Hereford, Sir Humphrey de Bohun, nephew to King Edward, who dwells at Gloucester.
He demanded this fair tale to be translated from French into English, for the convenience of Englishmen.

4

outstanding a chronicler as Froissart, were proud to acknow-
ledge themselves the servants respectively of Marie of Cham-
pagne and of Philippa of Hainault. And just as Marie indicated
the material and manner of treatment (*matiere et sen*) of the
story of the chariot (Lancelot) to Chrétien, so Lord Thomas of
Berkeley gave to his chaplain, John Trevisa, 'obedient and
buxom to work your will' explicit directions concerning the
translation of Ralph Higden's books of chronicles. Not only
did he select the subject-matter, but also laid it down that the
translation was to be in prose, 'for commonly prose is more
clear than rhyme, more easy and more plain to know and
understand'. The lord paid the piper, and was entitled to call
the tune! This he did; and a great part of the second-rate prose
and verse that was composed is as much a reflection of the
patron's taste as of the author's shortcomings. But at least the
wretched poet had a modest position in the household, and
could look with complacency on those who from time to time
appeared at his lord's castle and provided an evening's entertainment while they recited items from their repertoire. How
much of what they sang was their own is doubtful. In all
probability it was but little. These minstrels of the later Middle
Ages were for the most part only the peripatetic circulating
libraries of their day. Even if the early minstrels had been
original composers, the later ones were chiefly executants. The
man of letters could hope for no assured or happy way of
existence by sharing with them the life of the roads. What that
meant can be read in the graphic poems of the French minstrels
Rutebeuf and Villon.

Whether in monastic cell or in castled turret, these writers
were essentially men who wrote to order. The privilege of
writing what one liked was a more expensive hobby, and
postulated a source of income not dependent on one's writings.
Chaucer is the most famous of such authors in England, but we
are so accustomed to think of Chaucer the poet, that we forget
Chaucer the King's envoy, the controller of customs on wool,
hides and sheepskins, or the subforester of North Petherton.

Yet it was because of the economic security these offices gave him that it was possible for him to turn to poetry in his leisure. For this is what he did at the end of the day's work, as he himself tells us:

> For when thy labour doon al ys,
> And thast mad alle thy rekenynges,
> In stede of reste and newe thynges,
> Thou goost hom to thy hous anoon;
> And, also domb as any stoon,
> Thou sittest at another book
> Tyl fully daswed[1] is thy look,
> And lyvest thus as an hermyte.

It is worth while remembering, however, that while Chaucer wrote as a free agent, it may well be, that if we were fully informed, we should see that some of his works had at least an eye on royalty or the Court. It is hard to believe that *The Book of the Duchess* was written solely to commemorate the death of the wife of John of Gaunt without thought of how it would incline that great noble in the poet's favour. Similarly with other works of Chaucer's: there is some evidence that they were composed to fit in with some great Court occasion. Again John Gower, his contemporary, was an independent country gentleman, whose means allowed him to write in Latin, French and English verse in the hopes of edifying his countrymen. Even so, his English work, the *Confessio Amantis*, as he tells us, was written in reponse to a direct request by Richard II for 'som new thing', and when it was completed Gower wrote a final passage praising the King. Some years later, the poet found it expedient to omit this passage, and to insert a new preface, praising Henry IV! We have no reason to suppose that the Court definitely commissioned any of these pieces; but once they were written it is not difficult to believe that the royal favour (if not the royal purse) was bestowed upon the writers, and to that extent their fame increased and the demand for copies of their work grew.

[1] *daswed*, dazed.

Another group of writers, somewhere between these two classes, may also be discerned. In the late fourteenth and in the fifteenth centuries there was a body of men, for whom writing was a part-time occupation, as with Chaucer, but who, unlike Chaucer, made no bones about the fact that they wrote to supplement their incomes. Thomas Hoccleve is a good example of this. He was a clerk in the office of the King's Privy Seal, but led an extravagant and raffish life out of office hours; and, having some facility at verse-making, was constantly on the qui vive for a patron to whom he could dedicate a poem in return for a reward. He names various wealthy and influential patrons, such as Henry IV, Henry V, Humphrey, Duke of Gloucester and many other less important persons, and writes to various officials, such as the Lord Chancellor, exhorting them to make monetary payments to him. It is clear that Hoccleve lacked the assured official position of a Chaucer, with its fees, robes, annuities and butts of malmsey, or the economic security of Lydgate as a member of one of the richest monastic foundations in England. Such men as Hoccleve were dependent on their patrons only to a lesser extent than those like Trevisa, who spent their life in the service of their lord.

Conditions such as these prevailed until the fifteenth century. By then several radical changes were afoot, all of them more or less the result of the establishment of English as the recognized medium of official correspondence, of the law courts, and of our own literature. During Chaucer's lifetime it became clear that the long drawn out battle between English and French was over, and that henceforth English for the English was to prevail. French gradually ceased to be the language of the aristocracy, and the fifteenth century was not very old before the vernacular was everywhere in control. Once this was so, things began to move rapidly. The demand for reading-matter in English was insistent, and to meet this the multiplication of vernacular manuscripts greatly increased. Wherever we look the evidence confronting us shows writers and scribes eagerly at work seeking to satisfy the newborn demand. No longer was literature the closed preserve of the ecclesiastic and lord, but Latin and French works were hurriedly given an English dress, as books never before available in the vernacular were translated, copied and sent abroad. The growing reading public evidently absorbed this new-found literature with avidity as every known field of knowledge was laid under contribution.

Naturally the response was uneven and uncertain, but the author could make some reasonable assumptions. Religion held such a central place in medieval life that the number of those interested in works of a religious, moral or didactic character was immense. The religious houses required works of spiritual instruction and consolation in the vernacular in growing numbers, especially where nuns and anchoresses were concerned. Their inability to read Latin, or even French, is emphasized by writers who translate works into English for the benefit of their unlettered sisters in the faith. The reader of pious legends, such as those contained in that vast compilation *The Golden Legend*, or in smaller collections, such as those of Lydgate or Bokenham, was catered for. Volumes of pious stories; handbooks of practical help in church worship; books of systematized religious instruction; volumes of sermons and homilies; allegories and lyric poems—all were produced in considerable numbers; and, on the evidence of the number of surviving manuscripts of many of these, we may confidently believe that they achieved a wide circulation.

Works of information, on the other hand, had some preliminary difficulty in finding a public, for there was no such ready-made audience for them as there was for religious works. Even so, their obvious usefulness ensured their eventual circulation, so that grammatical works, glosses, and dictionaries survive in considerable numbers. So do works which provided information on the treatment of horses, hounds and hawks; or books of instruction on how to tend crops and gardens, or how to treat wounds and keep off the plague. Books of etiquette of every sort abounded, while technical

8

manuals concerning the terms and practice of carving, or the placing of a company in due order of precedence were plentiful. Matters of social, political and ecclesiastical interest were dealt with in a popular fashion in easily remembered verses, while the growing demand for English history was met by the production of the *Brut* and of many other national and local chronicles, all written in the vernacular. Finally, the needs of pure literature were far from being ignored. The fifteenth century is notable for the interest it displayed in the setting down of many of the old romances, in the production of the carol and lyric, in the recording of the ballad. The humorous tale and the fable flourished, as well as a mass of lyric poetry of every description.[1]

For us to-day it is impossible to do much more than to record these things in summary fashion, and to make what deductions we will on very general grounds. So much has perished, and in any case the number of manuscripts of any work was so comparatively small that statistics are useless. The proportion of the people to whom literature meant anything must have remained small, although there is evidence of a growing number of literates throughout the century, and Mr C. L. Kingsford's considered opinion may be accepted that

there has been too much readiness to undervalue the culture and civilization of the age. Certainly the capacity to read and write was no longer an accomplishment connfied to the clerical class... The wives and sisters of country gentlemen could often write as well as their husbands and brothers, and both they and their servants could and commonly did keep regular household accounts... In the merchant's office a capacity to read and write must have long been required.[2]

A reading public, in short, had been created, mainly during the fifteenth century, and the conditions were ripe for the

[1] For a fuller treatment of the above, see my article, 'The Production and Dissemination of Vernacular Manuscripts in the Fifteenth Century', *The Library*, Fifth Series, vol. 1 (1947), pp. 167–78.
[2] C. L. Kingsford, *Prejudice and Promise in Fifteenth Century England* (1925), p. 35. And see chapter II.

coming of printing. When Caxton began to make inquiries concerning the feasibility of setting up a press in England, he must have been told by the scriveners of London what a volume of work was occupying them. In their shops Caxton could have seen them making copies of every kind of book from the large folio with illustrations and illuminated borders down to cheap, rapidly executed octavos or smaller sizes, having no merits except a low price which put them within the reach of many. A little further inquiry on Caxton's part would have revealed to him the predominating interest in religious works, and a far from negligible interest in text-books and literary works in verse and prose. Nevertheless, it behoved him to move warily; and, thanks to the invaluable information he provides in the prologues and epilogues to many of his volumes, we have the opportunity of following the hopes and fears with which he put out his wares.

The story begins in the year 1468 at Bruges, where Caxton started to translate the work of Raoul Le Fèvre, entitled *Le recueil des histoires de Troyes*, written in 1464. 'To eschew sloth and idleness', he worked away until he had written five or six quires, when he grew discouraged and laid the work aside. Two years later, while talking to his patroness, Margaret, Duchess of Burgundy, he mentioned this cast-off work, and the Duchess asked to see it. When she had done so, she criticized the quality of the translation, but ordered Caxton to go on, and to complete the work. This 'dredefull comandement', he tells us, 'Y durste in no wyse disobey because y am a servant unto her sayde grace and resseive of her yerly ffee and other many goode and great benefets, and also hope many moo to resseyve of her hyenes'. So he 'forthwyth wente and labouryde in the sayde translacion aftyr my symple and pour connyng'.[1] In so doing, Caxton was following the normal course: the patron commands, the author obeys. A little later, in the epilogue to Book III, Caxton relates the circumstances

---

[1] *The Prologues and Epilogues of William Caxton*, ed. W. J. B. Crotch, Early English Text Society, Ordinary Series, no. 176 (1928), p. 5.

which removed him from the ranks of a mere composer, whose only hope of fame lay in the slow repetition of copies in the scrivener's shop, into the select company of printers who could put on to the market at any given moment, not one or two copies, but hundreds if necessary. He finished his translation on 19 September 1471, and between then and 1472, Caxton learnt the art of printing in Cologne where he helped to produce an edition of Bartholomew the Englishman's *De proprietatibus rerum*. He tells us that he did so because of the demand made to him for copies of his translation of the Troy book while he was still at work on it. He was getting old, and found the labour of copying a heavy burden.

Therfore I have practysed and lerned at my grete charge and dispense to ordeyne this said book in prynte after the maner and forme as ye may here see. And is not wreton with penne and ynke as other bokes ben, to thende that every man may have them attones, for all the bookes of this storye...thus empryntid as ye here see were begonne in oon day, and also fynyshid in oon day, whiche book I have presented to my sayd redoubtid lady...and she hath well acceptid hit, and largely rewarded me.[1]

It will not have escaped notice how important a part his patroness has played in all this. Not only had she seen his early effort at translation, but she had advised Caxton concerning its shortcomings and ordered him to continue. When he had finished it, she accepted it, and rewarded him handsomely. In addition, there can be little doubt that it was her interest that stimulated diverse gentlemen and friends to ask for copies, and so encouraged Caxton to take the momentous step of learning to print, and of putting forth his edition of *The recuyell of the historyes of Troye*, which he published at Bruges in 1475. This was a very substantial volume of just over 700 folio pages, so that it will be realized that its publication was a hazardous venture for a first attempt by a beginner at the craft.

[1] Crotch, *op. cit.* p. 7.

At much the same time,[1] Caxton published another work, *The Game and Playe of the Chesse*, translated again from the French. This was a smaller volume of 148 folio pages, but is further evidence of Caxton's confidence that there was a market for his wares. This time he did not work under a patron's direction; nevertheless, he realized that his chances of success would be increased if some great personage would show him favour, and he dedicated the work to the King of England's brother, Clarence, Earl of Warwick, despite the fact that the Earl was at that time to him 'unknowen'. His worldly wisdom was not misplaced; and this, together with the fact that 'thys sayd book is ful of holsom wysdom and requysyte unto every astate and degree', combined to sell the edition, and he reprinted it in 1483, more convinced than ever that it was 'ful necessarye for to be had in englisshe... to thende that somme which have not seen it, ne understonde frenssh ne latyn', might read it in the vernacular.[2]

These two ventures were both printed in Bruges, but towards the close of 1476 Caxton appears to have returned to England, and set up his press at Westminster, where on 18 November 1477 he published *The Dictes or Sayengis of the Philosophres*. This is worthy of note, since it was not a translation by Caxton himself, but was made by Earl Rivers, and given to Caxton to look over and correct where necessary, and afterwards to print at the Earl's command, 'in whiche I am bounden so to do for the good reward that I have resseyved of his sayd lordship'.[3] In publishing his first large book in England, therefore, it is clear that Caxton had written off a part of the risk incident on the production of a folio volume of 156 pages by accepting a 'good reward' from the Earl. In any case the work met a real demand, for Caxton published two further editions, and there was still another by Wynkyn de Worde in 1528. This was

---

[1] For discussion of the date see Curt F. Bühler's article on 'Caxton Variants' in *The Library*, Fourth Series, vol. XVII (1936), p. 63.

[2] Crotch, *op. cit.* p. 12.

[3] *Ibid.* p. 30.

probably the first book Caxton set up in England—certainly his first large book—and it is of interest to see how he proceeded from this point onwards in his first two years as a publisher. During this time he printed four folio volumes— the *Dictes*, *Boethius*, *The Canterbury Tales* and the *Jason*— nearly 700 leaves, or 1400 pages of print. In addition, he put out about twenty smaller volumes of quarto size, varying in length from little booklets of eight pages to slim volumes of 30–78 pages. These we may regard as efforts on his part to establish a market, while he was labouring on his great folio volumes. He showed considerable worldly wisdom in his choice, for he printed four poems by that popular fifteenth-century versifier John Lydgate, as well as Chaucer's *Anelida* and *The Parlement of Foules* (under the title of *The Temple of Brass*). More serious readers were given Benedict Burgh's translation of the distichs of Cato, Christine de Pisan's *Morale Proverbes* and a little *Book of Courtesy*. In this way he was able to test the strength and nature of the demand for printed books, and from this knowledge to make further plans. While he was willing to produce these smaller works at his own risk, it was a different matter when he was confronted with the printing of volumes each running to several hundred folio pages. Each of these was evidently carefully considered by Caxton before he started to work. The *Dictes*, the *Boethius* and the *Jason* he found by inquiry had little or no circulation in manuscript, despite their qualities, while *The Canterbury Tales* was always in demand, and a ready market could be expected for it. In publishing the *Dictes* he was doing what Earl Rivers had 'commanded' him to do, while he yielded to the 'requeste of a singuler frende and gossib' in spreading the rare work of Boethius. The *Jason* was the natural complement of *The recuyell*, but to minimize his risks, Caxton presented the work to the young Prince of Wales, and evidently counted on the favour of Edward IV and his Queen. All three works, therefore, were looked on by him as a fair business risk, while *The Canterbury Tales* was no risk at all—even though (as he learned later) the manuscript from which he set up his text was an imperfect one.

Caxton was evidently satisfied with the response made to his early efforts, and in his next two years continued his exploratory tactics. His works were designed to meet a variety of needs: the 'Cordiale', a Breviary, a Book of Hours, together with reprints of the *Dictes* and of Cato for the devout; a large volume on rhetoric for the learned, and a slim volume of vocabularies in French and English for the less learned. Those desiring information could explore the pages of *The Chronicles of England*, and *The Description of Britain*, while for the lover of poetry there was *The Court of Sapience*, at that time attributed to Lydgate. Only the 'Cordiale' had any outside backing of all these works, but he was clearly growing in confidence, as we can see by turning to his edition of *Tullius of Olde Age*, published on 12 August 1481. In his prologue Caxton tells us that he obtained a copy of the work, which had been translated in the middle of the fifteenth century, only 'with grete in-staunce, labour and coste'. Since he had never seen it elsewhere, he determined to 'put it in enprynte, and dilygently aftir my litil understandyng corrected it, to thentente that noble, vertuous and wel disposed men myght have it to loke on and to understonde it'.[1]

This he did, despite his knowledge that it was a work for a limited public only, since he says, 'this book is not requysyte ne eke convenyent for every rude and symple man whiche understandeth not of science ne connyng...but for noble, wyse and grete lordes, gentilmen and marchauntes that have seen and dayly ben occupyed in maters towchyng the publyque weal'. As with the *Jason*, he beseeches Edward IV to receive the book.

This valuable prologue helps us to understand Caxton's motives to some extent. We see that he is on the qui vive for works to print, but has to rely a good deal on his own inquiries concerning their general or special interest, and as to their

[1] Crotch, *op. cit.* p. 42.

14

manuscript circulation. Even though they have only a limited appeal he is prepared to go ahead, but canvasses the King's support as a valuable aid.

Caxton continued much in this way throughout his printing career in England. It was a testing time. He was carefully sounding his potential public; the variety of his publications is indicative of the way he explored many possibilities. By 1485 we can consider him as safely established. He had some fifty publications to his credit, and the new art of printing, thanks to him and to others at home and abroad, was winning converts, and the slow swing over from scrivener to printer was beginning. Caution remained his watchword: his publications were eminently 'safe', since they were almost exclusively confined to devotional works, reprints and volumes undertaken at the request of a patron.

It is this last group that is of the greatest interest. As we have seen, Caxton had commenced printing with royal encouragement, and had had aristocratic support from Earl Rivers for three volumes. For a number of his works supported by patrons we have only the shadowy 'requeste of dyverce gentilmen', or of 'a noble lady which hath brought forth many noble and fayr daughters', or of 'a gentyl and noble esquyer', which he tells us encouraged him to put them in print. We have no reason to suppose these characters to be fictitious, but it would have been more helpful had Caxton described them by name. The last ten years of his career, however, saw at least ten new publications expressly put forth at the request of a named patron. Royalty, the aristocracy, and rich citizens of London all made use of his services. Indeed, at times such patrons were indispensable. Caxton himself tells us that the gigantic task of translating and printing *The Golden Legend* soon left him 'halfe desperate to have accomplissd it', and that he was

in purpose to have lefte it, after that I had begonne to translate it and to have layed it aparte, ne had it be at thynstaunce and requeste of the puyssant, noble and vertuous erle, my lord wyllyam erle of arondel, whiche desyred me to procede and contynue the said werke, and promysed me to take a resonable quantyte of them when they were achyeved and accomplisshed.[1]

The Earl sent one of his gentlemen to Caxton with this message, promising him in addition a yearly fee of a buck in summer and a doe in winter. This, and other works, came from his press at the desire of the nobility. Perhaps even more significant, as a sign of the changing times, was the fact that he executed three books for eminent citizens of London. First Hugh Bryce, Alderman of London, asked him to translate *The Mirrour of the World* (1481) at his 'coste and dispense', so that he could present the work to Lord Hastings, the Lord Chamberlain. Then 'an honest man, and a specyal frende of myn, a Mercer of London named Wylliam Praat...delyvered to me in frenshe a lytel book named the book of good maners... and desyred me instantly to translate it in to englyssh'.[2] At much the same time he translated *The Royal Book* for another 'worshipful marchaunt and mercer of London'. Although Caxton does not say as much, save in speaking of Hugh Bryce, we may imagine that all three citizens underwrote to some extent the cost of these books, as did the Earl Rivers and many other aristocratic patrons.[3]

In addition to his efforts to limit his risks by the aid of patrons, Caxton showed a clear appreciation of the classes of readers to which various books would appeal. *Reynard the Fox*, he tells us, is meant 'for all good folk'; *Blanchardyn and Englantine* appeals to 'all vertuouse yong noble gentylmen and wymmen for to rede therin as for their passe tyme'; *The Order of Chyvalry* 'is not requysyte to every comyn man to have, but to noble gentylmen that by their vertu entende to come and entre into the noble ordre of chyvalry'. Certain books are unsuitable for every 'rude and unconnynge men to

---

[1] Crotch, *op. cit.* p. 70. *The Golden Legend* was one of the largest books Caxton ever printed, a folio volume of just under 900 pages.
[2] Crotch, *op. cit.* p. 99.   [3] See p. 45.

see', but are for 'clerkys and gentylmen that understande gentilnes and scyence'. Others again are for 'ladies and gentilwymen', or for 'every gentilman born to arms', while others make a wider appeal to 'all men', or 'every man livyng', or 'every cristen man'. Further, as we have seen, Caxton was careful to see that a large part of his output recommended itself to readers who wanted works of a religious and didactic nature. Nearly half his publications were of this kind (35 out of 77 original editions, or 56 out of 103 published items), and must have given him little anxiety. Indeed, nine of them ran into two or more editions—among them such substantial works as *The Golden Legend*, Maydeston's *Directorium sacerdotum*, Mirk's *Liber Festivalis* and the pseudo-Bonaventura *The Life of Christ*. His other largest venture was the publication of various poetical works, but here again he ran only a small risk. Chaucer, Lydgate and Gower were very popular at that time, and after Caxton had found a ready market for some of his little quartos of Chaucer or Lydgate's verses, he followed this up by the publication of *The Canterbury Tales* and the *Confessio Amantis* of Gower.

To sum up: our investigation of the work of our first printer shows him working within well-defined limits. He makes little attempt to educate or lead public taste, but prints what it was easy for him to know was popular by inquiry of the scriveners concerning manuscript circulation, or what the prevailing predilection for religious writings made a certain success. Romances and poetry were another reasonable venture, while a few works of instruction completed his list. To make assurance doubly sure, he worked under patronage in many instances, so that of seventy-seven original works published by him we know that for twenty-three of them he was assured of financial support, and the favour of influential personages. It was because of these considerations that he was able to put out this range of wares. Most of the other publishers in the earliest years of printing were much more conservative; their works were comparatively few in number and restricted in subject.[1] Caxton showed admirable judgement, energy and common sense. The business acumen gained by a lifetime of experience in the cloth trade in the Low Countries was of the utmost service to the printing trade in England. Where Caxton had pioneered, others could follow.

[1] See p. 181.

CHAPTER II

LITERACY

Before we turn to a detailed examination of the way in which Caxton's successors exploited their heritage, there are a number of questions calling for an answer, the most important being those concerning what we now call 'the reading public'. Who were the reading public of this period, and how large a proportion of the population did they represent? To answer this, we must survey the evidence concerning literacy, and the educational possibilities of the late fifteenth and early sixteenth centuries.

For a long time it was fashionable to regard the people of the fifteenth century as almost totally illiterate, and to look to the sixteenth century, and especially to the reign of Edward VI, 'the founder of the Grammar Schools' for the beginnings of education in England. Thanks to the labours of scholars such as A. F. Leach, James Gairdner, C. L. Kingsford and J. W. Adamson, much has been done to correct this view. Leach showed, with a wealth of examples, that the Grammar Schools had a history which stretches back to Anglo-Saxon times, while in addition many other schools of lesser importance were in existence throughout the later Middle Ages. Gairdner and Kingsford devoted their attention principally to the fifteenth century, and Kingsford only reinforced and emphasized Gairdner's opinion of fifty years earlier when he wrote so emphatically, as we saw above, concerning the state of literacy at that time.[1] In 1929, J. W. Adamson made a re-survey of the evidence concerning 'Literacy in England in the Fifteenth and Sixteenth Centuries', and concluded that:

it may be said of the English people of the fifteenth and especially of the sixteenth century that it was by no means an illiterate society

[1] See p. 9.

and that facilities for rudimentary instruction at least were so distributed as to reach even small towns and villages.... Where teaching existed there were candidates to receive it; and though we may not accept Sir Thomas More's estimate of the proportion of the population that could read,[1] we seem forced to believe that it was an appreciable proportion, and greatly in excess of the number frequently, perhaps usually, assumed to-day.[2]

If we turn from these general statements to examine the position more in detail, we may begin by noting that a little over 5000 volumes containing separate editions of works written in English were published before 1557 and still survive. This last phrase is important, for we cannot calculate how many works were printed during this period which for various reasons have perished altogether. Often what survives does so in such a way as to make clear the tenuous nature of the link between survival and destruction. For instance, there are a number of books which we know of only by the chance survival of a few strips, or of a single page. Others have come down to us in unique single mutilated copies, often lacking beginning and ending. Others, again, are found only in one or two examples—the sole evidence of an edition.[3]

For these reasons we may well believe that if we add 20% to the figure of 5000, we shall not be overestimating the number of publications before 1557. This gives us a figure of some 6000 volumes, and the existence of such a volume of work is in itself prima facie evidence of a considerable reading public. Further, as we shall see, these volumes served a wide variety of interests, and were made available in a number of forms, so that there were many cheap little pamphlets of a few pages as well as large and expensive folios.[4] Every kind of taste and every sort of public were catered for.

How widely throughout England these publications were distributed it is impossible to say. By far the major part of all

---

[1] See below, p. 28.
[2] J. W. Adamson, *The Illiterate Anglo-Saxon*, etc. (1946), p. 61.
[3] See below, p. 182.　　　　[4] See below, p. 183.

the printing was done in London, although it is true that at certain times the printers of France, the Low Countries and Switzerland made important contributions to the supply— principally of works of a religious nature.[1] Furthermore, various centres in England such as St Albans, Canterbury, Ipswich, Worcester, and York, together with Oxford and Cambridge, were responsible for some printing. Nevertheless, their total output was small, and it was to London that the would-be purchaser turned. There, in the little shops clustered for the most part around St Paul's, the printers themselves, and others who were booksellers only, offered for sale a variety of books, mainly in the vernacular, but also in classical and modern tongues. A graphic account of what was doubtless an everyday occurrence is given by William Salisbury, writing to his cousin, John Edwards, of Chirk in North Wales. Edwards had asked for a book in English dealing with the spheres. Salisbury tells him that

I walked my selfe rounde aboute all Poules Churchyearde, from shop to shop, enquyerynge of suche a treatyse, neyther could I here of any that eyther wrote of this matier proposely, nor yet occasyonallye. But what trowe you did I than? By my fayth syr, I returned backe even the same way (but wondrynge moche at the happe) and asked agayne for the same workes in laten, wherof there were .iii. or .iiii. of sondrye Aucthoures brought and shewed unto me.[2]

Readers who were unable to come to London, and who were without acquaintances there, had to rely on the provincial booksellers. These men ordered from London such books as they thought they could sell, with the result that the free choice of the would-be reader was limited by the stationer's selection, much as is that of the reader of to-day who finds himself benighted in a small provincial town with only the local bookseller's stock to select from. In such cases, not what he desires but what he can get has to suffice him. We have little

---

[1] See below, p. 65.   [2] *STC* 20399 [1550], sig. Aiiʳ.

evidence concerning provincial sales of books, so that much that we could wish to know about this, and what kinds of books were in demand, remains obscure. By far the most detailed information on such questions comes from the day-book of John Dorne, an Oxford bookseller of 1520. Dorne's account runs from 18 January to 31 May, and again from 3 August to the end of the year. During that time he accounts for 1850 items, for which he received a little over £100. As might be expected in a University town many of his works are in Latin, and are concerned with theological or classical studies. A number of English works, however, were to be bought. For beginners there were ABC's 'for to lerne rede', while the more advanced could enjoy a book of carols, or ballads such as 'Undo your dore', or 'Robin Hood', or poems such as *The Nutbrown Maid*. The romances of *King Ponthus* or *Robert the Devil* or *Sir Isumbras* were available for a few pence, while more serious readers found Dorne well stocked with religious works, such as the life of Christ and the lives of individual saints. On the practical side there were books on cookery and carving; on husbandry and the treatment of horses; on French and English vocabularies; and on prognostications of coming events. In short, Dorne had a fairly wide range of works even for those whose reading was confined to the vernacular. As soon as the reader was willing and able to turn to other languages a much wider range was available. Over 150 volumes of works by Erasmus were sold by Dorne in the year—a clear indication of the overwhelming position occupied by Erasmus in the minds of the educated of the time. Much indeed of Dorne's stock reflects the fact that he was catering for a University public. In few places would the proportion of foreign books on sale have been so large, or the selection in general so generous.[1]

There is an interval in his account-book from 21 May until 3 August, after which he begins again: 'Post recessum meum

---

[1] For all this see F. Madan, 'The Day-book of John Dorne'. *Oxford Historical Society, Collectanea*, vol. 1 (1885), pp. 71–178.

de ultra mare'—an entry which suggests that he had been abroad purchasing books to restock his shop. Whether or no this was a common custom among booksellers is doubtful. Most of them probably relied on agents who went to and from and who were aware of the needs of the English market which they endeavoured to satisfy. Reynolde Wolfe, for example, was a printer and bookseller who went backwards and forwards to the great Frankfort fair, for in 1538 we read from a letter that 'our friend Rayner did not come to this fair by reason of the recent death of his wife'.[1] Books arrived in barrels addressed to individuals, or were entrusted to an agent who supplied booksellers in London and in the provinces. For example, Thomas Hunte, an Oxford bookseller of 1483, found it convenient to deal with such agents, and heads his stock-list with the declaration:

Here follows the inventory of books which I, Thomas Hunte, stationer of the University of Oxford, have received from Master Peter Actors and John of Aix-la-Chapelle to sell, with the price of each book, and I promise faithfully to return the books or the money according to the price written below as it appears in the following list.[2]

These were the conditions in the early days of printing, but there is no reason to believe that the relation of agent and bookseller changed greatly throughout the period. Both in London, and in such places as Oxford, Cambridge, York, Hereford, Edinburgh and elsewhere, we find the booksellers were active, receiving their stock from their London agent.[3]

[1] E. G. Duff, *A Century of the English Book Trade* (afterwards referred to as *Century*), p. 171. See also E. G. Duff, *The Printers, Stationers and Bookbinders of London from 1476 to 1535* (1906) (afterwards referred to as *Printers*), pp. 82, 83, 91.

[2] F. Madan, *op. cit.* p. 142. Cf. Peter Kaetz's letter to John Siberch at Cambridge, telling Siberch that he is sending him a parcel of books for sale at Cambridge (*Proc. Camb. Antiq. Soc.* vol. VII, p. 186).

[3] Wynkyn de Worde was ordered by the Bishop of London's Vicar-General to recall all copies of a prohibited work that had been sent to the Universities of Oxford and Cambridge (A. W. Reed, *Early Tudor Drama*, (1926), p. 167).

Even this localized bookselling to a greater degree than was desirable, and enterprising booksellers made a point of attending the great fairs in their vicinity which were so common a feature of the time. John Dorne makes a special note of his takings at the two Oxford fairs of St Austin and St Frideswide, and no doubt the Barnwell Fair at Cambridge and others elsewhere did much to make books available to those unable to travel to London or to the great centres where booksellers were to be found. Gordon Duff records an entry on the fly-leaf of a Bible which reads: 'I gave to the Hereford bookseller called Ingelbert for this and the six other volumes of the Bible forty-three shillings and fourpence, which I bought at Ludlow the year of our Lord's incarnation, 1510, about the day of the Lichfield fair.'[1]

The provision of books on this scale postulates a considerable reading public, and some additional information concerning this may be obtained by investigating the facilities for education provided in this period. In the first place, however, we must beware of thinking that the foundation or prevalence of Grammar Schools is the best evidence for this purpose. The Grammar School was concerned with Latin, and Latin only. Its Master would have disdained the task of teaching the vernacular. That was the function of the lower schools—the ABC's and the Petty Schools, while the Grammar Schools were reserved for those who could already read in the vernacular. Thus Colet, in the foundation statutes of his new creation of St Paul's, requires of a boy at his admission 'that he knows the Catechism, and also that he can read and write competently, else let him not be admitted, in no wise'.[2] In this he was only repeating what was, and what for centuries had been, the common rule.

The provision of teaching below the Grammar School level was one of the many duties assumed for the most part by the Church. The education of the young was an important part of

[1] Duff, *Printers*, p. 83.
[2] J. H. Lupton, *Life of John Colet* (1909), p. 277.

the Christian ideal, and the Church was concerned to do what she could to this end. Unfortunately, this did not amount to very much in many places and over long periods, for nearly everything depended on the zeal and ability of the clergy scattered throughout the countryside. Where there was a curate willing and able to teach the boys of the village, there rudimentary education flourished. Happy the parish of which it could be said in 1548, 'The Incumbent hathe alwayes occupyed hymselfe in teaching of children'. The more able pupils learned to read, and in time could assist in the celebration of the Church services. They knew the elements of chanting and could even follow parrot-like the Latin words which had been drilled into them. Most of them, like the companion of the little 'clergeon' in *The Prioresses Tale*, challenged as to the meaning of the words, would have been forced to reply, 'I can but smal grammere'.[1] Reading and writing in the vernacular were their business—beyond that only a very few of them ever ventured.

In addition to the parish priest many churches had chantries served by a mass or chantry priest. These men were often enjoined not only to sing mass for the souls of the founder and others, but also in their spare time (which was very considerable) to instruct those parishioners who wished to learn to read and to write. In this way many boys—and possibly girls—got their early training, and helped to swell the number of those who could be pronounced literate.

As the sixteenth century progressed the number of new foundations grew, and schools of every kind were opened to provide for the demand which undoubtedly was fed by the output from the printing presses. After the first years when Caxton and his successors were struggling to make a living, the printers increased in number, and so did the output of books in English.[2] Those wishing for something to read in the vernacular found it was being provided in quantity and in

[1] I.e. 'I know very little Latin'.
[2] See below, p. 193.

25

variety. The little ABC's were the first step: from them more ambitious works could be attempted, and the schoolboy could look forward, for example, to the publications of de Worde wherein he would find jest books, such as the *Demands joyous*, or books of carols, or a variety of romances. These, no doubt, would have appealed to him more than those homiletic works, sermons and the like which were awaiting the devout adults who had mastered the elements. At the same time we must not underestimate the powerful effect on the growth of literacy produced by the dissemination of religious works. Throughout the fifteenth century, religious vernacular literature had a wide popularity, and it cannot be doubted that many pious souls found the greatest comfort and stimulus in the appearance on the market of comparatively cheap works in print which had been far beyond their means when they existed only in manuscript. Both these, and the mass of new works that came from the presses, must have encouraged many to make the effort necessary to acquire the art of reading.

Further we must take into account the tremendous impact made by the publication of the vernacular Bible. First surreptitiously, and later openly, the Bible was received with joy and greedily devoured by all sorts of people. No less than thirty editions of the Bible as a whole, and fifty editions of the New Testament, in English, were published by 1557—a striking indication of the zeal which welcomed the efforts of the translators. And, as with the Bible, so with the rest of the religious output. It obviously met a need, and obviously acted as the greatest encouragement to the devout to learn to read.

Lastly, when the days of controversy came, and men's minds and consciences were much exercised concerning what they should believe, they not unnaturally turned to the works pouring from the press for instruction and consolation. The authors of these works wrote for the man in the street, 'to help the rude and ignorant people to more knowledge of God and hys holy worde'. They adjure the readers to cast off 'their

importable burdens of hevey, unprofitable, superstitious ceremonies',[1] or advise them to 'sette a parte all blynde affeccion,
and read this boke with jugement'.[2] These, and many similar
pleas were made to the growing reading public, a body which
was numerous and which covered many classes, as may be
inferred from the Act of 1543 'for the advancement of true
religion and for the abolishment of the contrarie'. In this Act
the reading of the Bible in English was forbidden to women,
artificers, apprentices, journeymen, serving-men of the rank
of yeomen and under, husbandmen and labourers. Noble-
women and gentlewomen might read it to themselves, but not
to others. Only noblemen, gentlemen and merchants might
read it to their families.[3] The range of social classes indicated
in this Act will be noted, and shows clearly that the authorities
recognized that the ability to read was widespread.

This also is the impression given by many individual references to various people, such as the servant of an Essex tailor,
or a point-maker of Cheapside, both well known to their
friends as readers, or the maidens of an Essex village who read
their matins from an English primer, to the horror of the
sidesman who 'didde bidde the maydens to avoyde out of
Church [as] errent whores, with soche other odyous and spiteful
wordes more'.[4] Every official inquiry revealed the presence of
readers in many walks of life; ecclesiastical authorities feared
their influence on the non-literate; lists of books required by
such readers occur from time to time, and books are mentioned
in their wills, while lovers of the old ways frowned on these
'newfangled' activities.

When, however, we turn to inquire what proportion of the
population could read, say between the years 1500 and 1550,
we can find no satisfactory answer. The few pieces of direct
evidence are confusing and contradictory. For instance, John
Rastell, writing in 1527, says that 'the unyversall people of this
realm had greate plesure and gave themself greatly to the

[1] *STC* 14556, sig. B vii[r].   [2] *STC* 61, sig. A i[r].
[3] 35 Henry VIII, cap. i.   [4] A. W. Reed, *op. cit.* p. 180.

redyng of the vulgare Englyssh tonge'.[1] This, however, is something of a salesman's flourish to introduce his novel venture of an abridgment of the Statutes in English, and certainly must not be taken to mean that all people could read. Sir Thomas More in 1523 is more explicit, and his statement has been given great weight. He says in his *Apology*:

If the havyng of the scripture in englyshe, be a thyng so requisite of precyse necessitie, that the peoples soules shoulde nedes perysh but if they have it translated into their own tongue: then must there the moste part perishe for all that, excepte the preacher make farther provision besyde, that all the people shall be hable to reade it when they have it, of which people, farre more than fowre partes of all the whole divided into tenne, coulde never reade englishe yet, and many now too olde to begynne to goe to schole.[2]

It would be rash to follow some writers, and to deduce from this that 60% of the people could read. Sir Thomas only asserts that far more than four parts out of ten could not read, and leaves us in the dark as to what exactly is implied by the qualification 'far more'. At best his statement is only a guess, and it is highly improbable that the figures were meant to be more than a rhetorical flourish made to support his argument. This view is confirmed by another piece of evidence less well known, but written by one whose word carries authority almost equal to that of Sir Thomas. Stephen Gardiner, Bishop of Winchester, declared in a letter of May 1547 that 'not the hundreth part of the realme' was able to read, and therefore images (which are books for the illiterate) should be allowed.[3] Here again, no great reliance can be placed on the figure. It is an indication only of the Bishop's argument—but both More and himself cannot be right.

Other evidence is equally uncertain. One writer, after advising every man to read his book, is forced to add, 'or [those] that cannot rede to geve dylygent eere to the reder',[4]

---

[1] *STC* 9518, sig. A ii^r.   [2] *STC* 18076, p. 850.
[3] J. A. Muller, *The Letters of Stephen Gardiner* (1933), p. 274.
[4] *STC* 3186 (1530), sig. A i^r. A number of writers speak of those that read or hear their work.

while the parishioners of Rye state that their curate when reading the Bible reads 'scant a piece of the title', and even that may not be understood 'for he cannot rede the rethoryck wordes'.[1] On the other hand, some writers speak of the 'numbre of bokes ther be abrode in every mans hand of dyvers and sundry maters which are very gredely devoured of a greate sorte',[2] and of much translation into English. We are forced, therefore, to fall back on the general impressions left by a study of the period, namely that an ability to read was widespread; that it was to be found in all ranks of society, among both men and women, and that it was powerfully increased by the products of the printing press and by the strong religious emotions provoked by the action of Henry VIII and by later monarchs and their advisers.

While the growth of literacy cannot be exactly measured by the output of books from time to time, the two things are not altogether dissociated. The increase in the number of printers must be linked to the growing demand for their wares. Where the beginning of the century saw only a bare half dozen printers at work in England, by 1550 the number was about twenty. The *Short-title Catalogue* records the titles of 54 books printed in the year 1500, while the number has risen to 214 for the year 1550.[3] The Stationers' Company at the time of its incorporation in 1557 could feel assured that a considerable and eager reading public was awaiting its activities.

---

[1] *Letters and Papers of Henry VIII* (afterwards referred to as *L. & P. Henry VIII*), vol. xiii, no. 1150 (1538).

[2] *STC* 18576 (1548), sig. A iii^v.

[3] It must be remembered that these figures are not to be taken as absolutely accurate, since the *STC* includes the approximately dated items for the two years before and the two years after the end of each decade, thereby swelling the number of titles for these years by about 12%. For the purposes of my argument, however, this is immaterial.

CHAPTER III

THE REGULATION OF THE BOOK TRADE

In addition to the state of literacy in the first half of the sixteenth century there is another matter calling for inquiry—the various ways in which printing and the book trade were controlled at this time. Control arose mainly from two causes—economic and ecclesiastical—and, speaking generally, followed one another in that order. In the earliest days of printing no restrictions prevailed. The new art was free to flourish or languish as circumstances dictated; the Act of 1484 which regulated the conditions under which aliens might trade in England allowed complete freedom to printers, binders and scriveners to exercise their trade. The result is seen on looking at the list of printers in England for the first four or five decades of printing. With the exception of Caxton, Thomas Hunt of Oxford, and possibly the anonymous printer of St Albans, all the printers at work until 1513 appear to come from abroad. De Worde was a native of Wörth in Alsace; Pynson and W. Faques were Normans; W. de Machlinia came from Mechlin in Belgium; J. Notary was probably a Frenchman, and so on. John Rastell began to print about 1513, and from then onwards was joined by a growing body of native printers, encouraged, no doubt, by the ever increasing restraints placed on foreigners, whether trading in England as aliens or denizens.[1] Even so, it has been said that it would not be far from the mark to state that two-thirds of all persons residing in England connected with the book trade from 1476 to 1535 were aliens.[2] Their numbers were gradually decreased, first by the series of restrictive regulations on all foreigners, such as that of 1515

[1] *denizens*: foreigners admitted to residence and certain rights.
[2] E. G. Duff, *Printers*, p. 189.

which declared that a double subsidy was to be paid by all denizens, and secondly by Acts directly concerning the printing trade. Thus in 1523 all aliens were prohibited from having any but English apprentices, and were also forbidden to employ more than two foreign journeymen in their printing-houses. This restriction was found not to be sufficiently onerous to satisfy the growing body of English-born printers, and in 1529 a new Act prohibited the setting up of a press in England by any alien, although it did not forbid those already established from continuing to print. The net was drawn still tighter in 1534, when a further Act concerning printers and binders came into operation. The preamble to the Act speaks of 'a marvellous number of printed books' which from day to day had come into the country since the Act of 1484 'for that there were but few books, and few printers, within this realm at that time, who could well exercise and occupy the said science and craft of printing'. It goes on to declare that things have changed in the interim, so that at this day there be within this Realme a 'greatt number [of men] cunning and expert in the said craft of printing, as able to exercise the said craft in all points, as any stranger in any other realm or country'.[1] The Act of 1484 was repealed, and new clauses provided that aliens could only sell their wares wholesale to an English-born printer or stationer, and that no bound books were to be imported at all. With this new Act in force English printers were in a strong position: they had already secured that no new alien presses could be set up, and now no one other than a native or a denizen could retail foreign printed books. The English book market was entirely in their hands.

The severe check finally placed on aliens by the Act of 1534 may well be illustrated by noting the way it affected perhaps the most important of foreigners trading in books in England. Francis Regnault, the son and successor of the famous Paris bookseller, had been an active agent in the providing of books (especially service-books) ever since he succeeded to his

[1] 25 Hen. VIII, cap. 15.

father's business soon after 1516. He imported large quantities of books into England and prospered. After 1534, however, he found things so serious that he wrote to Cromwell in 1536 setting out his past history and recording his fears that the English booksellers wished to prevent him from printing and selling books in future, and to confiscate what he had already printed. He begged Cromwell to allow him to continue to sell his wares, adding that if his books were in any way faulty he would amend them.[1]

Apparently he got little out of Cromwell, and two years later took advantage of the fact that he was printing in Paris an edition of the Bible for R. Grafton and E. Whitchurch (overseen by Coverdale), to enlist their aid. Coverdale and Grafton then wrote to Cromwell as follows:

> Whereas of long tyme he hath bene an occupier into England more than xl yere, he hath alwayes provyded soche bookes for England as they moost occupied, so that he hath a great nombre at this present in his handes, as Prymers in Englishe, Misseles, with other soche like: wherof now (by the company of the Booksellers in London) he is utterly forbydden to make sale, to the utter undoyng of the man. Wherefore most humbly we beseke your lordshippe to be gracious and favourable unto him, that he may have lycence to sell those which he hath done allready, so that hereafter he prynte no moo in the English tong, onlesse he have an English man that is lerned to be his corrector.[2]

All this was of no avail, and no more foreign printed service-books of Regnault's appear to have been imported. There can be little doubt that from 1534 onwards the native printers had the upper hand, and that the foreigner was slowly being squeezed out.

The Crown, in making these enactments, was not guided solely by consideration for the native printer. The restrictions concerning the import of English printed books were but part of the campaign which by 1534 was in full swing against the

---

[1] *L. and P. Hen. VIII*, vol. xi, no. 1488.
[2] *Ibid.* vol. xiii, part ii, no. 336.

circulation of works which attacked the Church, or disseminated the doctrines of Luther and his followers. As early as July 1520 Leo X had issued a Bull against the writings of Luther, ordering their confiscation and burning, and Wolsey acted with vigour. In May 1521, in circumstances of the greatest ceremony and after a sermon by Fisher,[1] Luther was pronounced a heretic, and his works publicly burned at St Paul's Cross. Despite this, and despite action taken by the Bishops in their dioceses, Lutheran books found their way into England, and were disseminated in such numbers that the ecclesiastical authorities were forced to make further efforts. The researches of Professor A. W. Reed have shown that the booksellers of London were called together on 12 October 1524, and warned by the Bishop of London against importing or selling books containing the Lutheran heresies, and told that if they imported new books they were to show them to the Cardinal, the Archbishop of Canterbury, the Bishop of Rochester, or himself, before they were offered for sale.

Wolsey staged a second preaching[2] and book-burning on a wet Sunday in February 1525; and in the autumn of that year the Bishop of London reassembled the booksellers. This time his orders were more stringent. They were not to handle Lutheran works, either in Latin or in English, nor were they to sell imported works until they had been approved by Wolsey, Fisher, or himself. Further, no new book whatsoever was to be printed (except works hitherto approved by the Church) without authority. For the first time in England the printer was restricted in his choice of what he should print.[3]

This second warning was probably made necessary by the growing volume of heretical books in circulation. In 1525 de Worde was called on to show cause why he had printed

---

[1] *STC* 10893–4, and reprinted three times later.

[2] *STC* 10892: 'but for ye great noyse of ye people within ye churche of Paules...it myght not be herde.'

[3] We owe most of this information to the researches of A. W. Reed. See his *Early Tudor Drama* (1926), chapter VII.

The Image of Love, a translation made by John Gough,[1] alleged to contain heretical matter; while early in 1526, Thomas Berthelet was in trouble for printing translations of three works of Erasmus. Here there was no question of heresy, but Berthelet had failed to exhibit the works to the Bishop of London's officials, and thus had evaded control.

The anxiety of the authorities at this time was increased by their knowledge that not only were Lutheran pamphlets circulating fairly freely, but also that the first copies of Tyndale's New Testament were finding their way into England in considerable numbers.[2] From 1526 onwards, the Bishops fought unavailingly to stem the flood. Archbishop Warham and Tunstall, Bishop of London, were tricked by their opponents into buying up parcels of Testaments, thus providing funds for further editions.[3] The New Testament found its way into all sections of society, so that Bishop Nix of Norwich declared in despair: 'It passeth my power, or that of any spiritual man, to hinder it now, and if this continue much longer, it will undo us all.'

Bishop Nix was correct in one thing: it was impossible to stop the importation and reading of the Scriptures, and from 1530 onwards, much opinion within the Church led to a recognition of the need for a vernacular Bible. Fostered by ecclesiastics, such as Latimer and Cranmer, and by statesmen of Cromwell's party, steps were taken to produce a vernacular Bible which would be acceptable to the authorities. First Coverdale's Bible of 1535, then 'Matthew's' Bible of 1537,

[1] Gough was also examined in 1528 on suspicion of dealing in heretical books (*L. and P. Hen. VIII*, vol. IV, part ii, p. 1803), and was again in trouble in 1541, and was sent to the Fleet for printing and selling seditious books.

[2] For example, Hans van Ruremond, a London stationer, was forced to abjure in 1528 for causing 1500 of Tyndale's New Testament to be printed at Antwerp, 500 of which were brought into England.

[3] Cf. *STC* 1309, J. Bale's *Yet a course at the Romyshe foxe* [1543], p. 55: 'No lesse myght Harrye Pepwell in Paules churcheyearde have out of Michael Hillenius howse at Anwerpe at one tyme than a whole complete prynte at the holye request of Stokyslaye [the Bishop of London]. In a short space were they dyspached and a newe prynte in hande.'

followed by the Great Bible in 1539 marked the steps made to provide an 'open Bible'. The story of its reception by the laity is too well known to need repetition.

But if a change of attitude was shown to the vernacular Bible, that carried with it no softening of official hostility to books in English, mostly imported from abroad, which attempted to propagate Lutherism and heresy. As early as March 1529, the King issued a proclamation prohibiting certain books,[1] while in May 1530 a declaration by the Bishops denounced a number of works, such as *A supplicacyon for the beggars* [Antwerp, 1529?], while a royal proclamation of the following June prohibited the circulation of seven volumes, all condemned as heretical.[2] Nor was this all. The King's agents at home and abroad were active, and arrests for infringements of the embargo were frequent. For example, Richard Bayfield was taken in the autumn of 1531, charged with importing prohibited books, and was burnt on 14 December of that year. Many others during this decade were haled before the authorities, made to abjure from reading prohibited works, and forced to surrender them.[3] Many fled to the Low Countries, but even here they were not safe. Tyndale was harried from place to place—Cologne, Marburg, Hamburg, Antwerp—his surrender was demanded by Henry VIII, and when that was refused, plans were made to kidnap him. He was finally betrayed, and imprisoned by the Emperor Charles, who had him strangled and burnt at the stake at Vilvorde, in 1536.

A number of further proclamations followed,[4] culminating in one of 8 July 1546 comprehensively forbidding the reading

---

[1] R. Steele, *Tudor and Stuart Proclamations* (1910), no. 114.

[2] *Ibid.* no. 122.

[3] For example, in 1531 Michael Lobley bought a number of heretical works in Antwerp and returned with them. He was compelled to abjure. In the same year, Segar Nicholson of Cambridge was in trouble for possessing heretical books, while John Rowe did penance for selling the New Testament in English, etc. See Foxe, *Acts and Documents* (1877), vols. IV–VI *passim*.

[4] Steele, *op. cit.* nos. 155, 176.

of all works by Reformers such as Bale, Becon, Barnes, Coverdale, Frith, Joye, Tracy, Turner and Tyndale.¹ The coming to the throne of Edward VI did nothing to check the ardour of those wishing to control the activities of the printing-press, while the fanatical zeal of Mary made matters even worse, and the importation of books written by some twenty-five Protestant authors was forbidden.²

By means such as these the circulation of heretical books from abroad was made a dangerous and difficult affair. At home, the practice inaugurated by the Bishop of London in 1526 was continued. A proclamation of 1538 concerning heretical books declared that nothing was to be printed until it had been examined and licensed by the Privy Council or its agents. Henceforth the words *Cum privilegio regali ad imprimendum solum* began to appear at the end of books as a warrant that the law had been complied with.³ On the other hand, printers with strong religious feelings were prepared to take risks, and by using fictitious names and imprints they put a certain number of books on the market. Thus Melanchthon's *A very godly defense, defending the mariage of preistes* [1541] was printed with the types of John Oswen of Ipswich, despite its claim to come from 'Upright Hoff of Leipsic',⁴ and three books all without printers' names, each stating that it was printed in Wesel, actually were all printed in London.⁵ Coverdale was scandalized at the number of books in circulation all capable of corrupting the King's subjects. He asserted that many such books and a great 'sort of other most ungracious Popish

¹ Steele, *op. cit.* no. 295. For a full list of books prohibited by name in Henry VIII's reign, see R. Steele: 'Notes on English Books printed abroad, 1525–1548', *Trans. Bibl. Soc.*, vol. XI (1912), pp. 189–236.

² Steele, *op. cit.* no. 488.

³ A. W. Reed, *op. cit.* pp. 181–6. The meaning of the phrase *ad imprimendum solum* was discussed by Miss E. M. Albright in *Modern Language Notes*, vol. 34 (Feb. 1919), pp. 97–101, and by A. W. Pollard, *The Library*, Third Series, vol. X (1919), pp. 57–63.

⁴ *STC* 17798.

⁵ *STC* 1270, 17789, 21428. For other works with false imprints about this time, see *STC* 3760–4, 21804, and below, p. 209.

books' had been taken by him at Newbury in 1539, and he asks Cromwell, 'should I burn these Popish books at the Market Cross or not?'[1] R. Grafton was sent to prison in 1541 for printing a letter of Melanchthon's against the Six Articles, and was never after employed to print the Bible.[2] Then in 1543 there followed a series of actions by the Privy Council against printers who were transgressing the law. In April, eight of them were imprisoned 'for printing books thought to be unlawful',[3] and were only released after a fortnight upon recognisances to make a true declaration of 'books and balletes bowght wythin thiese iii yeres past, and what sold in gross; what merchants they know to have brought into the Realm any English bookes of ill matter'.[4] A few days later twenty-five other book-sellers were instructed to make similar returns.[5] The pro-clamation of 1538, requiring the sanction of the Privy Council or its agents prior to publication was reiterated in 1549 and 1551, while a little later Mary required her subjects not 'to printe any bookes, matter, ballet, ryme, interlude, processe or treatyse...excepte they have her grace's speciall licence in wrytynge for the same'.[6]

The growing control which was exercised throughout these years had another aim—it was political as well as religious. From the time of Henry's defiance of the Pope onwards it was necessary for the Crown to do everything possible to make the new position of the King acceptable and understandable. A considerable number of tracts and pamphlets, such as those of St German or Richard Morison appeared. The sinfulness of rebellion was assailed again and again; the Pope's rights in various ways were repudiated, and ridiculed in learned and popular treatises; the Crown's exact position with regard to

---

[1] *L. and P. Hen. VIII*, vol. xiv, part i, no. 444.

[2] *Ibid.* vol. xvii, p. v, n. 1 and vol. xvi, no. 422. In 1540 H. Tab (or Dabbe) was before the Privy Council for printing an addition of this work, but he was declared innocent.

[3] *Acts of the Privy Council*, vol. i, p. 107.

[4] *Ibid.* vol. i, p. 117.   [5] *Ibid.* vol. i, p. 120.

[6] *Ibid.* vol. ii, pp. 311–12.

political ideas and religious thought was carefully set out in works such as *The Institution of a Christian Man* (1537), etc. In short, the book trade was actively employed to further the ends of the Crown in its vigorous propaganda campaign.[1]

A further restriction of the liberty of printing is also to be seen in the practice which developed mainly under Edward VI and Mary of granting monopolies to certain printers. From the early days of printing there had always been individuals given the title of King's Printer, who had enjoyed the privilege of printing proclamations, and such other things as the Crown required. The first of them, Peter Actors, called himself 'Stationer to the King' (1485), but he was followed in 1503 by a working printer, William Faques, who took the title of 'Printer to the King', and his example was followed by his successors—Richard Pynson (1508), Thomas Berthelet (1530), Richard Grafton (1547), John Cawood (1553), and Cawood & Richard Jugge (1558).

The practice of giving exclusive rights of printing certain classes of books seems to have arisen with the granting of an exclusive patent to Grafton and Whitechurch for printing service-books. This was in January 1544, and in 1547 Reynolde Wolfe was appointed King's Printer in Latin, Greek and Hebrew, with an annuity of twenty-six shillings and eightpence. This was a much less valuable monopoly than that granted for service-books, for the volume of printing in these three languages was still small. On 16 January 1549 John Oswen received a privilege from Edward VI to print service-books, and books of instruction 'for our subjects of the Principality of Wales and the marches thereunto belonging' for the space of seven years. In the next few years a number of patents were granted. T. Gaultier was licensed to print French service-books about 1550, while in 1552 a similar patent was given to R. Tottel for law-books. The same year

---

[1] See also below, pp. 139–42. For a full treatment of this topic, see F. Le Van Baumer, *The Early Tudor Theory of Kingship* (1940), Appendix A, pp. 211–24.

John Day received the valuable right to print the Catechism in English and the ABC—a privilege he was still actively asserting as late as 1580. The next year saw John Wayland given another valuable patent for the sole printing of all primers and manuals of prayer howsoever denominated, and John Cawood, who also replaced Grafton as Royal Printer on the succession of Mary, was given the reversion of Wolfe's patent for printing in Latin, Greek and Hebrew.

Monopolies such as these clearly gave the Crown a useful, continuous control over various kinds of books, particularly it will be noticed over service-books and works of elementary religious instruction. This was not a serious handicap, perhaps, to the unprivileged printer at this time, but it was the beginning of a monopoly system that was to cause much trouble in the future.

It was under conditions and regulations such as these that the printing trade pursued its activities at this period.

CHAPTER IV

PATRONAGE

A survey of the relations between printers, authors and readers may well begin with some words written in 1548—nearly seventy-five years after the introduction of printing—by Nicholas Udall, dramatist, scholar and man of letters. He tells us that:

> In tymes past the studious wryters of bookes wer enforced with muche high suite and service to dedicate suche weorkes as thei wrote, to thentente that under the name and proteccion of suche noble personages the said weorkes might bee the better habled to the readers, and the better accepted of people: now dooe Kynges, Quenes, princes, and other piers (especially here in Englande) of their owne mere mocions and good zele not onely with their propense favour, and with their beneficial aide, comforte and liberalitee, help foreward the good endevour and sedulitee of studious wryters mindyng by their godly monumentes to edifie the feithfull congregacion, but also are diligent and peinfull, bothe to putte their owne handes to the endictyng and pennyng of many holsome traictises for that purpose, yea and ferther by their example and provocacion to sette others in hand with writyng or translatyng, to the fruictefull exercise of the learned, to the holsome enstruccion of Englishe readers, and to the effectual edifyng of the symple ignorant multitude.[1]

These, perhaps, are the words of a courtier, striving to put the best gloss possible on the state of affairs which he is seeking to increase and perpetuate by enlisting the royal support. At the same time, they serve to illustrate how close was the relation between patron and author, a relation which it has been shown goes back to the whole manuscript period, where an author inevitably looked to some lord or rich man for

[1] *STC* 2854, sig. ¶ 1ʳ (Acts) *The...paraphrase of Erasmus upon the newe testament* (1548–9).

support. The coming of printing had brought about no immediate or decisive change. It may well be that the new conditions had lessened the need for a patron, but it still remained advantageous to enlist the favour of some person, influential in Church or State, before publishing. It has been seen that Caxton adhered closely to medieval practice, and many of his books were published with the encouragement and support of some influential person.

Caxton's two chief successors, Wynkyn de Worde and Richard Pynson, seem to have shown little of his anxiety to find a patron. Each of them, it is true, published a limited number of books with the support of influential people, but on the whole they relied on their own skill in judging what the public wanted. Other publishers, both contemporary and later, were seemingly not so confident of their powers in judging the potential market; and, as a result throughout the period, many printers were influenced by the wishes or instructions of patrons who were responsible for the work in some way or another.

A good example of this is illustrated by the verses which the printer H. Pepwell composed and printed in front of Brian Anslay's translation of Christine de Pisan's work, *The Cyte of Ladyes* (1521). After saying that the noble man delights in reading and writing books to feed the minds of every gentleman, he goes on:

> So nowe of late, came in my custodye
> This foresayd boke, by Bryan Anslay,
> Yoman of the seller, with the eyght kynge Henry,
> Of gentylwomen the excellence to say.
> The whiche I lyked, but yet I made delay
> It to impresse, for that it is the guyse
> Of people lewde, theyr prowesse to dyspyse.
>
> But then I shewed the foresayd boke
> Unto my lorde, the gentyll Erle of Kente,
> And him requyred theron to loke

> With his counsayle to put it in to prente.
> And he forthwith, as ever dylygente
> Of ladyes (abrode) to sprede theyr royall fame,
> Exhorted me to prynte it in hys name.[1]

The patron shouldered an even greater responsibility when he actually commissioned the writing of a book. An early example of this is revealed by the Prologue to *The Contemplacyion of Synners* (1499), which tells us that:

> At the devoute & dylygent request of the ryght reverende fader in God, & lorde Rychard, Bysshop of Dureham and lorde pryvy seal of Englonde, this lytell boke, namyd Contemplacion of synners, is compylyd & fynysshed. The sayd blessyd fader in God desyryng gretly all vertue to encrease and vyce to be exiled, hath caused this booke to be enprinted.[2]

From this it is clear that Richard Foxe, Bishop of Durham, not only caused the book to be compiled, but was personally responsible for its printing by Wynkyn de Worde. Similarly, the 'exortacion and sterynge of the moost excellent princesse Margarete'[3] was the cause of Bishop Fisher's writing his treatise on *The fruytfull saynges of Dauyd*, and although it is not explicitly stated, it may be assumed that it was on her instructions that Wynkyn de Worde, 'printer to the mother of the King' produced the work in 1508.

Much more common than the command to write a book *de novo* was the request to translate a work into English. An informative preface by Thomas Paynell to his translation of U. von Hutten's *De morbo gallico* (1533) shows how this could happen. Paynell writes:

> Not long agoo, after I had translated into our englysshe tonge the boke called Regimen sanitatis Salerni (1528), I hapned being at London to talke with the printer (T. Berthelet) and to enquire of

---

[1] *STC* 7271, sig. Aaiv[r].   [2] *STC* 5643, sig. ii[r].
[3] *STC* 10902, sig. aa1[r]. For Margaret's activities see 'The Lady Margaret as a Lover of Literature', by W. E. A. Axon, *The Library*, Second Series, vol. VIII (1907), pp. 34–41.

hym, what he thought, and how he lyked the same boke: and he answered, that in his mynde it was a boke moche necessarye, and very profitable for them that toke good hede to the holsome teachynges, and warely folowed the same. And this moche farther he added therto, that so far forthe as ever he coude here, it is of every man very well accepted and allowed. And I sayd, I pray God it may do good, and that is all that I desyre.

And thus in talkynge of one boke and of an other,[1] he came forthe and sayde that if I wolde take so moche peyne as to translate into Inglysshe the boke that is intitled *De medicinia guaiaci, et morbo gallico*, wrytten by that great clerke of Almayne, Ulrich Hutten, Knyght, I shulde, sayd he, do a verye good dede. For seinge hit is sothe as this great clerk writeth of this medicine (for he hymself hath had the verye experience therof), how nedefull and howe beneficiall to the common welth were it?[2]

Encouragement such as this set the translator to work, just as Henry Watson undertook the translation of Sebastian Brandt's *Shyppe of Fooles* (1509) 'out of Frenshe at the requeste of my worshypfull mayster W. de Worde, thrugh the entysement and exhortacyon of the excellent prynces Margarette'.[3] At the same printer's request he translated *Valentyne and Orson* (1503-5) and the *Hystorye of Olyver of Castylle* (1518), while Robert Copland produced *Kynge Appolyne of Thyre* (1510), and other works, also for de Worde.[4]

The demand for a translation, however, did not usually come from a printer or publisher, as in these instances, but from individuals who thought that such a work would be useful. A good example may be seen in the preface written by Richard Foxe, Bishop of Winchester, to his translation of the Rule of St Benedict (1516?). He writes:

For asmoche as every persone ought to knowe the thyng that he is bounde to kepe or accomplisshe, and ignorance of the thynge that he is bounde to do cannot nor may not excuse him, and for so moche also as the reding of the thynge that a persone is bounde to

___

[1] See also p. 59 for another example.
[2] *STC* 14024, sig. [iʳ].   [3] *STC* 3547, sig. A3ᵛ.
[4] See also below, p. 162.

do and execute, except he understande it, is to the executinge then of no thyng vailliable.... We therfore Richarde, by the permission and suffrance of our lorde god, Bisshope of Winchester, revolvinge in our mynde that certayne devoute and religiouse women beinge within our Diocese and under our pastorall charge and cure, have not only professed them to th'observance of the Rule of the holy confessoure Seinte Benet, but also be bounde to rede, lerne, and understond the same when they be Novices and before they be professed. And also after their profession they shulde not onely in them selfe kepe, observe, execute and practise the sayd rule, but also teche other their sisters the same, in so moche that for the same intente they daily rede, and cause to be red, some parte of the sayd Rule by one of the sayd sisters... the which reding is alwayes done in the Latin tonge, wher of they have no knowlege nor understondinge, but be utterly ignorant of the same, wher by they do nat only lose their tyme, but also renne into the evident daunger & perill of the perdicion of their soules.

We the sayd Bisshope knowing and consideringe the premisses, and rememberyng that we may not without like peryll of our sowle suffer the sayd religious wemen...to contynue in their sayde blindeness and ignorance of the sayd Rule...and specially to thentent that the yonge Novices may first knowe and understande the sayde Rule before they professe them to it, so that none of them shall mowe afterward probably say that she wyste nat what she professed, as we know by experience that some of them have sayd in tyme passed. For these causes, and specially at thinstant requeste of our ryght dere and wel beloved doughters in our Lorde Jeshu, th'abbesses of the monasteris of Rumsay, Wharwel Seynt Maries within the citie of Winchester, and the prioresse of Wintnay: oure right religious diocesans, we have translated the sayde rule into oure moders tonge, comune, playne, rounde englysshe, easy, and redy to be understande by the sayde devoute religiouse women. And by cause we wolde not that there shulde be any lacke amongis them of the bookis of this sayd translation, we have therfore, above and besyde certayne bokes therof, which we have geven to the sayde monasteris, caused it to be emprinted by our wel beloved Rycharde Pynson of London, printer.[1]

---

[1] *STC* 1859, sig. A ii[r], and see the Colophon 'Imprinted (by the commaundement of the reverend fader in God, Richard [Foxe], Bisshope of

In this preface the Bishop shows clearly why he went to the trouble of translating the Rule for the nuns, and adds that he was not satisfied that 'certayne bokes therof which we have geven to the sayde monasteris' (presumably manuscript copies) would meet all their needs, so that he went further and caused his work to be put into print, 'bycause we wolde not that there shulde be any lacke amongis them of...this sayd translation'.

This is an unusually full account, but many other translations contain statements which make it clear that they were made for, or printed at the cost of, some wealthy benefactor, religious or layman. Among works of a religious kind we may instance *The Comparation of a Vyrgyn and a Martyr* (1537), translated at the request of the Prior of Merton,[1] or *The Summe and pith of the 150 Psalmes of David* (1539), translated at the request of Thomas Cromwell.[2] Secular works translated at request abound; for example, *The Four Sons of Aymon* [1489], translated by Caxton 'oute of Frenche...at yᵉ request and commandement of ye right noble and vertus Erle, John Erle of Oxford, my goode, synguler and especial lorde', or Sallust's *Cronycle of the warre...agaynst Jugurth* [1520?] put into English by Alexander Barclay at 'the commaundement of the right hye and mighty prince, Thomas, duke of Northfolke'. Barclay throws more light on the matter in his preface, where he tells us that he has translated it 'to [the] pleasure and profet of al gentylmen of this region: but manely of your hyghnes and of the noble men of your progeny and affynite'.[3] Similarly, *Xenophons treatise of housholde* (1537) was put into English

Winchester) by me Rycharde Pynson; printer unto the Kynges noble grace'. Cf. *STC* 17113, where Lyndewood's *Constitutions* are translated into English at the desire of one 'that myght upon my dewty have commanded me' (sig. iiiʳ).

[1] *Early Printed Books...at Lambeth*, S. R. Maitland, no. 439.

[2] *Ibid.* no. 454. Cf. *STC* 14553, sig. iiʳ (1534).

[3] *STC* 21626, sig. aivᵛ. Cf. Froissart's *Chronicles* (1523, 1525) made 'at the highe comaundement of my moost redoubted soverayne lord, Kynge Henry the VIII', or the *De immensa dei misericordia* (1533) of Erasmus, translated at the request of Margaret, Countess of Salisbury, *STC* 10475, sig. A iᵛ.

by Gentian Hervet, 'at the desyre of mayster Geffrey Pole',[1] of Melanchthon's *Apology* [1536?] by R. Taverner at Cromwell's order, 'to thende that the people for whose sakes his booke was commaunded to be translated may the more gredely devoure the same'.[2] Or, to take another example from a very different field,[3] Humphrey Lloyd's epistle to Lord Stafford makes clear the way in which translations could come into being. Lloyd writes:

When as this yere passeyd (Right Honorable and my singular good Lord) I dyd at your commandement translate a lytell treatise of phisicke, intitled ye treasurie of helthe...unto which boke... your lordshipe thoughte it necessary to adjoyne sum lytell treatyse, wherby the phisicyon shuld parfectly judge w^t what kynd of siknesse the pacient was greved withall....Wherupon your lordshyppe readinge over dyverse bokes entreatyng of ye same mater, dyd mete with one according to your owne desire, that is to saye, easy to understane, and very breffe and compendyouse wythall, whiche boke also (accordinge to your Lordships commandement), I have Englished after such simple knoledge and learnyng as I have...playnly and simply to declare ye meaning of ye auctor, so y^t hyt may as well profite ye unlernid, as suche as be endued w^t knoledge, as your lordshipes most godly entent was.[4]

Once the work was written, publication was the obvious next step, and the number of patrons whose names are mentioned as having desired or ordered the printing of original or translated works is of interest; although, in proportion to the number of books published, it is not very considerable. De Worde tells us how he printed Hilton's *Scala Perfectionis* (1494) because Margaret, 'the mighty princesse hath commanded me temprynt this boke, her grace for to deserve',[5] and similarly he printed Fisher's *Sermon at the Funeral of*

---

[1] *STC* 26071, sig. A 1^v.
[2] *STC* 17788·1, sig. A 2^r.
[3] *The iugemēt of vrynes* (1553), by J. Vasseus.
[4] *STC* 24595, sig. A ii^r, ii^v.
[5] *STC* 14042, fol. 135^r.

Henry VII (1509) at her demand.[1] Bishop's Alcock's *Mons perfectionis* (1497) was 'emprynted at Westmestre...at the Instaunce of...Thomas Pryour of the house of Saynt Anne...',[2] while Pynson's works also show a few books printed at request (in particular: the *Missal* produced at the expense of Archbishop Morton in 1500)[3] and the practice continued throughout the period,[4] although with decreasing frequency, until by 1530 it is rare to find that the printer needed this kind of special consideration to urge him to print a work.

This does not mean, however, that the patron had not an important part to play in book production. While he was no longer the sole arbiter of the writer's success or failure, he was still able to lend him powerful support, and a very large number of books published in this period contain specific (and often voluminous) accounts of what their authors hoped to gain from the favour of the person to whom their works were dedicated.

In the first place, authors hoped that ordinary men might be encouraged to read their books since outstanding persons had accepted them. In dedicating his book, *Comon places of scripture* (1538) to Henry VIII, the translator, Richard Taverner, declared that he did so in order that his work 'under your majesties protection and patromonie may the more plausibly, and gredyly be devoured of the people',[5] while that voluminous pamphleteer, Thomas Becon, dedicated his work *A potaciō or drīkynge for this holy tyme of Lēt* (1543) to Sir T. Neville, because 'in so doyng, I doubte not, but that both this and al my other workes shal be receyved wythe the more

---

[1] *STC* 10900, sig. A i^r. Cf. *STC* 10902, *The fruytfull saynges of Dauyd* (1508) quoted above, p. 42.

[2] *STC* 279, sig. E iii^v.

[3] *STC* 16173. 'Perhaps the finest book printed in England before 1501.'

[4] See, for example, *STC* 11396–7 (Froissart), 21626 (Sallust) mentioned above, 17242, *Myrrour of good maners* [1523?] and 13256, Hetoum's *Chronicle* [1520?], etc.

[5] *STC* 21753, sig. A vi^r. Cf. *STC* 12143, Gower's *Confessio Amantis* [1532], dedicated to Henry VIII for a similar reason.

grate, thankefull and acceptable myndes'.[1] Earlier in the preface Becon says:

> I have not forgotten to howe gentle and thanckefull mydne (as I maye passe over ye singuler beneficence and great liberalyte, which at that tyme ye shewed to me) your right honorable maystership did receive ye Christmasse Bancket which nowe of late (1542) I dedycated unto your name.[2]

It is not often that a writer definitely mentions the 'singuler beneficence and great liberalyte' that have accompanied the acceptance of a dedication, but it should be borne in mind, and is a clear link with earlier manuscript conditions.[3]

For a last example we may take William Baldwin's *A treatise of morall phylosophie* (1547), because his dedication to Lord Edward Beauchamp, Earl of Hertford, is so very explicit. He writes:

> Whan I had fynyshed thys tretise (ryghte honorable Lorde) I thoughte it mete, according to the good and accustomed usage of wryters, to dedycate it unto some woorthye persone, whose thankefull recyvyng and allowyng therof, myghte cause it to bee the better accepted of other. And forsomuche as it was not of value to bee given to anye auncient Counsailler, whiche are all therein sufficiently seen alreadie, I judged it moste conveniente to be given to some that were yonger: emonge whome for so muche as youre learnynge and vertuous towardness was greatlye commended of dyvers and sundrye credible persones, I doubted not but that your good disposition, naturally taken of your vertuous parents, woulde take in worthe the gifte of this simple treatise. . . .[4]

From time to time, especially in the forties and fifties, we come across books offered as New-Year gifts. 'The use of

---

[1] *STC* 1750, sig. A vi^r. Cf. *STC* 20091 (1556), sig. A ii^v.

[2] *STC* 1750, sig. A ii^r. Cf. the same author's acknowledgement of the 'liberality which your grace [Anne, Duchess of Somerset] hath most bounterously shewed unto me since I came first to your service' (*STC* 1720, p. 13).

[3] See, for example, the gift by Henry VIII to Polydore Vergil.

[4] *STC* 1253, sig. A ii^r.

gyvyng gyftes by men to theyr frendes the fyrst day of the newe yere', writes Sir Anthony Cope in 1547, 'hath of longe tyme continewed within this Realme of Englande, wyth an opinion that the luckie beginning is a good token of lyke prosperous successe duryng the rest of the yere', and he goes on to say that he warmly recommends the custom, but not as a 'token or presage of good fortune to come'[1]—the more especially when it is to come from the dedicatee!

The widespread custom of giving New-Year gifts to friends and acquaintances was seized on by some authors as an excuse to dedicate their book to some patron. In 1506 Erasmus wrote to Richard Foxe, Bishop of Winchester, saying that 'the fashion of distributing presents on New Year's Day...has come down to us from remote ages; and is thought to be of happy omen both to the persons to whom the presents go, and to those who receive them in return'.[2] The earliest example of this practice among English authors known to me is found in *The dyetary of ghostly helthe*, printed by de Worde on 20 November 1520, in which the anonymous writer speaks of the custom whereby

in the begynnynge of this newe yere, my good systers...so many frendes gyve tokens of custome one to another, whiche custome some use it for good lucke of a newe yere, some to procure carnal love, some to get a greater benefyte therby...and some with ryght godly intent to purchace ghostly love,

and goes on to say that he will return the presents he has received from many of the sisters by preparing this 'one token for you all, to profyte eche of you'.[3]

For these reasons or for others, the opportunity was too good a one not to be taken by a number of authors. Both T. Becon and R. Crowley entitle one of their books *A new*

---

[1] *STC* 5717, sig.*ii^r.
[2] F. M. Nichols, *The Epistles of Erasmus* (1901), vol. I, p. 391. For much information about this custom, see the article by H. W. Garrod, 'Erasmus and his English Patrons', in *The Library*, Fifth Series, vol. IV (1950), pp. 1–13.
[3] *STC* 6833, sig. aii^r.

yeares gyfte,[1] while other authors explicitly declare them to be so in their dedicatory letters or prefaces.[2]

Patronage was sought, not only that the general reader might be encouraged, but also that the author might be protected against the evil tongue of the detractor. The fullest statement (perhaps overstatement) of the feeling against such men is to be found in *The image of bothe churches* (1550) by John Bale, who writes: 'The other ("cruel enemy") is Momus or Zoilus,[3] yea rather one whiche playe it both partes under the cloke of a Christian. This cruel carper and malicious quarreller leaveth no mans worke unrebuked.'

For many years previous to Bale's diatribe, however, writers had feared the sons of Zoilus. Sir T. Elyot was constantly harping on the subject from his earliest work, *The gouvernour* (1531), onwards. There he implores Henry VIII to 'be patrone and defendour of this little warke agayne the assaultes of maligne interpretours; whiche fayle nat to rente and deface the renoune of wryters, they themselves beinge in nothinge to the publike weale profitable'.[4] Bartholomew Traheron sets forth his translation of J. de Vigo's *Chirurgerye* (1543) 'let some busie speakers, rather than doers, bable what they lyste';[5] William Hughe offers to the reader his work, *The troubled mans medicine* (1546) and adds at the end of his address to the reader: 'As for the Criticall censores whyche do nothynge them selfes that good is, but carpe and reprehende other mens doinges, we passe lytte of, doubtynge not but all honest hartes wyl gently accept it'.[6] Robert Record calls his critics 'monsters (I dare not call them men)...which delyte

---

[1] *STC* 1738 (1543); *STC* 6087 (1549).

[2] See, for example, *STC* 20062, *The preceptes of Plutarch for the preseruacion of good healthe* (1543); *STC* 25852, H. Wingfield, *A compendious treatise...of healthe* [1551?]; *STC* 191, W. Prat, *The description of...Aphrique* (1554).

[3] *STC* 1299, sig. a ii.ᵛ. Momus, 'a curious carper'; Zoilus, 'a poete, whyche envied Homerus: and therefore the enviers of welle lerned men are called Zoili' (*The dictionary of syr T. Elyot* (1538)). For the Zoili after 1550, see C. H. Conley, *The First English Translators of the Classics* (1927).

[4] *STC* 7635, sig. a iii.ᵛ.   [5] *STC* 24720, sig. *ii.ᵛ.

[6] *STC* 13910, sig. A i.ᵛ.

to deprave nature and hyr workes';[1] Thomas Phaer says that 'I never intended nor yet do entend to satisfy ye mindes of any suche pikfaultes (which wyll do nothynge but detract and judge other) snuffynge at all that offendeth the noses of theyr Momishe affeccions, howsoever laudable it be other wayes'.[2] Finally, Thomas Nicolls compendiously styles them as 'curyous, fantasticall parsons, pryvey diffamours of dylygent and vertuous laboure...grevously pynched wyth envye'.[3]

Indeed, nothing is more remarkable than this widespread fear that beset all who put their work into print. From the beginning of the century onwards, authors comment on the dangers they run, so that it is possible, despite the intemperate way in which they express their fears, that they believed them to be well founded.

It is against a background such as this that we must read the continuous series of dedicatory letters and addresses with which writers appeal to their patrons for protection. The matter is put clearly by Thomas Paynell in a dedicatory letter to Lord Mountjoy, prefixed to his translation of Agapetus (1534), in which he says that writers 'whan so ever any of them did either make worke, or translate any excellent mans worke, they are wont for ye defence thereof exquisitely to chose someone well lerned or noble parsone, to whome they shulde vowe and dedicate theyr laboure'.[4] This is what animates writers, such as Sir T. Elyot, to ask Henry VIII to be 'patrone and defendour' of his work,[5] or causes Richard Taverner to put forth his translation of Erasmus's *Epystle...in laude and prayse of matrymony* [1530?], under the 'noble protection' of Thomas Cromwell.[6] In fact, the 'protector' or 'protection'

[1] *STC* 20816, *The vrinal of physick* (1547), sig. Aii^r. Cf. his further attack on the 'besye brablynge' of such 'curyouse carpers' (sig. Aii^v), and *STC* 17502, *The Myrrour or glasse of maners* (1547) which speaks of 'cankerde and envyous stomakes' and of 'malencoly myndes replered wyth venym of intoxicate malyce' (sig. Avi^v).

[2] *STC* 11970, *The regiment of life* (1550), sig. Aii^r.

[3] *STC* 24056, *The hystory writtone by Thucidides* (1550), sig. Aiii^r.

[4] *STC* 193, sig. aii^r. Cf. *STC* 15218 (1560), sig. a3^v.

[5] See above, p. 50.　　　[6] *STC* 10492, sig. A1^v.

becomes a commonplace in the works of the next few decades.[1] Few writers felt they could afford to take the high line expressed by John Pilkington, Bishop of Durham, who wrote:

> Althoughe the commen usage... is to require the defense of some worthy personage of learnynge or aucthoryty for the thing that is written; yet the majestie of the matter in this booke [*Aggeus the prophete* (1560)] is suche that it rather defendes than sekes defense.[2]

What this general practice led to may best be seen by noting the dedicatory letter, addressed by an anonymous author to Lord Fitzwalter, son and heir to the Earl of Sussex. In offering him his work, *The institucion of a gentleman*[3] (1555), the author writes:

> it hath ben of long tyme ye maner of writers to dedicate their works to noble men, nothing considering before whether their works were fyt for courtly reading or no, but sought rather to occupye muche tyme in eloquente Epistles, in praysyng the parsone of the noble man, pronouncing the honoure of his predecessours, declaring ye genealogie of his noble house, w^t other like thinges, hardly avoyding the note of playne flattery, whereby such men have falne into a double abuse; th'one in geving unto noble men such presentes as are unfyt for their parsons, in the other they abused themselves: for of all coloured thynges flatery is soonest espyed.

It may be soon espied, but that did not prevent many writers, as this author says, from pouring out pages of wearisome panegyric, among which only now and then a note of sincerity is struck, as by Christopher Langton, who offers his benefactor, Sir Arthur Darcy the first-fruit of his study in recognition of his patron's 'kyndenesse and benevolence',

---

[1] See, for example, *STC* 11220, *The true dyfferēs between ye regall power and the ecclesiasticall power* (1548?); 20406, *The fal of the late Arrian* (1549); 5468, *The art of phisiognomie* (1556).

[2] *STC* 19926, sig. A ii^r.

[3] *STC* 14104, sig. *5^r. Cf. the remarks of John Major in his *History of Greater Britain* (trans. Constable, *Scottish Hist. Soc.* vol. x (1892), pp. cxxxiii ff.) on those who 'put on the mask of flattery rather than that of a historian'.

and as a token of his 'pure zele and love'[1] or by Bartholomew Traheron, who writes to 'good mayster Tracy' the following charming dedicatory sentences:

> As touching my laboure, applyed to ye translation of this present worke [J. de Vigo's *Chirurgerye*] in consideration of youre sondrye benefittes conferred unto me, I dedycate it unto youe....For whan I was destitute of father and mother, youe conceaved a very fatherly affection towarde me, and not onely brought me up in the universities of this and forayne realmes, with your great costes and charges, but also moste earnestly exhorted me to forsake the puddles of sophisters and to fetche water from the pure fountaynes of the scripture.[2]

The patron then may be found gracing a very large proportion of books printed before 1557. From Henry VIII's time onward many of them are dedicated to the sovereign—Henry VIII, the Protector Somerset, Edward VI, and Mary are offered tributes couched in every form of extravagant language, while their spouses and children are also lauded and asked to accept 'this cuppe of troubled water', or 'this frute of my spare houres'. Great statesmen, such as Wolsey and Cromwell, are pestered by men eager to dedicate their works to them, while the aristocracy in general are constantly asked to receive and favour the work of one of their retainers, or of some inferior gentleman. In short, anyone of position was fair game. His name at the head of the book, for the various reasons given above, made author and publisher feel more secure, and more hopeful that the work would receive a hearing.

---

[1] *STC* 15204 (1550?), sig. A iii^r. Cf. *STC* 1723, *The goldē boke of Christen matrimonye* (1542), dedicated to Anthony Gayse 'as a manifest testimony of myne unfayned love and ryght harty amite' (sig. B viii^v).

[2] *STC* 24720 (1543), sig. *ii^v. Traheron obeyed 'good mayster Tracy's' exhortations in later life, when he wrote *STC* 24168 (1557), *An exposition of a parte of S. Johannes Gospel*, which the troublous times made necessary for it to be printed abroad [Wesel?], and *STC* 24174 (1558), *A warning to England to repente* [Wesel?].

CHAPTER V

THE DEMAND FOR BOOKS

While the patron was a welcome figure in the printer's shop, and exercised a considerable influence on early book production, the printer was well aware that something more than patronage was necessary if he was to sell sufficient books to make a living. He knew that there was a growing reading public. The demands made upon the scriveners for manuscripts, both in the vernacular and in other languages, were considerable. The fifteenth century had seen the rapid growth of the manufacture of vernacular manuscripts to meet a great variety of needs, and from Caxton onwards, printers were aware of the desire of men and women for texts upon all kinds of practical matters, as well as upon others dealing with religious, legal, scientific, or educational topics. Even Caxton (despite his obvious leanings towards certain types of literature) showed from an early date that he recognized this, and catered for a wide variety of tastes and of people.

After his death, and as soon as de Worde and Pynson were able to settle down to their task, the books coming from their presses reflect their desire to serve the widest possible public, and throughout this period the same is true of most printers. While a few might specialize, most of them endeavoured to attract the attention of the 'ordinary reader' (if we may use such a term at this early date), or the 'lewd' as they were commonly called. To this end the printers spread their net wide, using every means in their power to find out what their readers wanted and how they could most successfully be attracted. Many books, as we have seen, came to them with a request that they should print them, and they did so, either feeling it to be a fair business risk, or hoping that they would have the support and perhaps the financial backing of the sponsor. When such books had a religious, educational or an immediate practical usefulness the printer had little to fear. In any case, many of these books were of no great size, and the cost of a moderate edition could not have been large. The heroic ventures of Caxton and of his immediate successors in putting forth large-scale folio volumes were not widely followed. Quartos, and later octavos, became the fashion, and even these often consisted of a few sheets only, so that the printers' risks were soon spread over a number of volumes of varying size and covering a number of subjects.

Unfortunately, few of the printers followed Caxton's example, and enlightened their readers as to the reasons leading them to put books into print, although as we shall see there are a number of prefaces by printers of a helpful nature. Things are better when we turn to see what prompted authors, although caution is necessary before always accepting what they say *au pied de la lettre*. Very few go so far as to say that the desire to see themselves in print has actuated them. They generally speak of their wish to benefit their country in some way or other, or to assert their belief that their work will be found comforting, helpful or even essential. If their assertions were taken at their face value we should be forced to regard these men as some of the most modest and humble folk who have ever lived. Here, however, they are but following medieval tradition. 'Go, little book', was the formula, accompanied by a variety of self-excusatory and denigrating phrases, with which the medieval author put forth his work, and the sixteenth-century writer conformed to this tradition. Hence, very many works contain a protestation of the writer's incompetence: 'I do knowledge mine owne reudnes to be such, that scant I can satisfie and please mine owne minde in the doinge therof, being often tyme displeased and offended with my selfe that I can do no better, &c.',[1] writes Nicholas Lesse, and many others are even more anxious to excuse their

---

[1] *STC* 10429, sig. Aii^r. *A very fruitful and godly exposition vpõ the XV. psalme* [1550?], translated by N. Lesse from the work of J. Epinus.

'rudeness', or the 'simple and illiterate treatise' that they have compiled. A good example may be seen in 'Lenvoy and excuse of Robert Copland, the translatour and imprynter of this boke'—*The secrete of secretes of Arystotle* (1528):

> In humble maner, and moost due reverence,
> Tremblynge for drede afore thy soverayne,
> Yf thy chaunce be to come in presence
> Where ony person shall the there retayne
> Submytte thy selfe as one that wolde be fayne
> His grace to please, in all maner degre
> And of thy rudenesse for to pardon the...
>
> Yf any man dyspyse the language rude
> Whiche barayne is of puryd eloquence,
> Desyre them that they do not delude
> Thy fronysate mater full of sentence,
> But in theyr hertes enprynt thy morall sence,
> Which compyled is by wysdome naturall
> Of prudent men, the veray governall.[1]

We need not take these protestations too seriously: they are all part of the literary convention which did not allow the author as yet any very exalted place in the commonwealth.

Some authors justified their works (especially their translations) by claiming that they had made them so that Englishmen might not lack what other men abroad might have. Sir T. Elyot translated *The doctrinal of princes* by Isocrates from the Greek, 'to the intent that thei, which do not understande Greeke or Latine, shoulde not lacke the commoditie and pleasure which maie be taken in readyng therof',[2] while Nicholas Grimalde's translation of Cicero's three books of duties was made 'to do likewise for my contrymen as Italians, Frenchemenne, Spaniardes, Duchemen and other foreins have liberally done for theirs',[3] and almost identical words are used by William Warde in his translation of *The secretes of Alexis of Piemont*.[4]

---

[1] *STC* 770, sig. 1 iii[v].
[3] *STC* 5282 (1558), sig. ¶ iii[r].
[2] *STC* 14277 [1534?], sig. Aii[v].
[4] *STC* 293 (1558), sig. *iv[r].

Nowhere was the desire to make works in foreign tongues available to Englishmen more strongly felt than by authors of religious and homiletic works. William Bonde, the reputed author of *The Pylgrimage of perfection* (1526), tells us that he commenced to write his treatise in Latin, but 'anone as I had sette the penne to the boke, it was put in to my mynde to drawe it in the Englysshe tonge, where by it myght be the more accepte to many, and especyally to suche as understande no Latyn'.[1] Gentian Hervet translated a treatise by Erasmus, entitled *De immensa dei misericordia* (1533) so that 'where as afore lerned men only dyd get out bothe pleasure and great frute in redynge of this boke, nowe every man, as welle rude as lerned, may have this sermon of the mercy of God as common unto him as the mercy of God it selfe is'.[2]

Sermons, homilies and devotional works of every kind were eagerly sought after, and translations made available much that would otherwise have had only a limited public. The *Imitatio Christi*, for instance, in its various translations was only the most famous of a large body of devotional writings which found their way into English homes of all classes of society.[3]

Not only works of this character, but also controversial pamphlets and books, many of them translations, were pressed upon the printers and often had a considerable sale. It was immensely important for the Reformers to get their 'New Religion' before as wide an audience as possible, and the trouble that Wolsey, Cromwell and their agents had in controlling or suppressing much of this literature is indicative of its pervasive

---

[1] *STC* 3277, fol. ii^r, and compare *STC* 5278, *Tullyes Offyces* (1534), sig. b3^r.

[2] *STC* 10475, sig. A2^r. *STC* 4410, Calvin's *Treatyse concernynye* [*sic*] *the sacrament* [1549?], translated by Coverdale, illustrates the care taken to help the 'lewd'. Coverdale says that he has made the translation 'avoydyng in all that I myght the darke maner of translatynge after the Latine phrases, to the intente the Englysshe readare myghte have the full understandynge herof, wythoute anye knowlege of the Latyne tonge'. Sig. Ai^r.

[3] See, for example, *STC* 1917, *The meditatōns of saint Bernard* [1499?]; *STC* 3259, *Speculum vitae Christi* [1486]; *STC* 3277, *The Pylgrimage of perfection* (1526); *STC* 3325, *The boke of Noblenes* [1550?], etc.

circulation. Book after book makes its appeal to 'all Chrysten people' or to 'the Christian reader'. John Fox tells us that he 'thought it not unprofytable to translate this golden boke of Urbanus' (*An instruccyon of christen fayth*, 1550?), since it was 'very fruytful for every christen man'.[1] Walter Lynne is even more explicit in his translation of *The true beliefe in Christ and his sacramentes* (1550) which he has made so

that al men, women and chyldren would read it. Not as they have bene here tofore accustomed to reade the fained storyes of Robinhode, Clem of the Cloughe, wyth suche lyke to passe the tyme wythal; neyther as of late dayes men have used to reade thinges for novellities: but for to spende the time wel, and to put away their newe errours (grounded upon the Romeish rock) by the knowledge of the olde fayeth, that is buylded upon the foundacion of the prophetes and Apostles.[2]

Religious works were only one (although the largest) class of books which were put into print more or less directly because their authors and the printers felt that there was a need to be met. The fields of law, education and information were profitable areas for publishing, as we shall see later, and many writers and readers must have brought pressure to bear on the printers to set out works of these kinds. For example, the prefaces to many law-books emphasize their usefulness to the student, or their value to the more advanced practitioner, or the way in which they can help the layman concerned with the law. Again, we have an admirable instance of the effect which individuals could have on publication told to us by Robert Copland, printer and translator of Guy de Chauliac's *Questyonary of cyrurgyens* [1542]. He says that

a certeyne yonge gentyllman enured in the sayd scyence [of surgery] had a boke of the same in Frenche [who] moved the ryght honest

[1] *STC* 20847, sig. A4ᵛ. Cf. *STC* 20131, *A postill or collection of moste godly doctrine* (1550) 'verye profitable for all Curates, Parentes, maysters of householdes, and other governers of youth'. And see, sig. X iiiʳ: 'Finally, the honest housholders, for whose sake principally thys booke is put forth'. See also, *STC* 11917, *A glasse for housholders* (1542).

[2] *STC* 14576, sig. Aiiᵛ.

persone, Henry Dabbe, bybliopolyst and stacyoner to have it translated in to Englysshe. At whose instigacyon...I have enterprysed to do it in folowynge dyrectly my copy.[1]

Dabbe shared the risk of the venture with another, for the book was printed by R. Wyer 'for Henry Dabbe and Rycharde Banckes'.

An even more instructive example is furnished by W. Waterman who translated *The fardle of facions* (1555). From his dedicatory letter to the Earl of Arundel he says

that a fewe yeres paste, at the instaunce of a good citizein (who might at those daies, by authoritie commaunde me), I had begonne to translate a little booke...but so corrupted in the printing, that aftre I had wrasteled a space with sondrie printes, I rather determined to lose my labour of the quartre translacion then to be shamed with the haulf. And throwing it aside, [I] entended no further to wearie my self therwithall—at the leaste untill I mighte finde a booke of a bettre impression. In searching wherof, at this my retourne to my studie, although I found not at the full that that I sought for, yet undrestanding among the bookesellers (as one talke bringes in another)[2] that men of good learning and eloquence ...had not thought it vayne to bestowe their time aboute the translacion therof...it kindled me againe, upon regard of mine owne profite, and other mennes moe, to bring that to some good pointe, that earst I had begonne....[3]

So Waterman made his version of part of a celebrated work on 'the aunciente maners, customes, and lawes of the peoples enhabiting the two partes of the earth, called Affrike and Asie'.

A slight change is noticeable, however, in the attitude of a few writers, mostly in the fifties, who began to express a belief that their writings (usually translations) would be of use to the country, since their contents would give readers a model on which to base their thoughts and actions. As early as 1544 Sir Anthony Cope translated from Livy *The historie*...

---

[1] *STC* 12468, sig. A1[v], and see p. 236.
[2] See also above, p. 43, where T. Paynell is conversing with T. Berthelet.
[3] *STC* 3197, sig. *ii[v].

of Anniball and Scipio, and in his dedicatory letter to Henry VIII said that his work is to do 'all noble men and gentilemen of the realme greate pleasure and commoditie', by putting into English the history of 'the two moste renoumed empires of the worlde...', whereby, 'bysyde the plesaunt bestowyng of tyme, in the readyng therof, men also may lerne bothe to dooe displeasure to theyr ennemies, and to avoyde the crafty and daungerous baites, which shall be layde for theim'.[1] A few years later was printed Thomas Nicolls' translation of Thucydides' *Peloponnesian War*, taken from a French version, which has much the same point of view, but it was left for John Brende in his version of Quintus Curtius's *Historie of...the actes of the greate Alexander* (1553) to state the case most fully. He writes:

Seing histories be then so good and necessary, it were muche requisite for mens instruccion, that they were translated into suche tounges as most men myght understand them: and specially the histories of antiquitye, whyche both for the greatness of the actes done in those daies, and for the excellencie of the writers have much majestie and many ensamples of virtue. I therefore havyng alwayes desired that we englishmen might be founde as forwarde in that behalfe as other nations, which have brought all worthie histories into their naturall language, did a fewe yeares paste attempt the translacion of Quintus Curtius, and lately upon an occasion performed and accomplished the same.[2]

This, of course, is not a new point of view. Much medieval literature was composed for the instruction and edification of its first hearers or readers. Charles the Bold as a youth listened to the exploits of Gawain and Lancelot being read to him, and later in life before returning to rest would listen for an hour or two to the lofty histories of Rome, especially liking to hear of Caesar, Hannibal and Alexander 'whom he wished to follow and imitate'. Froissart tells us he was entertained by the Earl of Foix 'and every night after supper I reed...to hym, and whyle I reed there was none durst speke any worde, bycause he

[1] *STC* 5719, sig. a iiiʳ.   [2] *STC* 6142, sig. A iiiᵛ.

wolde I shulde be well understande, wherin he tooke great solace'.[1]

Not only history, but other forms of literature were read for their 'message'. The preface to Brian Anslay's translation of Christine de Pisan's *Cyte of Ladyes* (1521) says that it is daily seen that noblemen 'do endyte and rede, In bokes olde, theyr worthy myndes to fede', and that when the work was shown to the Earl of Kent he exhorted the writer of the preface (H. Pepwell?) to print it.[2]

In addition to thinking of the needs of others, a number of authors also thought of themselves in explaining their reasons for writing. No plea was more favoured by authors than that they wrote 'to eschew idleness'. Fear of the 'peryllous infeccyon' as Chertsey calls it, was ever present in all men's minds, for idleness led to worse things. The anonymous author of *The institucion of a gentleman* (1555) tells us that 'idlenes is the Mistres of wanton appetites, and portres of lustes gates: for no man entreth into the pallace of Lust unles he be fyrst let in by idlenes, who after a man be entered, she bryngeth him strayght waye into the presence of Lust'.[3] Hence, Sir Thomas Elyot is unwearying in his insistence on the need 'to exercise my wytte and to avoyde idelnes', lest, as John Bankes says, 'I coulde not be justly rekened or taken for a membre of the mystical body of Christe, if that... I shoulde be founde ydle and unoccupied'.[4] So men turned to book-making, feeling as Robert Copland did when he praised an author with the words:

> The inflammate desyre of your good intent
> News to compyle, eschewynge ydelnesse,
> Cometh of grace.[5]

---

[1] *The Chronicles of Froissart* (Globe ed.), p. 329. And see Copland's prologue to his translation of *Apollonius of Tyre*, ed. E. W. Ashbee (1870) where he speaks of heroes whose 'glorie is eternally regystred in the boke of fame' by the aid of the historiographers.

[2] *STC* 7271, sig. Aaiv^r. 'And I obeyenge gladly his instaunce, Have done my devoyre'.   [3] *STC* 14104, sig. Kiii^v.   [4] *STC* 21065 [1550?], sig. Aiv^v.

[5] *Guystarde and Sygysmonde* (1532), sig. A2^r.

On the other hand those that disparaged such efforts were children of idleness, 'grevously pynched wyth envye that others shulde travayle to utter theyr talente to the commodytie of many'.

So much did the plea become a fashion that we have an amusing travesty of it in a mock-serious dedicatory letter, addressed by the translator 'Olyver Oldwanton to the ryght honorable and his especiall good lady, the lady Lust of Pawesforde'. He writes:

Callynge to mynde the oppinion of Aristippus, a certeyne Philosophre of thepicuriens secte, who by profounde argumentes and sundry authorities used to maynteyne that it was lawefull for man and woman at vacante tymes to exercise themselves with kyssinge and imbracynge (together with the suites and ceremonies therunto belongynge) rather than to syt styll and be idle. The same, my joly good lady, hath caused me so greatly to detest the wicked vice of idlenes, that in eschewynge thereof I have had sundry devyces howe I myght more conveniently be occupyed, and thereupon fyndynge myselfe more apte than able for the exercise aforesaide, and moreover as well ignoraunte in every crafte and facultie of bodely labour as destitute both of lernynge and knowledge, wherby to set forthe any worthy matter of newe, I determined at length, because I have understandynge in sundrye tounges, to take upon me the translation of some worke in Englyshe, and for that purpose, perusyng a numbre of bookes, I chaunced to fynde a lyttle queare intiteled the *Image of Idlenesse* wrytten many yeres past in the Troyane or Cornyshe speache, &c.[1]

The publication of books in this period would therefore appear to present few abnormal features. Once the printers began to gauge the size and diversity of their market they exploited it in various fashions, according to their temperaments and their resources. The King's Printer had obviously a special place among his fellows, and his output was con-

---

[1] STC 25196, *A lyttle treatyse called the Image of idlenesse, conteynynge certeyne matters moved betwene Walter Wedlocke and Bawdin Bacheler* [1558?], sig. A iii[v].

siderably controlled by the commands of the Crown. Apart from this (and within the limits imposed by the licensing authorities, from time to time) printers used their initiative in deciding what to print. A few of them, such as the Rastells and Redman, specialized in law publications, or in the production of small cheap handbooks of popular science and information, as did R. Wyer. The majority, however, knew very well that religious and devotional books had the best chance of selling, so that these bulk large in their lists. Other works appear less frequently, and often required the pressure of events or the influence of a patron to bring them into print.

A glance at some of the books printed about 1550 may serve as a useful indication of the diversity of reasons that brought books into circulation. *The twelfe steppes of abuses made by the famus Doctor S. Augustine* was printed by the pleading of the translator to his patroness, the Duchess of Richmond, that 'so godly, so frutful, so sound a work of good doctrine' should not perish.[1] John Larke translated *The boke of Noblenes*, 'because y^t all noble men be not very experte & instruct in the tonges, it semeth also profytable and necessary that the boke be had in the Englysshe tonge'.[2] *A boke of presidētes*, on the other hand, has a strictly practical purpose; and, as its title-page declares, is 'exactly written in maner of a register, newly imprinted and corrected, with addicions of diverse, necessary and sundery Presidentes, mete for all suche persons to knowe as desire to learne the forme and manner how to make all maner of Evidence and Instruments'.[3] Walter Lynne tells Edward VI that 'I have thought it my duetye...emongest all other to set forth thys shorte Cronicle',[4] which Carion 'gathered with great diligence of the best authours that have written in Hebrue, Greke or Latine'. Richard Sherry, 'at the request of some of my friends, and for the profit of such as understande no

[1] *STC* 84, sig. Aiv^r.   [2] *STC* 3325, sig. Ai^v.
[3] *STC* 3331. Cf. STC 14124 [1550?], *An introduction to the knowledge and understanding...to make indentures....*
[4] *STC* 4626, sig. *ii^r.

Latin...toke in hand to translat the exposicion of the sixte chapter of John...written in the Laten by ye right excellente clarcke John Brencius'.[1] R. Grafton printed a volume containing all the proclamations made in the reign of Edward VI up to 1550, so that men might know what they should do.[2] Nicholas Lesse translated an exposition on the fifteenth Psalm by Joannes Epinus 'for a certain peculiar deare friend of mine whom I perceived very desierous of the knoledge therof, which is unlerned and lamenteth him selfe much y^t he hath lacked the good, ye vertuous bringing up in lernyng y^t many men have had to their great confort'.[3] The translation of John XXI's *Treasury of healthe* was undertaken by Humphrey Lloyd as 'a meanes whereby I myghte profytte thys my natyve country' by making the treatise available 'and knowen in thys oure vulgare Englisshe tonge'[4] and so on.

These examples may be sufficient to show the variety of causes which are put forward by authors within a short space of time. They may not all be sincere, but on the whole they are to be trusted, and form a useful guide to the motives that actuated the authors in putting their wares before the public. Before this could be done, however, unless they were willing to pay the printer's bill (as was occasionally done), they had to persuade the printer that there was a public for their wares, and this they did, we may suppose, by reasons similar to those they put forward to patron or reader. What their contemporaries accepted for the truth we may accept.

---

[1] *STC* 3603, sig. A viii^r.
[2] *STC* 7758. For Grafton's preface see p. 135.
[3] *STC* 10429, sig. A ii^r.
[4] *STC* 14652^a, sig. A ii^r. Cf. *STC* 21065, sig. A vi^r.

CHAPTER VI

THE VARIETY OF BOOKS

The above chapters have given an account of the conditions and circumstances in which the book-trade made its way in these earliest years of its existence. It now remains to examine the variety of literary wares laid before the reading public.

1. *Religion*

A survey of the books published in English up to 1557 cannot fail to note the predominating position held by works of a religious and devotional nature.[1] Caxton, de Worde, Pynson and Berthelet were all publishers of such works on a large scale —about 40% of the output of de Worde and Pynson, and at least 45% of that of Caxton and Berthelet was of this kind. Other printers of this period, for the most part, show a corresponding preference for religious works, and we shall not be far wrong in thinking that the printers, as a body, gave something like half their output to this side of their business. The reason is obvious: the range and variety of religious works were considerable, and the printers could rely on a steady demand for such writings.

To begin with there was the need for all kinds of liturgical works necessary for the performances of the Church services. The demand appears to have been very heavy, and throughout this period the English presses alone were unable to cope with it, so that large numbers of works printed abroad were imported into the kingdom. Some of these were printed for individual stationers, while others were sent over by enterprising printers

---

[1] A preliminary survey of the earlier part of the period from this point of view will be found in 'The Bibliography of some Devotional Books printed by the earliest English Printers', by F. A. Gasquet, *Trans. Bibliographical Soc.*, vol. VII (1904), pp. 163–89.

from as far afield as Venice on the advice of their agents, and were readily accepted for sale by the stationers. Not less than 60% of all breviaries, books of hours (or primers), manuals, missals, etc. printed by 1557 came from overseas presses, despite the restrictions on the importation of books printed abroad from time to time.[1] Something like one book in ten printed in this period was of a liturgical nature, and formed a ready selling product for all concerned in its production and marketing.

In addition to these official service-books a mass of general religious literature was published. There were works intended for the instruction of the clergy; helps to priests in their parochial duties; books of moral instruction for the young; lives of Saints; treatises *de quatuor novissimis*; works concerning the conduct of monks, nuns and others devoted to the life of the religious;[2] books treating of the character of the life of the ordinary Christian; volumes of sermons, etc.[3] Furthermore, as the century went on, and the controversy arising from the separation of the Church of England from that of Rome developed, a great many works of an *ex parte* nature on this topic were issued.[4] The publication of the Bible in the vernacular, and the many commentaries and works of exegesis which followed, also kept the printers busy.

The nature and urgency of the demand for religious works can be seen from the introductory matter prefixed to many volumes. The needs of those professed to religion are met by works such as *The Pylgrimage of perfection* (1526) 'very profytable for all chrysten people to rede: and in especyall to all relygyous persones moche necessary'.[5] Or again there was

---

[1] See above, p. 31.

[2] Religious—i.e. men and women dedicated to the life of those living according to a rule, and members of some religious Order.

[3] For convenience of discussion and comparison, I have adopted the classification of Cardinal Gasquet, *op. cit.*, so far as books published by 1510 are concerned, and have added additional categories to deal with later developments.

[4] See below, p. 71.   [5] *STC* 3277, sig. Ai[r].

The Directory of conscience [1527] 'compyled by one of the fathers of Syon and now put in impressyon at the instant request of an other devout religyous man' for 'the gostly edifycacyon of all them that be, or entend to be, the spouses of our Redemour';[1] or lastly, *A deuoute epystle...for them that be timorous...in conscience* [1535?] 'compyled by a brother of Syon...and sent to a devoute relygiouse woman of Denney, at the instaunce of one of her spirituall frendes'.[2]

As an early example of works that appealed to a more general audience we can take *The medytacōns of saynt Bernarde* (1496), translated from Latin into English, 'by a devoute student of the universytee of Cambrydge...the which caused it fyrst to be put in prynt'. In his preface the translator tells us that he does so,

bycause I wold have so gode and prouffytable a thyng comyn to many, and also because that hastely after the translacyon hereof, before it was duely correcte and ordred, it was by devoute persons transumpte and copied, I wot not how ofte, ayenst my wyll. Therefore have I now...for to avoyde and eschewe the jeopardye and hurte that maye comme by that yt was not duly corrected, put it more dylygently corrected and ordered to the Imprinter, in lettynge and destrucyon of all other copyed after the foresayd uncorrecte translacyon.[3]

The translator's zeal to help his fellow Christians was evidently matched by their own zeal for spiritual guidance, so that they were even prepared to have manuscript copies made of the precious original translation, since they knew of no better means of obtaining it.

Many other examples might be given of the anxiety of men to share what they thought to be precious. R. Tracy translated a work entitled *The preparacyon to the crosse, wyth the preparacion to deeth* [1530?] because 'in the readynge of this boke I receyed such consolation and comfort that I thought it moste necessary, yea and expedient...to translate the same into

---

[1] *STC* 6904, title-page and sig. A ii[v].
[2] *STC* 3276, sig. A i[r].   [3] *STC* 1916, sig. A i[v].

englysshe and to put it forthe in printe'.[1] Another example may be seen in John Faukener's preface to *The troubled mans medicine* (1546), a work by William Hughe, which is of interest as showing how some books got into print. Faukener writes:

> Not long ago, it happened me to reade this boke then not printed which was written and dedicate unto a frende of myne, as a thyng whereby he myght be comforted in his adversities that then chaunced unto hym. By the whych he was comforted....Whyche thing did so greatly rejoyce us his frendes, and therfore we desyred a copye of the same boke, for one that neded in lyke case, lyke consolation....It was wished of al them that eyther dyd reade or heare this boke, that it might be prynted, and do good unto many, as it had done already unto a fewe: which thinge I toke upon me and thus boldly have caused it to be printed.[2]

A like zeal urged the publication of Katherine Parr's *The lamentacion of a sinner* (1547), which was put into print so that 'every Christian by ye reading ther of' might 'profit with increase from God'.[3] The Lord Protector, the Duke of Somerset, in publishing *A spyrytuall and moost precyouse pearle* (1550), tells us that

> thys man whosoever he be, that was the fyrst author of thys boke[4] (if oure judgement be anye thynge) goeth the ryghte waye to worck...and hereupon we have requyred hym of whom we had the copye of thys boke, the rather at our request and commendacyon to set thys boke forth and in prynte, that not onelye we or one or two more, but that all that be afflycted maye take profyt and consolacyon if they wyll.[5]

Examples such as these indicate how the enterprise of private individuals caused a number of works to be printed, but more important is the effect these private ventures had in indicating potential markets to the printers. We can see this very clearly by scrutinizing the output of de Worde and Pynson.

---

[1] *STC* 11392, sig. A iii[v]. Cf. *STC* 11211, *The foūtayne or well of lyfe* [1532?], sig. A 2[r].

[2] *STC* 13910, sig. A i[v].   [3] *STC* 4827, sig. * 2[v].

[4] I.e. Otto Werdmueller.   [5] *STC* 25255, sig. A vi[v]

Throughout de Worde's career as a printer a continuous stream of religious writings, amounting to some two hundred items, flowed from his press. Some were for the professed 'religious', while others were for 'all Christian men'. For the first group he printed works such as *A ryght profytable treatyse compendiously drawn out of many and dyvers wrytyngs of holy men, to dyspose men to be vertuously occupyed in theyr myndes and Prayers* (1500), which the author declared to be 'necessary and nedeful to them that ben come and shall come to Relygyon'.[1]

For the layman he printed a large number of works actuated by the belief that 'every good thynge the more it be communycate and disparsed abrode, the more fruyte and profyte cometh therof',[2] so that volumes such as *The myrrour of the chyrche* (1521) are put forth 'to all maner of people necessary and comfortable, to the edyfycacion of the soule and body, and the love and grace of God'.[3] What was done by de Worde was also done by Pynson, and by the printers that followed them, and it would be unprofitable to multiply instances of this common practice.

As with printers, so with writers and translators. As the author of *The fruyte of redempcyon* (1514) tells us, the work was translated by 'wretched Simon, anker of London Wall, for your ghostly conforte that understande no latyn',[4] and its value as a work of 'grete consolacyon and ghostly comforte' was vouched for by Richard Fitz James, Bishop of London.[5] *The floure of the commaundementes* (1510), 'the whiche is moche proffytable and utyle into all people, lately translated out of Ffrenche into Englysshe in the yere of our lord MCCCCCX',[6] was undertaken the translator tell us:

> Entendynge therby no sylver for to wyn,
> Ne yet none other temporall gayne;
> But welthe of soules, escapynge the engyn

[1] *STC* 1978, sig. A i^r.
[2] *STC* 4815, *The orchard of Syon* (1519), sig. B iii^r.
[3] *STC* 965, sig. A i^r. Two further editions soon followed.
[4] *STC* 22557, sig. A i^v.   [5] *STC* 22558, sig. D iv^r.
[6] *STC* 23876, sig. Xx vi^r.

Of the devyl of hell, his snares, and his chayne
Who ever is besy, gladde, and fayne
Soules to dystroye, whome god hath electe.
Who gyve us grace heven to attayne,
Of my hole mynde, this is theffecte.[1]

A large number of other works might be mentioned, all of which have as their avowed aim the strengthening of the spiritual life. The writers explicitly say that their works are 'righte necessary for troubled consciences, to the end that they shall not despayre in adversite and trouble' or 'to the gret profit and help of all such studentes in gods worde as have not had longe exercyse in the same'. The reading of them, it is hoped, will bring to every man 'frute and comforte' as well as a knowledge of 'what he shall beleve, what he shall hope, and why he shall love god'. On all sides there is convincing evidence that earnest, zealous Christians were using the printing press *ad maiorem honorem dei*.

So decade after decade pious souls were responsible, one way or another, for putting into print works of this kind. The demand seemed insatiable, and many reprints, as well as a continuing flow of new works, are evidence of this. And as the quarrel with Rome gathered momentum, the rival factions threw themselves into the fray with added vigour, and the passions excited by these and other agencies found one outlet in the composition and reading of controversial works. From the early days of the 'New Religion', when Lutheran and other heretical writings were printed abroad and secretly brought into the country, until the height of the struggle in the late forties and fifties of the century, when first one side and then the other had a momentary control, the printing-press was one of the most potent agents of propaganda, and the writers on both sides poured forth their tracts and treatises. Works of a highly polemical nature abounded, in many of which the conviction of the writers is equalled by the vigour of their prose.

[1] *STC* 23876, sig. A ii[r].

Consider, for example, the prologue of Thomas Swinnerton[1] to his translation of *A mustre of scismatyke bysshoppes of Rome* (1534). He tells us that there

chaunsed to come to my hande, the lyfe of Gregory yᵉ seventh, otherwise named Hyldebrande, wherin whan I had redde a lyttel way, as a man wolde say, one leafe and one syde in the Latyne tonge, and se the abhomynacion that there was writen, I begon some thyng to be moved, and bote the lyppe, scratched my heed, and wexed excedyng wery: yet forth I went.[2]

His indignation was such that in addition to his translation he writes a long preface, and after some pages declares:

In good fayth I was so besy with these popes, that I had almost forgotten my selfe, and have nye hand made halfe a worke in stede of a prologue: but I pray the of thy curtesye to pardon my forgetfulnesse, and than I wyll speake a worde or twayne of the deposycion of the Emperour, Henry the Fourth, with two or thre mo, and so make an ende.[3]

He does 'make an end', but it is not until he has indulged in 64 further pages of his own making, after which he says, not without justification: 'Thou dost lust and longe peradventure, to see it (the translation). Be of good comforte, for with all the spede that may be possible, it shall be imprinted. And in the meane whyle, fare as well as I wolde myselfe.'[4]

It is of such authors that Miles Coverdale complains when he prefaces his *Confutacion of that treatise...made agaynst the protestacion of D. Barnes* [1541?] by reminding 'all them that either reade or heare Gods holy worde', that 'there is now a wonderful diversite in writing bokes and balates in England, one enveyenge agaynst another, one revylinge and reprovyng another, one rejoysinge at anothers fall and adversite'.[5] Good tempered or bad tempered, a considerable volume of contro-

---

[1] Swinnerton wrote under the assumed name of John Roberts.
[2] *STC* 23552, sig. A iiiʳ.   [3] *Ibid.* sig. B vʳ.
[4] *Ibid.* sig. F ivᵛ.   [5] *STC* 5888, sig. a iiʳ.

versial works poured from the presses in the forties and fifties of the century. The clashes of opinion may be gauged from such exchanges as *George Ioye confuteth Winchesters false articles* (1543),[1] answered by the Bishop's *A declaration of such true articles as G. Joye hath gone about to confute* (1546),[2] which provoked Joye's *Refutation of the byshop of Winchesters derke declaratiō of his false articles* (1546).[3] Other titles, from many available, such as *A litel treatise ageynste the mutterynge of some papistis in corners* (1534),[4] or *A confutacion of that popishe a. anti-christian doctryne whiche mainteinith ye ministracyon of the sacrament vnder one kind* [1555?],[5] will further illustrate the vigour with which controversy on religious matters was carried on, and which was evidently enjoyed and read by enough people to make this sort of publication a commercial success.[6]

This great body of controversial literature engaged many of the best as well as some of the most prejudiced minds of the time. Great scholars and statesmen such as Sir Thomas More did not hesitate to throw themselves eagerly into the fray. Despite his many other interests, More wrote nine controversial works, several of them of considerable length, between 1529 and 1533, while his opponent John Frith was responsible for six volumes between 1530 and 1533. Others, not perhaps so eminent, but men of some position, such as George Joye and Thomas Becon in the next decade, were equally unflagging controversialists. Joye wrote six works between 1543 and 1549, while Becon, despite his plea that his labours left him but little leisure for pamphleteering,[7] and that he suffered from 'so grevous and troublous sycknesses',[8] nevertheless turned out no less than twenty-four works between 1541 and 1554.

---

[1] *STC* 14826.
[2] *STC* 11588.
[3] *STC* 14827.
[4] *STC* 19177.
[5] *STC* 17821.
[6] See also M. Channing Lenthicum, '*A Pore Helpe* and its printers', *The Library*, Fourth Series, vol. IX (1928), pp. 169–83, for a good deal of further evidence.
[7] *STC* 1742, sig. B iiii^r.
[8] *STC* 1738, sig. A iii^v.

Another prolific controversialist was Robert Crowley with an output of nine volumes in the three years 1548–51.[1] These writers may be regarded as exceptional, but many others were eagerly and actively engaged. Thus Crowley begins his *Confutation of the mishapen aunswer to the misnamed ballade called the abuse of y* blessed Sacramēt of the aultare* [1548] with these words:

> After I had perused this fonde aunswere (Christian Reader) and perceived howe greately the papistes gloried therin, thinckeinge (yea and making theyre crakes) that no man should be able to confute it, or if any man shoulde take in hande to writte agayne, he shoulde be aunswerede in lyke maner, I thought it my duti... to overthrowe thys theyr bullwarcke.[2]

In another work he refers to 'the blasphemous doctrine of Antichristes schole, as are in these articles' of the Bishop of Salisbury,[3] while Henry, Lord Stafford, speaks of his opponents as 'drowned in the dregges of popery and superstytion'—and so the wordy warfare continued.

Long before this it had become clear to all interested in the matter that the printing-press was a most potent instrument of propaganda, so that Roland Phillips (1465?–1538), Vicar of Croydon, was only expressing a widely held view when he declared that 'we must root out printing, or printing will root out us'.[5] In a little volume printed about 1530, entitled *A goodly dyalogue & dysputacyon betwene Pyers plowman and a*

---

[1] See below, p. 195. •

[2] *STC* 6082, sig. A i^v. Cf. *STC* 1309, *Yet a course at the Romyshe foxe* (1543), sig. A ii^r, in which John Bale stigmatizes his opponents as 'fylthye whoremongers, murtherers, thieves, raveners, idolatours, lyars, dogges, swyne...and very devyls incarnate'.

[3] *STC* 6083, *The confutation of xiii articles wherunto N. Shaxton subscribed* [1548], sig. a ii^r.

[4] *STC* 11220, *The true dyfferēs betwen y* regall power and the ecclesticall power* [1548], sig. a ii^v.

[5] Foxe, *Acts and Monuments* (1877), vol. VI, p. 804. Cf. *STC* 11797 (1547), *A godly inuective in the defence of the Gospell against such as murmure and woorke what thei can that the Bible shoulde not have free passage*.

popysh pryest concernyng the supper of the lorde, the upshot of the debate is crystallized by the priest's three colleagues as follows: 'If these hobbes and rusticals be suffred to be thus busy in readynge of Englysh heresy and to dyspute after this maner wyth us which are sperytual men, we shal be fayne to learne some other occupacion or els we are lyke to have but a colde brothe.' To which Piers replies, 'Amen'.[1]

Even earlier than this, as we have seen,[2] the King and the ecclesiastical authorities had taken severe action against those trading or printing heretical books, and with these rigorous measures in vogue it required a good deal of courage to deal in these works, and few but those impelled by strong religious convictions were likely to do so. Printers at home for the most part left it to overseas presses to put out these dangerous works, and it was to Antwerp and Zürich, in particular, that the Reformers sent their works, from whence, as we know, they found their way into England.

For those less eager to share in religious controversy and propaganda there were many other opportunities, for the various types of religious literature listed above all had their public. A few words about one or two of these categories may serve as sufficient illustration.

The output of lives of the Saints was considerable, especially in the first decades of printing. Caxton first published his translation of the *Legenda Aurea* in 1483 in a large folio volume of 898 pages, and it was not until it reached its eighth and last edition by 1527 that the market was satisfied. In addition to this, a smaller compilation made in the fifteenth century by John Capgave, the *Nova legenda Anglie*, was published by de Worde in 1516, and Pynson printed an abridged version in English translation in the same year. Volumes such as these were expensive affairs, and the printers saw that something smaller was called for. To meet this demand a series of slender quartos (for the most part) began to appear. Caxton printed the *Lyfe of Saynt Wenefryde* (1485), while de Worde printed

---

[1] STC 19903, sig. A8ʳ. [2] See above, p. 33.

the *Lyf of saint Katherin of senis* [1493?] and the *Lyf of saynt Ursula* (n.d.). Pynson made a speciality of such works, and from his press survive the lives of St Margaret (1493), St Francis [1515?], St Bridget (1516), St Thomas à Becket [1520?], St Werburgh (1521), St Radegund [1521?], St Armele (n.d.) and St George (n.d.). These lives, in verse or prose, were often accompanied with crude woodcuts, and were so popular that they have been wellnigh thumbed out of existence. Few examples of this kind of production appear to have been printed after about 1525, although we may note that the life of St Alban, translated by John Lydgate, was printed at St Albans by J. Herford in 1534, and that J. Waley printed a life of St Catherine of Siena about 1550.

It is perhaps unnecessary to speak in detail of the work provided for the printers by the translation into English first of the New Testament by Tyndale (1525), and later of the whole Bible by Coverdale (1535).[1] Although it was the overseas presses, especially those of the Low Countries and Germany, that were responsible for the earliest editions, it was not long before the Bible, the New Testament and the Psalms, with commentaries of every kind, were forthcoming from English presses. Books of selections, such as *Certain praiers and godlye meditacions of holy men and women: taken out of the byble* [1550?],[2] or *The foundacyon and the summe of the holy scripture* [1535?];[3] or aids to the study of the Bible, such as *The concordance of the new testament, most necessary to be had in ye cõmunicacion of any place* (1535);[4] or metrical versions of the Psalms appeared. Commentaries were an obvious necessity for a lay public struggling with the innumerable difficulties presented by the open Bible. Bishop Ridley wrote *A commentary in Englyshe upon Sayncte Paules epystle to the Ephesyans, for the instructyon of them that be unlearned in tonges* (1540),[5] and this was accom-

---

[1] See A. W. Pollard, *Records of the English Bible* (1911) for the best account.
[2] *STC* 2996.   [3] *STC* 3034.
[4] *STC* 3046. Cf. *STC* 17300, Marbecke's *Concordance* (1550).
[5] *STC* 21038.

panied by further commentaries on a number of other epistles.[1]
Other aids followed such as G. Joye's *Exposicion of Daniel the
prophete* (1545),[2] or A. Scoloker's translation of *A bryefe summe
of the whole byble* [1548?].[3]

Finally we may note *A briefe and compendiouse table, in a
manner of a concordance* (1550) which Walter Lynne translated,
and in his dedication to the Duchess of Somerset, said he did
so, since

> I perceived it to be moost diligently gathered out of the holy
> Byble and set in suche order that wyth in it lyghtly as much maye
> be founde by it as by a great concordaunce I ceassed not tyll I had it
> translated and sette in lyke order in the Englysh tounge that your
> grace myghte not be destytute of so necessarye an instrumente in
> your goodlye studie.[4]

Enough, perhaps, has been said to illustrate the overwhelming part played by works of religious, didactic and
moral interest in the publications of this period. It was of
great importance to the early printers that they could rely on
this constant demand which gave work to their presses, and
enabled them to look about and venture from time to time on
more speculative undertakings.

2. *Law*

It was clear from the early success attending the publication
of service books that works aimed at a special, but not too
restricted a public, had a good chance of success, and the needs
of lawyers and those connected with the law offered an obvious
opportunity to enterprising printers. Caxton did not avail
himself of this opening, for he printed only one work of a legal
nature, and allowed his contemporary, W. de Machlinia, to
develop this market. This he did with some success, so that

---

[1] *STC* 21039 (*Colossians*, 1548); 21040 (Philippians, 1550?); 21042 (Jude,
1538).
[2] *STC* 14823. Cf. *STC* 2788 (Jonas, 1531?); 14499 (Jeremiah, 1539?).
[3] *STC* 3017.   [4] *STC* 3015, sig. A ii[v].

eleven of his thirty known publications are law books, but it was left to Pynson to enter the field with such enthusiasm that nearly 150 legal works—that is, one-third of his total output—was the result. Later on, other printers—the Rastells, Redman and Berthelet—joined in, but not every printer wanted to undertake this type of work, whatever its rewards. These books required expert handling, and were liable to cause much difficulty in the printing-house. In the first place, it was a never-ending business to keep some law books, such as the Statutes, for example, up to date, and secondly, a great many texts needed by lawyers were in Norman-French or Law Latin, often of a highly contracted nature, and these gave endless possibilities for compositors' errors.

Nevertheless, there was a considerable business to be done, and Pynson, Redman and J. Rastell were all keenly aware of one another's output, and each made efforts to keep their own wares up to date and attractive to the legal public. It was probably to counter the complete abridgement of the Statutes to 18 Henry VIII, published by Redman in 1528,[1] that Pynson reissued his 1521 edition of the abridgements with a new title-page, and four folios of 'newe addicions of the last parliament an. XV. H. VIII' (1528).[2] The other outstanding legal publisher, J. Rastell, could not let these actions go unchallenged, and replied with his *Magnum abbreviamentum*,[3] a work containing the statutes down to 1523 abridged in their original languages, Latin, Anglo-French and English.[4]

In addition to producing their wares in keen rivalry one with another, publishers took care, through statements on title-pages and elsewhere, that the public should learn of the efforts they were making. Hence we read on the title-pages of many editions some such words as 'amended nowe at this impryntynge...and [things] added to, that were never before printed

---

[1] *STC* 9519.   [2] *STC* 9517.
[3] *STC* 9520.
[4] See J. D. Cowley, *A Bibliography of Abridgments* (Selden Society, 1932), pp. xxii, xxiii, xxv.

in the sayde boke';[1] or, as Henry Smith claimed for his edition of the same book some years later, 'never so well and diligently set forthe'. Publishers were sometimes not content with a mere statement on the title-page, but elaborated on this in prefaces, such as that of Robert Redman to his edition *The greate abbrydgement* [1540?]. There he was careful to draw attention to the fact that

in this presente booke the whiche is callyd the great abredgiament of al yᵉ statutes of England, dyvers estatutes be here abredgyd whiche have not ben abbredgyd before this tyme past, and many statutes that have ben abbredgyd before tyme be herein enlargyd and be more openly and more pleynly couched then they were before, as to the reder it wyll appere; desyrynge the reders not to thynke it tedyous though they fynd some tyme one statute twyes abbredgyd, syth many statutes serve convenyently for dyvers chapiters.[2]

Few law-printers, with these considerations clearly before them, found themselves able to write as confidently as did Robert Redman in 1534 when, after speaking of the way that some Year Books were 'greatly defaced and emblemished', not being 'truely wryten or prentyd', went on to say 'dyvers have done theyr payne and laboure about the prentyng of sondrye yeres [i.e. Year Books], wherof (I thynke I may say) some have ben fynyshed so that nothyng lacketh which industry myght have holpen'. He goes on to attack Pynson and other earlier printers for their incorrect version of the Year-Book he proposes to reissue. Here, perhaps, he is only paying off an ancient grudge against Pynson, who had vigorously attacked him as an incompetent printer in a note at the end of his edition of Littleton's *Tenures* (1525).[3]

Redman had had ample experience previous to this of the

---

[1] *STC* 14876, *The Boke for a Iustice of peace*...[1539?], sig. Aiᵛ.

[2] *STC* 9522, sig. *2ʳ.

[3] *STC* 9587, sig. Aiᵛ. See p. 223 for text of Pynson's outburst. No edition of Littleton by Redman is extant before 1528, and Pynson seems to have had a monopoly of the work since 1496 at the latest. Hence, possibly, his indignation.

labour entailed in keeping his abridgements up to date. In 1528 he had published *The hole abrygemẽt of al the statuts*,[1] and soon after began to issue a series of small supplementary pamphlets. About 1530 he published two editions containing an abridgement of the statutes of 21 Henry VIII (1529–30).[2] Further supplements appeared in 1531? (two),[3] 1532? (one),[4] 1534 (two),[5] 1535? (three),[6] 1538? (two),[7] and 1540? (four)[8] by which time he was dead and his business was being carried on by his widow Elizabeth. The fact, however, that he was willing to set up two or three independent editions of the same work in any given year shows that there was a considerable demand for these booklets—a conclusion which is strengthened when we note that in 1530, 1531 and 1534 W. Rastell was also issuing similar abridgements.

It was the same with other legal publications: all the law-publishers strove to keep abreast of the times, but it was not always a simple matter. The famous work known as Littleton's *Tenures* affords an interesting example of this, and of the care which had to be taken to gauge what was wanted. The work was originally published in 1481 by J. Lettou and W. de Machlinia, so that it was not an unreasonably hasty action of Pynson to publish an edition in 1510 which was entitled *Leteltun teners newe correcte*. Fifteen years later he thought it time to overhaul the work again, and it was published as *Lytylton tenures, newly and moost truly correctyd and amendyd*, printed in the handier octavo form in place of the folio hitherto used. Redman and others put out editions from time to time after this, merely claiming them to be 'newly imprinted', or 'newly revised'. In 1553 the title-page of W. Powell's edition claimed them to be 'newly revised and truly correcte', while the 1557 edition went further and claimed to have been

---

[1] *STC* 9519.
[2] Cowley, *op. cit.* pp. 17, 18. Not in *STC*.
[3] *Ibid.* pp. 22 (*STC* 9534), 23.   [4] *Ibid.* p. 24.
[5] *Ibid.* pp. 27, 28 (*STC* 9537).   [6] *Ibid.* pp. 29 (*STC* 9539), 30, 31.
[7] *Ibid.* pp. 32, 34.
[8] *Ibid.* pp. 35 (*STC* 9542), 36 (*STC* 9541), 37 (*STC* 9535), 38 (*STC* 9543).

'conferred with divers true wrytten copies, and purged of sondry cases, having in some places more than ye autor wrote, and less in other some'.[1] In so doing the printer, R. Tottel, went further than his conservative clients thought proper. The excisions may have been a justifiable purging, but the profession thought otherwise, and in later editions the outcast passages were restored.

The special problems confronting the printer of law books were not easily solved, and we may well imagine that those printers who specialized in such work surveyed the field carefully before embarking on publication. Such a survey would undoubtedly have revealed that one of the prime needs was for copies of the actual statutes. This they met, in part, by the production of volumes containing collections of statutes of various dates. The first of these volumes, the *Nova Statuta*, was published by W. de Machlinia in 1484, and contained the statutes from 1 Edward III to 22 Edward IV.[2] Pynson improved on this about 1505 when he printed an edition of the statutes from 1 Edward III until 1505,[3] and in a later edition of 1508 added the text of Magna Carta to the book.[4] Up to this time and later these texts were in Latin or Norman-French, and it was not until 1534 that a translation of Magna Carta and other statutes was printed by R. Redman.[5] Such a work the translator claimed was necessary,

bycause the moste part of them (i.e. the statutes) retayne theyr force, and bynde the Kyngs subjectes unto this day, me thought it necessary to set them forth in suche sorte as men myghte beste have knowledge of them, and knowledge can they have none excepte they rede them, and what dothe it avayle to rede, yf they understande not, and howe shulde they understande the meanyng which understande not the texte? For this cause, I saye, was this boke translated into the Englyshe which though percase it shal not satysffye the lerned, yet shall it be a good helpe for the unlerned.[6]

---

[1] *STC* 15738, title-page.
[3] *STC* 9265.
[5] *STC* 9272.
[2] *STC* 9264.
[4] *STC* 9266.
[6] *STC* 9275 [1541?], sig. +ii^v.

Some thirty editions more or less complete of the statutes in Latin, French and English, were published before T. Berthelet in 1543 issued two large folio volumes containing the statutes from the time of Henry III to that of Henry VIII,[1] and subsequently W. Rastell brought the matter up to date by his edition of *A collection of all the statutes...unto...1557*, published by R. Tottel the same year.[2]

In addition to these general collections, separate works containing the statutes for one or more years were published. Pynson, Berthelet, Redman and Grafton were particularly active here, and altogether some 150 little books were published. The number of these is sufficient indication of their popularity. They generally consisted of a few pages only, but were indispensable for those actively engaged in the law, who presumably placed them with their larger general collections, and as they were generally of the same format, it was easy from time to time to bind them together.

Busy men, however, required something shorter than the complete statutes, and abridgements were popular. The first of these in Norman-French and Latin was issued about 1481 by Lettou and de Machlinia, and was followed by other and fuller abridgements from time to time by Pynson, the Rastells, Redman and others. John Rastell published in 1527 an edition in translation 'as farre as my symple wytt and smal lernynge wyll extende...which conteyn forfeytours and penaltes' made before 1485, 'by the knowlege wherof and by the dylygente observyng of the same [every man] maye the better do hys dewte to hys prynce and soveraynge, and also lyve in tranquylyte and peace wyth his neyghboure'.[3] Further editions by William Rastell, Redman and others followed, the last in 1551 digesting the statutes until 1544.[4]

As well as making use of volumes of statutes and their convenient abridgements, all actively concerned with the law

---

[1] *STC* 9301.   [2] *STC* 9306.   [3] *STC* 9518, sig. Aii.

[4] *STC* 9525, 9526. There was also an identical edition published in the same year by R. Kele (not in *STC*).

were in constant need of the Year Books. These volumes, written in French, contained reports of cases Term by Term from the reign of Edward I onwards. 'Written by lawyers for lawyers, they are by far the most important source of, and authority for, the medieval common law', writes Sir William Holdsworth,[1] who goes on to say:

Probably the earliest printer of Year Books was W. de Machlinia....Pynson was their earliest systematic publisher. Fifty editions certainly, and perhaps five more, bear his name. Sixteen others are also attributed to him....Rastell, Redman, Berthelet, Myddleton, Henry Smyth and Powell were their chief publishers during the first half of the sixteenth century...In 1553 Richard Tottell began his publications of the Year Books...Early in his publishing career Tottell began to publish the separate years in groups. Thus in 1553 he printed the years 1–14 Henry IV as one book, etc.[2]

Before 1560 at least 260 volumes of Year Books had been published.

Sir William emphasizes the importance of these volumes when he says, 'The printed Year Books were absolutely necessary to all students of the law; and the printed abridgements were useful indices to the Year Books themselves'.[3] The first of these was probably made by Nicolas Statham, and carries us down to the end of Henry VI. It was printed in Rouen for R. Pynson in 1490. Ten years later Pynson printed another compilation by an anonymous hand, and of less general utility. Then about 1513 J. Rastell put on the market his *Liber Assisarum et placitorum Corone*. This, says Sir William Holdsworth, contains 'reports in a style very different from that of the other Year Books of Edward III's reign. They are more concise than the Year Books usually are, giving rather the gist of the argument and the decision than a report of the actual proceedings.'[4] Finally, there was *La Graunde*

---

[1] *Hist. Eng. Law* (1923 ed.), vol. II, p. 525.
[2] *Op. cit.* vol. II, pp. 528–9. [3] *Op. cit.* vol. II, p. 543.
[4] *Op. cit.* vol. II, p. 537. For the date, see A. W. Reed, *Early Tudor Drama,* p. 206.

Abbregement de le Ley (1516) by Sir Anthony Fitzherbert (a work in three large folio volumes published at forty shillings).[1] The second edition contained an index by J. Rastell which greatly increased its usefulness, despite Rastell's plea for consideration, seeing that he had 'so smale lerning and so lytell leyser to performe so grete a worke'.[2]

Nor did this complete the demands for legal aid which the printers tried to satisfy. In addition to the source material, various types of legal treatises were forthcoming. Some of these were compiled in Norman-French and were mainly intended for lawyers. Perhaps the most famous was Littleton's *Tenures*, first printed by Lettou and Machlinia about 1481. It was ostensibly written by Littleton to assist his son, and rapidly became the most popular book for those beginning to study law, so that by 1560 some twenty editions in Norman-French, and beginning from 1532 twelve editions in English had been printed and are extant.[3] Then again, as 'the learning of writs was both the foundation of law and the ABC of legal education', tracts containing selections of writs, such as the *Natura Brevium*, *Novae Narrationes*, *Articuli ad Novas Narrationes* and *Diversite des Courtes* were printed in considerable numbers; for, as W. Rastell says in his preface to his edition of twelve law tracts (1534):

How commodyous and profitable unto gentil men studentes of the law be these thre bokes, that is to wit, Natura Brevium, The olde tenures, & the tenures of mayster Lyttylton, experience proveth and the bokes them selfe declare. For lyke a chylde goyng to scole, fyrst lerneth his letters out of the a.b.c.: so they that entende the study of the law, do fyrste study these .iii. bokes.[4]

---

[1] *STC* 10954, and see below, p. 229.
[2] *STC* 10955, sig. A i[v].   [3] See above, p. 79.
[4] *STC* 18394, sig. +i[v]. This volume contains *Natura brevium, The olde tenures, Lyttylton tenures, The new talys, The articles uppon the new tales, Diversyte of courtes, Justyce of peace, The chartulari, Court Baron, Court of hundred, Retourna brevium, The ordinance for takynge of fees in the escheker.* 'Thus have y[e] these xii small bokes into one volume, ryght studyously corrected.' Sig. +i[v]. The whole makes a small octavo of about 450 pages. Cf. *STC* 11008, sig. A i[v].

Help in the form of various treatises was also necessary for those who had to administer justice up and down the country. There were, for example, those invaluable handbooks for the amateur lawyer, such as is indicated by the title of one of them:

The Boke of Justices of peas, the charge with all the processe of the cessions, warrantes, supersidias, and all that longeth to ony Justice to make endytementes of haute treason, petyt treason...with dyvers thynges more as it appereth in the Kalendar of thsame boke.[1]

There were also books dealing with the court baron, the court leet or the hundred court. These treatises enabled the lord of the Manor to follow with some assurance the proper forms of procedure, and over twenty editions were printed by a variety of publishers during this period—evidence enough of their popularity. Another useful work which also had considerable popularity was *The offices of sheryffes, bailliffes of the Liberties, Escheatours...drawen out of bokes of the comon lawe and of the statutes* [1535?].[2] This had a more limited appeal, but obviously was a work likely to be in demand, and here again a number of printers each ventured to put out an edition.

The fact that Rastell[3] and others found it worth while to assemble these composite volumes is of interest to us in our inquiry concerning the demands the publishers were attempting to meet. Thus, in 1539, Berthelet also issued a volume of six well-tried legal treatises with a title-page: *The Boke for a Iustice of peace, the Boke that techeth to kepe a court baron, or a lete. The boke teaching to kepe a lete*, etc., and found the response sufficient to call for another edition in 1544.[4]

In addition, a variety of helps to old and young were forthcoming. J. Rastell explicitly tells us that his *Expositiones terminorum legum anglorum* (1525) are

for the helpe and erudicyon of them that be yong beginers whych intend to be studyentys of the law...for as mych as the law of thys

---

[1] *STC* 14862 [1506?], title-page.
[2] *STC* 10984. There were more editions by 1560.
[3] See above, p. 81.   [4] *STC* 14876, 14877.

realm of englond is ordeynd and devysyd for augmentacion of justyce and for the quietnes of the peple and for the common welth of the same; ergo, it is convenient that divers bokes be made wherby the studentis of thys law may the soner come to the knowlege therof.[1]

To take two other classes of treatises: R. Redman reprints the Year Book of Edward III, 40 'for as moche as this yere...is greatly bosted and noted of some studentes', but heretofore only a poor text has been provided.[2] Then again, in his preface to Britton 'on the laws of England', he tells us that it is printed 'to the great profyt (I trust) of the studentes of the same', although he is aware that the manuscript versions of the treatise vary considerably.[3]

This brief survey of some of the principal categories of legal works printed in this period is sufficient to show how continuous and widespread was the demand. It must have been a boon to the legal profession, and to those connected with it, to know that cheap, handy texts of statutes, year books, special treatises, etc. were readily available. At the same time the printers were well aware that their market was a critical one, so that their efforts were continually bent on producing better and more up to date texts. There can be little doubt that the printing-press at this period was a most valuable friend to the legal profession.

3. *Education*

Another of the more obvious fields open to the printer was the provision of books for educational purposes. The need for text-books, at Oxford and Cambridge, and still more at grammar schools, was very great, and grew greater as the sixteenth century went on its way. Caxton showed little interest in this market, but other printers seized the opportunity. At Oxford, Theoderic Rood catered for the needs of those

---

[1] *STC* 20701, sig. Aii^r. [2] See above, p. 82.
[3] *STC* 3803, sig. +iii^r.

who had mastered the rudiments of grammar by his edition of Alexander de Villa Dei's *Doctrinale* [*c.* 1490]. This work has been called 'the most important school book of the later Middle Ages', and successive editions by de Worde and Pynson kept the book in circulation until 1516.[1] Other famous grammars, such as the *Accedence* of Donatus [1495], and treatises deriving from it—the *Donatus melior* [1487], the *Donatus minor cum Remigio* [1510?], and the *Donatus pro pueris* [1500],[2] as well as the 'Equivoca' (1496) and 'Synonyma' (1496) of John of Garland were frequently reprinted.[3]

All these works belonged to the Middle Ages, and the time was ripe for text-books more suitable to contemporary conditions. It was to meet this need that a number of teachers set to work. The three outstanding names of this early period are those of John Anwykyll, John Stanbridge and Robert Whittinton—all three Informators in succession of Magdalen School, Oxford. The Latin Grammar of Anwykyll, entitled *Compendium totius grammaticae* [1483], was printed at Oxford by T. Rood and T. Hunte.[4] Anwykyll's successor, John Stanbridge, was responsible for a large number of books for schoolboys, while Robert Whittinton was even more productive. Another Magdalen grammarian, John Holt, completes the list of those writers who so successfully exploited the elementary text-book market for some fifty years.[5]

Their output and the demand for their writings were remarkable. The works of the two most popular—Stanbridge and Whittinton—received a wide circulation. Stanbridge wrote five works which in all were printed and reprinted at least fifty times,[6] while Whittinton's more numerous compilations have survived in at least one hundred and fifty editions.[7] De Worde and Pynson profited by this demand, for de Worde

---

[1] *STC* 315-20.   [2] *STC* 7009-18.
[3] *STC* 11601-17.   [4] *STC* 695-6.
[5] Note, for example, the demand for their works as evinced by the entries in the account book of John Dorne, the Oxford stationer (1520). See p. 231.
[6] *STC* 23140-99.
[7] *STC* 25444-581, and this is far from all the editions now known.

published three-quarters of Whittinton's works, and printed over half of the known editions of Stanbridge, while Pynson was responsible for a considerable proportion of the remainder of the work of these two authors. The steady market provided by these successful text-books, and its importance to de Worde (and to a lesser extent to Pynson) is obvious.

Stanbridge and Whittinton did not have matters all their own way, however, for the early years of the sixteenth century saw a new stirring of the waters. Under the powerful influence of Erasmus, and in particular of his *De Ratione Studii*, the new principles which were to underlie the grammar-school teaching for many generations to come were set forth. Not only this, but the courses of study, the authors to be read and the text-books to be followed were prescribed. The old grammars were cast aside, and new ones put in their place. Colet, the founder of St Paul's, prepared a treatise in English on the eight parts of speech, while the first Headmaster, Lily, compiled another on the rudiments of construction. These two parts, the *Aeditio* and the *Rudimenta*, thus provided beginners with the elements of accidence and syntax, and were published in one volume. A statement by Colet in the *Aeditio* indicates the new attitude to the teaching of grammar and Latin. He says:

> Of these viii partes of speche in ordre well construed, be made reasons and sentences, and longe oracyons. But how and in wat maner, and with what construccyon of wordes, and all the varietees, and diversitees, and chaunges in Latyn speche (whiche be innumerable), if ony man wyl know, and by that knowlege attayne to understande Latyn bokes, and to speke and to wryte the clene Latyn, let hym above all besyly lerne and rede good Latyn authours of chosen poetes and oratours, and note wysely how thy wrote, and spake, and study alway to folowe them, desyryng none other rules but their examples.
>
> For in the begynnynge men spake not Latyn, by cause suche rules were made, but contrari wyse, bycause men spake suche Latyn, upon that folowed the rules were made. That is to saye, Latyn speche was before the rules, not the rules before the Latyn speche.

Wherfore welbeloved maysters and techers of grammer, after the partes of speche [be] sufficiently knowen in your scholes, rede and expounde playnly unto your scholers good authours, and shewe to them every worde, and in every sentence what they shal note and observe, warnynge them besyly to folowe and to do lyke, bothe in wrytynge and in spekynge, and be to them your owne selfe also spekyng with them the pure Latyn...and leve the rules. For redyng of good bokes, diligent informacyon of taught maysters, studyous advertence and takynge hede of lerners, heryng eloquent men speke, and finally [besy] imitacyon with tongue and penne, more avayleth shortly to gete the true eloquent speche, than all the tradicions, rules, and preceptes of maysters.[1]

These words of Colet were probably written about 1510–12, but only survive from an edition of 1527, entitled *Ioannes Coleti...aeditio, una cum quibusdam G. Lilii Grammatices rudimentis.* By this time, however, the book had won such a position for itself that when Wolsey adopted it for his new school at Ipswich under the title *Rudimenta grammatices et docendi methodus* (1529),[2] the title-page asserted that the work had been prescribed for all schools in England. Certainly a movement towards a single grammar was gaining ground, and not long after this the rival grammars of Stanbridge and Whittinton ceased to be printed.

The production of a Latin syntax in Latin was also taken in hand. Lily was asked by Colet to prepare this, and he did so, but it was revised so thoroughly by Erasmus that Lily refused to claim it as his own. It was finally published under the title *Libellus de constructione* (1513)[3] without any author's name being attached, but with a letter from Colet, commending its use to Lily! A further treatise by Lily, *De generibus nominum, ac verborum præteritis* [1520?][4] sets out the rules for distinguishing the genders of nouns and for the inflexion of verbs. These two works, together with the *Aeditio* and *Rudimenta,*

---

[1] *STC* 5542, reprinted in *Shakespeare Jahrbuch*, vol. XLV, pp. 55 ff.
[2] *STC* 25944.
[3] *STC* 5544, and there ascribed to Colet. See also, *STC* 15602–4.
[4] *STC* 15607.

gave boys a fairly complete grammatical grounding, and they were widely adopted.

Furthermore, this composite work gradually became known as 'Lily's Grammar', and was revised and supplemented by a royal commission ordered to produce a complete Latin grammar for general use. This was done by 1540, and in the edition of 1542, entitled *An introduction of the eyght partes of speche*,[1] the King himself in a preface addressed to 'all schoolemaisters and teachers of grammar within his realm', laid it down that this was the sole text-book which they were to use.

Grammatical text-books were well enough, but their users were in need of help such as could be provided by dictionaries, and the printers soon produced Latin-English and English-Latin dictionaries to meet this need. The two most generally used were works which had been compiled in the fifteenth century, known as the *Promptorium parvulorum sive clericorum* and the *Ortus vocabulorum*. The *Promptorium* was printed by Pynson in 1499; it gave the English word with its Latin equivalent, and was a most convenient volume for all *parvuli* or *clerici* to consult. As Pynson's preface announced, 'humble grammarians and boys may look on this short volume as in a mirror, and find freely and immediately the common words which belong to the Latin tongue'. Its sister work, the *Ortus vocabulorum*, was a Latin-English dictionary, first printed by de Worde in 1500, and the two were often bound up together, since as de Worde wrote 'ad lectorem':

And yf ye can not fynde a laten worde, or englysshe worde accordynge to your purpose in thys present boke [*Promptorium parvulorum*] so shall ye take *Ortus vocabulorum*, the wyche is more redyer to fynden a latyn worde after the ABC... And because that no man or chylde shall hereafter have any dyffyculte more to serche for ony latyn or englysshe worde, therfore we have ordened this lybell in smal volum for to bynde with *Ortus vocabulorum* moost necessary for chyldren.[2]

---

[1] *STC* 15605.   [2] *STC* 20438, sig. Miv^r.

These dictionaries were the heritage of the Middle Ages, and not unnaturally in time it was felt something new was required. This was first produced by Sir Thomas Elyot, who by 1538 had compiled a Latin-English dictionary

> wherin I dare affirme may be founde a thousande mo latine wordes than were togither in any one Dictionarie publyshed in this royalme at the tyme whan I fyrste began to write this commentarie, whiche is almost two yeres passed. For beside the conference of phrases or fourmes of speakynge latin and englishe, I have also added proper termes belongynge to lawe and phisike, the names of divers herbes knowen among us, also a good number of fishes founden as wel in our occean as in our rivers; moreover sondrie poysies,[1] coyne, and measures sometymes used among the aunicent Romaynes, Grekes, and Hebrues.... Nor I have omitted proverbes callyd Adagia, or other quicke sentences.[2]

Despite its size (a folio of about 450 pages in double columns) it was very popular and was reprinted in 1545, and later revised by T. Cooper (afterwards Bishop of Lincoln) in 1548, 'enriched' by him in 1552, and 'the third tyme corrected' in 1559.

It was not until 1552 that an attempt was made to put another dictionary on the market, but in that year John Veron, a well-known teacher of French, adapted the Latin-French dictionary of R. Estienne (Paris, 1538) by adding an English column and published his *Dictionariolum puerorum tribus linguis*.[3] He addresses his work 'ad puerum linguarum studiosum' in Latin verses, and his dictionary was the most useful of Latin-English dictionaries produced after the *Promptorium*.

At much the same time two English-Latin dictionaries appeared. Richard Huloet compiled an *Abcedarium Anglo-Latinum pro tyrunculis* (1552),[4] a task which had occupied him for ten years, he tells us, and which he promised to improve if another edition was called for. His volume provided useful lists of equivalent words and phrases, such as 'Laboure. *Cura, Industria*; or Lacke of crafte or science. *Inertia*, &c.' but had

---

[1] poysies, i.e. weights.   [2] *STC* 7659, sig. Aiii^r.
[3] *STC* 10555.   [4] *STC* 13940.

to wait twenty years before being reissued 'newelye corrected by J. Higgins'.[1] In 1553 a much more elementary work, *A shorte dictionarie for yonge begynners*,[2] compiled by J. Withals, was published. This was a vocabulary rather than a dictionary, and evidently met with favour, for with corrections and augmentations it continued to be printed until 1634, by which time there had been fourteen editions.

The new educational ideas, however, demanded something more than grammars and dictionaries. Erasmus had laid it down that composition was an essential to Latin studies, and at the earliest moment boys were set to work to write sentences and proses. To help them Erasmus had composed his huge collection of colloquies on all sorts of subjects, his books of adages, apophthegms and similes, and his *Copia* as a guide to the making of orations and the use of all this material. Many of these works were translated into English, such as the *Prouerbes or adagies...gathered out of the Chiliades of Erasmus*, by R. Taverner (1539)[3] or the *Apophthegmes, that is to saie, prompte saiynges*, by N. Udall (1542).[4] Other school-books, such as *Floures for Latine spekynge Selected and gathered out of Terence*, by N. Udall (1533), were 'verie profitable and necessary for the expedite knowlage in the latine tounge'.[5]

While all this attention was devoted to the learning of Latin little seems to have been done to put Greek on an equal footing. Indeed, despite the recognition of its importance by many of the early humanists, no grammar in English appears to have been published in this period. Various school statutes prescribe for the learning of the Greek grammar and the reading of selected Greek authors; but Greek was come by via Latin, not English.

Once the elementary text-book stage was past, other works were needed, and the *Libellulus secundarū intentionū logicalium*

---

[1] STC 13941.   [2] STC 25874.
[3] STC 10436. For other translations from Erasmus by Taverner, see STC 23711, *The garden of wysdom* (1539); STC 23713, *The secōd booke of the garden of wysedome* (1539); STC 10445, *Flores aliquot sententiarum ex variis collecti scriptoribus* (1540).   [4] STC 10443.   [5] STC 23899 title-page.

[1498?] or the *Libellus sophistarum ad vsum Oxonien* [1499–1500] furnished texts for the undergraduate at an early stage of his career. His more advanced studies were aided by works such as J. Seton's *Dialectia* (1545), or Thomas Wilson's *The rule of reason* (1551) or his *Arte of rhetorique* (1553).[1] Other aids to the art of persuasion were the books of R. Sherry, *A treatise of schemes & tropes* [1550], and *A treatise of the figures of grammer and rhetorike* (1555). It was not only the undergraduate, but the 'vulgare people' that Wilson and Sherry hoped to interest and to instruct. Whether their hopes were misplaced is another matter; the fact remains that both they and their publishers thought the attempt worth making— indeed, Wilson tells us that his *Rule of reason* was 'provoked' by the printer R. Grafton, and adds:

> For considering the forwardnesse of this age, wherein the very multitude are prompt & ripe in al Sciences that have by any mans diligence bene sett forth unto them: weighing also that the capacitie of my country men the English nacion is so pregnaunt and quicke to achieve any kynde, or Arte of knowlege, wherunto it may attayne, that they are not inferiour to any other....I thoughte that Logique among all other beyng an Arte as apte for the English wittes, & as profitable for there knowlege as any the other Sciences are, myght with as good grace be sette forth in thenglishe, as the other Artes, heretofore have bene.[2]

Similarly Sherry puts into English his *Treatise of schemes & tropes*

> bicause longe ago, I was well acquainted wyth them when I red them to other in ye Latin, and that they holpe me verye muche in the exposicion of good authoures, I was so muche the more ready to make them speak English; partli to renew the pleasure of mine old studies, and partelye to satysfy your [his friend's] request.[3]

[1] As early as 1524 L. Cox had written *The arte or crafte of rhethoryke* for use in the grammar school at Reading.

[2] *STC* 25810, sig. A iii[r].

[3] *STC* 22428, sig. A iv[v]. For the study of rhetoric at this time see F. R. Johnson, 'Two Renaissance Textbooks of Rhetoric', *Huntington Library Quarterly*, vol. VI (1942–3), pp. 427–44.

So far we have been discussing the provision of books for the grammar schools and universities. There were other demands, however, particularly for aid in the learning of French,[1] and these, as a practical man, Caxton saw were worthy of attention. Many merchants and others wanted a simple conversational manual which would help them on their way, and provide vocabulary and phrases for everyday situations. It was to meet this need that Caxton produced his 'Dialogues in French and English' [1480]. The work is in French with an English translation in a parallel column, and an introductory section thus recommends the book:

Mais sachies pour voir	But knowe for trouthe
Que es lignes de cest aucteur	That in the lynes of this auctour
Sount plus de parolles et de raysons	Ben moo wordes and reasons
Comprinses, et de responses	Comprised, and of answers,
Que en moult daultres livres	Than in many othir bookes.
Qui cestre livre vouldra aprendre	Who this booke shall wylle lerne
Bien pourra entreprendre,	May well entreprise or take on honde.
Marchandises dun pays a lautre,	Marchandises fro one land to anothir,
Et cognoistre maintes denrees, etc.	And to knowe many wares, etc.[2]

Save for an introduction and epilogue the work is not original, and comes from one of the versions of the *Livre des Mestiers* that were freely circulating in the fifteenth century. With this little volume in hand the traveller could inquire the way, buy and sell, make his reckoning at fair or inn, and so on. Caxton's example was followed by his disciples de Worde and Pynson, for they each published 'a good book to learn to speak French for those who wish to do merchandize in France, and elsewhere in other lands where the folk speak French'. It is in the form of a dialogue, with conversations on buying and selling, gossip with the landlady, etc., as before, but the dialogues are followed by a vocabulary, then a little treatise on manners for children in English and French, and finally by

[1] I am greatly indebted in what follows to the admirable work of Kathleen Lambley, *The Teaching and Cultivation of the French Language in England during Tudor and Stuart Times* (1920).
[2] STC 24865. See H. Bradley, *Caxton's Dialogues, French and English*, E.E.T.S. Extra Series, vol. LXXIX (1900), p. 3.

commercial letters in both languages. Only four editions of this handy work have survived, one by de Worde in 1497, and three by Pynson all before 1505.[1]

All these works are eminently practical. How to *speak* French is what they have to impart, so that merchants and others may prosper in their ventures. They afford material for conversational practice, and the enlargement of vocabulary, but make no attempt to teach the elements of French grammar. That was left for later writers, and had to wait for some decades, until the study and teaching of French was placed on a better footing. This was slowly being effected in the early part of the sixteenth century, when a number of teachers of French were active in London and elsewhere, some attached to the Court and the nobility, some teaching as free-lances. French was freely spoken at Henry VIII's Court, and it was only a matter of time before manuals of French grammar were called for. The earliest of these, as far as we know, was compiled by Alexander Barclay, who composed a grammar at the request of the Duke of Norfolk and of other gentlemen. This was a comparatively short book of 32 folio pages, printed by R. Copland in 1521.[2] Barclay says his treatise is for all Englishmen that are not 'experte in the sayd langage', for now that there is peace between France and England it is not expedient that men should be 'utterly ignorant in yᵉ Frenche tonge'. He goes on:

> And though the sayde tratyse hath been attempted of dyvers men before my dayes: yet I trust with the ayde of God to make the same more clere, playne and easy, parte by reason that I have sene the draughtes of others made before my tyme, and parte for that I have bene in my youthe and hytherto accustomed and exercysed in two languages of Frenche and Englysshe.[3]

---

[1] *STC* 24866–8, and Duff, *Fifteenth Century English Books* (1917), no. 407 note.

[2] It was partially reprinted by A. J. Ellis in his *Early English Pronunciation*, E.E.T.S. Extra Series, vol. XIV (1871), part iii, pp. 804–14.

[3] *STC* 1386, sig. A ii^r.

His work is plain and easy, mainly because it is very limited in its aim, and sets out to be little more than a collection of notes, and concludes: 'Who so desyreth to knowe more of the sayd language must provyde for mo bokes made for the same intent.' Among other books were *Introductions in Frensche for Henry the Yonge Erle of Lyncoln (childe of greate esperaunce) sonne of most noble and excellent princesse Mary, etc.*, a work probably written by Pierre Valence, French tutor to the Earl of Lincoln [*c.* 1530], and another work of 1528, of which only two leaves survive. Far exceeding these in importance, however, were the volumes of the two great teachers of their day, Giles Duwes and John Palsgrave. Duwes was a Frenchman, and his *Introductorie for to lerne to rede, to pronunce and to speke French trewly, compyled for the right high excellent and most vertuous Lady Mary of Englande, daughter to our most gracious soveraign, Lorde Kyng Henry the Eight* is a small quarto of 204 pages, printed about 1534.[1] After giving an outline of the rules of grammar, Duwes devotes over half his book to practical exercises in the form of letters. His work is a practical, entertaining, competent manual, and was three times reprinted in the next ten years.

The most notable sign of the importance attached to French studies at this time is seen in the work of John Palsgrave, who published in 1530 his *Lesclarcissement de la langue francoyse*, a monumental folio of over 1000 pages. The first two books, dealing with the rules for pronunciation and accidence are comparatively short, but in book three, Palsgrave devotes some 950 pages to the formulation of rules to govern every inflection, arranged according to the parts of speech, with illustrative phrases and idioms. Nothing like it in size or thoroughness had yet appeared in English—but these very things helped to limit its sale, and no second edition appeared.[2]

Twenty years were to elapse after the publication of Duwes's

[1] *STC* 7377.
[2] *STC* 19166. For the interesting history of the printing and sale of *Lesclarcissement*, see below, p. 226.

work before another aid to the student was printed. About 1553 Pierre du Ploiche, a Frenchman, wrote his *Treatise in Englishe and Frenche right necessary and proffitable for al young children*, published by R. Grafton. In his preface (printed in parallel columns in English and French) du Ploiche says he wrote the work 'for the better and more evident declaryng of the diversite of one toung to the other: and it is turned almost worde for worde, and lyne for lyne, that it may be to his young scholers more easy and lyght'.[1] He resorts to the dialogues that were so popular in the earliest manuals, and evidently relied on conversation and practical exercises more than on grammar. His is the first of a series of French books that were to follow, in which the rules are condensed as much as possible and the largest part of the volume devoted to lively dialogue and familiar scenes and objects. The time was not yet ripe for the serious study of the language such as Palsgrave had attempted.

No other language received attention comparable with that given to French. Translations from German were frequently made for the English market, while a number of Spanish and Italian works were put into English, but no attempt was apparently made in print to help Englishmen learn these languages until 1550 when *Principal rules of the Italian grammer, with a dictionarie for the better understandyng of Boccace, Petrarcha and Dante, gathered into this tongue by William Thomas* appeared. In an interesting foreword we are told that

after William Thomas had bene about three yeres in Italie, it happened John Tamworth, gentleman, to arrive there, who beynge desyrous to learne the tongue, intreated the sayde William Thomas to drawe him out in Englishe some of the principall rules that mighte leade him to the true knowlage therof.... And aboute two yeres after maister Tamworth lente this booke so written to Syr Walter Mildmaie, knighte, who thinkyng it a necessarie thynge for all suche of our nacion as are studious in that tong, caused it thus to be put in printe for their commoditiee.[2]

[1] *STC* 7363, sig. A i^v.
[2] *STC* 24020, sig. A i^v. It was reprinted in 1562 and 1567.

The book is very well arranged and put together, but did little to inspire others, and no such works for German, Spanish or other modern languages appeared in this period. The most that we can point to is the licence granted to Edward Sutton in 1557 to print 'a boke intituled Italian, Frynsche, Englysshe and Duche'. This work was probably a polyglot phrase-book (similar to those put out in French and English earlier) for the use of merchants and traders and looked no further than that in its interests and instruction.

Such in brief was the contribution made by the book trade to formal learning at this time. Indirectly, of course, the publication of works of history, geography, medicine, and the like were an even greater contribution to the civilization of Tudor England, as will become evident as our survey proceeds.

4. *Medicine*

The fifteenth century had seen a considerable expansion in the provision of works on science and information, and in due course this interest was reflected in the output of the printers. At first, however, progress was slow. From Caxton's time until 1525, a period of fifty years, only some fifteen volumes of such works are extant. All save one of these (Tunstall, *De arte supputandi*, 1522) are little treatises concerned with health. The famous pamphlet on the plague, attributed to Canutus, a Danish bishop, which had circulated freely in manuscript, was first printed by W. de Machlinia about 1486,[1] and was reprinted five times by 1520. In the next decade, Thomas Paynel, a canon of Merton Abbey, translated another short treatise (*c.* 1534),[2] and about 1539 Thomas Moulton produced a larger work, *The myrrour or glasse of helth*, 'necessary and nedefull for every person to loke in that wyll kepe theyr body from the seknes of the Pestylence'.[3] Although he frequently

[1] *STC* 4589.
[2] *STC* 24226, *A moche profitable treatise against the pestilence.*
[3] *STC* 18214.

appeals to 'every Surgyon', at the end of his prologue Moulton says that he has 'set it in prynt so in Englysshe yᵗ every man both lerned, and lewde, rich and pore may the better understand it and do therafter'.[1] He evidently satisfied his readers, for the work was reprinted thirteen times by 1550. Another treatise that enjoyed some popularity was the translation by Thomas Phaer of a French work which he entitled *The Regiment of life, wherunto is added a treatise of the pestilence, with the boke of children* (1544).[2] The book describes the nature of man's body, the inward and outward diseases, with the most wholesome and expert remedies; then goes on to deal with the pestilence, then to discuss blood-letting, and finally the treatment of children.

Another group of books destined to have a wide popularity were the herbals. These volumes not only contained a description of various plants, but also gave instruction for the making of potions, salves or lotions from their leaves and flowers. They were invaluable first-aid books of reference, and to those far from medical care, often served as the only means whereby a patient's ailments might be treated. Of course, they were far from scientific in many particulars; but, expressed in simple language, and at times adorned with crude woodcuts of the plants, they met an obvious need, and 'Bankes' Herbal', published in 1525[3] was reprinted at least fifteen times by 1560. The public were encouraged to buy new editions by statements on the title-pages attributing the work to Macer, or more daringly as 'Macer's Herbal practised by Dr Linacre', or by the untrue statement that there were 'certayne addicions at the ende of the boke'. Later editions also catered for a wider public by adding information concerning lucky and unlucky days, or by inserting an almanack, etc. These small octavo

[1] *STC* 18219, sig. A vii*ʳ*.
[2] *STC* 11967. *STC* 11969 (1546) 'Newly corrected and enlarged'. And see also, *STC* 4039, W. Bullein, *A newe booke entituled the gouernement of healthe* [1558], 'for the better understanding of th'unlearned'.
[3] *STC* 4720. The attribution of this herbal to W. Cary or W. Copland has now been abandoned.

volumes were cheaply produced, and probably all derived in the main from one of the many herbals circulating in manuscript in the fifteenth century.[1] For those able to afford a larger work there was the folio volume published in 1526 called *The grete herball*.[2] This contained 372 pages, and, in addition to the 207 sections on the virtues and properties of herbs, trees and minerals, had an 'exposicyon of wordes obscure', and a treatise on urines. It was for the most part a translation of *Le grand herbier* (Paris, n.d.), and included a large number of woodcuts of botanical specimens, 'many fictitious and many misplaced'. It was sufficiently popular to call for a reprint in 1529, and another without illustrations in 1539.

From the herbals it was but a short step to books on the preparation of tinctures from herbs and flowers, for 'as Avicenna testifieth, the waters be better than the Herbes...to the profyte, cure and remedy of all maner dyseases and infirmytees apparent and not apparent'. Hence the translation of so large a work as Jerome of Brunswick's *Vertuose boke of distyllacyon* (1527) may have been considered a fair risk. This folio volume of about 200 pages, adorned with cuts of stills, was written 'not only to the synguler helpe and profyte of the Surgyens, Phisycyens, and Pothecaryes, but also of all maner of people'.[3] The translator, Laurence Andrewe, appeals to the 'favorable reader' to

lerne the hyghe and mervelous vertu of herbes, knowe how inestymable a preservatyve to the helth of man god hath provyded growyng every day at our hande; use the effectes with reverence, and gyve thankes to thy maker celestyall. Beholde how moche it exceedeth to use medicyne of eficacye naturall by god ordeyned then wycked wordes or charmes of efycacie unnaturall by the devyll envented. Which yf thou doste well marke, thou shalt have

---

[1] For an account and list of these, see my 'Science and Information in English Writings of the Fifteenth Century', *M.L.R.* vol. XXXIX (1944), pp. 2–3.
[2] *STC* 13176. [3] *STC* 13435, sig. ¶ i[r].

occasyon to geve the more lovynges and prayse to our savyour, by redynge this booke and knowlegynge his benyfites innumerable....[1]

Three editions, published within some three years, indicate the commercial success of this considerable venture, while two other works of a similar nature published by other printers show that the demand was not fully met by Andrewe's version alone.[2]

It was not until nearly the end of our period that the herbal was given a scientific basis. William Turner, Doctor of medicine, and Dean of Wells, spent much of his leisure in the careful study of plants which he sought for in their native habitat, and described with an accuracy hitherto unknown in England.[3] Earlier herbals meant little to him and it was presumably to 'Bankes' Herbal', or to *The grete herball*, that he was referring when he wrote in 1568:

> Above thyrtye yeres ago...beyng yet felow of Pembroke hall in Cambridge wher as I could learne never one Greke, nether Latin, nor English name, even...in simples at that tyme, and as yet there was no Englishe Herbal but one, al full of unlearned cacographees and falselye naminge of herbes.[4]

Thirty years earlier, Turner had published his first botanical treatise, *Libellus de re herbaria nouus* (1538).[5] This was in Latin and reached a limited public. Turner made a wider appeal in his next botanical work, *The names of herbes in Greke, Latin, Englishe, Duche and Frenche wyth the commune names that herbaries and apotecaries use* [1548]. This he published, as he tells us, because

certeine scholars, poticaries, and also surgeans, required of me if that I woulde not set forth my latin herbal...at the least to set forth

---

[1] *Ibid.* sig. ¶ii[r].

[2] See *STC* 1180. 'This boke doth treate all of the beste waters artyfycialles' [1530?]; and *STC* 11800, *The treasure of Euonymus* [1559].

[3] For a detailed account of all that concerns Turner as a scientist, see C. E. Raven, *English Naturalists from Neckam to Ray* (1947), pp. 48–137.

[4] *STC* 24367, sig. Aii[v].   [5] *STC* 24358.

my judgement of the names of so many herbes as I knew. Whose request I have accomplished, and have made a little boke, which is no more but a table or regestre of such bokes as I intende, by the grace of God to set forth hereafter.[1]

The promise he fulfilled by the publication of his *magnum opus*, *A new herball*, in three folio volumes, the first of which appeared in 1551, the second in 1562, and the third after his death, in 1568.[2] These volumes gave the first clear, systematic survey of English plants, and with their admirable woodcuts, and detailed observations based on Turner's own field studies put the herbal on an altogether higher footing than in earlier works. At the same time, however, Turner included an account of their 'uses and vertues', and in his preface admits that he knows that some will accuse him of divulging to the general public what should have been reserved for a professional audience, and that it is

Unwysely done, and agaynst the honor of my art that I professe [as a doctor]; and agaynst the comon profit, to set out so muche knowledge of Phisick in Englyshe, for now (say they) every man ...nay every old wyfe will presume, not without the mordre of many, to practise Phisick.[3]

These words of Turner echo what had been said by a number of writers in this period who put forward books of medical instruction, whether in the shape of herbals, guides to health, simple manuals of medicine or surgery. Works such as these in English had not gone unchallenged, and their authors felt it necessary to reply with vigorous counter-attacks. Thus Sir Thomas Elyot, in *The castel of helth* (1541) wrote:

If physitions be angry that I have wrytten physyke in englyshe, let them remembre that the grekes wrote in greke, the Romayns

[1] *STC* 24359, sig. Aiii[r]. A few years later [1551?] Humphrey Lloyd declared that all interested in the herbals were 'muche beholden to Mayster Wyllyam Turner, who wyth no small diligence hath in both his herballes most truly and syncerly set forth the names and natures of diverse herbes' (*STC* 14652, sig. Aiii[r]).
[2] *STC* 24365–7.   [3] *STC* 24365, sig. Aiii[v].

in latyne, Avicenna and the other in Arabike, which were their owne propre and maternal tongues. And yf they had bene as moche attached with envy and covetyse as some nowe seeme to be they wolde have devysed somme partycular language with a straunge cypher of fourme of letters wherein they wolde have written their scyence, whyche language or letters noo man shoulde have knowen that hadde not professed and practysed physyke.[1]

In 1551, as we have seen, Turner justified his right to publish in English, even if it meant throwing open the secrets to 'every olde wyfe'. He declared that few were able to understand the classical writings of Galen and Dioscorides, and that to translate them would do no harm. After all, to their original readers, they *were* in the vernacular, and

if they gave no occasion unto every olde wyfe to practise Physick, then give I none. If they gave no occasyon of murther, then gyve I none. If they were no hynderers from the study of lyberall sciences, then am I no hynderer, wrytyng unto the English my countremen an Englysh herball.[2]

About the time Turner was writing this, Humphrey Lloyd, in publishing his translation of John XXI's work *The treasuri of helth* [1550?], puts the case for the vernacular version in more cautious words, designed to allay the criticism of the profession. He knows

what a perlyous thyng it is for them that be not lerned both in the complectyons of men, Age, Regions, and tyme of the yere, with the knowledge of the Orygyne and causes of the diseases, to take upon them the cure of any pacient...and therfore I wold that all such rash & temerariouse persons shuld perfectly knowe that it was never my mynde or wyll that thys worke should be set forth to mayntayne there fylthy lucre and blind boldness...I wold that it shuld be for ye use and profyte of suche honest persones as wyll modestly and discretelye (either in tyme of necessyty when no lerned Phisicion is at hande, or els conferryng wyth some lerned man and usynge hys councel) mynyster the thynges herein conteyned.[3]

---

[1] *STC* 7643, sig. Aiv^r (second ed. 'Corrected and augmented').
[2] *STC* 24365, sig. Aiii^v.   [3] *STC* 14652, sig. Aiii^r.

Earlier in his preface Lloyd had noted that 'dyverse lerned men...have herebefore translated and set forth sundry bokes, conteyning the moste holsome and profitable preceptes of Physicke...in thys oure vylgare Englisshe tonge', and from the earliest days of printing treatises giving simple rules of health had appeared. In 1489 Caxton had printed *The Gouernayle of helthe*, a little quarto of 36 pages, the first of such works.[1] This was followed about 1526 by a volume printed by R. Bankes: 'Here begynneth a newe boke of medecynes intytulyd...the Treasure of pore men.' This contained an account of a number of diseases, and gave an appropriate remedy for each of them. At least nine editions had appeared by 1560.[2]

There were also other works of a popular kind. One of these, Sir Thomas Elyot's *Castel of helth*, has already been mentioned. Although the author was not a doctor, he had studied the great medical classics with care, and the ordinary man found in his pages an explanation of the humours, advice on hygiene and diet, etc., which he could understand, so that the work was reprinted many times in the sixteenth century. Another outstanding popular success was the *Schola Salernitana*; *Regimen sanitatis Salerni* (1528), translated by Thomas Paynell.[3] The *Regimen* was 'a boke techyng al peple to governe them in helthe', and set forth a number of precepts on diet and hygiene that had acquired great popularity from the time of their first formulation in the twelfth century. Once printed, the work had considerable success, and the printer T. Berthelet told Paynell in 1533 that 'so far forthe as ever he coude here, it is of every man very well accepted and allowed'.[4] Half-way

[1] *STC* 12138.   [2] *STC* 24199–206.

[3] *STC* 21596. The work was reprinted throughout the century, and even into the next, an edition being printed in 1634. See also the next note.

[4] *STC* 14024, sig. *i*. As late as 1584 Thomas Cogan in *The Haven of Health* admits that he has quoted whole sentences from Elyot, 'and speciallye out of *Schola Salerni*'. *STC* 5478, sig. ¶4ᵛ. With the *Schola* we may class a translation made about 1540 of a little treatise of Arnold de Villa Nova, called the *Defence of age and recouery of youth* (*STC* 777). It consists of 16 pages only, of simple rules of health.

through the century the demand for general works of a popular nature was considerable. About 1550, Christopher Langton wrote *An introduction into phisycke, wyth an universal dyet,*[1] superseding his earlier work, *A very brefe treatise, ordrely declaring the prīcipal partes of phisick* (1547),[2] while Humphrey Lloyd had appealed to the 'Gentilharted Reader' with a translation of John XXI's *Treasuri of helth* [1550?],[3] and Henry Wingfield had ready his *Compendious treatise... conteynynge certeyne preceptes necessary to the preseruacion of healthe* [1551?]. Wingfield tells the 'gentle reader' that he has 'gathered of the moste principall writers of physick, this compendious extract, wherein are conteyned certein observacions and preceptes very necessary and profitable to the prolonging of lyfe'.[4] Lastly there was *The breuiary of healthe* written by Dr Andrew Borde and printed in 1552. After a long prologue, addressed to the 'egregious doctours and maysters of the Eximiouse and Archane Science of phisicke', in which he extols the doctor's art, and reproves those who 'wyll enterprise to smatter and to meddle to mynister medecynes',[5] he goes on to say, 'I do not wryte these bokes for learned men, but for simple and unlerned men that they may have some knowledge to ease them selves in theyr diseases and infirmities'.[6] With this in mind he writes a comprehensive but brief treatise, so that

there is no sickenes in manne or womanne, the whyche may bee frome the crowne of the heade, to the soole of the foote, but you shal fynde it in thys boke, as well the sycknesse the whyche doth pertayne to Chierurgy as to physycke, and what the sycknes is, and howe it doth come, and medecynes for the selfe same.[7]

In addition to these general works there were a number of treatises dealing with special diseases. One destined to have

[1] *STC* 15204.
[2] *STC* 15205.
[3] *STC* 14652.
[4] *STC* 25852, sig. A vi^r.
[5] *STC* 3375 (1557), sig. A ii^r. An early version of this seems to be the same author's little treatise of 32 pages, published by R. Wyer about 1540, entitled *The boke for to lerne a man to be wyse in buyldyng of his howse for the helth of body* (*STC* 3373).
[6] *Ibid.* sig. R i^v.
[7] *Ibid.* sig. A v^v.

much popularity was *The seynge of uryns* (1525) which reached its tenth edition about 1555.[1] The title-page announced the work as one 'moche profytable for every man to knowe', and added at the end, 'All they that desyre to have knowledge of Medycyns for all suche Urynes as be before in this boke, go ye to the Herball in Englysshe, or to the boke of Medycynes, and there you shall fynde all suche Medycynes that be most profytable for man'. These little books, in octavo or more rarely in quarto, were evidently used as 'first aid' manuals, or as the compiler of the edition of 1527? writes, 'for the comen welt of peopell',[2] since 'phisicyons do afferme that the surest and most generall way of judginge the nature and place of the siknesse is by ye Uryne'.[3] With such a volume in hand, as Dr Record tells us, 'all men... may lerne to have sum knowlege in their owne urines, and therby may be the better able to enstructe the phisicion... what sort of urine they have made from time to time'.[4]

This highway to knowledge did not go unchallenged, as is to be seen from some remarks by Christopher Langton in his book on physic [1550?]. There he deplores the empirical methods followed by those that

wer never Galennes scholers: for he teacheth them not to judge all dyseases by the uryne, where as the moste parte of them (I do not saye all) after that they have ones sene the water of the sycke, yea though they never knewe hym, nor can not be enformed by the bearer in what state he is in, wyll not stycke to wryte the Appotecarie a byl for such maner of drugges y^t if they were layed before theyr eyes, they coulde not tell whether they were the same y^t they write for or no. How is it possible for these Phisitions to do any lesse then kyll theyr pacientes; but it maketh the lesse matter,. seinge they be hyred to it wyth golde and sylver.[5]

---

[1] *STC* 22153ª, sig. H3ʳ. Repeated in *STC* 14834, *The judgemēt of all vrynes* [1540?], sig. Iivʳ.
[2] *STC* 14836, *The iudycyall of vryns* [1527?], sig. Siʳ.
[3] *STC* 24595, *The iugemēt of vrynes* (1553), sig. Aiiʳ.
[4] *STC* 20816, *The vrinal of physick* (1547), sig. Bivʳ.
[5] *STC* 15204, sig. Biiʳ.

A few more special treatises may be noted, the most popular being Richard Jonas's translation of a German treatise on childbirth, which he entitled *The byrth of mankynde* (1540). This Jonas says he has translated

> for the syngular utilite and profete that ensueth unto all such as rede it, and moste speciallye unto all women (for whose onely cause it was wrytten)...so that there be fewe matrones and women... but yf they can rede, wyll have this booke alwayes in readynesse... if it be set forth in the Englyshe speche.[1]

The early popularity of this work encouraged the physician Thomas Raynalde to correct and augment the first edition, so that later editions are twice as long.[2] Another treatise of some importance was Thomas Paynell's translation of a book on syphilis by U. von Hutten, *De morbo gallico* [1533]. This work set forth the nature of the disease, its causes and its cure, and became a standard work, so that Paynell feels bound to add the following declaration to 'a remedy for the frenche pockes' which he prints as part of a little medical treatise. He writes:

> It may be, that this remedy for the frenche pockes before wryten, was at the begynnyng the beste that men had by experience proved: but I thynke it is nothyng nowe comparable to that Hutten wryteth *de signo guaiaco*, yet notwythstandynge we have put it to, that men may se what thynges are good, yf the other coulde not be had.[3]

These works were all of semi-popular nature, intended for the layman. There was also a market to be served by the printing of medical manuals for professional use. The fifteenth century had seen the translation of a number of these into English, and so far as surgery was concerned it was to English versions that the early printers turned. The first of these was a translation of Jerome of Brunswick's *Noble experyence of the*

---

[1] *STC* 21153, sig. AB ii[v].

[2] For an account of the fortunes of this work throughout the sixteenth century and later, see Sir D'Arcy Power, 'The Birth of Mankind or the Woman's Book', *The Library*, Fourth Series, vol. VIII (1927), pp. 1–37.

[3] *STC* 24226, sig. B 4[r].

vertuous handy warke of surgeri (1525), a small folio with a number of full-page woodcuts, showing in gruesome detail the surgeon at work. It appeals to

ye yonge studentes, maysters and servantes of barbers and surgyens that entende this noble arte and connynge, [to] beholde, overse and rede with diligence this lytell boke.... Thynke y^t ye may now for a lytell money have gret lernynge and connynge to your honour and profyte, the whiche herafter ye myght fortune nat to gett for ten tymes so moche golde as it sholde coste you now.[1]

Next in 1542 Robert Copland addresses 'all yonge and pregnaunt prattycyens as fayne wolde attayne to the perfytenes of every suche scyence' as surgery, and says that Guy de Chauliac's *Questyonary of cyrurgyens* which he has translated has 'ben often requyred and soughte for to be had in englysshe (as well of me as of other) by dyvers and many persones of the sayde scyence'.[2] Two years later Edward Whitchurch printed *The most excellent workes of chirurgerye, made...by maister John Vigon* [i.e. Joannes de Vigo],[3] a work commended a few years later by Dr Robert Record as 'most surest for you to follow in the arte of surgery...that I know'.[4]

A more critical note is struck by the anonymous author of *The practyse of cyrurgyons of Mountpyller: and of other that neuer came there* [1540?]. This little eight-page quarto discusses adversely current surgical practice, and says that 'many men hath ben thus used that Cyrurgions may have a lyvynge. And they make the people to beleve that they have done a great cure, and that they maye be called greate connynge men.'[5] The limitations under which much surgery was performed will be appreciated if it is remembered that surgeons were working from the point of view, and using the text-books of men such as Guy de Chauliac who had flourished centuries earlier, and

---

[1] *STC* 13434, sig. Aii^r.
[2] *STC* 12468, sig. Ai^v.
[3] *STC* 24720.   [4] *STC* 20816, sig. Avii^r.
[5] *STC* 18052, sig. A4^r.

whose works were already outmoded by the great Renaissance investigators.[1]

This point is well illustrated by the history of anatomical studies. There was no good book of anatomy in English available for the use of young students of surgery until 1548 when Thomas Vicary published *A profitable treatise of the anatomie of mans body*. This, again, was mainly based on the work of a thirteenth-century surgeon, Henri de Mondeville, and approached the subject in a strictly academic way. Despite this, it was a popular text-book and ran to some ten editions. It remained for Thomas Gemini, surgeon to Edward VI, to provide a more practical manual, which he did in his *Compendiosa totius anatomie delineatio* (1545) in which he follows Vesalius, 'but whatever he produced very diffusely in many prolix books, I, in accordance with my ability, have put into a compendium, so to speak'.[2] But since he wrote in Latin, he realized that this still left a need, and in 1553 Nicholas Udall translated the *Compendiosa*, so 'that the same worke beeyng set foorth in the Englishe tounge might greatly availe to ye knowlage of the unlatined Surgeons, & by meane of them, should bee muche more beneficiall, than in Latin it is to an infinite nombre of people in thys your Majesties Royalme of Englande'.[3] The two versions of the *Compendiosa* rank among the most important anatomical works of the sixteenth century, and were of the greatest value in the orderly and practical study of dissection, since they were based on the modern ideas and teaching of Vesalius—one of the greatest names in the history of medicine.

Medical works—as distinguished from surgical—had far less vogue. A number of works in Latin by Galen were published. In 1521 J. Siberch printed at Cambridge the 'de temperamentis et de inaequali intemperie libri tres, T. Linacro

[1] Cf. 18217 [1540?] where Thomas Moulton's prologue (sig. A ii^r) says: 'Do you well to wytte, that this Boke profyteth greatly to every Surgyon, for to knowe in what Sygne, or in what degree of the Sygne of the Sonne and the Moone settethe every daye.'

[2] *STC* 11714, sig. A i^v.   [3] *STC* 11716, sig. *i^r.

interprete', and this was reprinted in 1527. Pynson also printed four other treatises of Galen between 1522 and 1524, but none of these appear to have been reprinted, and little else in English or in Latin of a medical character appeared in this period. If Langton is a reliable witness this is not surprising, for he says of his contemporaries:

> But alas, there is no mans Physycke so lytle regarded nowe a dayes as Galennes is, and in deede, to saye the truthe, it maye very well be perceyved by theyr doinges that they wer never Galennes scholers. . . . Yf I were disposed I coulde prove that there is as moch jugglyng and deceyvyng of the people now a dayes amongest our phisitions. I wyll nam none, (but everye man knoweth his owne weakenesse and infirmitie) as ever was amongest the Popysh preestes, and a redresse myght be had, yf it pleased the kynges hyghnesse, yᵗ none might be suffered to practyse but suche as be learned.[1]

On the whole, as might have been expected, the printers exploited the popular market and ignored to a large extent the professional one. The great success of some of their ventures, such as the herbals, the books on urine, or the work on childbirth, provided them with a valuable source of income, and at the same time gave the public access to first-aid information which seemed perhaps of greater value than it really was.

5. *Information*

It is obvious that once a considerable body of people were able to read, a demand for a variety of works of a practical nature would soon reach the printers. They would be urged to produce handy, practical manuals, easily understood and dealing with every-day information. These ranged from the large folio encyclopaedias to the small octavo or quarto pamphlets which told in a few pages the way to treat a sick horse or to graft a tree.

Caxton was enterprising enough to blaze the trail with a large-scale work *The myrrour of the worlde* [1481].[2] This was a

---

[1] *STC* 15204, sig. Biiʳ.   [2] *STC* 24762.

prose translation of a work originating in the thirteenth-century French poem by Gautier de Metz, and falls into three parts. The first treats of God and of the Seven Liberal Arts; the second of the Four Elements, of Geography and Meteorology, while the third is mainly concerned with Astronomy. It is a typical example of the encyclopædia so beloved of the Middle Ages, and here made available to the ordinary reader with no attempt to bring it up to date. Caxton furnished it with a number of woodcuts, and was called on to reprint it in 1490, and there was another reprint in 1529. It remained the best popular exposition of astronomy until the middle of the century.

A work of far greater range and importance was the *De proprietatibus rerum* of Bartholomaeus Anglicus. The Latin original was translated into English in the last years of the fourteenth century, and this version was first printed by Wynkyn de Worde in 1495. It is a storehouse of information on every subject from the nature of God to the proper way to lay a table. The work remained in demand throughout the sixteenth century, and it was reprinted by T. Berthelet in 1535

with many places therin amended by the latyne exemplare; wherby ye shall nowe the better understand it, not onely bycause many wordes & sentences that were here & there lefte out be nowe restored agayne, but also by reson the propre names of men, landes, cites...be trwely ortografied.[1]

There followed a slightly enlarged and corrected edition of Stephen Batman printed by T. East in 1582.

These works contributed little or nothing that was new. Their compilers were content to reproduce knowledge that had been current for centuries, and the stationers traded in these wares confident that their customers would not be put off by their old-fashioned contents. They were much more likely to demur at their size and cost, and it was inevitable that smaller manuals each dealing with some separate field of knowledge would be required.

[1] *STC* 1537, sig. ⲣ ii^r.

It was to meet such a demand as this that books on a wide variety of topics were forthcoming. For the farmer, John Fitzherbert[1] produced his treatise on *Husbandry* [1523], a work seven times reprinted by 1560. Here might be found a discussion of the best methods of farming, and of the tools and capital required. The qualities desirable in the farmer and his servants and their daily life were discussed, and the whole formed a useful, eminently practical manual. Side by side with it went the same author's *Surveying* (1523)—a work full of information useful for farmers and others, set forth, as the author tells us 'to thentent that the lordes, the freholders nor their heyres, shulde not be disheryt, nor have their landes loste nor imbeseled, nor encroached by one from another'.[2] When he printed it in 1539, Thomas Berthelet commended it as good and profitable 'for all states that be lordes and possessioners of landes, and for the holders or tenauntes of the same landes to have dayly in hande, to knowe and beare awaye the contentes'.[3]

A number of works of a similar nature were published. The celebrated medieval treatise on farming by Walter of Henley, *The boke of husbandry*, was printed by de Worde about 1510,[4] while at the end of the period the versified *Hundreth good pointes of husbandrie* (1557) by Thomas Tusser made its appearance. The first of these is a severely practical manual, while the second is a medley of country lore and housewifery:

> Housekeping and husbandry, if it be good
> Must love one another, as cousines in blood.
> The wife to must husband, as well as the man,
> Or farewel the husbandry, doe what those can.[5]

Between these two ways of dealing with country matters a number of little treatises found a place. At the end of Walter of

---

[1] There is still much controversy over the authorship of *Surveying* and *Husbandry*—some authorities claiming them for Sir Anthony, some for his brother John. I have followed the *STC* ruling.

[2] *STC* 11006, sig. b ii^v.

[3] *STC* 11008, sig. A i^v. Cf. *STC* 1873, a work by R. Benese [1537?] which 'sheweth the maner of measurynge of all maner of lande'.

[4] *STC* 25007.   [5] *STC* 24372, sig. A ii^r.

Henley will be found some directions on the planting of trees,[1] and about 1520 another treatise, *The crafte of graffynge & plantynge of trees* was published anonymously.[2] Both these works appear to derive from the well-known treatise on husbandry by Palladius, and are very elementary. Thomas Hill's famous work on *The proffitable arte of gardening*[3] was not forthcoming until the sixties. Nor was the farmer well served in other departments. Horse-keeping might have been thought worthy of attention, but little printed matter appeared on this subject before about 1560, when *The arte of ryding and breakinge greate horses* by Thomas Blundeville was printed. This was said to be 'very necessary for all Gentlemen, Souldyours, Servingmen and for every man that delighteth in a horse'.[4] Horse-lovers until then had to be content with a few pages hidden away in the large *Book of St Albans* (1486), or a pamphlet of about 1500, issued by de Worde: 'Here begynneth the Proprytees and medycynes for hors.'[5]

Outdoor sports received but little attention after their first splendid eulogy in the *Book of St Albans*:[6] 'The book of Hawking, hunting and blasing of arms', save that in the second edition of this work, printed by de Worde in 1496, a new section on 'fysshynge wyth an angle' was added. In this we are told that if a fisherman fail of one fish,

he maye not faylle of a nother yf he dooth as this treatyse techyth: but yf there be nought in the water. And yet atte the leest he hath his holsome walke and mery at his ease, a swete ayre of the swete savoure of the meede floures: that makyth hym hungry. He hereth the melodyous armony of fowles. He seeth the yonge swannes: heerons: duckes: cotes and many other foules wyth theyr brodes. Whyche me semyth better than alle the noyse of houndys: the blastes of hornys and the scrye of foulis that hunters: fawkeners & foulers can make.[7]

---

[1] *STC* 25007, sig. Biii[v].   [2] *STC* 5953.   [3] *STC* 13491 (1563).
[4] *STC* 12387, sig. Ai[r].   [5] *STC* 13827 +.   [6] *STC* 3308.
[7] *STC* 3309, sig. iv[v]. A third edition was printed by H. Tab in 1540, and there were three subsequent editions before it was 'reduced into a better method', by G. Markham in 1595.

Apart from the *Book of St Albans* there is a little treatise on hunting printed by de Worde [1515] and again in [1530?],[1] while John Waley printed another small work on hawking [1550?].[2] These seem to be all that have survived, and it is perhaps important to emphasize this latter point, since most of these treatises were small, and by their practical usefulness, constantly thumbed over, and quickly worn to fragments and discarded. There may have been many more editions, or additional works, of which we know nothing.

6. *Arithmetic, Astronomy and Popular Science*

For those at work indoors, and concerned with commercial affairs of all kinds, a number of handbooks became available. The keeping of accounts and the art of computation had been dealt with by a number of medieval authors, but the science of numbers was still in its infancy. Elementary books on arithmetic were an obvious necessity, but were slow in appearing. In the earlier part of the century, the only work published in England dealing wholly with arithmetic was Cuthbert Tunstall's *De arte supputandi* (1522).[3] Tunstall was made Bishop of London, after holding the office of Master of the Rolls, and wrote his book as a farewell gift to the sciences. He tells us in the preface that he took up the study of arithmetic because he suspected the accuracy of accounts laid before him, and he wished his book to be a practical manual for the help of merchants. He did not succeed in making it this, but it sets out the principles of arithmetic with skill and learning. It did not catch on in England: the fact that it was all in Latin probably telling against it, but it was frequently reprinted in Paris and Strasbourg.

A book of much greater practical importance was *The grounde of artes*, 'teachyng the worke and practise of arith-

---

[1] *STC* 3317–18.   [2] *STC* 3316.
[3] *STC* 24319. It should be noted that Caxton's edition of *The myrrour of the worlde* (1481), contained a chapter on 'Arsmetrike and wherof it proceedeth'—probably the first English printed matter on the subject.

metike, both in whole numbers and fractions, after a more easyer and exacter sorte than any like hath hithertoo bin set foorth'.[1] It was written by Dr Robert Record, a great popularizer of his day, and was intended for the 'simple ignorant', for whose sake was 'plainly set forth the Examples, as no Booke that I have seen hath done hithertoo'. In making this remark Record may have been referring to a volume published by N. Bourman in 1539, 'An introduction for to lerne to recken with the pen, or with the counters accordyng to the trewe cast of Algorisme, in hole numbers, or in broken...'. The preface to this work emphasizes 'howe profitable and necessarye this feat of Algorism is to all maner of persons, whiche have rekenynges or accountes, other to make elles to receyve', and adds, 'Neyther is this arte onely necessarye to these, but also...to all maner of sciences and artificyes'.[2] The author goes on to advise readers to work methodically through the book, 'for if you lepe to the seconde parte before you have sene perfectly the fyrst...you shal never prosper ne profette in this arte'.[3]

Record's book was written in the form of a dialogue between master and pupil and became the most influential work of its kind in the sixteenth century. As late as 1662 an introduction to a new edition claimed with some justice that it was 'entail'd upon the People, ratified and sign'd by the approbation of Time'.

Record followed up his first book by another, entitled *The whetstone of witte* (1557). In a rhyming verse he declares

> The *grounde of artes* did brede this stone:
> His use is greate, and moare than one,
> Heere if you list your wittes to whette,
> Moche sharpenesse therby shall you gette.

---

[1] *STC* 20798.
[2] *STC* 14119 (1546 ed.), sig. Ai^v. There was also *A brief instruction and maner howe to keepe bookes of accompts* written by Hugh Oldcastle, schoolmaster, and printed in August 1543, which only survives in the edition of 1588. See *STC* 18794, sig. A3^v.   [3] *STC* 14119, sig. Aii^r.

Dulle wittes hereby doe greatly mende,
Sharpe wittes are fined to their fulle ende.
Now prove, and praise, as you doe finde,
And to your selfe be not unkinde.[1]

His 'preface to the gentle Reader' is more explicit and in it
he says:

Many praise it [the benefit of number] but fewe dooe greatly
practise it: onlesse it bee for the vulgare practice concernyng
Merchaundes trade, wherein the desire and hope of gain, maketh
many willyng to sustaine some travell, for aide of whom I did sette
forth the firste parte of *Arithmetike*. But if thei knewe how farre
this seconde parte dooeth excell the firste, thei would not accoumpte
any tyme loste that were imploied in it.[2]

His treatise follows, and is again thrown into the form of
question and answer, so that the difficulties encountered by the
pupil step by step, can be elucidated by the master. After he
had set out the elements of arithmetic, Record turned to write
his work *The pathway to knowledg* (1551), which as the title-
page tells us contains 'the first principles of Geometrie as they
may moste aptly be applied unto Practise, bothe for Use of
Instrumentes Geometricall, and Astronomicall; and also for
Projection of Plattes in everye kinde, and therefore much
necessarie for all Sortes of Men'.[3] In his dedication to
Edward VI, Record claims that this is the first time a book on
geometry has been written in English, but he says that he does
so as many, and especially those about the Court, do not
understand Latin. In addition to showing how to work out
various questions in geometry, Record gives a list of astronomical instruments at use at the time, and estimates the earth
to be some 21,600 miles round. He expresses the hope that
many gentlemen 'will fall in trade with this easie forme of
teachyng in their vulgar tong, and so employe some of their
tyme in honest studie, whiche were wont to bestowe most part
of their time in triflyng pastime'.[4]

[1] *STC* 20820, sig. a1ʳ.
[2] *Ibid.* sig. biiiʳ.
[3] *STC* 20812, sig. ¶iʳ.
[4] *Ibid.* sig. 3iiiʳ.

Finally, after a study of all these works, Record advises his readers to turn to *The castle of knowledge* (1556), where they will find 'the explication of the Sphere, both celestial and material',[1] and much that is useful to merchants with overseas business and to mariners. The work is a handsome folio volume of some 300 pages, in which for the first time in English, a clear scientific account is given of the elements of astronomy instead of the hotch-potch of truth and superstitious falsehood that had hitherto prevailed. Record's book rightly remained the standard authority throughout the remainder of the century. It was carried by Martin Frobisher as part of his ship's library, for works such as this were useful as aids to navigation, and it is significant that Record dedicated his *Whetstone of witte* 'To the right worshipfull, the governers, Consulles, and the reste of the companie of venturers into Moscovia'.[2]

Astronomy, as we have seen, was touched on, both in Caxton's translation of *The myrrour of the worlde* and in Trevisa's translation of Bartholomew's *De proprietatibus rerum*.[3] The history of the next extant publication dealing with astronomy is instructive. Under the title *Le Compost et Kalendrier des bergiers* there was published at Paris in 1493 a miscellany of information, the concluding sections of which deal with astronomy and astrology. In 1503 a translation of this with the title *The kalendayr of the shyppars* was made into a pseudo-Scottish dialect, and was published by A. Verard in Paris; in 1506 an independent translation was made for R. Pynson, and in 1508 R. Copland's translation was published by de Worde. These volumes with their many woodcuts and variety of information evidently met a popular need for information and instruction, for about 1518 Julian Notary published another edition, based mainly on Copland's translation supplemented by that contained in Pynson's edition, and in 1528 this text was republished by de Worde.[4]

Additional evidence of the popularity of *The Shepherds'*

[1] *STC* 20796, sig. A i^v.　　[2] *STC* 20820, sig. a ii^r.
[3] See above, p. 110.　　[4] *STC* 22407-11.

Kalendar may be seen in the activities of Robert Wyer in the thirties. He was a rising publisher of small handbooks of popular science and everyday information. Wyer abstracted that portion of the *Kalendar* which dealt with astronomy and astrology, and gave his work an air of authority and novelty by replacing the word 'Shepharde' wherever it appeared by the word 'Ptholomeus' or 'Astrologian'. He labelled the result *The compost of Ptholomeus Prynce of Astronomye*, and put out at least three editions of it between 1532 and 1540.[1] These small octavo books, poorly printed and adorned with cheap woodcuts, reached a market untouched by the more expensive products of de Worde and Pynson, so much so that Wyer produced another book of the same kind, consisting of questions and answers on matters astronomical, or as it was called in a later edition, *The boke of demaundes of the scyence of Phylosophye and Astronomye, Betwene kynge Boctus, and the Phylosopher Sydracke.*[2] This again is taken from another work, *The history of kyng Boccus & Sydracke* [1530?], a verse translation from the French.[3] Wyer selected from this the questions dealing with astronomy, and turned them into prose.

Other ventures by Wyer of a similar nature at this time were a vernacular version of one of Aristotle's supposititious works, the *De Astronomia*, which told of 'the Nature and Dysposycion of the dayes in the weke...with the course and dysposcyon of the dayes of the Moone: whiche be good, and whiche be badde';[4] a *Boke of knowledge of thynges vnknownen apperteynynge to astronomye*;[5] *The seven dialogues* 'of the sonne and of the Moone...of Saturne and of the Clowde', etc.,[6] and *The dyfference of astronomy.*[7]

These books were popular during the 1530's and even in the 1540's they were challenged by nothing more serious than

---

[1] *STC* 20480–1. For a full account of this theft, see H. B. Lathrop, 'Some Rogueries of Robert Wyer', *The Library*, Third Series, vol. v (1914), pp. 349–64.
[2] *STC* 3188 [1535?]; 3188ᵃ [after 1536].
[3] *STC* 3186.   [4] *STC* 768 [1530?]; 769 [1535?].
[5] *STC* 11931 [1530?].   [6] *STC* 6816 [1530?].   [7] *STC* 6837 [1535?].

Andrew Borde's *Pryncyples of astronomye*.[1] Although Borde made great claims for the importance of Astronomy in a two-page preface, his work merely sets out the names of the twelve signs of the seven planets, and similar well-known lore, and then goes on to discuss 'when and what tyme a phisicion sholde minister medycynes', or when they should proceed to the 'sowing of seedes and plantynge of trees and setyng of herbes'.[2] Borde's pamphlet was followed in 1550 by a translation of an account by the fifth-century Greek astronomer Proclus of the structure of the world. This was made by William Salisbury and was entitled *The descripcion of the sphere or frame of the worlde*,[3] and was intended for those whom he tells us in his dedication are 'almoste ygnoraunte (for the seldomnes of the science) in the speculation of the wonderfull, goodly and devyne fabricature of the world'.[4] Another serious work was published in 1552, written by Anthony Ascham, a Cambridge physician and astronomer, under the title, *A lytel treatyse of astronomy*.[5] In this Ascham discusses the way in which the exact length of the year is to be calculated, and the adjustments to the calendar that are required.[6]

Finally, we may notice the series of prognostications and almanacs that had a very wide circulation.[7] Prognostications on single sheets had existed from the early days of printing, and they appealed to the man in the street by their foretelling of events to come. They seem to have been sold for a penny,

---

[1] *STC* 3386 [after 1547].
[2] *STC* 3386, sig. A iii^v. [3] *STC* 20399.
[4] *Ibid*. sig. A iii^r. [5] *STC* 857^a.
[6] The subject-matter of this section is admirably treated by F. R. Johnson in his *Astronomical Thought in Renaissance England, 1500–1645* (1937).

[7] For a detailed bibliographical survey of these books, see E. F. Bosanquet, *English Printed Almanacks and Prognostications: A Bibliographical History to the year 1600* (1917), and also for supplementary information, *The Library*, Fourth Series, vol. VIII (1928), pp. 456–77. See also, Carroll Camden, 'Elizabethan Almanacs and Prognostications', *The Library*, Fourth Series, vol. XII (1931), pp. 83–108. A list of the majority of these prognostications, etc. will be found under the heading *Almanacks, Kalendars and Prognostications*, Appendix II, pp. 278 ff.

and were very popular. The attitude of the learned to this kind of pamphlet is shown by Sir T. More's epigram to one Fabianus:

> The crowd proclaims thee wondrous wise,
> If out of all thy prophecies
> One only proveth true.
> Be, Fabianus, always wrong,
> Then I will join the gaping throng,
> And call thee prophet too.[1]

The authorities frowned on these publications, for they were a means of circulating veiled political prophecy, and of fomenting unrest. The ambassador Chapuys, writing to Charles V of Austria, related how a prognostication lately made in Flanders threatened Henry VIII with war and misfortune that year. As a result, the translation and publication of this piece had been forbidden, since members of the Council feared that affairs in England were so uneasy that such an event would set the realm topsy-turvy.[2] Some time after this, in 1541, and again in 1549, statutes were enacted forbidding the publication of any false prophecy with intent to cause trouble, and there can be no doubt that the authorities had good reason for their action, for these prophecies made a deep impression on men during these troubled times.[3]

The earliest prognostication surviving was printed by de Worde in 1497, and concerns the year 1498, while another printed by Pynson probably belongs to the year 1500. Both are fragmentary and Pynson's is a translation, probably from one of Jasper Laet's prognostications. Mr Bosanquet has shown that all the early prognostications were translations, and that it was

---

[1] Translated by J. H. Marsden, *Philomorus. A Brief Examination of the Latin Poems by Sir T. More* (1842), pp. 68–9, quoted by C. Camden, *op. cit.* p. 87.

[2] *L. and P. Hen. VIII*, vol. XI, p. 2.

[3] See R. Taylor. *The Political Prophecy in England* (1911), and M. H. Dodds 'Political Prophecies in the reign of Henry VIII', *M.L.R.* vol. XI (1916), pp. 276–84.

not until 1545 that Andrew Borde compiled an English
'pronostycacyon or an almanacke', now known only by its
surviving title-page.

Closely allied to the prognostications were almanacks, which
contained much useful information concerning the weather,
the proper days in every month for blood-letting, the dates of
movable feasts, the eclipses, etc. The two began to be issued
together about 1540, and a large number of editions of these
little pamphlets (often in mangled form) exist to testify to their
popularity. In 1555 Leonard Digges produced a perpetual
almanack, or as his title-page has it: *A prognostication of right
good effect, fructfully augmented, contayninge playne, briefe,
pleasant, chosen rules, to judge the wether for ever, by the Sunne,
Moone, Sterres, Cometes, Raynbowe, Thunder, Cloudes, with
other Extraordinarie tokens, not omitting the Aspectes of Planetes,
with a brefe Judgement for ever, of Plentie, Lacke, Sickenes,
Death, Warres, &c.* In his address to the reader Digges says
that in order to help men 'to avoyde the yearly care, travailes,
and peines of other, with the confusions, repugnances, and
manifold errors, partly by negligence, and ofte through
ignorance committed, I have agayn breefly set forth a Prognostication general, for ever to take effect'.[1] His work won an
immediate popularity, and was constantly reprinted throughout
the century.

7. Geography

The growing interest in exploration, and the provision of
works such as *The castle of knowledge* as aids to navigation,
was accompanied by works more suitable for the ordinary
reader which would give him an account of various countries,
and of what might be seen there. Unfortunately no attempt at
first was made to bring these up to date; so that when Caxton
printed his 'Description of Britain' as a supplement to the
'Chronicles of England' (1480), he lifted the 'Description'

---

[1] *STC* 6860, sig. A iii^v.

straight from Higden's *Polychronicon*, compiled in the early fourteenth century. Nor could much be said for the slender geographical information given in *The myrrour of the worlde* [1481], for this again was sadly out of date.[1] A much more exciting work made its appearance in 1496, when Pynson printed the first of a series of editions of Sir John Mandeville's 'Travels',[2] a book purporting to be a guide to pilgrims to Jerusalem, but also to contain an account of the wonders of the East in the realms of the Great Cham. This work is written in such a lively fashion, and combines truth and fiction with ease and apparent good faith. Its popularity is shown by the fact that it was four times reprinted between 1494 and 1503. It was over one hundred and fifty years old when first printed, but as an absorbing account of travel it remained for a long time unrivalled. With it may fittingly be coupled the Antwerp edition *Of the new lãdes and of yᵉ people founde by the messengers of the kynge of portȳgale* [1520?], containing an account of the travels of Prester John.[3]

Something a little more valuable as a guide to travellers, and especially seamen, had appeared about 1503 when an Antwerp edition of 'Arnold's Chronicle' was issued containing 'A copy of a Carete Composynge the Circuet of the Worlde and the Compase of every yland'.[4] About thirty years later [1535?] Robert Wyer thought it worth while to reprint this book, since as he says, it is 'very necessary for all Marchauntes, and Maryners, and for all such as wyll labour and traveyle in the countres of the worlde'.[5] Then in 1553 appeared J. Peele's *Maner and fourme how to kepe a perfecte reconyng*, dedicated to 'Sir W. Densell...and all the worshipfull felowshippe of Merchaunt adventurers', which he tells us he has been pressed to publish, since it is 'as necessary unto the worshipfull felowshippe of the Marchantes as either is meate or drinke to

---

[1] See above, p. 109.   [2] *STC* 17246–9.
[3] *STC* 7677.
[4] *STC* 782; 783 (1521). Carete, i.e. a chart, map.
[5] *STC* 17297, sig. Ciiiᵛ.

hym that dooeth thirst or hunger'. Peele concludes his dedication with the following verse:

> Sith knoweledge then, is of suche price and grace,
> And tyme ones loste wyll not agayne renew,
> Learne well this booke, while you have time and space,
> That you the lacke dooe not lamente and rewe.[1]

A more scientific and useful work was R. Copland's translation of Pierre Garcie's *The rutter of the see, with the hauens, rodes, soundings, kennings, windes, floods and ebbes, daungers and coastes of divers regions.* In his prologue Copland says that all science is endowed with reason, and men do not undertake to build without a plan, so 'in like maner I conject that in the feate and course of Navigation or sailing a man may presume and take upon him by his speculacion to conduct a vessel as a blinde man in a desolat Wildernes doth walk till he be lost. But ye sure, wise and enured maister mariner, or lodesman, not ignorantly trusting his own sensual reason',[2] takes advice, such as will be found in the work he has translated.

These last two works were obviously designed for seamen and would have had little interest for the average layman, even if he were one of those, like some of Chaucer's pilgrims two centuries earlier, who had crossed many a 'straunge flode' in their various journeys. For such amateurs of travel there were a number of little books whose sole aim was to give practical information about the countries the traveller would traverse, such as may be found in *Informacōn for pylgrymes vnto the holy londe*[3] printed by de Worde about 1498, or *The pylgrimage of M. Robert Langton clerke to saynt Iames in Compostell* (R. Copland 1522).[4] Less limited in their aim were books appearing later in the century. In 1554 W. Powell printed *The description of the countrey of Aphrique*, a translation from the French by William Prat, being the first part of a projected work on 'Aphrique, Asie and Europia, the three

---

[1] *STC* 19547, sigs. A iii^r, B v^v.　　[2] *STC* 11552 [1555?], sig. A i^v.
[3] *STC* 14081.　　[4] *STC* 15206.

parts of the worlde'.[1] The next year saw another translation of the same work by William Waterman.[2] Both these publications gave the public for the first time a scientific approach to ethnology, as well as portraying a 'pleasant variety of things, and yet more profit in the pith'. In the same year (1555) appeared Peter Martyr of Angliera's *Decades of the newe world or West India*, translated by Richard Eden. The work contains an account of the recent discoveries in the New World, and of the voyages in search of America as well as a 'particular description of the most ryche and large landes and Ilands lately found in the West Ocean perteynyng to the inheritaunce of the Kinges of Spayne'.[3]

Such is the meagre material that had to serve those interested in matters geographical before 1557. Despite much coming and going overseas by Englishmen, the time had not yet come for their adventures to be belauded in the glowing pages of Richard Hakluyt's *Diuers voyages touching the discouerie of America* (1582), and *The principall navigations, voiages and discoueries of the English nation* (1589).

8. *History*

Whereas geographical enterprises or knowledge of the world meant but little in this period, few subjects presented a more favourable opportunity to the printer than history. Renaissance writers were all in accord in extolling the claims of history on the educated. The sentence of Cicero 'An hystore is the recorder of tymes passed: the lyght of verite: the maistress of mannes lyvenge: the presydent of memorie: the messanger of antiquite'[4] was constantly quoted or paraphrased by authors in introducing their wares. Moralists and those concerned with the training of gentlemen; busy merchants and citizens who wished to know of past events as a guide to the present, or as an inspiration for future action—all turned to the histories of

---

[1] *STC* 191, sig. A vi^v.   [2] *STC* 3197.
[3] *STC* 645, title-page.   [4] Cicero, *de Oratore*, II, 36.

the world, of England, or of their own city, for guidance. Where other forms of literature, such as poetry or romance, were suspect, history was praised, and printers found a steady market for various types of historical writings. These works covering world history or recording local annals, were put out in a variety of forms, from large folio volumes, running to many hundreds of pages to the little pamphlet of eight pages. Some are bare records of fact, in a strictly chronological form, while others attempt a consecutive narrative. Most are content to accept the material provided for them by their predecessors, but a limited number made independent investigations and put together their own version. Few have any claim to be impartial; they set out their story to favour a cause or a country, and their readers accepted what thay had to say without any attempt to check their statements. Most chroniclers could be thought of in the words of Edward Hall as 'men worthy to be praysed for theyr diligence, but farshotyng wyde from the butte of an historie'.[1]

Among the earliest works to be printed by Caxton was Higden's *Polychronicon* (1482), and Caxton's preface to this states admirably the view held throughout this period of the nature of history. He writes:

> Grete thankynges, lawde and honoure we merytoryously ben bounde to yelde and offre unto wryters of hystoryes which gretely have prouffyted oure mortal lyf, that shewe unto the reders and herers by the ensamples of thynges passyd what thynge is to be desyred, and what is to be eschewed.... Historyes ought not only to be juged moost proffytable to yonge men, whiche by the lecture, redyng and understandyng made them semblable and equale to men of greter age, and to old men to whome longe lyf hath mynystred experymentes of dyvers thynges, but also thystoryes able and make ryght private men digne and worthy to have the governaunce of Empyres, and noble Royammes, historyes moeve and withdrawe Emperours and Kynges fro vycious tyrannye, fro vecordyous

---

[1] And see *STC* 785, Arsanes, *Orations* [1560?], sig. *ii^r, for a long justification of the reading of history.

sleuthe unto tryumphe and vyctorye in puyssaunt bataylles.. . .
Historye is a perpetuel conservatryce of thoos thynges that have be
doone before this presente tyme, and also a cotydyan wytnesse of
bienfayttes, of malefaytes, grete Actes and tryumphal vyctoryes of
all maner peple. And also yf the terryble feynded Fables of Poetes
have moche styred and moeved men to pyte, and conservynge of
Justyce, how moche more is to be supposed that Historye, asser-
tryce of veryte, and as moder of alle philosophye, moevynge our
maners to vertue, reformeth and reconcyleth ner hande alle thoos
men whiche thurgh the infyrmyte of oure moral nature hath ledde
the mooste parte of theyr lyf in ocyosyte and myspendeth theyr
tyme passed ryght soone oute of remembraunce, of whiche lyf and
deth is egal oblyvyon.[1]

Higden's *Polychronicon*, composed in the mid-fourteenth
century, was translated in 1387 by John Trevisa, and it was his
translation (with a continuation up to 1460) that was printed
by Caxton in 1482.[2] Save for Caxton's new matter, which he
derived from the *Brut*, the *Polychronicon* gave a view of the
historical, geographic and scientific knowledge of the age in
which it was written. Out of date, as it was, however, it
was the best general history of the world then available, and
notwithstanding its great bulk (900 folio pages) it was reprinted by de Worde in 1495 and by P. Treveris in 1527.

Among the 'many dyverse paunflettis and bookys' that
Caxton tells us lay about in his study, we may well imagine
that there was a copy of the *Brut*—by far the most popular
historical chronicle yet written in English, and one that
circulated in manuscript in very considerable numbers. The
growth of a vernacular historical literature was a feature of the
fifteenth century. After the Anglo-Saxon Chronicle had ceased
to be written at Peterborough in 1154, little historical writing
in English had been attempted, and the great chronicles of
William of Malmesbury or Matthew Paris were hidden in the
Latin tongue. The fifteenth century saw a great change, for the

---

[1] Crotch, *op. cit.* p. 64. *vecordyous*: mad; *cotydyan*: daily; *ocyosyte*:
idleness.   [2] *STC* 13438.

only continuous chronicle of this century (the *Brut*) was in English, and manuscripts of it abound.

When, therefore, 'divers gentlemen' asked Caxton to print a history of England it was to the popular *Brut* that he turned. Here, in chronicle fashion, was given an account of our history from the time that 'Albyne with his susters entred into this isle, and named it Albyon' until the accession of Edward IV. It was written in a simple English, easily followed by the most ordinary of readers, and from its first publication in 1480 down to 1528 'the Chronicles of England' were always in demand, and not less than twelve editions survive.[1] In the main these are a plain copy one of the other with only small additions, as in 1485, when an edition was issued by the schoolmaster printer of St Albans which also contained a history of the Popes, and some other ecclesiastical matter.

Among the strangest of works given the title of 'Chronicle' was the compilation by Richard Arnold, Londoner and haberdasher. He evidently put together from time to time a commonplace book in which he recorded a wide variety of things that interested him, and this was first printed at Antwerp about 1503, in a folio of some 250 pages, and in a later edition by P. Treveris in Southwark in 1521.[2] He starts off with a list of Mayors and Sheriffs of London from the time of Richard I, 'with dyvers maters good and necessary for every citizen to understand and know', but wanders off to describe 'the craft of grafting and planting of trees', or to give 'the Copy of a Carete Cumposynge the Circuit of the World and the Compace of every Yland', and best of all includes the only known text of the famous fifteenth-century ballad 'The Nut Brown Maid'. It was not until the eighteenth century when Thomas Hearne, the antiquary, first labelled the work 'Arnold's Chronicle' that attention was drawn to the collection of ordinances, charters and London municipal documents which it contained.

More worthy of the name Chronicle was the work of Robert Fabyan, draper and sometime Sheriff of London. This took the

---

[1] *STC* 9991-10002.   [2] *STC* 782-3.

form of a substantial folio volume in two parts, running to some 800 pages in double columns, first published by Pynson in 1516. 'The new Chronicles of England and of France', as the colophon terms them, sets out the history of the two countries until 1189 in the first part, while the second is in the form of a regular London chronicle, the record of each year having at its head the names of the Mayors and Sheriffs of that year. The work has no original value, but was to the taste of many readers, so that William Rastell reprinted it in 1533, and it was put out again in 1542 by two publishers 'nowe newely printed and in many places corrected'. It was finally issued in 1559 'continued to thende of queene Mary'.[1]

Rastell's father had published in 1529 his illustrated volume, *The pastyme of people; the croncyles of dyvers realmys, and most specyally of the realme of Englond*.[2] He follows closely Fabyan's Chronicle, and adds little of importance. His work is a brief outline of history, and derives part of its interest from the series of woodcuts of the kings of England from William I to Richard III. Only one edition was published, and as we have seen his son William reverted to the full edition of Fabyan in 1533, but had shown his interest in things historical, by publishing very early in his career *Iulius Cesars commentaryes. Newly translated owte of laten into Englyshe as much as cōcernyth thys realm of England sumtyme callyd Brytayne* (1530).[3] Caesar, he tells us, 'ys the eldyst hystoryen of all other that can be found that ever wrote of thys realme of England', and his little volume of 40 pages contains both a Latin and an English text, the latter by himself.

The interest in English history was growing, and the time ripe for a work which would set out fully the events, still fresh in the minds of many, known as the Wars of the Roses, and epitomized later by those two poignant stage directions in 3 *Henry VI*: *Enter a Son that hath killed his father, with the dead body*, and following that *Enter a Father that hath killed his Son, with the body in his arms.* Edward Hall set about to provide a history of those and of earlier times, and in *The union of the two noble and illustrate famelies of York and Lancaster* (1542) produced a work of lasting importance. Intended as a glorification of the House of Tudor, Hall wrote in a dramatic style with an eye to making his narrative effective and favourable to the Yorkist cause. Unlike earlier publications, his work was an artistic whole. He abandoned the simple chronicle form, and following the example of Polydore Vergil wrote a narrative of events, coloured of course by partisan feeling, but alive and full of vivid phrase and drama. His picture of events and of their causes profoundly influenced future historians and others interested in our national fortunes. A short passage from his introductory epistle to Edward VI will indicate Hall's attitude:

> What mischiefe hath insurged in realmes by intestine devision, what depopulacion hath ensued in countries by civill discention, what detestable murder hath been committed in cities by separate faccyons, and what calamitte hath ensued in famous regions by domesticall discorde and unnaturall controversie: Rome hath felt, Italy can testifie, Fraunce can bere witnes...and especially thys noble realme of Englande can apparauntly declare and make demonstracion.[1]

After recounting the works of earlier chroniclers, Hall proceeds:

> Sithe the ende of Frossarte whiche endith at the beginninge of kynge Henry the fourthe, no man in the Englishe tounge, hath either set furth their honors accordinge to their desertes, nor yet declared many notable actes worthye of memorie doone in the tyme of seven Kynges, whiche after Kynge Rycharde succeded: Excepte Robert Fabian and one without name, whiche wrote the common Englishe Chronicle [the *Brut*], men worthy to be praysed for theyr diligence, but farre shotyng wyde from the butte of an historie.[2]

[1] *STC* 12721, sig. A i^r.   [2] *Ibid.* sig. A ii^v.

Hall's estimation of the need for a new history was accepted, and five editions of his work were printed between 1542 and 1552, and when Holinshed and his collaborators came to write the *Chronicles* that go by his name, they helped themselves freely from Hall's work.

A work of a very different character was published in 1543 by Richard Grafton. This was John Hardyng's metrical *Chronicle* 'from the firste begynnyng of Englande, unto the reigne of Kyng Edward the fourth when he made an end of his chronicle'. This is a work of nearly 500 small quarto pages, and is followed by another 300 pages in prose by Grafton, in which he brings the work up to the reign of Henry VIII. Two editions were printed, both bearing the date January 1543 on their title-pages, but they are far from identical in content. What is presumably the first edition[1] contains only two pages dealing with the reign of Henry VIII, while in the second edition this is enlarged to 31 pages, while the text in other places is altered.[2] Hardyng's *Chronicle* has little of value to commend it to the historian save that it contains for the first time 'the History of Richard the Third', written by Sir Thomas More. This admirable piece of English historical prose served as a pattern for future historians, for in it More makes his characters move and speak like living men, and examines not only their deeds but the causes that motivated them. His writing is full of drama, and his portrait of the king has remained the popular conception of Richard ever since.[3]

Another work, popularly known as 'Cooper's Chronicle', was printed in 1549 by T. Berthelet. This was *An epitome of cronicles of England*, which Cooper tells us was begun

not many yeeres passed by a studious yonge man named *Thomas Lanquet*, and now of late by me finished, and continued from the

---

[1] *STC* 12768. [2] *STC* 12767.

[3] Grafton also printed an edition of Hall's *Chronicle* in 1548 with additions by himself which brought the story down to the end of the reign of Henry VIII. This proved sufficiently popular, despite its size, to call for three further editions by 1552.

incarnacion of Christ to the seconde yere of the reigne of our soveraine lord *kyng Edward the sixte*. In suche forme and ordre that a diligent reder may as in a mirrour behold the state and condicion of all realmes at all tymes...when the *Britaines*, and likewise the *Scottes*, came first into this land, with the succession of their kinges, and the whole discourse of the histories of both countreis.[1]

This work was very popular, and easy to be read, so that in 1559 Marsh and Seres printed an edition of it without Cooper's leave, which called for another edition by Cooper with a prefatory note inveighing against 'certaine persons, [who] for lukers sake contrarie to honestie, had caused my chronicle to be prynted without my knowlage'.[2]

It was not everyone, however, who could afford the time or money necessary to enjoy one of these longer histories, and some attempt was made to meet the needs of those for whom a mere outline would suffice. The earliest extant was *A lytell shorte Cronycle...of all the kynges, with the sayntes and martyrs that have ben in this lande'*, printed by de Worde in 1530.[3] This is an eight-page quarto and is only a list of names from the time of Brute, who came 'into this lande after the makyng of the Worlde' until the time of the Conquest. It is a well-nigh worthless list of names and dates, with woeful omissions and errors, but it had had a wide circulation in manuscript for a hundred years. In publishing it for a penny or twopence at most de Worde was certain of his market.

Another pamphlet, printed in 1539, was little more than an *aide-memoire* whose usefulness is suggested by its title: *A short cronycle, wherin is mencioned all names of all the kings of England, and mayors and sheriffs of the cytye of London, and of divers and many notable actes and things done in and sith the time of King Henry the fourth*.[4] A rather more substantial work in 80 pages duodecimo, was a riming *Chronycle with a*

---

[1] *STC* 15217, sig. A iii^v.
[2] *STC* 15218 (1560), sig. a i^v. The full text of Cooper's note will be found below, p. 237.
[3] *STC* 10012, sig. A i^r.   [4] *STC* 10021.

genealogie, declaryng that the Brittons and Welshemen are lineallye descended from Brute. Newly and very wittely compyled in meter,[1] by Arthur Kelton in 1547. The running-title, 'A Chronicle of the Brutes', more exactly describes the work: its wit may be judged from the following specimen:

> We Welshemen saie for our defence
> That yᵉ Romayns, surmountyng in pride
> With your Imperiall magnificence,
> Supposyng therby the hevens to devide,
> Came long after our noble tribe:
> So that we maie write of your estate,
> Not ye of us; ye came all too late.[2]

As an additional source of interest, from not later than 1541 publishers sometimes added a few pages setting out the names of nine main roads, and the distances from place to place. Thus W. Myddelton's edition of 1544 states that it is 'newely augmented, & corrected: where unto is added the length, bredth, and compasse of England...and also the wayes leadynge to the most notable places: and the dystaunce betwyxte the same'.[3]

This new feature perplexed John Mychel, 'boke Prynter' of Canterbury when he came to issue his *Breuiat cronicle contaynynge all the Kynges from brute to this daye* [1551]. In this he has by his 'poor laboure somewhat augmented and enlarged wyth more matter' the 'littell shorte Cronicle' of his predecessors, he tells us, but when it comes to the roads he hesitates. 'Here I should have put in the notable waies from certaine cities to London, but some of them be not marked truly, wherefore I left them out till such tyme as I have more knowledge in these waies.' They were in the next known edition of 1552, however, and the popularity of this little work is attested by the existence of nine editions in ten years, and still more perhaps by Mychel's unavailing plea to his fellow-

---

[1] *STC* 14918.   [2] *STC* 14918, sig. eivᵛ.
[3] *STC* 9988, sig. Aiʳ.

printers to allow him to enjoy the fruits of his labours. He requires and prays his

> frendes and brothers of the occupacion of printing to suffer me quietlye to enjoye the benefite of these myne owne labours, and to have the advantage of myne owne invencion, as I shall gladly suffer every[one] of them to enjoye the commodities of his, and then we shal brotherlike live in concorde, one by another.[1]

In addition to chronicles of English history, printers turned to the records of other countries for material to interest their public. Perhaps the most famous of these were the Chronicles of Jean Froissart, translated by Lord Berners, and published by Pynson in two large folio volumes, the first in 1523 and the second in 1525.[2] Here men could read in the vernacular the vivid, detailed story of the French wars and of the part the English played in them. Berners adopted a plain, straightforward style, without straining for effect or using an elaborate and pretentious diction. The narrative moves well, with plenty of action, and gives the reader a constant sense of being actually present at the events or the conversation. His work is a classic. It was reprinted in 1545, and has never lost its interest, both as a source of outstanding importance, and as a work of high literary art.

Not only their own history interested English readers. That of Greece and Rome was not entirely neglected. In the early 1520's Alexander Barclay translated Sallust's *Jugurtha*.

> I have attempted [he writes] to translate into our maternal language the auncient cronicle and famous hystorie of the warre and dyvers batayls which the romayns dyd agaynst the tyran Jugurth, usurper of the Kyngdome of Numidy. It is [he tells us] a ryght fruytful historie: bothe pleasant, profitable and ryght necessary unto every degre; but specially to gentylmen whiche coveyt to attaine to clere fame and honour by glorious dedes of chyvalry.[3]

---

[1] *STC* 9970, sig. x3[r].   [2] *STC* 11396-7.
[3] *STC* 21626, sig. aiv[v].

Pynson soon reprinted his work, and in 1557 it was included by Thomas Paynell with his translation of the work of Constantius Felicius, *The conspiracie of Lucius Catiline*, at the desire of his patron Viscount Mountague, who wished to have both works in one volume. Paynell claims that he has corrected Barclay's text 'somewhat mangled and corrupted through unlearned correctors', but in fact he made but a few insignificant changes before he launched the two works on the reading public,

trusting the matters of these histories to be so cherefull and pleasaunt, the oracions so ingenious and wyttie, the strategemes so close and craftie, the answers of the prudent and polytike Romaines so ingenious...that no man (except envie rule hym) can myslyke the historie or the translacion of the same.[1]

Paynell had made his translation some years before (1541), when it was dedicated to Henry VIII. At that time, in the course of his dedicatory epistle, Paynell declared that his object in undertaking the work was 'that all that be unlerned maye se if God amonge the gentiles wold not suffer riottous rebelles to overrunne rulers and distroye common weales: howe moche less then wyll he suffer them to prevayle ageynste a chrysten prynce, his veray image in erthe.'[2]

Similar reasons provoked Sir Anthony Cope to translate *The historie of...Anniball and Scipio* (1544), and to dedicate it to Henry VIII. It was a time of war with Scotland and France, and Cope feels that

well ponderyng the tyme of warre to be nowe in hand, as a thyng so much nedefull for many consideracions, I (for my poore part) thought that I should dooe, not onely to your hyghnesse acceptable service, but also to all noble men and gentilemen of the realme greate pleasure and commoditie, if gatheryng to gyther...the marciall actes of...Anniball of Carthage and Scipio...into our englysh toung: wherby...men may learne bothe to dooe displeasure to theyr ennemies, and to avoyde the crafty and daungerous baites, which shall be layde for theim.[3]

---

[1] *STC* 10752. sig. *i*v*.
[2] *STC* 10751, sig. A ii*v*.
[3] *STC* 5719 (1548), sig. a iii*r*.

John Brende, who translated *The historie of Quintus Curcius,
conteyning the actes of the greate Alexander* (1553), thought that
his work would be useful and instructive, for the history
recorded the deeds of the great and set an example of manly
virtue.[1] His work evidently commended itself to the age, for
it was constantly reprinted until 1614, and was one of the most
frequently consulted of Elizabethan histories.

Lastly, we may note Herodian's *History of the Roman
Emperors*, which was translated from a Latin version by
Nicholas Smith about 1555, possibly because it gives a good
general account of the empire, and possibly because it gives
some information about early Britain. To help the reader
Smith has annexed 'the Argumentes of every Book at the
begynnyng thereof, with Annotacions for the better understandynge of the same Historye'. The Annotations are in
alphabetical order and form an 'exposytion of many wordes,
Histories, Fables, sytuacions of places, and descriptions of
Countreyes, servynge to the more easye understandynge of
the presente Hystorye'.[2]

It must be confessed that the early translations of historical
works are not impressive either in number or in importance.
The attention of English writers of genius found full scope
in the religious works inviting attention, and the massive
quarries of antiquity to be exploited had to wait to the latter
half of the century for workers worthy of them. What was
translated, it will be noted, had a perfectly clear practical aim.
History was a mirror wherein men might gaze and see reflected
the successes and failures of the past, and from these they could
learn how to conduct themselves and their countries' affairs
in the present.[3]

[1] *STC* 6142, sig. Aiii^v. For the full text, see p. 60.
[2] *STC* 13221, sig. Ddii^r.
[3] For a fuller treatment, see Lily B. Campbell, *Shakespeare's Histories*
(1947), and H. B. Lathrop, *Translations from the Classics into English from
Caxton to Chapman, 1477–1620* (1933).

9. *News*

What newes? or here ye any tidinges
Of the pope, of the Emperour, or of kynges
Of Martyn Luther, or of the great Turke,
Of this and that, and how the world doth worke?[1]

Such we are told, was the cry constantly made to the printer in early sixteenth-century England where the absence of any kind of newspaper made it almost inevitable that he would be called on from time to time to publish news, information and other matter which was thought to be of sufficient interest and importance to warrant it. Much of this was issued by the authority of the King in the form of broadside proclamations. These were generally printed off on a single sheet, and were thus very easily affixed to walls, doors, etc. They were of ephemeral importance, in many cases, and a large proportion of those issued in this period have perished entirely, and are known only from manuscript sources.[2] Even in their own day they were often not so widely circulated as could have been wished, a condition glanced at by Richard Grafton in a note 'to the Reader', prefixed to his edition of *All suche procla-macions, as haue been sette furthe by the kynges maiestie (and passed the Print) from the last daie of Januarii, in the firste yere of his highnes reigne, unto the last daie of Januarii, beeyng in the iiii. yere.* Grafton says:

Forasmuche as many Proclamacions set furthe by the kynges majestie are penall, and diverse good and lovyng subjectes do often offende theim, whiche happeneth either by ignoraunce, or els for that when the print is passed thei cannot come by theim, I thought it therefore very mete and nedefull to gather them together, and to imprint them wholy in one volume...intendyng here after every second yere (or oftener, if it shal be requisite) to adde hereunto

[1] *STC* 5734, sig. A i^r.
[2] For a full account of the history of these documents, and a most valuable list of them, see R. Steele, *Tudor and Stuart Proclamations*, 2 vols. (1910).

suche other Proclamacions as shall happen to bee published by like authoritee.[1]

The volume was a small octavo, easy to slip in the pocket, and was furnished with a table of contents for easy reference. Apart from these proclamations, however, there was much material calling for print. Only a part—probably a very small part—of this has come down to us, for much of it was put before the public in little quarto pamphlets of 8, 16 or 32 pages, and was easily destroyed, or used for wrapping, or otherwise discarded. As with the broadside proclamations, for the most part these little booklets had an immediate appeal, but once the occasion which provoked their appearance was over, they rapidly faded in interest, and only the care of some collector (such as Humphrey Dyson) has enabled them to survive at all. Many of these works, therefore, are known by single copies, or by fragments only.

'Now a dayes especially (I know not by what motion)' writes Peter Ashton, 'we desyre of all thinges to heare newes and tydinges, and to know of strange ambassadours what is done in farre landes',[2] and it was to meet such a demand that the printers sought eagerly for material. News concerning royalty is always welcome, and it was no less so in the time of the Tudors, especially news of Henry VIII, whose personal popularity was so marked a feature of his reign. This he was at pains to preserve, and a series of publications was forthcoming in which outstanding events, both personal and political, were described. Naturally, personal news was the most exciting, and it is for this reason that a number of small publications describing such events as marriages, coronations, state celebrations or funerals were issued.

---

[1] *STC* 7758, sig. A i^v. Grafton's promise was not kept, for he was deprived of his office of Royal Printer by Mary in 1553.

[2] *STC* 11899 (1546), sig. *4^v. Cf. T. Becon's statement to Sir T. Wyatt, *STC* 1775 (1542), sig. A iii^r: 'Howe glad is an Englyshe man beynge in Fraunce, Germany or Italy, or elsewhere to knowe by the transmission of mutuall letters what is done in Englond.'

These had no official sanction in many cases, but the material on which they were based was obtained from the royal officers and then worked up, or even printed in its crude state. For instance, in 1501 Pynson printed *The traduction & mariage of the princesse*, which was nothing more than the memoranda compiled by the officials in charge of the ceremonies consequent on the arrival of Catherine of Aragon and her marriage to the Prince of Wales. The document sets forth how the Queen was to be received at Southampton, and how she was to go in progress to London, and so on until the ceremony was complete, and the wedding party arrived at Westminster Palace. The incomplete nature of the document may be seen from the last entry:

Md. to knowe betwene the kynge and the byshop of London howe the byshops paleys shal be repaired.[1]

Despite this, however, public opinion was evidently sufficiently strong for Pynson to print this early forecast of the proceedings in a little 8-page pamphlet, adorned with a woodcut.

Similarly, the betrothal in 1508 of the Princess Mary to Prince Charles of Castille, was the occasion of two works, one of 24 pages in English, and one of 48 pages in Latin. The Latin account sets out in full the elaborate ceremonies which led up to the marriage by proxy, and is accompanied by woodcuts, one showing the King and the Prince's ambassadors, and another showing the princess under a canopy, receiving the compliments of the nobility.[2] This little book, compiled by Petrus Carmelianus, Latin secretary to Henry VII, is a finished piece of work, and was no doubt read eagerly by the many who were unable to be present. The fact that Pynson thought it worth while to produce a reduced version in English is indicative of the interest such events aroused, and the way in which an astute publisher took advantage of them.

Other major events in the life of royalty furnished material

---

[1] *STC* 4814, sig. Biii^v.   [2] *STC* 4659.

for ephemeral publications.[1] Bishop Fisher's sermon at the funeral of Henry VII was printed at the desire of Margaret, his mother, but in general, the publication of these little books was a fair business risk which the printer undertook. Thus de Worde printed an 8-page quarto, containing a poem by Stephen Hawes, being *A joyfull medytacyon to all Englonde of the coronacyon of our moost naturall soverayne lorde kynge Henry the eyght* [1509],[2] and a 12-page quarto setting out *The noble tryumphaunt coronation of quene Anne, wyfe vnto the moost noble kynge Henry the viij* [1533]. This tells in detail of the events of the three days which culminated in the coronation service at Westminster on Whitsunday. The citizens of London, and still more those in the provinces, rejoiced to read of such scenes as that at

Grasechurche where was a ryght costly pagent of Apollo with the nyne muses amonge y͏ᵉ mountayns syttyng on y͏ᵉ mount of Pernasus....And so she passed forth with all her nobles tyll she came in Chepe and at the great condyt was made a costly fountayne whereout ranne whyte wyne, claret and reed, great plenty all that after noone, and ther was great melody with speches.[3]

Again the ceremonies leading up to the coronation of Elizabeth were recorded, together with the various pageants and Latin verses that were part of the magnificent progress through the city. These events took place on 14 January 1559, and by the 23rd Richard Tottel had printed a 40-page quarto, hoping to catch the interest of his public while excitement of the coronation was fresh in their minds.[4]

While the printers were trying to make money from the personal affairs of their rulers, the King and his advisers were

---

[1] See, for example, *STC* 5017, *Of the tryūphe, and the vses that Charles themperour, & the kyng of England...were saluted with, passyng through London* [1520?] or *STC* 4350, *The maner of the tryumphe at Caleys and Bulleyn* [1532].

[2] *STC* 12953. [3] *STC* 656, sig. Aiv͏ʳ.

[4] In order to meet the expected demand, Tottel had the piece set up in two editions, both dated 23 Jan. See *STC* 7590, 7591.

turning to them on their own account. Henry VIII, for example, found in the press a valuable instrument in waging his campaign against the Church of Rome, both in his quarrel over divorce, and later in his defiance of the Pope. One of his main objects was to muster public opinion on his side; and, as part of his campaign, he sought the opinions of the Universities, both at home and abroad, concerning the validity of his marriage with his brother's widow. Once these were obtained, he had them printed by Berthelet, the King's Printer, both in Latin and in English.[1] In addition, the instructions given to counsel who pleaded the King's cause at Rome, were printed by authority.[2]

Many private individuals, however, also intervened. On the King's side there was the anonymous *A glasse of the truthe* (1530), which justified the divorce by reason of the necessity of a male child to inherit.[3] Others (sometimes discreetly writing from abroad) opposed the King in treatises such as Tyndale's *The practyse of prelates* (1530),[4] or T. Abell's *An answere that by no maner of lawe it maye be lawfull for... Kinge Henry the Ayght to be diuorsid* (1532). In this book Abell answers the Universities, and calls on the Christian reader to 'sette a parte all blynde affeccion and [to] read this boke with jugement, conferring it with the tother boke agenst which this is written: and I doute not but thou shalt stande on the quenes parte as a favourer of the firme and invincible verite'.[5]

The King had the last word in his *Articles deuisid by the holle consent of the kynges counsayle not only to exhorte, but also to enfourme his lovynge subjectis of the trouthe*—that is, the truth according to Henry VIII.[6] As in his personal quarrel, so with the growing opposition to Rome, Henry caused to be put on the market a number of works of an anti-papal nature. To this

---

[1] *STC* 14286 (1530); 14287 (1531).
[2] *STC* 5399 (1532).   [3] *STC* 11918.
[4] *STC* 24465.
[5] *STC* 61, sig. Ai^r. For this Abell was imprisoned in the Tower (1532) and after much delay executed (1540).
[6] *STC* 9177 (1533); 9178 (1534).

end four books were published by Berthelet in 1537 and 1538, all inveighing against the Pope's proposal to call a General Council.[1] The King's lead was eagerly taken up by members of the reform party, who from this time onwards were active in putting into print works favourable to these tenets which told of the progress of the new religion overseas. The life and death of leading members of the Church were described; accounts given of the assemblies and congregations which met to draw up confessions of faith; the creeds, liturgies and forms used by reformed Churches abroad were set forth—in short every means was seized to impress upon Englishmen the growing revolt against Rome.[2]

The usefulness of the press quickly became apparent, and the King and his advisers frequently sought its aid so as to disseminate their views, sometimes in works put out under their authority, and at other times making use of their secretaries, friends, and hangers-on to produce what was wanted.[3] As an example, we may notice some of the works dealing with sedition and rebellion that Henry VIII's policy so readily provoked. Somewhere about 1535 Cromwell recommended a certain Sir Richard Morison to the King as one 'redy to answer, and take up such as wold crake or face with literature of lernyng, or by indirectyd wayes, if any such shall be, and as I think there shal be fewe or noon...I knowe his hert so good that he is worthy favour in dede'.[4] Circumstances soon called for his aid, and his pen was active in the King's service. He wrote *A lamentation in whiche is shewed what ruyne and destruction cometh of seditious rebellyon*,[5] and *A remedy for*

---

[1] *STC* 13080–2; 13090.

[2] It would require considerable space to list all the volumes under this head. As examples, see *STC* 14717, *The true hystorye of the departynge of M. Luther* [1546?]; *STC* 23553, *The confescion of the fayth of the Sweserlādes* [1548?]; *STC* 16560, *The forme of common praiers vsed in the churches of Geneua* (1550); *STC* 17798, *A very godly defense, defending the mariage of preistes* (1541).

[3] For an extended treatment of this topic, with a list of the works it called forth, see F. Le Van Baumer, *The Early Tudor Theory of Kingship* (Yale Historical Publications, no. xxxv, 1940), Appendix A.

[4] *State Papers, Henry VIII*, vol. I, p. 603.   [5] *STC* 15185.

sedition, wherin are conteyned many thynges concernyng the true and loyall obeysance that commons owe,[1] both published by Berthelet in 1536. The first of these works was probably occasioned by the rebellion in Lincolnshire which broke out in October. This was quickly suppressed, but a more serious rising known as The Pilgrimage of Grace occurred shortly after, and this called forth *A remedy for sedition*. Both these works were produced by Morison under conditions of great haste, and hurriedly put into print. The first is a little quarto of 24 pages written, as Morison relates in a letter to Master Phylippes, 'in my botes as my lord and the king also doth know in a after none and a nyght. Thowght it be not done as it myght have ben done, yet the litel tyme maketh my great scuse.' The second volume runs to 52 pages, and Morison adds, 'I am compellyd to do thynges in such haste that I am ashamed to thynke they be myn when I se them a brode'.[2]

Morison's pen was active on the same topic a little later, when a more extended work *An inuective ayenste the great and detestable vice, treason* (1539) once more outlined the wickedness of rebellion.

Rede this lyttell invective that foloweth, I truste by thynges past ye shall perceyve it very unlyke that any traytour here after maye or can hurte his highnes. Ye shall see who is his gracis protectour, from what daungers he hath preserved hym, and therby gather an assured assyuance that traytours can but worke their owne confusion, when so ever they seke to do his highnes any displeasure.[3]

In addition to these works, a number of other manifestos were put out by authority. Answers to the petitions of the rebels in Lincolnshire and Yorkshire were printed in 1536,[4] and

---

[1] *STC* 20877.

[2] *L. and P. Henry VIII*, vol. xi, no. 1482. For further discussion and information, see 'Two Anonymous Tracts on Sedition', by C. R. Baskervill, *The Library*, Fourth Series, vol. xvii (1936), p. 83, and W. G. Zeeveld, 'R. Morison, Official Apologist for Henry VIII', *P.M.L.A. America*, vol. lv (1940), pp. 406–25, and the same author's *Foundations of Tudor Policy* (Harvard, 1948), chapter vii.

[3] *STC* 18111, sig. a vi^r.   [4] *STC* 15185; 13077.

Starkey's *Exhortation to the people instructynge theym to unitie and obedience* followed shortly.[1] In the reigns of Edward VI and Mary, similar means were employed to combat risings and rebellions. The King's message to the people of Devon was printed by R. Grafton in 1549,[2] and a broadsheet ballad on the defeat of the rebels was circulated;[3] while the more formidable rebellion of Sir Thomas Wyatt in 1554 was the occasion of a work of some 220 pages, which was popular enough to call for a second edition within a month. This was written by J. Proctor who was outraged by the false accounts given of the rising. In dedicating his book to the Queen he says:

hearing the sundry tales therof farre dissonant in the utteraunce, and many of them as far wide from truth...and understandyng besydes what notable infamie spronge of this rebellion to the whole countre of Kent...I thought these to be speciall considerations wherby I ought of duetie to my countrey to compyle and digest suche notes as I had gathered...and to publishe the same in this age and at this present.[4]

War as well as rebellion provided the printing presses with material. The defeat of the Scots at Flodden Field produced an exultant whoop from Skelton,[5] while a more sober prose account was forthcoming, giving names and details, under the title *Hereafter ensue the trewe encountre or Batayle lately don betwene Englande and Scotlande* [1513].[6] A later campaign against Scotland produced first of all a *Declaration, conteynyng the just causes...of this present warre with the Scottis* (1542)[7]

---

[1] *STC* 23236 [1536?]. There can be little doubt that the work was in circulation early in 1536. By April, Pole received a copy in Italy. See *L. and P. Henry VIII*, vol. x, no. 600.

[2] *STC* 7506. [3] *STC* 6795.

[4] *STC* 20407, sig. aiv[r].

[5] *STC* 22593, *Ballade of the scottysshe kynge* [1513].

[6] M. A. Shaaber, *Some Forerunners of the Newspaper in England, 1476–1622* (Philadelphia, 1929), p. 121. This earliest English news-pamphlet is fully described by J. C. T. Oates in *Trans. Camb. Bibl. Soc.* vol. I (1950), pp.126–9.

[7] *STC* 9179.

which set out 'to notify unto the world his (the Scottish King's) doinges and behaviour in the provocation of this warre, and lykewyse the meanes and wayes by us used to exchue and advoyde it'. This was followed by 'certain bookes printed of Newes of the Prosperous successe of the Kings Majesties armie in Scotland', describing the campaign of May 1544, and later in that year an eyewitnesses account, sent to the Lord Privy Seal, was printed by Reynolde Wolfe the King's Printer.[1] Without books such as these to inform them, the best men could do was

to spend a quarte of wyne or two of a caryer or servingman that commyth out of the northe partyes to heare tel what skyrmisshes hath ben betwixt us and the Scottes, and to know which of our warryours played the valyauntest parte and pretyest feate.... It dyd rejoyce us Englisshe men not a lytle (and that justly) to heare tell when our warriours at Bulleigne, Dammes, or Gynes, had the better hand and mastrie of the Frenchemen, and when we knewe the contrary, o lord, how pensyve and sad wolde we be for a season, and (as ye wolde saye, without joye or comforte).[2]

The next campaign of 1547-8 produced the most famous of early eyewitness accounts, that of William Patten, 'Londoner', written at 'the Parsonage of S. Mary hill in London, this xxviii. of January, 1548'. Patten accompanied the expedition in 1547 and was made 'one of the Judges of the Marshelsey'. 'Havynge in these last warres againste Scotlande (that never wear any with better succes acheved) made notes of actes therat doon, and disposed the same since my cummynge home, into order of diarie', Patten sent them to Sir William Paget, Controller of the Household, 'his moste benigne Fautour and Patron', and they were published by R. Grafton on 30 June 1548. His book gave the reader a day-to-day account of the campaign, and accompanied it with three plans of various actions, as well as a long introduction (which might well have

---

[1] *STC* 22270, *The late expedicion in Scotlande* (1544).
[2] *STC* 11899, *A shorte treatise vpon the Turkes chronicles* (1546), sig. *4[r].

been omitted). If men asked how he knew all he reported, he says that William Cecil and himself 'not beynge bounde soo straightly in daies of travel to ordre of marche: nor oother while, but when we sat in Courte; too any great affayres, had libertie to ride, to see things that wear doon, and leysure too note occurrences y[t] came'.[1] Any reader of his work must have allowed that Patten made good use of his opportunities, and Holinshed and Sir John Hayward were glad to make use of his material in writing their histories.

The contention between Scotland and England at this time brought forth a number of other works. Both James Harrison (1547)[2] and Nicholas Bodrugan (1548)[3] wrote treatises to show that the crown of Scotland was properly subject to that of England. J. Harrison, 'Scottish man', writes from 'love of my country...and desire of concorde and quietnes'. 'Armed with truth, moved with honestie, and provoked by love towards God and my country', he shows his fellow-countrymen the error of their ways, and at the end of his work warns them that 'the lord protector is comyng towardes you, with a puissaunt and invincible army, having on his side God and the just cause, and an intent to receive to mercy, grace and favor, so many of you...as wil come in to him. And contrarily, &c.'[4]

The authorities also put out *An epistle, or exhortacion to vnitie & peace...to the nobility and commons of Scotland* (1548).[5] This was issued first in English and later in Latin,[6] and adopted a conciliatory note, suggesting a royal marriage between the two houses to end the strife. It went on, however, to add that if the proposals were not accepted 'we shall not wyllyng, but constrained, pursue the battaill, chastice the wicked and malicious, by the angrie Angells of God, &c.'[7]

---

[1] *STC* 19479, *The expedicion into Scotlāde of prince Edward* (1548), sig. Piv[v].
[2] *STC* 12857, *An exhortacion to the Scottes.*
[3] *STC* 3196, *An epitome of the title that the kynges maiestie of Englande hath to the souereigntie of Scotlande.*
[4] *STC* 12857, sig. hvii[v].   [5] *STC* 22268.
[6] *STC* 22269.   [7] *STC* 22268, sig. Cli[r].

While all these things were news, and welcomed as the only means for many of knowing what was going on, the printers not unnaturally seized any opportunity that came their way to put before the public sensational news of murder, sudden death, earthquake—anything that would interest a credulous, ill-informed audience. Wynkyn de Worde imported a broadside, describing a 'horryble monster...cast of a Sowe' in Prussia. De Worde cut off the German text at the top and printed his own in between the cuts showing the two animals joined at birth,[1] and another broadside, published about 1550, related the birth of 'Siamese twins'. Nicholas Bourman printed an 8-page description of an earthquake in Italy which occurred in June 1542. The account takes the form of a letter from an eyewitness who describes the seven quakes which shook the little town near Florence where he was lodging 'in an ynne of the suburbes, neare to the gates, which was a great fortune for us that we were not closed in'.[2] There was another edition by another printer, probably in the same year.

Such was the variety of ephemeral literature put out by the printers in this period. Both they and those in authority realized that there was a ready public for such wares, especially if they were produced quickly and cheaply. Few of these works, therefore, are of any great size, and we are fortunate that so many have survived.

10. *Literature*

Most of the publications which we have been discussing were concerned with the edification or instruction of the reader. Not unnaturally, however, some readers looked to the printers for entertainment and relaxation for their spare hours. For reasons which need not detain us here, this period is not one of the great productive eras of English literature. Neither in

[1] See A. W. Pollard, *The Library*, Fourth Series, vol. IX (1929), p. 98.
[2] *STC* 21807 *Heuy newes of an horryble earthquake in Scharbaria* [1542], sig. [x] 2ᵛ.

verse nor in prose are we confronted with an outstanding work, although the names of Skelton, Wyatt, More, Tyndale, Elyot and Berners will remind us that we need not take too sombre a view of the matter.

In any case we must remember that the early sixteenth-century reader started wellnigh from scratch. His library was all to be formed, and he was only too ready to stock it with pieces old and new. This was particularly true of literary works. However meagre the contemporary output, all educated men knew by repute of the great ones of the past—'worthy Chaucer glorious', and many others—and it was entirely reasonable of Caxton to respect the feeling, and to print the works of three outstanding medieval poets—Chaucer, Gower and Lydgate, as well as Malory's great prose romance. The work begun by Caxton was continued by his successors who extended their search for masterpieces of English literature, so that by 1557 the printers could feel that they had done fully as much as could be expected of them in providing the public with a variety of verse and prose by English authors.

In the first place the works of Chaucer had been printed in a variety of forms. As early as 1526 Pynson had printed a large folio in three parts which could be sold separately, but bound together (as in the Greville copy in the British Museum) they gave the reader the bulk of Chaucer's important pieces, and the volume may be looked on as a first attempt to collect his works. Six years later, Thomas Godfray printed a folio volume of nearly 700 pages containing most of Chaucer's works, and many 'Chaucerian' pieces. These had been assembled by the zeal of William Thynne, clerk of the kitchen of Henry VIII, an enthustiastic collector of manuscripts and early prints of Chaucer's work.[1] With this volume at hand the

---

[1] In his 'pistle to the reader', prefixed to *The auncient historie...of warres betwixte the Grecians and Troyans*...translated by John Lydgate, R. Braham writes that it was 'by the dylygence of One Willyam Thime, a gentilman who laudably studyouse to yᵉ polyshing of so grete a Jewell with ryghte good judgement, travail and great paynes, causing the same to be perfected, and stamped as it is nowe read, otherwise yᵉ sayde Chaucers workes had utterly

reader had a splendid anthology to browse in. Despite its size, the demand was evidently greater than the supply, so that in 1542 a third edition 'with dyvers workes whych were never in print before' was printed by Richard Grafton for two stationers—W. Bonham and J. Reynes. Yet a fourth edition followed about 1545, this time shared by four stationers, each of whom had his name and place of business attached to part of the stock. It is clear, therefore, that the sale of Chaucer's work was a good speculation, and one in which a number of men were prepared to participate.

For those with smaller purses a number of editions of individual works by Chaucer were published. Caxton put out texts of *The Canterbury Tales* (1478), *Troilus and Criseyde* [1482?], *The Hous of Fame* [1486?] and *The Parlement of Foules* [1478?], and after his death later printers did the same, although it must be confessed, not so freely as we should expect. The fact is that their potential clients were not able to discern clearly the superiority of Chaucer over all other English poets, so that it was the works of Lydgate, not Chaucer, which were to be found freely on the book-stalls. While (fortunately) there was no collected edition of Lydgate's 145,000 lines of verse, no less that fifteen works of his were put into print, many of them in three or four editions. Something over thirty separate editions of items of his work survive to attest his popularity. Against this Gower's *Confessio Amantis*, first printed by Caxton in 1483, only struggled into print again on two occasions. To these poets of earlier times we must add Langland whose very different work was not published until 1550, when R. Crowley printed three editions in one year, thus completing the efforts of the printers to give the public the best of our medieval poetry. As we look back and consider the difficulties, it must be admitted that we have no reason to accuse Caxton and his successors of any neglect of their literary heritage.

peryshed, or at yᵉ lest ben so depraved by corruption of copies, that at the laste there shoulde be no parte of hys meaning have ben founde in any of them' (*STC* 5580, sig. *Biʳ).

As for writers who were at work after the introduction of printing, Hawes, Barclay, Skelton and Wyatt are the most important of the poets and a number of editions of works by them were put on the market. These were in quarto or octavo form, and in general were far less of a burden on the printers' resources than were the editions of Chaucer's *Works* or Gower's *Confessio Amantis*. Hawes probably interested those fond of old poetry, while the novel and audacious verses of Skelton, with their contemporary satire and comment on current events, kept readers in a state of excited expectancy. Altogether some fifteen editions of individual or collected poems by Skelton were printed before 1557.

Verse was also used to meet the contemporary taste for works of a satirical and humorous nature dealing with domestic and general affairs. *The Shyppe of Fooles* (1509) set a fashion that was popularized in a little quarto of de Worde's *Cocke Lorelles bote* [1510?], which presented a selection of low-life figures in humorous fashion. Again, a series of mock wills enabled writers to put out some racy and amusing verses, such as *Wyl Bucke his testament* [n.d.], or *Gyl of Braintford's testament* [1560?]. The most lively series of such pamphlets, however, concerned women. Both in verse and in prose a running controversy was kept up from the early days of the century onwards. One of the chief manifestations of the growing bourgeois interest in literature in the late fourteenth and the fifteenth centuries had been the *fabliaux*, and the short, racy, stories of women's rights and wrongs, their duplicity and their faithfulness. The printers did not fail to exploit this market, and about 1510 de Worde printed *The gospelles of dystaues*, a translation of a German work which ironically purports to reveal 'the grete noblesse of ladyes'. This he followed about 1525 by *The boke of mayd Emlyn that had V husbandes and all kockoldes*. Then in 1541 came the most famous of this group, *The schole house of women*, a vigorous and comprehensive attack on the sex, which appears to have provoked two replies—*A dyalogue defensyve for women*

148

agaynst malycyous detractoures (1542), and *The prayse of all women called ' Mulierum Pean'* [c. 1542]—and so the *querelle* went on.[1]

During his years as an apprentice in Caxton's printing house, de Worde must have worked on the large prose romances which his master loved to translate and publish. Such work was probably beyond de Worde's competence as a translator, and outside his interest as a printer. But in addition to these late examples of romance, there were the many earlier works, mostly in verse, which were still in manuscript circulation and still with power to command attention. 'Herknet to me, godemen, Wives, maydens, and alle men'—the opening appeal by the minstrel did not fall on deaf ears, and de Worde saw that here was a possible market, so that from time to time throughout his career he printed little quarto volumes, containing such famous romances as *Bevis of Hampton, Sir Degare* and *Ipomydon*, as well as a number of others, at least four of which are unique, and it is to de Worde's enterprise that we owe the first editions of ten or eleven of the romances.[2] No one else showed so keen an interest in this field, although some decades later W. Copland found the market still brisk enough for him to print editions of a dozen or more romances between 1548 and 1557. At least fifty editions of the romances exist, but this only partly tells of their popularity. Few forms of literature have been thumbed to pieces more completely than these slender quartos. When we speak of fifty editions we are not speaking of perfect copies, but of those remains which enable us to say that once an edition existed. Some of these editions we know of only by the survival of a leaf or two, or by a few tattered pages. Their enthusiastic readers were concerned only with having them at hand for a spare hour: they cost but a few pence, and it was far from anyone's mind that these simply executed pieces would ever become collectors' items. The early

---

[1] For an account of this subject, with detailed biographical information, see F. L. Utley, *The Crooked Rib* (Columbus, Ohio, 1944).

[2] See below, p. 191.

printers found them of value among their stock of wares which the reader readily bought 'to while away the longe nyghtes blak'. Once that was done, it was almost inevitable that they would gradually shed their outer leaves, thus becoming useless, and in due time were thrown away, or used for scrap.

As for drama, it will be remembered that the early sixteenth century saw the flourishing of the interlude. These little plays, instinct with morality as they were, nevertheless often contained enough humour or rough comedy to make them palatable, and a group of writers of whom Sir T. More, J. Rastell, J. Heywood and H. Medwall were the chief, produced a number of these 'new and very mery enterludes', which were printed by Rastell and others. A more truly dramatic note is struck in two farces by Heywood, *A mery play betwene Iohan Iohan the husbande, Tyb his wyfe, & syr Jhān the preest* (1533) and *A mery Play betwene the pardoner and the frere, the curate and neybour Pratte* (1533);[1] and also in *The beauty and good properties of women* [1530?], 'a new comodye in englysh...ryght elygant and full of craft and rethoryk'.[2] All these, and others, to the number of twenty-six were printed by 1550, some of them in more than one edition. They are little quarto volumes, of varying lengths, the longest *The thre lawes*[3] by J. Bale running to 104 pages, the shortest *Iohan Iohan, Tyb, and syr Jhān* by J. Heywood only occupying 16 pages. As with the romances, they survive in a fragmentary or imperfect condition in many cases, and few copies of any one play are known.

In a prefatory letter to *The true beliefe in Christ* (1550), Walter Lynne asks that his work may be read by men, women and children, 'not as they have bene here tofore accustomed to reade the fained stories of Robinhode, Clem of the Cloughe, wyth suche lyke to passe the tyme wythal',[4] but so as to spend

---

[1] *STC* 13298–9.
[2] For a complete bibliographical account of these plays, see W. W. Greg, *A Bibliography of the English Printed Drama to the Restoration*, vol. I (1939).
[3] *STC* 1287.   [4] *STC* 14576, sig. Aii^v.

their time well. As early as 1500, both de Worde and Pynson had printed the 'lytell geste of Robyn Hode', and a number of later editions attest its popularity,[1] while the ballad of Adam Bel, Clym of the Clough, and William of Cloudesle was certainly in print by 1536, and was reprinted about 1550 and many times later.[2] Again, old Robert Copland, the printer, tells us how inquiries are made of him:

> Have ye the balade called *Maugh Murre*,
> Or *Bony Wenche*, or els *Go from my durre*,
> *Col to me*, or *Hey downe dery dery*,
> Or *A my hert*, or *I pray you be mery*?[3]

These references are few enough, but sufficient, perhaps, to remind us of this body of ballad literature, so popular at the time yet so fugitive that only a fragment of it remains as evidence of the part it played in reading matter of the cheaper sort.

[1] *STC* 13687–90.   [2] *STC* 1806–7.
[3] *STC* 5734, sig. Ai͏ʳ.

CHAPTER VII

TRANSLATIONS AND TRANSLATORS

1. *Translations*

It will not have escaped notice how frequently the works mentioned in earlier chapters have been translations from ancient or modern authors. The wealth of writings which the printing-press had made available was apparent to all who moved about on the Continent, and during the time that the importation of all kinds of books into this country was permitted, many such works came into the hands of Englishmen, and from this it was but a small step to the translation and printing of some of them.

It is easy to appreciate what were Caxton's motives in making translations so large a part of his output. In the first place many of them were works executed to meet the wishes of some patron, who could reasonably be expected to bear some part of the financial risk of the venture. Then again, as we have seen, he had a shrewd idea of the potential market he might interest with various kinds of books, and the variety of his translations is in part, no doubt, a reflection of his own tastes, but it is also an index of the skill with which he surveyed the uncharted desires of an incipient reading public.

Caxton was his own translator for the main part, and his successors continued to rely on translations to a considerable extent, although they were not often translators themselves. We may imagine that for some time after Caxton's death the potential market for books was extremely difficult to assess. The scriveners' shops in the course of centuries had established for themselves a clientele, and had some notion of what custom they might expect. The change over to the printing-house left all in doubt. In the 1490's, and the first decade or two of the sixteenth century, it must have been mainly by trial and error that certain sides of the printer's business went forward. No doubt some things, such as religious manuals or service-books, had a fairly safe sale, but if new classes of books were to be got into circulation greater risks had to be taken. Even if most editions were small, compared with modern ideas, the printer had several hundred copies of the book on his hands, and only the most rudimentary of publishing and distributing systems to help him to sell them. Caution was therefore an essential to success, and it was in this spirit that the printer turned to the writings already available in other tongues, hoping to find among them wares suitable for his English market. If he could make them fit in with the kinds of books he was most interested in publishing, so much the better. Pynson, for example, published a whole series of Lives of Saints, so that it was natural for the translator of the life of St Werburgh (1521), and of St Radegund [1521?] to bring his work to Pynson, rather than to de Worde or J. Notary. Robert Wyer's long list of cheap manuals of popular science, or Robert Copland's list of ballads, plays and romances marked them out as likely publishers of such wares, and it was in their interest to add new items to their catalogue whenever possible.

As we have seen, there is no lack of evidence that many of these new works were produced at the 'command', or 'exhortation' of the printer, and it is reasonable to assume that he did the same with translations because the original convinced him that it was a work upon which he might take a fair risk. When Berthelet the printer was talking to Thomas Paynell about his translation of the *Regimen sanitatis Salerni* (1528), after a while,

talkynge of one boke and of an other, he [Berthelet] came forthe and sayde that if I wolde take so moche peyne as to translate into Inglysshe the boke that is intitled *De medicina guaiaci, et morbo gallico*, wrytten by that great clerke of Almayne, Ulrich Hutten, Knyght, I shulde, sayd he, do a verye good dede.[1]

[1] *STC* 14024 [1533], sig. [i^r]. See above, p. 43, for the full quotation.

Clearly here was a case where Berthelet knew the book and the possible market, and the same was generally true for most publications. As the early printers were usually their own publishers also, it was possible for them from their stalls in Paul's Churchyard and elsewhere to learn what was needed, and to estimate the demand for any particular kind of work. In addition to this, it was necessary for the printer to take note of the general, widespread demand for books of all kinds which came as a result of the introduction of the printing-press. An earlier chapter has shown how every kind of knowledge was laid under contribution and made into books for our early printers, and translations as well as original works were all grist to the mill. 'I se many yonge persones. . . very studyous of knowlege of thynges, and be vehemently bente to rede newe workes, and in especyall [those] that be translated into the vulgare tonge', writes Robert Whittinton, and it was this desire the printers strove to fulfil.[1] Much of religion, of information and of literary interest was provided by translation. Not only the translation of the Bible itself, but of a host of foreign commentators, both old and new, together with rival bands of eager controversialists kept the printers busy.[2] At the same time, the devout writings of great saints and churchmen, such as Thomas à Kempis or Erasmus, were not likely to be overlooked. Nor were the claims of other moralists, old and new, neglected. All were swept up in the great net of the printers who eagerly competed one with another to meet the market created in part by the vehemence of rival religious opinions, and in part by the traditional belief in the outstanding importance of works of the spirit. These things being so, authors and translators were at one in their desire to see their writings as widely spread as possible, and translations in particular have for their aim the informing of those only able to read the vernacular. This is borne out by the prefaces to a large number of religious works which expressly say that they are written 'to helpe the rude and ignorante people to more

[1] *STC* 5278 (1534), sig. b 3ʳ.   [2] See above, p. 70.

knowledge of God and of hys holy worde',[1] or to know what to believe,[2] or to their great profit and edification.[3] Indeed, the words *profit, comfort, fruitful, help, edification* are everywhere to be found—in part, no doubt, 'common form', but as the whole tone of the prefaces makes apparent, far more as key words, indicating the force driving the writers. 'All men, women and children', are appealed to, but especially 'oure common people', the 'more ignoraunte and unlerned persones', for whom these translations have been made, and by whom it was hoped that they would be 'greedily devoured'. As one title-page puts it, the readers of the work were asked to

> Rede it dylygently, Marke it perfectly,
> Revolve it thorowly, Beare it equally,
> Beholde the auctours simplicitie
> And prayse God Almyghty.[4]

As we have seen, translations of works dealing with religious controversy had a ready sale. Opponents of the English ecclesiastical authorities, writing in exile, eagerly translated books and documents of the Reformed religion which were smuggled into England, and found many readers, despite all efforts to prevent their circulation.[5] In this way many Englishmen first learnt of Charles V's rebuff of the summons of Paul III to the Council of Trent,[6] or of the 'Confession of Faith of the Germans in the Council at Augusta',[7] or of the Acts of the Council of the Empire at Regensburg.[8] The faith and words of leaders such as Luther[9] or Zwingli[10] were spread by translations from abroad, while the creeds, liturgies and forms of

---

[1] *STC* 21038, sig. *i^v [1540?].   [2] *STC* 3015, sig. ii^v (1550).
[3] *STC* 14553, sig. *ii^r (1534).   [4] *STC* 191, sig. A i^r (1554).
[5] See above, p. 33. See also R. Steele, 'Notes on English Books printed abroad, 1525–48', *Trans. Bibl. Soc.* vol. XI (1912), pp. 189–236, and M. E. Kronenberg, 'Notes on English Printing in the Low Countries (Early Sixteenth Century)', *The Library*, Fourth Series, vol. IX (1929), pp. 139–63.
[6] *STC* 5014 (1543).   [7] *STC* 908 (1536).
[8] *STC* 13612 (1542).   [9] *STC* 16984 (1543); 14717 (1546).
[10] *STC* 26136 (1548); 26140 (1555).

worship used by the Reformers were set out in a number of little books.[1]

In other fields the supply of various kinds of translations was considerable. For example, the fifteenth century had shown a remarkable zeal for vernacular works of information,[2] and the coming of print stimulated this desire. There are few topics of this kind that were not provided for by translations from Latin, French, German, Italian or Spanish sources. The art of warfare, the treatment of horses, the preparation of medicinal waters, or the ways of the stars, were made plain in translation, as were treatises on medicine, chiromancy, surgery, navigation or foreign travel. Authorities, ancient and modern, were ransacked, and often ruthlessly adapted to provide a cheap handbook on astronomy, dietary or popular medicine. While we cannot always approve of the methods of the translators, we must freely admit the zeal and enterprise with which they made all knowledge their province.

Further, we may note that, apart from religious and utilitarian ends, translators endeavoured to improve the body politic by their wares. Men believed firmly in the good to be derived by the reading of works of moral and civic virtues. Sir Thomas Elyot expressed the widely held view of his era, in the preface to his translation of *The image of gouernance compiled of the actes of Alexander Seuerus* (1541) where he speaks of his own labours as author and translator as follows:

My boke called the *Governour*, instructinge men in suche vertues as shalbe expedient for them, which shal have authority in a wele publike. The *Doctrinal of princis*, which are but the counsayles of wyse Isocrates, inducinge into noble mens wittes honest opinions. *The Education of children*, whiche also I translated oute of the wise Plutarche, making men and women, which will folow those rules, to be wel worthy to be fathers, and mothers. The litel *Pasquill*, although he be mery and playne, teching as well servantes how to be faythfull unto their maisters, as also masters how to be circumspect in espying of flaterars. Semblably thoffice of a good councel-

---

[1] *STC* 23553 (1548); 6609 (1550); 11723 (1556). [2] See above, p. 7.

lour, with magnanimity or good courage in tyme of adversity, may be apparantly founden in my boke called, *Of the Knowlege belonging to a wise man*. In reding the sermon of saynt Cyprian by me translated the devout reder shal fynd no little comfort in plages or calamities. *The banket of Sapience* is not fastidious, and in litle rome shewith out of holy scripture many wise sentences. *The Castel of Helth* being truly rad shal longe preserve men (being some phisicions never so angry) from perillouse siknes. My little boke callid *The defence of good women*, not only confoundeth villainous report, but also teachith good wives to know well their dueties.[1]

It was in this spirit that men turned to ransack the works of foreign writers, and if we bear this in mind we shall not be so surprised when we see what they found to be of most value, for example, in the writings of classical authors. Thus Cicero, Cato and Boethius were translated because of the help they gave as moralists, while Plutarch was found valuable as a guide to health, or to the education of children, or as a political philosopher. A number of chronicles of classical times by Caesar, Herodian, Livy, Plutarch and Thucydides were translated, while military affairs as discussed by Frontinus or Valerius were considered worthy of attention.[2] Marcus Aurelius and Xenophon were translated because of their kindly, worldly wisdom, but the great poets and tragic writers were practically untranslated. The *Andria* of Terence appeared in English about 1520; otherwise Terence was only rifled to provide materials for school-books, viz. a *Vulgaria ex Terentio* (1483), and *Floures for Latine spekynge* (1533), 'selected and gathered out of Terence and translated by N. Udall'. Virgil fared but little better. Caxton translated a French prose version of the *Aeneid*—*The boke of Eneydos* (1490), and a later version by Gavin Douglas survives in one edition of 1553. The Earl of Surrey translated the second and fourth books of the *Aeneid* in 1557, and the next year saw the metrical version of the first seven books of Thomas Phaer. As for Aeschylus, Sophocles and Euripides they still had long to wait for an

---

[1] *STC* 7664, sig. aiii[r].   [2] See p. 132.

English dress, but Seneca was more highly favoured, and in 1559 Jasper Heywood translated the *Troas*, and this was followed in the next decade by several more of tragedies, the whole being translated by 1581.[1]

Compared with the conditions abroad this poverty is staggering. France, for example, had translations of a large number of Greek and Roman classics made available, so that whole authors could be read and appreciated by the 'lewd'. Speaking of historical literature only, Professor H. B. Lathrop writes:

> In France whole works were translated, not mere scraps or fragments: and a body of translators each adding his own contribution to what had already been done, carried through the enterprise of providing French versions of all the important classic historians. A half century or more before... Philemon Holland had given the country gentleman stately volumes of history, de Seyssel and his collaborators had done the same service for French gentlemen. The French had Livy, Caesar, Sallust, Tacitus, Suetonius, Quintus Curtius, Justin, Herodotus, Thucydides, Xenophon, Polybius, Arrian, Aelian, Appian, Herodian. Amyot's Plutarch was the capstone of an already stately pile. England had not yet the public, the wealth, or the ideas for such large undertakings.[2]

England had to wait until the second half of the century, and even longer, before some of the outstanding classical works became available; while, as we have seen, the plays of the three great Greek tragedians still remained unpublished in translation even then.

This, perhaps, was in keeping with contemporary opinion, for it will have been noted from Sir Thomas Elyot's list of his translations how strongly he emphasizes the moral or instructive appeal that they are to make. 'Works of solas', as the medieval author would have called them, have no place in his scheme of things, which lays all the emphasis on 'works of

---

[1] For a detailed examination, see H. B. Lathrop, *Translations from the Classics into English from Caxton to Chapman, 1477–1620* (1933).

[2] Lathrop, *op. cit.* p. 91.

sentence'. Hence it was that translations of works destined to while away an empty hour were comparatively few. Prominent among them were the romances, but even these were there to some degree by reason of the picture they gave of 'gentle' manners, and because of their encouragement to would-be aspirants to gentility and nobleness.

The position of England was summed up (with some exaggeration perhaps) by Udall when he wrote:

> What Royalme almoste (Englande excepted) hath not all the good authours that ever wrote translated into the mother toungue, whereby the people are made prudent and expert men in the traicte of all affaires, either touchyng any discipline, orels any civile matiers? And in Germanie, what good worke of divinitee is there whiche thei have not in their owne language to the unestimable edifying of the people in the due knowelage of God?[1]

2. *The translators*

To turn to the translators themselves is to be confronted by a body of men who have little in common. They were recruited from many ranks of society, and were usually men of education —some religious, some lay—but the preponderance among them of members of the Inns of Court, which was a characteristic of the translators of the next period, is not so noticeable before 1557. A considerable number, more particularly the translators of religious and controversial works, preferred to remain anonymous. Of the remainder, as would be expected, there are the 'professional' translators, so to speak, and those whose output is confined to one or two pieces. The latter group far outnumber the former, and we may assume that to make a living by translating alone was a precarious and not often practised occupation. Nicholas Udall lamented the small rewards given to the translator, 'the hyre nothyng at all', so that few would undertake the work. Nevertheless, there were

---

[1] *STC* 2854, *The paraphrase of Erasmus upon the newe test.* (1549), sig. B iii^v.

men who devoted much of their time to the making of translations, although it must be noted that they generally had some
other activity, such as a clerical office, or an appointment at
Court or elsewhere, which gave them a means of livelihood even
if their literary skill went for little. In the early decades of the
sixteenth century a number of these men were closely associated
with the printers, translating from ancient or modern languages
as required. Such a man was Andrew Chertsey, 'gentylman'.
A poetical prologue by Robert Copland to de Worde's edition
of Chertsey's translation of *The passyon of our lorde Jesu
cryst* (1521) tells us:

> Of late howe besily with his pen
> The translatour of this sayd treatyse
> Hath him indevered, in most goodly wyse
> Bokes to translate, in volumes large and fayre,
> From Frenche, in prose, of goostly exemplayre.

In execrable verse, Copland then names Chertsey's five
translations, 'with dyvers other, to mannes lyfe profytable',
and continues:

> And nowe this boke of Christes passyon,
> The which before in langage was to rude,
> Seyng the mater to be of grete compassyon,
> Hath besyed hym, that vyce for to exclude,
> In englysshe clere, with grete solycitude,
> Out of frensshe, at Wynkyn de Wordes instaunce
> Dayly desiryng of vertues the fortheraunce.[1]

All Chertsey's translations were printed by de Worde, and there
is little reason to doubt that they were made (as was the
passyon) at the printer's 'instaunce'.

The two names most closely associated with de Worde as
translators for his press are those of Henry Watson and Robert
Copland. Both appear to have been apprentices of his, and he
left to Copland 'as many printed bookes as shall amounte to
the value of ten markes sterling'. Both speak of him as

---

[1] *STC* 14558, sig. ai^v.

'worshipful master', and work at his 'exhortation', or 'commandment', or 'request'. Once de Worde had established himself, and was seeking for openings in the London market, he began to use both of them. Henry Watson's name first appears in connexion with a translation of *Lystoire des deux vaillans cheualiers Valentin et Orson* which was made in all probability soon after the production of the third French edition of 1505, and in a preface the translator writes:

> I, Henrye Watson, symple of understondynge have translated out of Frenche [the lyfe of the two chyvalrous Lordes, Valentyne and Orson] in to our maternall tongue of Englyshe, at the instaunce of my worshypfull mayster, Wynkyn de Worde, prayeng all the reders or hearers here of to have my youth for excused, yf I have fayled in any thyng.[1]

A more important task was given him soon after, for on 6 July 1509 de Worde published Watson's translation of a French text of Brandt's *Narrenschiff*, under the title of *The shyppe of fooles*. This was a considerable undertaking, for the work made a quarto volume of about 200 pages, adorned with many woodcuts, and at the end of the work Watson appeals to 'you Lectours humbly...to pardon me yf that I have erred in ony thynge, for ye tendernes of my yeres hathe so offusked me that I have not applyed me unto the letters as I ought to have done'. He goes on to excuse his method of translation by saying that 'the language is not autentyke, to the ende that every body may understande some thynge, for folkes unlyttered demaundeth not thynges obscure'.[2]

Two years later de Worde published Watson's translation from the French of a sermon of St Bernard of Siena, *The chirche of the euill men and women*, and again Watson prays 'all the reders or herers of the same to have my robuste language devoyde of undepured eloquence for excused'.[3] In *Olyuer of*

---

[1] *STC* 24572 , sig. A ii^r.   [2] *STC* 3547^a, sig. A 3^v.
[3] *STC* 1966, sig. B i^v.

Castylle (1518)[1] Watson translates another French work, with similar apologies for his 'little and obscure understanding'. Since this phrase is in his French original, however, we may perhaps regard most of his excuses as conventional flourishes. Two other works, 'The noble history of King Ponthus' [1501?][2] and *The gospelles of dystaues* (c. 1510)[3] were also probably translated by Watson and complete his known output on behalf of his sometime master. They are not sufficient in number to allow us to make any very significant deductions, but afford valuable evidence of the care and energy shown by de Worde to provide the public with new wares.

Robert Copland was also closely associated with de Worde, first as translator, and later as a printer of some of de Worde's publications. His first known translation was *The Kalender of shepeherdes* (1508), a work of sufficient popular interest as a *vade mecum* of popular lore concerning the seasons and the weather, etc., to be worth while re-translating, despite its size and the existence of two earlier editions.[4] The next undertaking was also one of considerable size, and Copland tells us that

> my worshypfull mayster, Wynkyn de Worde havynge a lytell boke of an auncyent hystory of a kynge, sometyme reygnynge in the countree of Thyre called Appolyn, concernynge his malfortunes and peryllous adventures right espoventables, bryefly compyled and pyteous for to here, the which booke I, Robert Coplande have me applyed for to translate out of Frensshe language into our maternal Englysshe tongue at the exhortacyon of my forsayd mayster.[5]

Some ten years later he translated St Edmund of Canterbury's *Myrrour of the chyrche* (1521), commencing with a 'petycyon'.:

> Eternall grace of .iii. in one substaunce
> Be now my guyde, in this my besynesse
> Unto thy laude, this lytel werke tavaunce.[6]

---

[1] *STC* 18808. [2] *STC* 20107.
[3] *STC* 12091. [4] See above, p. 116.
[5] *STC* 708.1. Facsimile of the Devonshire copy, ed. E. W. Ashbee (1870), p. 2. [6] *STC* 965, sig. ai[v].

Finally, among the latest productions of de Worde's press, came translations by Copland of *The Complaynte of them that ben to late maryed* [1535?] and *The Complaynte of them that be to soone maryed* [1535?].[1] This variety of output characterized Copland's work throughout his long life. As well as making translations for his own press on dancing, on navigation, on popular science, he worked for a number of printers, turning his hand to whatever came his way, and often adding epilogues and prologues which give us welcome details of his aims and of the reasons actuating him.[2]

Another translator, who was of considerable help to de Worde was Richard Whitford, a member of the Brigittine house at Isleworth, known as Syon House. The 'olde wretche of Syon', as he called himself, furnished de Worde with a number of translations, the earliest of them having for titlepage the following description of its contents: *The rule of saynt Augustyne, bothe in latyn and englysshe, with two exposycyons. And also y*e *same rule agayn onely in englysshe without latyn or exposycyon* (1525). He made the translation he tells us at request, which he 'rather and more lyghtly dyd graunt therunto, that [he] had not before y*e* tyme seen or herde of ony other translacyon but that was olde, scabrouse, rough and not of the Englysshe comynly used in these partyes'.[3] The next year saw the publication of his *Martiloge in englysshe after the vse of Salisbury*, translated out of Latin for the devout reader.[4]

In the preface to his next translation, *A werke for housholders*, Whitford reveals that he wrote the work for 'a private persone and speciall frende', but that the copy came into the hands of others who pressed him to 'put it newly forth in commune, supposyng in theyr devoute mynde it shulde be unto other persones as it semed unto them, edificatyve and

---

[1] STC 5728–9.
[2] A number of Copland's verses are printed by Percy Simpson in his *Proof-reading in the Sixteenth, Seventeenth and Eighteenth Centuries* (1935), Appendix II: 'Musa Typographica'.
[3] STC 25417, sig. Ai*v*. [4] STC 17532.

profitable'.[1] His connexion with de Worde made it reasonable, no doubt, that he should take the work, which contains much from St Bernard and others, and ask de Worde to publish it. That he was not ill-advised in doing so we may surmise from the fact that the edition of 1531 is said to be 'newly corrected and prynted agayne', and is followed by another of 1553. After the death of de Worde, Whitford had to seek other publishers, for he continued translating for another ten years. His works are all devotional in character, the outstanding one being his translation of the *Imitatio Christi*, published about 1531 by Robert Wyer. This replaced the earlier version of William Atkinson and the Lady Margaret (1503), and remained in favour for a generation, until yet another translation took its place.

Richard Pynson does not seem to have relied on any particular translators for his publications, but in the next generation of printers Thomas Berthelet was indebted to a number of such helpers—in particular to Sir Thomas Elyot and Thomas Paynell. Sir Thomas Elyot published all his works, original and translations, with Berthelet, and between 1531 and 1545 some fourteen or fifteen books by him appeared. Of these six were direct translations, while others were based on classical works, or contained large quotations from them. Plutarch, Isocrates, Severus, Lucian and Cyprian of the ancients, and Erasmus of the moderns, were laid under contribution, while Elyot's other works rested heavily on his reading of foreign authors. He provided Berthelet with some of the earliest translations into English from Greek, as in his *Doctrinal of princes* [not before 1534] by Isocrates, which he made, 'not presumyng to contente with theim whiche have doone the same in Latine, but to thintent onely that I wolde assaie if our Englisshe tonge mought receive the quicke and propre sentences pronounced by the greekes'.[2]

---

[1] *STC* 25412 (1531), sig. A i^v. The earliest extant edition is *STC* 25422, dated 2 May 1530.

[2] *STC* 14277, sig. A ii^r. For Elyot's list and comments on his translations, see above, p. 156.

Thomas Paynell, an Austin friar, and Canon of Merton Abbey, Surrey, was another active translator. He made a number of translations, mainly of religious works, although he was also responsible for at least three medical treatises published by Berthelet. After 1541 his translations were published by a number of printers, and by 1557 at least a dozen works had come from his pen. He enjoyed the patronage of some of the great nobles, and had dedicated works to three sovereigns, so that many of the works came to the printer with the prestige attaching to them from their influential recipients. This may have recommended them to the printer, or turned the scales in favour of their publication, but it is more likely that the printer thought them a fair risk, and acted accordingly. The fact that many of Paynell's works (in common with those of Sir Thomas Elyot and other translators) ran into several editions is prima facie evidence that the printer had not misjudged his market.

A number of other translators have several works to their credit, and appear to have written as dependants of aristocratic patrons, or because of strong religious opinions. It is more important, perhaps, to note that occasionally the printer or bookseller followed Caxton's example, and was his own translator. This we have seen was what Robert Copland did, and other names can be added. For example, Laurence Andrewe translated a work on distilling (1527), and another on *The wonderful shape and natures of man* [1527?], both for the Antwerp printer Jan van Doesborch. In the prologue to the first of these, Andrewe speaks of other works of his: 'dyvers and sondry small volumes and tryfles of myrth and pastaunce, some newly composed and some translated and of late finished'.[1] Then again, Walter Lynne, bookseller, tells us that he is 'one who spendeth all hys tyme in the settynge forth of bokes in the Englyshe tounge',[2] and was responsible for at least eleven translations published between 1548 and 1550. He was an ardent reformer who enjoyed the patronage of Cranmer, so

---

[1] *STC* 13435, sig. ¶ii^r.　　[2] *STC* 4626, sig. *ii^r.

that his works are drawn from writers such as Bullinger, Luther and Urbanus Regius.

While these and other translators, such as Chaloner, Lesse, Lloyd, Morison, Taverner and Scoloker rendered substantial aid to the printers, so far as the evidence allows us to judge, a great deal of material came into the printing-house from individuals who have left no evidence of their literary abilities other than a single item or two. The number of such translators in the period runs into hundreds—and, as might be expected, their work deals with every kind of subject—and their skill ranges from distinction to mediocrity or worse. On the whole, however, English prose was greatly aided by this body of undistinguished practitioners, whose efforts to make the language express a great variety of ideas and concepts hitherto unknown to it helped to create a healthy living tradition of writing, not overloaded with rhetorical devices, nor crushed by the elaborate use of foreign words and phrases.[1]

3. *The translator's art*

The body of work, produced as it was by so various a corps of translators, carries with it a good deal of information concerning their aims and methods, since they often seek to justify themselves in preface or dedication. An early example will be found in *Terens in englysh*. (*The translacyon of the furst comedy, called Andria*) which was printed by John Rastell about 1520. This has some illuminating verses at its beginning and end, vilely composed and mismetred though they are. After praising the translations of Chaucer, Gower and Lydgate the poet continues:

> By these men our tong is amplyfyed, so
> That we therin now translate as well may
> As in eny other tongis other can do;
> Yet the Greeke tong & Laten dyvers men say
> Have many wordys can not be englyshid this day.

---

[1] In Appendix II will be found a list of such translations as I have been able to trace.

So lyke wyse in Englysh many wordys do habound
That no Greke or Laten for theym can be found.

And the cause that our tong is so plenteouse now
For we kepe our Englyshe contynually
And of other tongis many wordys we borow
Which now for Englysh we use & occupy;
These thingis have gyven corage gretly
To dyvers, & specyally now of late
To them that this comedy have translate.[1]

Again at the end of his translation the poet writes:

The translatours now require you this,
Yf ought be amys ye wold consyder
The Englysh almost as short as the Latten is,
And still to kepe ryme a dyffycult matter;
To make the sentence oppenly to appere
Which yf it had a long expocysyon
Then were it a comment & no translacon.[2]

Not everyone perhaps would have agreed with this anonymous
poet that English was at this time sufficiently copious and
flexible enough to serve the translator's purpose.[3] Whether it
was so or no, many, as we shall see, were so aware of their own
inferiority as translators that they said as little as possible about
this, but emphasized the value of their work to the commonwealth, since it brought before their countrymen the culture
and achievements of other lands and civilizations, and by so
doing held up a mirror to their own comparatively backward
condition. As early as 1539 Richard Taverner says he has put
part of the *Adagia* of Erasmus into English for 'the love I bear

---

[1] *STC* 23894, sig. A i[v].   [2] *Ibid.* sig. D v[v].

[3] In 1547 Bishop Gardiner expressed himself concerning the future of the
English language in the following words: 'As for the English tonge, it selfe
hath not continued in one forme of understanding CC yeares; and without
God's work and speciall miracle it shall hardely containe religion long,
when it cannot last it selfe' (J. A. Muller, *Letters of Stephen Gardiner* (1933),
p. 289).

to the furtheraunce and adornment of my native country',[1]
a view more fully expressed by Humphrey Loyd in his preface
'To the Gentil harted Reader', affixed to the translation of
John XXI's *The treasury of healthe* [1550?], where he writes:

> I, callynge to memory the notable sentence of Cicero, that every-
> man is not al only borne for hym selfe but chifely to profit his
> native Countrye, then his parentes, afterwards hys chyldren and
> frendes, sekynge a meanes whereby I myghte profytte thys my
> natyve Country, thought it best to translate this lytle treatyse. . . .[2]

We have already seen the view of John Brende on this
matter.[3] Brende's statement expresses admirably what was in
the minds of many men. They wished not to lag behind other
countries, and at the same time to instruct or inform their
fellow-countrymen of things not readily available otherwise.
This they could do only by means of the printing-press. The
days when a translation was made for a rich patron, and afterwards got into limited manuscript circulation were over.
Nicholas Lesse, having translated a treatise of St Augustine
(1550), remained unwilling to leave it at that:

> Even so me thoughte that I hadde not done as much as I was
> bound to do good, in that I broughte so goodly a worke forthe of a
> strange tonge to be understanded of oure common people, excepte
> I myghte se them have it in their hands, rede it and also understand
> it in dede. But, to use the phrase and maner of spekyng of the
> Apostle, howe can they rede it and understand it except they have
> bokes? How can they have bokes except it be put into print?[4]

To this purpose (which does not necessarily exclude more
personal desires for public recognition) Brende, like many
others, did everything he could to persuade patron and
publisher to print his work.

[1] *STC* 10436, sig. Ai^v. Cf. 15204 (C. Langton, 1550?); 18312 (R.P. 1555);
25875 (J. Withals, 1556).
[2] *STC* 14652^a, sig. Aii^r.   [3] See above, p. 60.
[4] *STC* 84, sig. Aii^v.

It is for reasons such as these that many prologues to translations seem to oscillate between vaunting the worthiness of the translation and deploring the incompetence of the translator. Most translators are at one in this: they are consumed with an anxiety that the reader should realize that they are but tyros in the art of translating. This convention has a long history, going far back into the manuscript period, and need not be taken too seriously. It was part of the writer's convention—he trembled, but still he wrote![1] There was, perhaps, more substance for his plea that he wrote for the unlearned. Barclay asserts that he writes for the 'rude people', for whom he has therefore couched his translation in 'common and rural terms', and the particular public aimed at has, from the time of Caxton, been a consideration in the translator's mind. *Ex hypothesi,* the need for a translation at all showed that there was a sufficient public, 'unclerkly' or 'lewd' as it was called, which was awaiting reading matter. This, no doubt, was the motive leading some to make their translations easily understandable by an unlearned audience. The translator of the Exposition of the Creed by Erasmus says that his patron wished the work to be useful to 'ignoraunte and unlerned persones. And therfore I have so handeled the thynge that I have shaped and ordred al myne oratyon and speche after suche forme and maner as myght be moste mete and agreynge to the capacyte of those that are symple.'[2]

This was not always easy. In the first place a large number of works were only translations of translations. Much that was originally in Latin was first translated into French, and sometimes into German, and from one of these at a later date into English. In doing so the second translator accepted perforce the errors made by the first, unless he was unusually scrupulous, or had reason to believe that his text was corrupt or imperfect. When Miles Coverdale translated a treatise by Calvin he did so from a Latin version, but took care not to allow this to impart

---

[1] See my *Chaucer and the Fifteenth Century* (1947), pp. 126 ff.
[2] *STC* 10504, sig. A ii[r] [1533].

to his rendering the characteristics of the Latin style and word order, but throughout set himself to follow the true meaning of the author. He expressed his purpose as follows:

> As the authoure of thys lytle booke, moved with the desyre to profite as wel the rude and unlerned as the lettered and professers of knowledge, wrote it in hys vulgare tonge, even so I...moved also with the desyre to profite my naturall countremen so much as shall lye in my lytle power, have thought it my bounden dutie to employe my dylygence to the translatyng therof. And because it hath pleased the lorde to geve me more knowledge of the Latyne tonge then in the French (wherin thys boke was fyrste wrytten) I have translated it after the Latyne copy, puttyng the faythful reader out of doubt that I have not in any poynte gone frome the true meaning of the auctour, but have thorowlye observed the phrases of bothe tonges, avoydynge in all that I myghte the darke maner of translatynge after the latine phrases, to the intente the Englysshe readar myghte have the full understandynge hereof wythoute any knowlege of the Latyne tonge.[1]

We cannot but admire such scrupulousness, or that of R. Whitford who re-translated the *Imitation of Christ* about 1531. In doing so he had before him the previous translation made by the Lady Margaret a generation earlier, which he observes,

> for as muche as it was translatyd by the sayd noble prynces out of frenche it coulde not folowe the latyn so nyghe ne so dyrectly as if it had ben translated out of latin. And therefore it is nowe translated out of latyn, and yet nevertheless it keepeth the substaunce and the effect of the fyrst translation out of frenche, though sometyme it vary in wordes.[2]

Most translators, however, kept to the text that they had before them. Whether the original were in Greek or Latin, or in a contemporary language, was a matter with which they

---

[1] *STC* 4410, sig. Aii^r.
[2] *STC* 23961, sig. aii^r.

were unconcerned and of which they were often ignorant. They were not scholars, far less textual critics, but for the most part men who were making the translation, as we have seen, for the good of the commonwealth. So John Bankes, after reading 'two lytle bokes whiche John Rivius, an excellent lerned and godly man, compiled on the latyne tongue...and marveylynge muche that such two bokes coulde be kepte hyd so long, and not translated into Englyshe',[1] undertook to do so; and claims for his work that 'although it is not so fynely translated, yet I trust that the mynde of the authore is so expressed that mine industrye and labour herein cannot justly be reprehended'.[2]

'The mynde of the authore', or as another translator puts it, the 'right declaration of the history', are the aims men set before them. 'I dydde not regarde, nor had respecte, how eloquently I coulde translate this boke, but how faithfully and truely I could do it',[3] writes Turner in a preface dated 24 February 1523, and we may accept this as a fair account of the spirit animating many translators.

Nicholas Udall, one of the most influential translators of our period, declared, 'I have laboured to discharge the duetie of a translatour, that is kepyng and folowyng the sense of my boke, to interprete and turne the Latine into Englysshe with as muche grace of our vulgare toung, and in my slendre power and knowelage, hath lyen',[4] but few translators would have dared to claim much 'grace of our vulgare toung' for their work. Indeed, Thomas Key, who worked on the Paraphrases of Erasmus with Udall, expressly disclaimed that there was any grace in his translation, since he 'minded nothyng lesse then to contende with hym [Erasmus] in ornate speach and eloquence, but have done my dilligent endevour so to enterprete ye said worke, that it should be both plain and pleasaunt unto the

---

[1] STC 21065 [1550?], sig. A iv^v.
[2] Ibid. sig. A vi^r.
[3] STC 25127, fo. 6^v. Cf. 17113, sig. +iii^r.
[4] STC 10443 (1542), sig. ¶ ii^v.

171

reader...and faithfully to translate and expresse every thyng accordyng to the true sence and meanyng of thauctour'.[1]

It was one thing, however, to talk of the faithfulness of a translation, and another to achieve it. A vivid example of the difficulties besetting the would-be translator is found in the words of William Salisbury, who was asked by his cousin John Edwards to provide him with an English book, treating of 'the Sphere or Frame of the World'. Failing to find one in English, Salisbury discovered a Latin version by Proclus, the Greek mathematician and philosopher. 'And this, a Goddes name', he says,

entended I then (for the accomplyshement of your wyll) to traducte into the Englysshe tonge. But wolde God that he whiche translated it in to the Latin, had taken so moche payne, as for his countrie sake, as to englysshe the same. Also Englisshe was his natyve tonge, Greke and Laten as well knowen, wheras Englysshe to me of late yeares was wholly to lerne, the Latyn not tasted of, the Greke not once harde of, whom although even at this present I might rather and truelye with lesse reproche denye to have any knowledge in it at all then to professe the perfet phrase of any of theym three. Why then shall I attempte for any mannes pleasure, to go aboute to translate a Scyence unknowen, out of a tonge unknowen, into a tonge no better knowen to me?[2]

What wonder after this if he says that he will do his best, for the love he bears his cousin, but warns him that he 'wyll wrest it rather than truely torne it'.[3] Salisbury, perhaps, should never have tried his inexpert hand at a work for which he was so imperfectly equipped, yet the absence of any English work on the subject, and his cousin's entreaties, overcame him. So we may suspect did this or that reason persuade others whose wiser moments would have bid them pause before they undertook so difficult a venture. Robert Copland, old hand at

---

[1] *STC* 2854, sig. ⟨ii[r] (St Mark). Cf. J. Old, the translator of Ephesians, sig. ⟨ii[r]. 'I thought it better to seke the edification of the playne unlerned by playne termyng of wordes than by tedious circumlocution...and by that meanes not onelye to leave the simple vulgare people untaught...but also in vayne sekynge after curiositie to be justly laught to scorne.'

[2] *STC* 20399, sig. A ii[v] (1550).   [3] *Ibid.* sig. A iii[r].

THE TRANSLATORS' DIFFICULTIES

translating as he was, hesitated before venturing to translate *The rutter of the sea*, but after 'a sad, ingenious and circumspect Mariner of the City of London' had brought a French copy of the work to him, and said that it was 'necessary for all English men of his facultie to have it in their owne language to the erudition and safeguarde of our merchantes', Copland gave way, despite the difficulties,

me not knowing the termes of maryners and names of the costes and havens for I never came on the sea, nor by the coste therof. But folowing my copye by the advise and oversight of certaine cunning men of that science which bolded and informed me in many doutes, I did undertake in dooing my diligence, as a blinde horse in a mill turning the quern ignorantly, save by conducting of the Milner that setteth him on woork.[1]

Occasionally we hear of the translator's difficulties when confronted with an earlier version which he is asked to amend before reprinting. When Richard Whitford was brought the Rule of St Augustine by some nuns to 'amende and reforme the englysshe' he found that they had set him an impossible task.

For to amende your translacyon passed my power and wyt. It seemeth unto me so scabrouse, rughe, or rude, and not after the commune englysshe of this countrie. And also the translatour dyde lene over moche unto the strayte lettre, whyche thynge in translacyon doeth (many tymes) render the mater very blynde, and moche unsaverye. Therefore have I chosen here a playne style, without ynkehorne termes.[2]

The mention of 'ynkehorne termes' reminds us of a difficulty which beset translators, as well as other writers, throughout this period. Caxton was always aware of the dangers which he ran if he employed 'fair and strange terms',

---

[1] *STC* 11551, sig. Ai[v].
[2] *STC* 25417, sig. Aii[v]. Cf. *STC* 5574 where Whitford says that *The thre kynges of coleyne* (1511) was brought to him 'in englysshe of an olde translacyon rugh and rude'.

or went to the other extreme and used 'old and homely' ones. He was also aware that 'comyn Englysshe that is spokon in one shyre varyeth from a nother', and decided, after much trial and error, to use 'Englysshe not over rude, ne curyous, but in suche termes as shall be understanden by goddys grace'. His successors, as we have seen, relied on a wide range of individuals for their translations, and the kind of English they used varied accordingly.

The most vigorous criticism of the use of language by contemporary translators comes from Peter Betham. In dedicating *The preceptes of warre, set forth by James the erle of Purlilia* (1544) to Sir Thomas Audley he delivered himself as follows:

> I wil be bolde, under your lordeshyppes licence, somthyng to wander from my fyrst mattyer, and to speake a lytle of the translatours of thys age, whych after my pore judgement do marre and misframe our Englysshe tounge through theyr termes unnedefullye borowed of other languages. For lyke as the carpenter that goth abowte hys worke doth occupye for the most parte hys owne instrumentes, and hath lytle nede to borowe of anye other craftesman, so I thynke that all translatours ought to use the usuall termes of our Englysshe tounge, which of itselfe is ryche and plentyfull and not to breke wythout all judgemente into the boundes of the Latyn tounge, to steale termes of it, as yf our Englyshe tounge had not in hymselfe suffysaunce of woordes to set fourth all our speakynges.
>
> But suche men as do unadvisedly desyre other long termes would be taken (to my judgement) as authours of our woordes, therby to enlarge our language (whyche rather they do make poore and barrayne) so that manye good mattyers be dusked and defaced wyth theyr newe borowed ynkehorne termes, and the common people of Englande do not understand the wrytynges ne yet the speache of them, for theyr trycke termes, of theyr own brayn shaped . . .
>
> Yet lette no man thyncke that I doo damne all usuall termes borowed of other tounges, when I doo well knowe that one tounge is interlaced with an other. But nowe to be shorte, I take them beste

Englyshe men which folowe Chaucer and other olde wryters, in whyche studye the nobles and gentlemen of Englande are worthye to be praysed whan they endevoure to brynge agayne to his owne clennes oure Englysshe tounge, and playnelye to speake wyth our owne termes, as our others dyd before us.[1]

While this criticism has some validity, in the main it may fairly be said that the majority of translators realized the necessity for using good, clear English, unencumbered with crude words and not unduly complicated by stylistic tricks and ornaments. Peter Ashton, in his preface to his translation of *A shorte treatise vpon the Turkes chronicles* (1546), says that his 'simple translation, althoughe it be...but rudely and groslye turned', should be read,

not so muche to regarde and loke for picked termes and strange Englishe wordes (whiche indeed be not here) as for the playne setting forthe of the sentence and right declaration of the history. For truly, throwgheout al this simple and rude translation I studyed rather to use the most playn and famylier english speche, then ether Chaucers wordes (which by reason of antiquitie be almost out of use) or els inkhorne termes (as they call them) whiche the common people, for lacke of latin, do not understande.[2]

This unusually clear statement of his aims may be taken to exemplify the considerations in the minds of many translators. If they failed (as they often did) it was not through any lack of goodwill towards their readers, but rather from inability to express themselves any better. English prose was still in an experimental stage, and it was useless to expect that any one way of expression would command general consent. Further, the translator had to face the fact that the art of

[1] *STC* 20116, sig. Avi[r].
[2] *STC* 11899, sig. *vi[v]. Cf. 17113 (1534), sig. [+iiii[r]], where the translator of Lyndewood's Constitutions says: 'I have nat sought anye prayse in the translation, but was contentyd so to set it forth rudely and playnly without any straunge termes that it myght be well understond of y[e] unlerned layete in englyshe as it was before of the lerned clergy in latyn, which thing I doubte nat but I have broughte to passe.'

translation had its own difficulties, and that a wide divergence of opinion on the merits of any translation was possible—even probable. Once the translator allowed his work to be put into print, he had to be prepared for criticism. As Nicholas Lesse wrote (1550), the work

> once abroad, muste nedes come under many mens judgments, must susteine and abide yᵉ opinions of mani, of whom some wyl saie this might be more cleane translated: this word or that is not in his own kind: this sens or that is not given according to the minde of the author as it hath ben alway sen.[1]

To such criticism the author was inevitably (and rightly) exposed. His best answer was to reply, as did Nicholas Udall, that

> these translations [of the paraphase upon the *New Testament* by Erasmus (1549)] are not to be depraved because some reader would perhaps otherwyse have turned some thynges, when he shall here rede it. For no twoo would agree in all poyntes of style or endityng.... And the same interpreter yᵗ would have translated some parte here of better then it now is, would in some pointes perchaunce have doone it wurse.[2]

We may allow Nicholas Udall to sum up the case for the translator in the following passage, taken from the Introductory letter to the King, prefacing the Erasmus paraphrases. After some remarks on the art of translation, he goes on:

> Now besydes that suche a translatour travailleth not to his owne private commoditee, but to the behouf and publique use of his countrey, besydes that the thyng is suche as must so throughly occupie and possesse the dooer, and must have hym so attent to applye that same exercise onely, that he maie not duryng that season take in hande any other trade or buisinesse whereby to purchase his livyng: besydes that the thyng cannot bee dooen without bestowyng of long tyme, great watchyng, muche paines,

---

[1] *STC* 10429, sig. A ii^v.
[2] *STC* 2854, sig. B 7^v. Cf. Udall's remarks in his translation of Erasmus' *Apophthegmes* (1542), *STC* 10443, sig. *ii^r.

diligent studie, no small charges as well of meate, drynke and bookes, as also of other necessaries: the labour (it) self is of itself a more peinefull and a more tedious thyng then for a man to wryte or prosecute any argumente of his owne invencion. A man hath his owne invencion readie at his owne pleasure without lettes or stoppes to make suche discourse as his argumente requireth, but a translatour must of force in manier at everie other woorde staigh and suspende bothe his cogitation and his penne to looke upon his autour, so that he myght in equall tyme make thrise so muche as he can bee hable to translate. But whether of bothe a man shall applye hymselfe to dooe, he can in the mean whyle dooe nothynge els: he cannot duryng the season bestowe hymself on any other occupacion for his living, and his necessitees and also charges in the meane tyme neverthelesse dooe growe as well as other mennes. Wherof it cometh to passe that a noumbre of suche as would bee right willyng and diligent to dooe good in the common weale with this kynde of service, yet through defaulte of necessarie maintenaunce cannot; and certain that have bothe livyng and vacaunt tyme enough, forasmuch as thei see the peines of this travaill so great, the hyre nothyng at all, and the capciousnesse of some maligners against the trueth so readie to deprave the diligent labour of studious wryters, are for the moste parte of theim better contented (accordyng to the accustomed proverbe) to plaie for naught then to weorke for nought. And by this meanes lye almoste all good bookes hidden from the people.[1]

[1] *STC* 2854, sig. Biiii^v.

CHAPTER VIII

THE PRINTERS

The history of printing in England during this period has been carefully surveyed by a number of writers, and it is unnecessary to set it out in detail again. The accomplished bibliographers[1] to whom we owe so much have naturally concentrated upon typographical and bibliographical problems and minutiae, and have left it to their successors to explore such matters as the interrelations between various printers, the different markets exploited by them, the extent to which they led or followed popular taste, and so on. To these topics we now turn, and for convenience may divide the period into four sections: the era of Caxton (1476–91); the immediate heritage and work of his successors (1491–1500); the development of printing until the death·of de Worde (1535), and the progress made by subsequent printers until the incorporation of the Stationers' Company in 1557.

Before we begin our chronological survey, a few general remarks are necessary. It must be remembered that in speaking of the printers before 1557 we are speaking of a comparatively small body of men. It would be rash to think that more than a hundred master-printers in all existed between 1476 and 1557, while only some dozen or so of these printed outside the City of London, or in the provinces, or in Scotland and Ireland. For the rest their numbers grew slowly at first, but with growing strength in the second half of the period. Thus between 1541 and 1550 at least thirty-five printers hitherto unknown began to print.

It is deceptive, however, merely to count heads, for many of these names appear on imprints for a few times within a

---

[1] See in particular, E. Gordon Duff, *Century* and *Printers*, and also H. R. Plomer, *Wynkyn de Worde and his Contemporaries...to 1535* (1925).

brief space of years, and then are gone. Of the thirty-five printers identified between 1541 and 1550, at least a dozen seem to have been at work for two or three years only, and to a lesser extent this is true of the next decade. Then again, although some printers were at work over a considerable period they have only a handful of volumes to show, whereas de Worde has over 700 to his credit. As we shall see, a number of printers turned out at least 100 volumes in the course of their careers, but the output from various presses was very varied, and generalizations are difficult and unrevealing. Our best course is to remember that we are dealing with the development of a new industry, which had to feel its way slowly, with little to guide it save the demands of the public and the perceptiveness of the printers.

What is known of the lives and circumstances of the printers and booksellers has been epitomized by Mr Gordon Duff in his *A Century of the English Book Trade, 1457–1557,* and although some additional material has been added since he wrote, it has not substantially altered our knowledge of the subject. From his pages, and from the evidence provided by the books themselves, we can see something of the way in which these early books were produced and put on the market. We naturally hear most about the printers themselves, although they were necessarily assisted by a number of helpers about whom we are far less clear. We know, however, that they were divided into apprentices and 'servants', and that the apprentices who served fo. a number of years, had to complete their apprenticeship by the age of twenty-four, and formed a part of their master's household. They are frequently mentioned in the printers' wills where they are left sums of money or other tokens of regard. Their number in any one workshop varied; de Worde mentions six of them in his will, as well as two 'late my apprentices'; R. Kele mentions five, and several other printers two. The other workmen in the printing-house were known as 'servants'—a term which covered the apprentice who had served his time as well as the journeymen, many of whom were foreigners and had served no apprenticeship in England.

With the aid of his 'servants' and the apprentices the master-printer produced his wares at his printing-house which usually had a sign outside it to denote its whereabouts. For example, de Worde's books after 1500 were 'printed in London in Flete-strete, at the sygne of the Sonne', while John Wayland printed 'in saynt Dunstones parysh at the signe of the blewe Garland next to the Temple bare', and so with the other printers. Anyone wishing to purchase their books had only to make for their sign, and outside their works would sometimes be found a stall, for we read of a man taking refuge 'under T. Berthelet's stall in Fleet Street'.

Fairly early in the history of English printing, however, booksellers began to congregate round St Paul's, and had there either a stall or a small house and shop for their business premises. This concentration was obviously a convenience both for customer and bookseller. The would-be purchaser could walk from one stall to another in search of the book he wanted, as we saw that William Salisbury did when he was looking for a book on the spheres.[1] Here again, each trader had his own sign, which was sometimes different from, sometimes the same as that of his printing-house. De Worde's sign in St Paul's was that of our Lady of Pity, while J. Notary tells us in the title-page of his edition of *Sermones discipuli* (1510) that they

are to be sold (when they have been printed) in London in the suburb of Temple Bar near the porch of St Clement's in the house of Julian Notary, printer and bookseller, carrying on business under the sign of the Three Kings. And they will also be found for sale in St Paul's churchyard in the same man's little shop (cellula) from which also hangs the same sign of the Three Kings.[2]

These signs being an important clue to the printer's whereabouts, it is not surprising that when he changed his premises he often took his sign with him, as did J. Rastell or J. Day.

[1] See above, p. 21.   [2] *STC* 13226.

By the time the Stationers' Company was incorporated in 1557 the printing trade was well established, with a considerable body of printers mainly concentrated in St Paul's Churchyard and in the vicinity. The four phases which led to this state of affairs may be summarized as follows.

1. *The age of Caxton* (*1476–91*)

Caxton began to print 'at the sign of the Red Pale at Westminster' in 1476, with the knowledge that no rivals were in the field, and throughout his lifetime he was little bothered by competition. The new art of printing made its way very slowly. In London only one rival printing-house was set up—that established by John Lettou in 1480, in which he was joined by William de Machlinia in 1482, and which de Machlinia carried on alone from 1483 to 1490. Their wares were theological treatises, scholastic works and law-books, and did not seriously compete with Caxton's interests.

Outside London two printing-houses were at work. At Oxford Theodoric Rood about 1478 began printing scholastic works, and was joined about 1481 by an Oxford stationer, Thomas Hunte. We know of seventeen books issued by them, but here again they were trenching but little on Caxton's market, and probably found their main custom in Oxford and round about. Only one other press is known, that at St Albans, which dealt mainly in scholastic works, but is famous for two outstanding volumes, *The Chronicles of England* [1485] and *The Book of St Albans* (1486). Both these works were of considerable general interest: Caxton had already published two editions of the *Chronicles*, and the St Albans printer was able to make use of these in putting out his enlarged edition, while *The Book of St Albans*, with its sections on hawking, hunting and heraldry, had a wide appeal, and in various forms was reprinted throughout the next century.

It must not be forgotten, of course, that it was not only home competition that Caxton had to consider. Books were being imported from France, Germany, Holland, Switzerland and Italy. We are very imperfectly informed as to the extent of this trade, nor do we know the titles of more than a limited number of books.[1] In the main, however, they are the kinds of books we should expect to be imported—that is, books which had an obvious market such as missals, books of hours and legendaries. A small number of grammatical text-books also came into England from overseas, but all these importations did not seriously compete with Caxton's wares, which in the main were of a different class, and made appeal to the reader of literature rather than to the student of learning.

2. De Worde and Pynson (1491–1500)

The death of Caxton in 1491 was a blow from which the newly established craft took some time to recover, and the next decade may conveniently be isolated, for it was a period in which Caxton's successors were but slowly feeling their way forward. Neither de Worde nor Pynson were men of Caxton's stature. They were both active and reasonably enterprising business men, but without Caxton's flair, or his personal interest in this or that type of book. During this decade, as was reasonable, they ventured forward slowly. The potential book-buying public was still uncertain both in size and in interests, and they were forced to limit their risks in exploring the nature of the public tastes.

As we survey the total output of these two printers it is clear that de Worde produced more in quantity than his rival, but that his work was generally inferior in quality. We are able to identify a little over a hundred items from each press during this decade, though how many works have perished it is impossible to say. As it is, a number of extant works survive only in a fragmentary state. For example, *The Ghost of Guy*

---

[1] Gordon Duff, in his *Fifteenth Century English Books* (1917) lists sixty-nine books printed abroad for the English trade by 1500. Not more than a quarter of these were printed in Caxton's lifetime. For the remainder, see below, p. 184.

(1492) is known only from two small strips taken from a binding, and many other works exist in a page or two only, having been used as waste by binders of that period.

Pynson's folio volumes are in general much less bulky than those of de Worde. Where de Worde averaged 360 pages a volume, Pynson was content with 180. Among de Worde's largest folios (all in double columns) were Bartholomew's *De proprietatibus rerum* (1495) in 956 pages; two editions of the *Golden legend* (1493 and 1498) of 878 and 896 pages respectively; Higden's *Polychronicon* (1495) of 796 pages; Jerome's *Vitas Patrum* (1495) of 712 pages; Malory's *Morte Darthur* (1498) of 652 pages, besides twenty other folios, ranging from 12 to 532 pages. All these books were put out between 1493 and 1500 and must have taxed the resources of his printing-house severely. On the other hand Pynson seldom printed folios of such bulk. If we exclude the eleven Year Books (ranging from 28 to 184 pages), we have to consider eighteen volumes, the largest of which, *The Canterbury Tales*, made a book of 648 pages. He never ventured on so large a book again in this period, although his Missal of 1500 ('perhaps the finest book printed in the fifteenth century in England') was only 32 pages shorter. With the exception of Lydgate's translation of Boccaccio's *Falle of Princis* (1494), Pynson's remaining folios were comparatively small, and he seems to have kept his output of these volumes much more regular than did de Worde. He seldom printed books totalling more than 600 folio pages in any year, whereas de Worde reached 2464 pages in 1495, and 1990 pages in 1498, but only 404 pages in 1497.

Both printers produced a large number of quarto volumes—seventy-five coming from de Worde, and fifty-five from Pynson. These ranged from a little school text-book, or a short poem of 8 pages, to considerable volumes, such as Maydeston's *Directorium sacerdotum*, which in de Worde's edition ran to 464 and Pynson's to 452 pages.

To turn from bulk to subject-matter, we find that each printer is catering for a wide variety of interests. Both naturally devote about half their attention to religious works. Pynson makes a successful attempt to capture the market for legal works, while de Worde has not yet realized the insatiable public waiting for grammars, vocabularies, etc., which he was to exploit so successfully in the sixteenth century. Both published works of general interest, such as chronicles, encyclopaedias, poems, travels, etc., for it was inevitable that many of their productions should be of a common character, competing for the favour of the same people. Thus both printed editions of well-known scholastic manuals—the *Equivoca* and *Synonyma* of John of Garland, or popular works such as Lydgate's *The churl and the bird*, or Sir John Mandeville's *Travels*. Similarly, it was essential for both of them to have on sale well used religious manuals—Lyndewood's *Provinciale*, Maydeston's *Directorium sacerdotum*, or Mirk's *Festial*.

Competition between them at this period was no doubt keen, but at the turn of the century they could both look back on their first decade as printers with satisfaction. There was a public for all their various wares, and as yet no serious rival had arisen to challenge them at home. Julian Notary, of Westminster, it is true, had a bare half-dozen books on the stalls for sale, but most of these had already been printed by his rivals. Such competition as there was came from overseas. Even so this competition was limited in scope and volume. In the main it contented itself with supplying missals, primers or grammatical text-books, just as it had done in Caxton's lifetime, and evidently the book market was buoyant enough to absorb all that came from abroad, as well as the limited home supplies. The titles of about fifty volumes from foreign presses have survived, and the records from time to time make laconic mention of the importation of 'one hogshead of printed books', or 'three fattes containing twelve dozen primers', etc.[1] We

---

[1] H. R. Plomer, 'The Importation of Books into England in the Fifteenth and Sixteenth Centuries', *The Library*, Fourth Series, vol. IV. (1924), pp. 146–50; and 'The Importation of Low Country and French Books into England, 1480 and 1502–3', *ibid.* vol. IX (1929), pp. 164–8.

know that in 1479–80, according to a Customs House return for the Port of London, over 1400 books were imported during the year, so that the trade was not insignificant, bearing in mind the small output of books by printers working in England. Although the scope was limited, there is evidence that foreign printers were eagerly watching the market, and if printers here were not ready to supply books thought to have a chance of circulation, then the foreigner stepped in. For instance, after the death of Caxton, Gerard Leeu of Antwerp quickly printed editions of three of Caxton's works, *The History of Jason, Paris and Vienne* and *The Chronicles of England*, together with a tale *The Dialogue...between Solomon and Marcolphus*. Caxton's successor, de Worde, was caught by these reprints at a moment when he was reorganizing his printing-house, and completing those works left unfinished by his master, and so had little time for new ventures.

The real challenge, however, which de Worde and Pynson had to face arose from the greater superiority of the work of their continental rivals to their own. England lacked the skill and technical resources, together with the funds, that made possible the work of the printers of Paris, Rouen, Venice, and half a dozen other centres. Paris specialized in the production of beautifully executed little books of Hours, surrounded on every page with woodcut borders, attractively filled with a variety of designs, and these were imported in large numbers. Other liturgical and devotional works also came from overseas, and set a standard altogether beyond anything usually achieved by printers in England, and no doubt formed a healthy incentive at a time when competition within the country was so limited.

3. *From 1500 to the death of de Worde (1535)*

During the last decade of the fifteenth century de Worde and Pynson carried on the heritage which Caxton had left them in so far as they were capable. De Worde lacked Caxton's literary interest and typographical skill, and was also without those contacts with the aristocracy and the higher bourgeoisie which had been so important an influence on Caxton's output. The move in 1500 of his printing-house from the comparative quiet of Westminster to the bustle of Fleet Street is indicative of what was going on in his mind at this time. He saw—or perhaps sensed—that his success as a printer lay among the citizens and petite bourgeoisie, rather than in higher circles. Caxton's imposing series of works were beyond him in every way, and we may imagine that by 1500 he was looking about him for new ways in which to make a living as a printer.

A series of experiments during the first few years of the sixteenth century showed him how to proceed, and determined the main lines of his output for the next thirty years. Briefly it was to give the public a variety of books on subjects known to have a popular appeal—religious and homiletic, practical and instructional—and to issue these in easily handled volumes likely to attract readers who would recoil from large and expensive volumes. These comparatively small books, generally in quarto form and seldom exceeding a hundred pages, met a real need. A few pence bought a small-sized book; indeed, Robert Copland tells us that some were unwilling to pay as much as fourpence, and thought that a penny was enough. 'Hast thou a book', asks his customer:

> Hast thou a boke of the wydowe Edith
> That hath begyled so many with her wordes,
> Or els suche a geest that is ful of bourdes?
> Let me se; I wyll yet waste a peny
> Upon suche thynges and if thou have eny.

COPLAND

> How say ye by these; wyll ye bestowe a grote?

CUSTOMER

> Ye syr, somuche? Nay, that I shorowe my cote.
> A peny I trow is ynough on bokes.
> It is not so soone goten, as this worlde lokes.[1]

[1] *STC* 5734, sig. A ii^r.

186

The change of front adopted by de Worde was also followed by Pynson to a lesser extent, for Pynson was a better educated man, and had higher typographical standards than his rival. Nevertheless, he too realized that the number of people ready and able to buy works such as Caxton had printed was limited, and that a larger public must be sought elsewhere. This in part he found by providing books similar to those de Worde was printing and also by turning his attention to the production of books for lawyers.

Both printers then, in the first decade of the sixteenth century, without being fully conscious of what they were doing, brought the printing-press into closer contact with a body of readers whose needs were great. At the same time, however, it must be noted that the standards of such readers were low, such education as they had leaving them with little appreciation of fine book production or typographical skill. They wanted the maximum of reading matter for the minimum of outlay. Caxton had told the public that some of his wares were for sale 'good chepe'; the Tudor printers likewise were ready to meet their readers by providing cheap rather than well turned-out books.

So while de Worde, and more particularly Pynson, could and did produce a number of works not without merit as pieces of printing, it is true to say that their output as a whole shows them more concerned with material than with aesthetic ends. De Worde's vast output was achieved by an indifference to good printing and by a knowledge of the considerable demand which existed for works of limited size and small price. If the characteristic work of Caxton is the large folio, running to hundreds of pages, the typical volume of de Worde is the quarto of 24 or 32 pages.

Pynson died early in 1530, and de Worde early in 1535 (although the latter does not seem to have been very active after about 1532) and the history of printing during these first three decades of the sixteenth century is largely the history of these two men, for they outdistanced all rivals who from time to time appeared. Their overwhelming position may best be estimated by the following figures: in the first decade of the century they were responsible for 70% of the entire output of books in English. Of the remainder, over half were the work of foreign printers. In the next decade they produced 73%, foreigners 17%, and the other printers only 10% of the output. In the third decade they suffered a setback. Only 55% of books came from their presses, but their English rivals increased their output to 30%.[1]

While both of them throughout their careers printed books of every kind, particularly religious works, each of them specialized to some extent. Wynkyn de Worde paid great attention to the books required for the new curriculum of the grammar schools, so that some 40% of his publications were designed to meet this need. The printing of the various types of Latin grammars devised by Robert Whittinton was largely his monopoly, and he shared with Pynson the printing of many editions of John de Garland's *Equivoca* and his *Synonyma*. He printed about half of Stanbridge's grammatical primers, produced editions of old favourites, such as Donatus or Sulpitius, or works by new candidates for scholastic favour —Colet, Lily and Erasmus. Pynson, on the other hand, while he did not neglect the educational world, ventured into a field virtually neglected by de Worde, and tried to meet the needs of lawyers and those connected with the law. No printer before 1557 has so many legal works to his credit as Pynson, who indeed seems to have started his career by printing a number of legal works. He continued to print various types of matter useful to lawyers, both original documents such as the *Statutes* and *Year Books*; compilations of legal material as in Littleton's *Tenures*, *The Abridgement of the Statutes*, and the *Natura Brevium*, or helps to amateur lawyers, whether they were Justices of the Peace, or manorial lords holding a Court Baron, or a Hundred Court. Not less than one-third of the books printed by Pynson are connected with the law, and it

[1] See below, p. 189.

was evidently a successful type of venture, for nearly every law-book he published was reprinted at least once. Of the other printers at work in the first decades of the century little need be said. We have already seen that their output was slight, especially before 1520,[1] and in general it followed lines of least resistance, consisting as it did mainly of religious works, and to a lesser degree of scholastic manuals. One figure stands out, that of John Rastell, 'Printer, Lawyer, Venturer, Dramatist and Controversialist', as he has been termed by Dr A. W. Reed who has so admirably explored his career.[2] Dr Reed's summary description of Rastell reminds us that printing was only one of his activities, and probably because his livelihood was not controlled by the printing-house, he was able to put out legal treatises, religious and contro-versial tracts, jest books or popular plays, as it pleased himself without stopping to consider whether they would please the public or not.[3]

For forty years then from the death of Caxton until about 1532 de Worde and Pynson were the overwhelmingly impor-tant figures in the printing industry. How had they exercised their power? We have seen how each of them specialized to some extent, and Pynson's appointment as the King's Printer about 1508–9 meant that he had to use his resources when so commanded to print proclamations, books of statutes, etc.[4] Nevertheless, each of them could look back on a body of publications touching very many interests and offering some-thing for every literary appetite. Here we part company, to some extent, with the bibliographers and students of typo-graphy who have allowed their admiration of Pynson's superior

[1] See above, p. 188.

[2] A. W. Reed, *Early Tudor Drama* (1926), *passim*.

[3] In a letter to Cromwell, written in the last years of his life, however, Rastell admits that his printing used to bring him in more than his pleading (Reed, *op. cit.* p. 24).

[4] The extent of the King's Printer's official work is hard to assess as so many proclamations, etc., have perished, but we can see from Berthelet's account rendered for 1541–4 and reproduced in Arber's *Transcript*, vol. II, pp. 50–60, that it was considerable.

press-work to mask the debt we owe to de Worde for the mass and variety of his output. Gordon Duff says that de Worde was 'not skilful as a printer', while H. R. Plomer accuses him of a lack of artistic feeling in his choice and arrangement of woodcuts, of stupid mistakes and carelessness in composition and press-work, and of being a man of no literary tastes.[1] We may readily admit all of this (although Plomer's last phrase is a little hard), and at the same time assert that de Worde's services to literature, to religion and to the popularization of the printed word were very considerable.

In the first place the magnitude of his output was remarkable. Between 1492 and 1532 his imprint appears on over 700 works. Even allowing for the fact that many of these were reprints, or small pamphlets rather than books, his activity and enterprise are worthy of respect. We may estimate his achievement in another way when we recall that the total number of works recorded in the *Short-title Catalogue* before 1557 is about 5000, so that de Worde contributed some 15% of this total single-handed.

If we turn from mere bulk to other considerations, de Worde is even more worthy of respect. Far more works have survived, largely because of his efforts, than most bibliographers suggest. So far as I can judge by an examination of samples of his output at various times, 70% of the books printed by him were printed for the first time. To list their names would be to recall a number of items famous in our literary history, while many other works (most of them admittedly of little literary value) have survived only in de Worde's edition. Something over 30% of his output consisted of such works. In other words, over 200 works printed by de Worde were never again reprinted before 1640, and most of them have never been reprinted at all. While (as said above) many of these works are of small value to the student of masterpieces, they are important items of evidence in the history of taste, and in the investigation of the growth and appetite of the early reading public.

[1] H. R. Plomer, *Wynkyn de Worde and his Contemporaries* (1925), pp. 70 ff.

Not all, by any means, of de Worde's pioneer editions can be written off as of comparatively little value. If we examine his contribution to romance literature, for example, we find that de Worde had a real understanding of what was required. He printed fifteen romances in all, and of these twelve appear for the first time under his imprint, and three of these— *Appolonius of Tyre* (1510), *Melusine* [1510?], and *Olyuer of Castylle* (1518)—are unique. As with romance, so with other forms of literature: de Worde was ever ready to print some new thing. He had little literary judgement of his own, and relied on his friends and helpers, such as Robert Copland and Henry Watson, for advice; but whatever his methods, his solid contribution to our literature (despite its demerits typographically) cannot be gainsaid.

Pynson's work from 1500 to his death shows him to have been a systematic, careful man of business. Until his appointment as King's Printer about 1509 he devoted nearly half his output to religious works of various kinds—all 'safe' lines. After that he rapidly developed the legal side of his business, for he had a privileged position with regard to the publication of statutes, and perhaps of the Year Books, printing over seventy editions of the latter. These two great classes of books, religious and legal, accounted for some two-thirds of his total output. The rest of his time was spent in producing a considerable number of scholastic manuals, while general literature occupied but little of his attention. Thus he may be looked upon as being less adventurous than de Worde, catering for a more educated public, and producing more expensive and better printed works.[1] At the same time, his shrewdness as a business man is indicated by the fact that very many of his books were reprinted, some of them many times over. Thus he reprinted Littleton's *Tenures* at least eight times; the *Natura Brevium* six; the *Sarum Horae* eight, and other liturgical manuals on several occasions.

[1] Pynson was an innovator in his craft, always eager to introduce a new device, such as pagination, catchwords, roman type, etc.

This did not prevent him from printing the first editions of many books. Between 50 and 60% of his productions fall into this category, and we are indebted to him for the first editions of such famous works as Froissart's and Fabyan's *Chronicles*, Lydgate's *Troy Book*, Barclay's translation of *The ship of fools* and for *Everyman*. For the majority of his works he preferred the quarto form, reserving the folios for his editions of the Statutes, Bulls, Proclamations, etc., and for a select body of books which remain among the glories of our early printing. The *Missal* of 1500, *The ship of fools* (1509), the *Intrationum excellentissimus liber* (1510), and the *Missal* of 1520, may serve as examples of Pynson's best work in this format. The quartos, however, absorbed much of his attention, for these convenient little volumes were growing in favour, and both he and de Worde used them both for works of a few pages, or for large-scale productions with lavish illustrations, as may be found in *The castell of laboure* [1505?].

It may be asked how far these two printers trespassed upon one another's market. The answer is very little, when one considers their total output. Not more than five works were printed by them in common in the same year, or indeed within a period of up to five years, and their rivalry (such as it was) is more notable in their early years as printers when they were unsure of the extent of the public demand.[1] The most interesting of their clashes occurred in 1509 when de Worde published a prose version of *The ship of fools* in July, and Pynson followed with one in verse the following December. Here de Worde was acting with the encouragement of the Lady Margaret, while Pynson undertook the edition at his own 'coste and charge'. For the rest the books they printed in common were religious or scholastic works much in demand, and most of them were reprinted again and again. In other words, the combined labours of both the printers were scarcely sufficient to satisfy the market. At times one, at times the other, was first in the field; but, as they became more firmly established, the race for

[1] See above, p. 186.

priority declined very considerably, each printer going his own way and carrying out his programme without fear of being out-distanced by his rival.

We have already seen that the importation of books was felt to be a menace by the English printers, since many of these foreign books were admirable examples of the printer's craft. Few English books of this time could claim much typographical distinction: at best there was a reasonable competence about them—at worst a slovenly disregard of any typographical standards. The spur of foreign competition was therefore a healthy one, but the printers could hardly be expected to appreciate this view. At this moment they were unexpectedly aided by two things: first the desire of the Church and the King to control the heretical literature coming into the country, and secondly by the determination on the King's part to keep a strict eye on all books touching the question of his divorce and his constitutional position in Church and State. After various ineffective methods had been tried, as we have seen, an Act was passed in 1534 which made foreign competition wellnigh impossible.[1]

Henceforth the English printer had things all his own way. The public found it increasingly difficult to compare his wares with the finer products of foreign presses. The market for books was growing and the nature of the demand was becoming clearer. The great pioneering days were over. Instead of the trade being concentrated largely in the hands of two men, at the time of de Worde's death there were some ten printers actively at work, and their number was to increase rapidly in the next two decades.

4. *From the death of de Worde to the incorporation of the Stationers' Company (1535–57)*

From the passing of the Act of 1534 and de Worde's death early in 1535 until the incorporation of the Stationers' Company in 1557 was a period of growing prosperity for the printers.

[1] See above, p. 31.

They were freed of much foreign competition just at the moment when the King's quarrel with the Pope presented them with magnificent opportunities for developing their trade in religious and controversial literature. The output of books steadily rose. For the years 1520–9 we have recorded the titles of 550 books; in the next decade this rose to 739; then to 928, and in 1550–9 to 1040.

With the increase in output went an increase in the number of master-printers at work. Not less than seventy persons are known to have printed books in the period 1535–60. While it may be true that a few of them were not actually printers, despite the colophons on their books, in the main they all had presses, and turned out few or many volumes. They present a complicated picture, for their output and range varied tremendously. Several are known by a single book only, or were in business apparently for a brief period of a year or two. It is hard to understand how these fugitive ventures came into being, although occasionally we can make a guess. For example, the sole work printed by Roger Madeley (1553) was *An invective against treason*, a ballad 'imprynted at London...and are to be sold at Paules church yearde at the sygne of the Starre'. Now this was the printing house of Thomas Raynalde until 1552, and when we observe that Madeley was printing with the same types as Raynalde had used, it is reasonable to assume that Madeley had taken over Raynalde's press. In general, however, we have no clue to the reasons animating these men to take up printing. In a number of cases, although their presses were at work over a number of years, the output (so far as it has survived) was far too small to be more than an additional—not a main source of income. Perhaps these men were booksellers first, and printers only to a secondary degree.[1] Others again were printers for a brief period only, and were

---

[1] See, for example, Henry Smith (1543–50), who specialized in law books, shared editions with Kele and Toye, printed by N. Hill and sold Fortescue's *De politica administratione* 'excusum Londini tipis Edwardi Whitechurche, et veneunt in edibus Henrici Smyth Bibliopole'.

generally inspired by strong religious convictions. For example, we cannot think of Robert Crowley as a professional printer, despite his output of fifteen books between 1549 and 1551. He was sometime a Fellow of Magdalen College, Oxford, and later rector of St Giles, Cripplegate. His publications were mainly of a religious nature, and he probably acquired a press to further his anti-papal activities. On it he printed five theological treatises and a metrical psalter of his own, as well as Wycliffe's Prologue to the Bible, and five works (mainly theological) in Welsh. Even this limited output strained the resources of his press, and there is evidence that he had to call on two more substantial printers—Jugge and Day—to help him out.

A number of other printers were rather more ambitious, but were content with what was still a modest output (in nearly every case almost exclusively religious) which they felt sure would meet a demand and give them a reasonable return. They printed translations of the great foreign divines and reformers, as well as a number of didactic works, sermons and treatises on special points by native theologians. Thomas Raynalde, for example, is known to have printed thirty-four works between 1540 and 1552. Of these, no less than thirty were of a religious nature—works by Bale, Hooper, Joye, Turner, Tyndale and Zwingli; Bibles, metrical versions of the Psalms, service-books, etc.—a mixed output meeting a variety of religious needs.[1] Another printer of much the same calibre, Thomas Petyt, put out forty-two works of which twenty-five were of a religious nature. For the rest he printed seven popular law-books, and six works of general information, such as Hugh Rhodes's *Boke of nurture* [1545?] and Thomas Moulton's *The glasse of helthe* [1550?]. He took a share of the 1542 edition of Chaucer, printed by R. Grafton and part of Taverner's version of the Gospels, printed by R. Bankes in 1540. In part printer, in

---

[1] Cf. J. Mayler who printed some twenty-nine volumes, all of a religious nature but one, or even more striking, J. Day who only printed five non-religious books out of a total of one hundred.

part bookseller, he endeavoured by these means to make ends meet.

So it would be possible to survey group after group of these printers until we reach the most productive group of all—T. Berthelet with over 350 items to his credit, followed *longo intervallo* by W. Seres (187), R. Grafton (180), R. Redman (180), R. Tottel (129), R. Jugge (108), R. Wyer (102) and J. Day (100). As we look at their output we see that they threw their net wide—some catering for one interest, some for another. While each had one or two kinds of books he particularly fancied, on the whole they were more catholic in their choice than were the smaller printers. Berthelet, for example, although he devoted nearly half his output to works of a religious nature, contrived to print over one hundred legal books or pamphlets. To some extent, however, his legal work came to him as King's Printer, and better examples may be seen in the output of R. Redman and R. Wyer.

Redman clearly made legal works his main interest. As we have seen, he was in competition with Pynson and with J. Rastell in this field, but well over half his output went into the provision of all kinds of law-books. The rest of his energies were given over almost entirely to religious works, so that only a handful of books of other kinds came from his press. On the other hand R. Wyer's claim to fame rests on the wide variety of works of general interest that he published. He realized before anyone else that there was a demand for small, cheap little volumes giving information on the weather, the planets and their influence on mankind; on popular medicine; on the properties of a good horse, etc., and at least half his output went into these. As we should expect, most of the rest went into religious works, but, even so, among his other productions are the translation by W. Marshall of *The Defence of Peace* by Marsilius of Padua (1535), a folio of 282 pages, which we know cost £34 to print, and is the finest specimen of his work, and *The C. Hystoryes of Troye* [1540?], the most copiously illustrated of his books, now surviving in the unique copy in the British Museum. Wyer's books for the most part are poor specimens of typography, but that must not blind us to the enterprise and energy he showed in exploiting a hitherto little-worked market in the provision of handy, easily-read, popular guides of various kinds.[1]

The period 1535–57, then, shows the printing trade in England actively exploiting the market to the best of its ability, according to the predilections of individual printers, to their responsibilities as King's Printers, or holders of special patents,[2] and to their material resources. We have now to see what was implied by the production of a book at this time, and how the printers endeavoured to cope with the many practical problems of printing and selling their wares.

[1] For a more detailed account of Wyer's work, see the monograph by H. R. Plomer, *Robert Wyer, Printer and Bookseller* (1897).
[2] See above, p. 117.

CHAPTER IX

THE PRINTING OF THE BOOK

One of the major problems which beset the printer, then as now, was to decide what to print. We have already seen some of the ways in which 'copy' came into his hands, placed there directly by authors, or their patrons, or even by hacks commissioned by the printer to translate, abridge or sometimes to write books for him. As printing became more widespread and a larger reading public developed, the problems confronting the printer became easier of solution, but at their head, however much they changed in some respects, remained the vital question 'what shall I print?'. Suggestions, as well as manuscripts, were offered to the printer, and some of these he felt were worth following up—and there his difficulty began. At times he could not get hold of a copy of the manuscript he was asked to print: at times it was an obviously imperfect text. In the earliest days of printing Caxton tells us from time to time of his difficulties. He found that a text of Tully *Of old age* (1481) was only to be obtained with great difficulty, and 'is comen in to myn honde' with 'grete instaunce, labour and coste';[1] while after he had printed *The Canterbury Tales* (1478) 'one gentylman cam to me and said that this book was not accordyng in many places unto the book that Gefferey Chaucer had made', and that his father had a true copy. This Caxton borrowed, and hastened 'to emprynte it agayn, for to satysfye thauctor where as to fore by ygnouraunce I erryd in hurtyng and dysfamyng his book in dyverce places in settyng in somme thynges that he never sayd ne made, and levyng out many thynges that he made whyche ben requysite to be sette in it'.[2]

This Caxton wrote in his preface to the second edition of 1483, and perhaps it was the lesson he learnt over the text of

---

[1] W. J. B. Crotch, *op. cit.* p. 42.   [2] *Op. cit.* p. 91.

The Canterbury Tales that urged him to take considerable pains when he produced Gower's *Confessio Amantis* in the same year. He managed to obtain at least three manuscripts, each having a different recension, of this poem. He used the third recension for the first half of the work, and then turned to make use of the second and then of the first recensions in the later half.[1] On what principles he worked we are unable to decide, but at any rate it cannot be denied that he took trouble in the matter.[2]

The sequel to this is instructive. In 1532 Berthelet found that a new edition was wanted, but when he came to consider the text he soon found himself in difficulties, for the manuscript copy of the poem to which he had access differed in many particulars from Caxton's print. In the first place some seventy lines of the prologue were different, for Caxton had printed this from the third recension, while Berthelet had a text of the second. Further serious differences appeared as Berthelet compared the two texts. In Caxton's version

there were lefte out in divers places of the warke lines and columes, ye and sometyme holle padges, whiche caused that this moste pleasant and easy auctour coude not well be perceived: for that and chaungeyng of wordes, and misordrynge of sentences wolde have mased hys mynde in redyng that had ben very well lerned: and what can be a greatter blemisshe unto a noble auctour?[3]

In the end Berthelet satisfied his conscience by printing the seventy variant lines of the prologue in his preface, and by inserting all the omitted passages. This done,

although the bokes that be written [i.e. the manuscript copies] be contrarie, yet I have folowed therin the print copie, for as muche as

---

[1] Gower, *Confessio Amantis*, ed. G. C. Macaulay, vol. I, p. clxviii. In *The Library*, Fourth Series, vol. XII (1931), pp. 284–306, Mr Gavin Bone has given evidence which suggests that the text now in Magdalen College, Oxford, was the one used by Caxton for the first 4525 lines, and that it has been 'marked up' by the printer for the guidance of his compositors.

[2] Cf. *STC* 5085, fo. li, where de Worde says that 'I have ryght dilygently serched my dyvers copies' for the missing portion of *The Squire's Tale*.

[3] *STC* 12143, sig. *ii^v^.

it maie serve bothe waies, and because moste copies of the same warke are in printe: but yet I thought it good to warne the reder that the writen copies do not agree with the printed.[1]

Another of our great medieval classics was treated with equal care by Robert Crowley when he first printed *Piers Plowman* in 1550. Before he did so,

beynge desyerous to knowe the name of the Autoure of this most worthy worke, and the tyme of the writynge of the same, I did not onely gather togyther suche aunciente copies as I could come by, but also consult such men as I knew to be more exercised in the studie of antiquities then I myselfe have ben.[2]

Later in the same year he printed two further editions 'wherin are added certayne notes and cotatiens in the margyne, gevynge light to the Reader. And in the begynning is set a brief summe of all the principall matters spoken of in the boke.'[3] A close examination of these three editions convinced Professor Skeat that Crowley had access to four manuscripts at least— testimony enough to the pains he took to produce a correct text.[4] Similarly, John Wayland explains how, after determining to reprint Lydgate's *The Fall of Prynces*, he 'caused the copy to be red over & amended in dyvers places wher it was before, eyther through the wryters or Prynters fault, corrupted. . . . Yet is it not so throughly well corrected as I would have wyshed it, by meanes of lacke of certayne copies and authours which I could not get by any meane.'[5]

The printer's difficulties are put in a more picturesque way by Robert Copland, himself a printer, in his verses appended

---

[1] *STC* 12143, sig. *ii[v]*.
[2] *STC* 19906, sig. *ii[r]*.   [3] *STC* 19907[2], title-page.
[4] W. W. Skeat, ed. *Piers Plowman* (1886), II, p. lxxvi. An examination of the three editions shows that Crowley was continuously correcting the work as it came from the press.
[5] This is taken from the verso of the unique general title-page, now in the Dyce collection. See W. A. Jackson, 'Wayland's Edition of *The Mirror for Magistrates*', *The Library*, Fourth Series, vol. XIII (1932), pp. 155–7.

to an edition of Chaucer's *The assemble of foules*, printed by de Worde in 1530. There he says that he found a manuscript

Layde upon shelfe, in leves all to torne,
With letters dymme, almost defaced clene,
Thy hyllynge rotte, with wormes all to worne
Thou lay, that pyte it was to sene.
Bounde with olde quayres, for age all hoorse & grene,
Thy matter endormed, for lacke of they presence;
But nowe thou arte losed. Go, shewe forth thy sentence.

And where thou become, so ordre they language
That in excuse thy prynter loke thou have,
Whiche hathe the kepte from ruynous domage
In snoweswyte paper, they mater for to save
With thylke same langage that Chaucer to the gave,
In termes olde, of sentence clered newe,
Than methe muche sweter, who can his mynde avewe.[1]

If manuscripts of a purely literary nature gave trouble to the printer, his task was even more difficult when he was endeavouring to print works of learning. Legal manuscripts, for example, were notoriously difficult to get into an accurate form. Nearly all the law-publishers, at one time or another, draw attention to the labour they have been put to, in order to provide a good text. Something of what was involved can be seen in the preface to the first edition [*c.* 1540] of a famous medieval law-treatise by John Britton. The editor of this tells us:

I have (moste gentyll and lovynge redars) imprynted this boke, not without my great charges accordyng to the letter of the more part of my sayd copyes, to the great profyt (I trust) of the studentes of the same.... And though this myne emprynt be not without some fault, or at lest variable from some of your copyes, marvel you not: consyderyng this is the fyrst empryntyng of the same, and some of myn owne copyes have varied from the other, haply by negligence or misprision of yᵉ fyrst wrytars of thes same copyes.[2]

---

[1] T. F. Dibdin, *Typographical Antiquities*, vol. II (1812), p. 279; *hyllyng*: covering.   [2] *STC* 3803, sig. +ii^v.

This (like many other legal works) was a treatise written in Norman-French, and it is easy to see the difficulties it presented, first to the editor in his task of establishing a text, and secondly to the printer in dealing with a manuscript which gave little or no help to the ordinary compositor. The difficulties of both parties were admirably stated in a prefatory note to an edition of *The great charter* [1541?]:

Here hast thou gentyl reader the lawes of Magna Carta with dyvers other olde statutes of this realme, conteyned in thys boke, which though it were ons imprynted afore, yet what through mystakynge of the translator and what through neclygence of the prynter, there escaped sundry apparent faultes, whiche nowe in this seconde prynt are well weedyd out....For yf thys yse [ice] were to be cutte agayne, men shulde fynde it no easy pece of worke to take in hand, specyally when many of the termes as well French as Latyn be so ferre out of ure [use] by reason of theyr antyquyte, that scarsely those that be best studyed in the lawes can understande them, much less then shal suche as come rawly to the redynge therof perceyve what they meane.[1]

This edition was eagerly purchased, so that the work was reprinted in 1542. After this, it had to wait until 1556, when it was reprinted by T. Marsh, with a preface by I. T., which tells us how scarce the work had become in the interim. On 12 June of the same year R. Tottel published his edition, with a preface 'To Gentelmen studious of the lawes of Englande', which is full of interest and information on the law-publisher's problems. He writes:

To stuffe a preface with praise of this boke, or with exhorting you to reading of it, werein a matter not doubtfull to take fond peine not nedefull, and for sundry just respectes not unworthy to be scorned. Onely touching my selfe, and my labours in this and other, I praye ye suffer that I maye somewhat use your pacience, as ye shall alway use my diligence....What so lay in me to do for your profit, ye have alway used it, and shall do (God willing) so longe as I that live able to doo anything. How unperfit the bokes of the

[1] *STC* 9275, sig. +ii[r].

lawes of England were before, what price the scarcenes had raysed, the most part mervelously mangled, and no smale part no wher to be gotten, ther be enow, though I rehearse it not, y^t do freshlye remember, and can truely witnes. Likewise how, sithens I toke in hand to serve your uses, ye imperfections have ben supplied, the price so eased as the scarcenes no more hindreth, but that ye have them as chepe (notwithstanding the common dearth of these times) as when thei were most plentiful; the print much pleasanter to the eye in the bokes of yeres than any y^t ye have ben yet served with; paper and margine as good & as faire as the best, but much better and fairer then the most; no smal nomber by me set forth newly in print y^t before were scant to be found in writing,—I nede not myself to report it. For ye exact truth therof, my copies I might wel folow as thei were, but I could not my self correct them as they ought to be. Therfore in some workes where I could, with my entreatie or cost, procure learneder helpe, ye have them not smally amended: in some other where I could not, yet dare I answer they are nothinge appeired: so as (seeing other mennes default, which should one helpe another, is not my fault, whiche woulde gladly helpe you all) though I shoulde not impudentlye crave thankes, considering my living therby to be my sufficient recompence: yet if I be so bold as to desire that ye contentedly accepte so muche frute as my good will can bringe unto you, I suppose I may seme to ask no wrong at all, and (I trust) no greater righte than your own good natures woulde graunt even undesired, being not altogether undeserved. That obteined, I must nedes think my certain travail, adventured expenses, and al wherin otherwise I may be able to pleasure you, to be wel employed for ye behofe of such men, as your names promise of you. . .

But now to say also somewhat of this present work: albiet it might seme superfluous and nedelesse to have emprinted it now againe so sodeinly, being so lately done in so faire paper and letter by another [i.e. Thomas Marsh]: yet when ye shal wey how in sundry places much here is added out of bokes of good credit, as examined by ye roules of parliament; how eche (where the truth even of the best printes is overmatched by theire faultes not fewe) not a little reformed; the light of pointing adjoyned, ye chapters of statutes truly devided and noted with their due nombers; the alphabeticall table justly ordred and quoted; the leaves not one falsly marked, with mani other help to correct it when (I say) ye shal have weyed both al these by me performed, and the want of these in al other heretofore, I hope your wisedoms wil sone espie that nether I have newe printed it for you causelesse, nor ye shall bye it of me frutelesse. This thought I fit in min own behalf first to have sayd unto you: and so now I cesse further to trouble you from your more earnest studies.[1]

Comment on this is needless. Even when we have made full allowance for a tradesman's temptation to make the most of his wares, and to stress the difficulties incident on their production, we cannot but respect the energy and care shown by printers such as Tottel to produce a worthy text.

Difficulties such as these faced the master-printer in his quest for copy, even when it took the shape of a professionally produced manuscript, or of an earlier print. No such difficulties faced the compositor of such works. He had only to follow his copy: if this was defective, so much the worse for those whose duty it was to provide him with corrected copy of the best version to be obtained. The compositor set up what was put before him, but the matter was not so simple when what was put before him was a manuscript in the author's handwriting. If the copy was 'good', i.e. clearly written and free from interlineations and corrections, all was well, and composition went forward smoothly. But the printer could not rely on receiving such copy, and then difficulties arose. For example, T. Berthelet, in an address which he inserts in a translation of *The table of Cebes the philosopher* [1525–7?], warns the reader that 'if any faute be therin, I knowe well it is mistakyng, for my copie was somewhat combrouse, what for the enterlinyng and yll writyng'.[2] A more excusable instance of how bad copy could be handed in is provided by the work of Sir Richard Morison, a man who was employed as a mouthpiece for the Crown and who was at times forced to write quickly. He tells us how he composed *A lamentation in whiche is shewed that ruyne and destruction cometh of seditious rebellyon*,[3] a work that

---

[1] *STC* 9278, sig. *iv.   [2] *STC* 4891, sig. Ai^v.   [3] *STC* 15185 (1536).

filled 24 quarto pages in print, 'in my botes...in a after none and a nyght. Thowght it be not done as it myght have been done, yet the litel tyme, maketh my great scuse.....I am compelled to do thynges in such haste, that I am ashamed to thynke they be myn when I se them a brode.'¹ Copy produced under such conditions must have presented problems to the compositor, and manuscript drafts of other works by Morison show much revision and interlineation.² Another quick worker, Andrew Borde, confesses that he wrote *The pryncyples of astronomye* [1547?] in four days 'with one olde pen with out mendyng'.³ As this work runs to 58 octavo pages of print, the printer is unlikely to have received a particularly clean piece of copy!

A different kind of difficulty confronting some authors in the days of religious persecution is mentioned by George Joye at the end of his reply to the Bishop of Winchester (1546). There he writes,

it was Easter ere I had your boke, and then had I little tyme, skant xx dayes to read it and to make this answer, and lesse quietnes to wryte. For in dede ye made me a runner about into uncertaine seates and under, and other whiles above uncertaine sower elements.⁴

Another kind of copy is met with in *The seuen sorrowes that women haue when theyr husbandes be deade*. Although this work exists only in an edition of 1565 or later, it contains a prologue of Robert Copland which probably dates from the 1520's. In this Copland is asked to print a satire on women, and his interlocutor is asked:

> have ye any copy
> That a man myght imprynt it therby?

¹ C. R. Baskervill, *The Library*, Fourth Series, vol. XVII (1936), p. 84, quoting from Record Office—SP. 1/113, p. 212.
² *Ibid.* p. 86, and see F. Le V. Baumer, *op. cit.*   ³ *STC* 3386, sig. D vᵛ.
⁴ *STC* 14827, fo. cxciᵛ. Cf. Tyndale's words in similar circumstances in *STC* 24460, *The parable of the wycked mammon* (1528), sig. Kiʳ: 'Be not offendyde moost dere reder, that dyvers thynges are oversene thorowe neclygence in this lytle treatyse. For verely yᵉ chaunce was suche that I mervayle that it is so well as it is.'

To which he replies:

> I have no boke, but yet I can you shewe
> The matter by herte, and that by wordes fewe.
> Take your penne, and wryte as I do say;
> But yet of one thyng, hertely I you pray[e]
> Amende the Englysh somwhat if ye can,
> And spel it true; for I shall tel the, man,
> By my soule ye prynters make such Englyshe,
> So yll spelled, so yll poynted, and so pevyshe,
> That scantly one can rede lynes two.

Copland must have had his work cut out to produce a good text under such conditions, but he probably set about it without those nagging scruples which beset a modern editor. He will do his best, he says; nevertheless,

> I can it not amende
> I wyl no man ther of dyscommende,
> I care no greatly, so that I nowe and then
> May get a peny as wel as I can.[1]

That authors were aware of the necessity for handing in clean copy is illustrated by some remarks made by John Gwynneth in the preface to *A declaration of the state wherein all heretikes dooe leade their lives* (1554). There he tells us how some seventeen or eighteen years earlier he fell sick after a few sheets of a work of his had been printed off, and was forced to go to London

for helpe of mine infirmitee. And before I was able to go abrode, the printer (as I suppose for lacke of worke) beeing where he myght come by my scrowes [scrolls] and papers, printed up the reste of that I had doone, after suche sorte as he coulde pike it out of my fyrst draught therof—before I had perused and dewly examined that I had written, as that and other like thynges dothe alway require.[2]

This valuable reference makes it clear that the 'foul papers' of authors were as dangerous to print without revision as were

[1] *STC* 5734, sig. A ii[r]. [2] *STC* 12558, sig. A i[v].

those of the Elizabethan playwrights of whose scribal habits we are more fully informed. Gwynneth's first printer (J. Herford of St Albans) was storing up trouble for his printing-house when he went ahead in 'suche sorte as he coulde pike it out', without waiting until the work had been 'perused and dewly examined'—a practice evidently common among authors even as early as this.

When at length the copy was ready the printer had to decide whether the demand was sufficiently keen for him to produce the work with the utmost speed or in the greatest possible number. If speed was the all-important factor, two compositors might be set to work. This may have been the reason for the setting of *The vision of Pierce Plowman* 'nowe the seconde tyme imprinted' (1550) from two different sets of types—presumably by two compositors. Again, in 1557 T. Powell printed an edition of Vives, *The instructiõ of a christen womã*. Two founts of type were used, the first two sheets being of Type I, followed by four sheets of Type II. Then Type I was used continually, until the last four sheets were reached, which were set in Type II. This would appear to be a clear case of two compositors at work.[1]

If, however, the printer required a large number of copies for immediate sale, he might have set up the work in duplicate so as to save time,[2] since the custom of the trade apparently forbade the production of more than a limited number of copies from one set of types. The publication of *The First*

---

[1] See F. S. Isaac, *English and Scottish Printing Types, 1535–58* (hereafter described as *Types II*) under Crowley and Powell. For another example see *STC* 3327, *A newe boke of presidentes* [1543]. An earlier example may be seen in *STC* 17102, Lyndewode's *Constitutiones* (Oxford, 1483), where there are two issues of the first 72 leaves, and *STC* 17103 (1496), where de Worde's edition of the same work has also two issues of the first 32 leaves.

[2] See R. B. McKerrow, *An Introduction to Bibliography* (1927), p. 214, n. 1. For other examples, see *STC* 9514–15, *Abbreviamentum statutorum*, where Pynson printed two editions both dated 9 Oct. 1499; and *STC* 4407–8, *An epistle...of godly consolacion*, also printed in two editions by E. Whitchurch, both dated 5 April 1550, and *STC* 7590–1, two editions both dated 23 Jan. 1559, printed by R. Tottel to describe Elizabeth's coronation festivities.

Book of Common Prayer in 1549, for example, necessitated the appearance of a large number of copies very quickly, and Whitchurch and Grafton who held the exclusive privilege for the printing of service-books were hard pressed. Whitchurch printed five editions in 1549: two of these were dated 4 May, and two others 16 June, while Grafton printed four editions, two of them in March. It seems that their presses must have been fully occupied in producing these volumes, and speed was obtained by setting a number of compositors to work simultaneously, or at least in rapid succession.

In setting up his copy the compositor was often unable to space it out so that he exactly filled the sheet or half-sheet at the end of the book, and rather than leave a number of blank pages, the printer resorted to 'fill-ups' of various kinds. This is often frankly avowed; for example, Sir T. Elyot, in his translation of Plutarch's *De capienda ex Inimicis utilitate* [1533?], says: 'To fylle up the padges that els wold have ben voide, I thoghte it shuld nother hurt nor displease to adde hereunto a fewe sayenges howe a man shulde chose and cherysshe a frende',[1] and then proceeds to use up the remaining seven pages of the sheet. Similarly the same writer, at the end of his translation of *The doctrinal of princes* (c. 1534), begins an 'addicion, to fill up vacant pages'[2] in the middle of the last half sheet, and with some sayings of Solomon fills up the remaining space.

A more practical purpose was served in the use made of a spare page of *Pierce the Ploughmans crede* (1553), for the author tells us that 'to occupie this leaffe, which els shuld have ben vacant, I have made an interpretation of certayne hard wordes used in this booke for the better understandyng of it'.[3]

---

[1] *STC* 20052, sig. B v^v.

[2] *STC* 14277, sig. C ii^v. Cf *STC* 18849 (1537); 22820 (1546); 11587 (1553) and 25251 (1553).

[3] *STC* 19904, sig. D iii^v. The colophon follows on D iv^r. Cf. *STC* 2826, Tyndale's *New Testament* (1534), sig. Ee vii^v: 'These thinges have I added to fill up the leffe with all', which is a note on certain terms, such as *Infernus*, *Hell*, etc.

John Bradford, finding that he has four pages blank at the end
of his 'letter... declaring the nature of the Spaniards, and
discovering the most detestable treasons which they have
pretended most falsely against our most noble kingdom of
England' (1555), fills them up with 'A tragicall blast of the
Papisticall trompette for maintenaunce of the Popes kingdome
in Englande'—a stirring series of six line stanzas.[1]

The printer was careful, however, not to fill up every scrap
of space at the end of the book, and usually left the last page
blank on which he printed his device or sign, and also the
colophon—that is, a brief statement containing the name of the
printer and his place of business, and often the date on which
the work was finished at the press. As an example we may take

Imprynted by me Robert Wyer dwellynge at the sygne of saynt
John Evangelyste in saynt Martyns parysshe, in the field of the
Bysshop of Norwytche rentes besyde Charynge crosse. In the yere
of our Lorde God a MCCCCC.XXXII. The viii daye of the moneth
of Octobre.

Before the title-page became well established after 1530,
these colophons gave the inquirer the information he wanted
as to the whereabouts of the printer, and they were never
entirely abandoned by printers, although shorn of much of
their former glory, and often only recording that the volume
was 'At London Printed by John Daye'. Verbose or terse, the
colophons have been of the greatest use to bibliographers in
their efforts to place and date the work of individual printers,
although at times the information they give is misleading, and
the colophon not to be trusted.

Sometimes, for example, in order to avoid trouble with the
authorities, a false colophon was added. We see the beginning
of this practice in the early days of the religious controversy,
when Tyndale found it expedient to issue his books with a
false colophon. Many of them were published as being printed

[1] *STC* 3480, sigs. G vii^r–viii^v.

'at Marlborow [or Marburg] in the lande of Hesse', although we now know that they were actually printed by John Hoochstraten of Antwerp.[1] Furthermore, this false colophon was allowed to stand in later years when English printers reissued some of Tyndale's works. During the 1540's and 1550's a number of books were printed in England by men who called themselves Upright Hoffe, M. Boys, J. Troost, etc. Others used false colophons, such as 'Rome before the Castell of St Angel at the sign of S. Peter', or 'Strassburgh at the sign of the Golden Bibell'. An obviously false colophon might be attached, such as 'Printed at Jerico in the land of Promes by Thome Truuth', to which the British Museum catalogue prosaically adds '[London, 1542]'.

Other colophons are misleading in other ways. De Worde constantly employed J. Skot and R. Copland to print for him, but the books contain de Worde's colophon and device, as in *The Mirror of gold* (1522) which is printed throughout in Skot's types. Similarly *The Royal Book* (1507) was published jointly by de Worde and Pynson. It was printed by de Worde, but a copy in the British Museum has a colophon attributing it to Pynson's press.[2] A similar instance may be observed in the edition of the *Returna Brevium* (1546), printed by N. Hill for H. Smith, R. Toye and J. Waley. Although the type used is solely that of Hill, copies are in existence in which the colophon is that of one of his three partners in the venture.

Again, in 1549 a number of broadside ballads inveighing against Cromwell appeared, and the colophon of several of them stated that they were printed by Richard Banks. When Banks was brought before the Privy Council he denied that they were his, but attributed them to Robert Redman deceased and

---

[1] See R. Steele, 'Hans Luft of Marburg', *The Library*, Third Series, vol. II (1911), pp. 113–31; 'Notes on English Books printed abroad, 1525–48', *Trans. Bibl. Soc.* vol. XI (1912), pp. 189–236, and M. E. Kronenberg, 'Notes on English Printing in the Low Countries (Early Sixteenth Century)', *The Library*, Fourth Series, vol. IX (1929), pp. 139–63.

[2] See F. S. Isaac, *Types I* and *Types II* for examples of this practice, *passim*.

Richard Grafton. This was admitted by Grafton, who had printed 'part of the sayd invectives'.[1] For this Grafton was committed to the porter's ward, and not unreasonably, for there was little security for any printer if his name could be taken in vain in this way.

Lastly, it may be noted that at times a colophon containing a date is reprinted from an earlier edition without change.[2] This is a piece of carelessness on the part of the printer for the most part, but it may mislead, unless something in the book itself betrays its true date.

It must be emphasized, however, that although much has been said here about misleading colophons they form only a small proportion of an otherwise honest trade device. The vast majority of colophons mean what they say, and are to be accepted at their face value.

Last to be set up (as is the custom to-day) were the 'pre-liminaries'—that is, the title-page, dedicatory epistle or letter to the reader, preface, etc. These matters filled the first few pages, and gave the author a chance to explain himself and his work. Such pages have formed the bulk of the evidence brought forward to substantiate many of the statements in this book, so their importance and interest need not be further laboured here. A few words, however, may be said about what went before them—the title-page.

Our earliest books were without title-pages. Here as else-where typographers were greatly influenced by manuscript practice, and Caxton saw no reason to break with this. Hence the nature of his publications had to be gathered from the opening words on the second leaf, such as:

This book is intytled the pylgremage of the sowle, translated oute of Frensshe into Englysshe, whiche booke is ful of devoute maters touchyng the sowle, and many questyons assoyled to cause

[1] E. G. Duff, *Century*, p. xxiv.
[2] See, for example, *STC* 16701, 24354, 24460, while a number of T. Berthelet's books have a compartment bearing the date 1534 which has caused much confusion, since it was used for a number of years.

a man to lyve the better in this world. And it conteyneth fyve bookes as it appereth herafter by Chapytres.[1]

Almost at the end of Caxton's lifetime, however, it was evidently felt that this was not enough, and about 1490 W. de Machlinia printed a book with the first known title-page in English, which read: 'A passing gode lityll boke necessarye & behovefull agenst the Pestilence'.[2] De Worde saw the value of this device, and in *The Chastising of God's Children* [c. 1492] printed a three-line description of the book on the title-page. In later works he developed a title-page which gave the name of the work, sometimes enclosed in a scroll,[3] sometimes above a large woodcut,[4] and as time went on the title-page began to bear the name of the printer, and the date of publication.[5] In this way much that hitherto was contained in a short opening paragraph (as in Caxton's *Pilgrimage of the Soul*), or in the colophon, slowly found itself on the title-page.

This practice seems to have been established about 1530, and after this the printer began to use the title-page as a place whereupon to advertise his wares which he describes as 'very necessary for all relygyous persones',[6] or 'moche necessarye to be redde of al the kynges true subjectes',[7] or more particularly 'necessary and nedeful for every person to loke in that wyll kepe theyr body from syckenesse and dysseases',[8] or 'very behovefull and profytable to all Professours of scyences, Grammaryens, Rethoryciens, Dialectyke, Legystes, Phylosophers and Theologiens',[9] etc. The reader is told 'thou wylt repent that this came not sooner to thy hande',[10] or that 'Truthe is comynge home, longe afore beynge in captyvytye,

---

[1] *STC* 6473, fo. ii[r].   [2] *STC* 4591, fo. i[a].
[3] See, for example, *STC* 6833, *The dyetary of ghostly helthe* (1520).
[4] See *STC* 5136, *The wyse chylde of thre yere olde* [1520?].
[5] See *STC* 12143, Gower's *Confessio Amantis* (1532).
[6] *STC* 17542, *The Myrroure of oure Lady* (1530).
[7] *STC* 23552, *A mustre of scismatyke bysshoppes of Rome* (1534).
[8] *STC* 18217, *The glasse of helthe* [1540?].
[9] *STC* 24112, *The art of memory* [1548?].
[10] *STC* 20061, *The gouernaūce of good helthe* [1530?].

steppe forthe and meete her by the waye',[1] or is abjured to 'refrayne from laughynge'.[2]

The value of the title-page as a means of advertising the book caused many printers to forget the importance of brevity in this respect, and instead they would flood the page with type (destroying its effectiveness in so doing), as may be seen in such a title-page as Berthelet's which reads: *A spirituall consolation, written by John Fyssher, Bishoppe of Rochester, to hys sister Elizabeth, at suche tyme as he was prisoner in the Tower of London. Very necessary, and commodious for all those that mynde to leade a vertuous lyfe. Also to admonishe them to be at all tymes prepared to dye, and seemeth to bee spoken in the person of one that was sodainly prevented by death.*[3] As might be expected, it is religious (and particularly controversial) books that most commonly and freely indulge in this practice, but works of instruction are frequently verbose in their title-pages, as is Robert Record's *The pathway to knowledg, containing the first principles of geometrie, as they may moste aptly be applied unto practise, bothe for use of instrumentes geometricall, and astronomicall and also for projection of plattes in everye kinde, and therfore muche necessary for all sortes of men.*

Geometries verdicte.
All fresshe fine wittes by me are filed
All grosse dull wittes wishe me exiled:
Thoughe no mannes witte reject will I,
Yet as they be, I wyll them trye.[4]

Occasionally, to advertise his wares, the printer placed some rough verses on the title-page, as in de Worde's edition of *Thystory of Iacoby and his twelue sones* [1510?]:

All yonge and olde that lyste for to here
Of dedes done in the olde tyme
By the holy patryarkes that there were

[1] *STC* 13081, *An epistle to the Emperours maiestie* (1538).
[2] *STC* 14842, *The dyalogue betwene Jullius...and saynt Peter* (1535).
[3] *STC* 10899 (1533).   [4] *STC* 20812 (1551).

> Whiche descended of olde Adams lyne
> Often the sonne of grace on them dyd shyne.
> For to rede this story, it wyll do you moche gode
> Of Abrahams sone that was syth Noes flode.[1]

Another example of a more serious nature occurs on the title-page of the anonymous *Treatyse shewynge howe that we ought to haue y* scripture in Englysshe* (Antwerp, 1530). This reads:

> The excusacyon of y* treatyse.
>
> Though I am olde, clothed in barbarous wede,
> Not beynge garnysshed wyth gaye eloquency,
> Yet I tell the trouth yf ye lyst to take hede
> Agaynst theyr frowarde, furious frensy
> Which reken it for a great heresy, etc.[2]

In other books the verses will be found on the back of the title-page, as in *The olde learnynge & the newe* (1537) where we have:

> To the reader.
>
> Some ther be that do defye
> All that is newe, and ever do crye
> The olde is better, awaye wyth the new
> Because it is false, and the olde is true
> Let them thys boke reade and beholde
> For it preferreth the learnynge most olde.[3]

Or again in Langton's brief treatise on physic (1547) we are asked not to despise the book:

> Whiche smal though it seme, contayneth as much
> Of arte to be knowen of them that are wyse,
> As byg myghty bokes agastfull to tuche
> As well for the wayght as for the heavy pryce.
> Reade it therfore all ye that love your healthe,
> Learne here in an houre, elles where in a yere.[4]

---

[1] *STC* 14323, sig. Aiʳ.   [2] *STC* 3021, sig. Aiʳ.

[3] *STC* 20840, sig. Aiᵛ. Cf. *STC* 13439 (1495); or 19904 (1553), sig. Aiᵛ, where the printer says: 'To read strange news, desires manye, Which at my hande they can not have, For here is but antiquitie', and *STC* 5719, printed on p. 133.

[4] *STC* 15205, sig. *iᵛ. Cf. *STC* 5719 (1548), sig. Aiᵛ, and *STC* 10464 (1553), sig. Aiᵛ, both by T. Berthelet.

In their endeavours to attract public attention, printers made use not only of title-pages, but also of ornamental borders, printers' ornaments, or woodcuts. Some of these had a certain artistic merit, but for the most part our early woodcuts are sorry things compared with those of foreign printers. Even so, they had a meretricious attraction and de Worde and others provided them in plenty, with little attention to their relevance or lack of artistry. For those who could not read, or were struggling with the art, there can be no doubt that these drawings, crude as most of them were, had a great sales value, and it is estimated that de Worde used nearly a thousand of these blocks in the course of his printing career.[1]

As the composition of a work went forward, galley pages of proof were struck off from time to time, and the necessary corrections made on them both within and without the printing-house. The earliest proof of an English book yet known is a fragment of *A lytyll treatyse called the boke of lytyll John*, printed by de Worde in 1492. This is printed on one side only, and has no corrections. Of greater interest is the proof sheet of *The Grete herball*, published by P. Treveris of Southwark on 27 July 1526. This sheet is printed on both sides: the outer forme has already been corrected and printed off in its correct state, but the inner forme bears marks of the corrector's red pencil—'watrr' to 'water', 'helped' to 'helpeth', 'the' to 'of', etc. Missing words are supplied and attention is drawn to irregularity in printing by marginal signs.[2] Another example is to be seen in the imperfect sheet from R. Record's *Vrinal of physick*, published by R. Wolfe in 1547. Here again a number of misprints on Dii[r] and Diii[v] are corrected: 'about' to 'aboue' or 'somtymes' to 'fattynes', while words imperfectly inked are noted.[3]

A different kind of proof-sheet is to be seen in the trial

---

[1] The subject is exhaustively dealt with by E. Hodnett in his *English Woodcuts 1480–1535* (Oxford, 1935).
[2] Strickland Gibson, *The Library*, Fourth Series, vol. XII (1932), p. 430.
[3] U.L.C. Syn. 8.54.185.

title-page for Higden's *Polychronicon*, printed for John Reynes by P. Treveris and published in 1527. Within an ornamental border, surmounted by a crown, the original design was in three parts. The first had the title and Reynes's trade-mark in red; the second medallions of the royal arms, the King and the arms of the city of London: the third a large woodcut of St George and the dragon. This layout was evidently not considered satisfactory: the block was cut, and the title *Polycronycon* in much larger red characters was inserted between the second and third compartments, and an enlarged form of the trade mark placed at the bottom of the page. A far more striking effect was thus obtained, and this version was adopted for the edition.[1]

A few fragments such as these are all that seem to have survived, but they afford precious evidence of the actual corrections themselves which otherwise we should have to infer from statements by authors and others, and from the fact that different copies of the same book show that the sheets were corrected while they were being printed off. For instance, Dr Curt Bühler has shown that 'someone in Caxton's shop would change the set-up of a line or two or correct an obvious error after a number of copies of a quire had come off the press',[2] and this practice persisted throughout the period and beyond.

Such corrections as these were probably the work of members of the printer's staff, but outside correctors were also involved as may be seen from the agreement of 1523 between Pynson and Palsgrave, concerning the printing of the latter's French grammar. The agreement declared that Palsgrave contracted to deliver to Pynson 'hys copye corrected...that

[1] Strickland Gibson, *op. cit.* p. 430.
[2] *The Library*, Fourth Series, vol. XVII (1936), p. 62. For examples in this period, see the two copies of *STC* 1537, Bartholomew's *De proprietatibus rerum* (1535), in the University Library at Cambridge. The title-page of one reads 'Impressrois' and gives the number of pages as ccclxxxvi. The other reads 'Impressoris', and numbers the pages correctly as ccclxxxviii. *STC* 15271–3 has three states of the title-page, with variant readings of the word 'majestie'; *STC* 15274 has also two variant title-pages, while *STC* 18111–3 gives the catchword on sig. A 4ᵛ as 'brink', 'brinke' and 'brynke'.

the worke shall not be stopped on hys behallff', while Pynson agreed to 'suffer the said John Palsgrave or hys assignes to correct the proff, or ever that he for any hast print the hole nomber off any off the saide levys'. This valuable statement helps us to understand the early printing practice which recognized the right of the author to oversee the printing of his work. Abroad, Erasmus had shown much concern over the corrections of his work, and had even gone to live with the printer for a time so as to ensure a correct version.[1] In so far as the printer might (and frequently was) engaged in setting up work in a language unknown to him,[2] it was essential that a competent scholar should attend at the press, to oversee the proofs as they appeared. Thus when he was setting up a difficult legal text, the *Abbreviamentum statutorum* (1499), Pynson required the three members of the Inner Temple for whom he was printing copies to 'gyve attendaunce in Correctyng, examenyng ev[er]y lefe after the pryntyng of the seid bokes when they were there to required'.[3] Similarly, John Bale stated that 'three learned correctors which took all pains possible' were at the disposal of the printer of *The Ymage of both churches*, so that an accurate text might be set up. It was this concern to secure accuracy that caused careful authors to go to considerable pains to watch over the progress of their work. Sir Thomas More wrote to Erasmus in December 1515 to tell him that 'as soon as Christmas is over, Linacre is going to send what he is translating from Galen [i.e. *de sanitate tuenda*] to Paris to be printed there. Lupset will go with it, and stay to correct the press'.[4] While he was in Paris on this business, Lupset also supervised the printing of the second

[1] P. S. Allen, 'Erasmus' Relations with his Printers', *Trans. Bibl. Soc.* vol. XIII (1916), pp. 307, 309.

[2] See, for example, the absurd errors in the Latin of the Lord's Prayer, as set by J. Notary in his edition of the St Alban's Chronicle (1515), *STC* 10000, fo. xxiii^r.

[3] H. R. Plomer, 'Two Lawsuits of Richard Pynson', *The Library*, New Series, vol. X (1909), pp. 130–3.

[4] J. A. Gee, *The Life and Works of Thomas Lupset* (New Haven, 1928), p. 59.

edition of More's *Utopia*. Similarly in England authors or their agents acted as correctors. Alexander Barclay, at the end of his translation of *The Ship of Fools* (1509), tells us that he has corrected the proof, but by oversight and negligence, in addition to the imperfect workmanship of the printers, who work 'hedelynge and in hast', some faults have nevertheless escaped notice.

What could happen when correction of proof was omitted or carelessly done may be seen from two earlier examples. The first comes from de Worde's edition of *The Golden Legend* (1498). In setting up the colophon, the compositor omitted a whole line from his copy-text, thus making nonsense of the entire colophon. The error remained unnoticed in all subsequent editions—three by de Worde and one by J. Notary. De Worde's workshop was also responsible for another blunder when it set up an edition of Lydgate's poem, *The hors, the sheep, and the ghoos* (1500), from a copy of Caxton's text, without noticing that one leaf was missing![1]

Closer supervision of the compositors was obviously necessary, and this was sometimes given. For example, the *Apothegmata* of Erasmus were translated by R. Taverner, and contain the colophon: 'Printed in Flete strete very diligently under the correction of the selfe Richard Taverner, by Richard Bankes.'[2] At the close of this period we find similar conditions prevailing. Jasper Heywood, in the preface to his translation of Seneca's *Thyestes* (1560), complains bitterly that in issuing a second edition of his translation of the *Troas*, the printer, Richard Tottel, had 'corrupted all', despite the fact that Heywood had 'perusde their prooves the fyrst tyme'. His verses run:

> For when to sygne of Hand and Starre[3]
> I chaunced fyrst to come,

---

[1] For an example of a careless and inexpert compositor's work, see J. Notary's edition of *The lyfe of saynt Barbara* (1518), *passim*.

[2] *STC* 10445 (1540).

[3] The Hand and Star was the sign of Tottel's printing-house.

To Printers hands I gave the worke:
 by whome I had suche wrong,
That though myselfe perusde their prooves
 the fyrst tyme, yet ere long
When I was gone, they wolde agayne
 the print therof renewe,
Corrupted all: in suche a sorte,
 that scant a sentence trewe
Now flythe abroade as I it wrote.[1]

What was said by Barclay and Heywood concerning the
printer was repeated in various ways by many authors of this
period.[2] One of the most extreme of such critics was John
Bale, who prefaces his work *The Ymage of both churches* (1550),
by commenting on 'two cruell enemies' who have hindered
him, and goes on to say that 'the printers are the fyrst, whose
heady haste, negligence, and covetousnesse commonly cor-
rupteth all bokes'.[3] Another vigorous critic was John Hooper,
who in his *A godly confession* [1551?] speaks of 'wordes and
sillables evil placed...both agaynste my copye and the state
and argumente of my matter', but adds resignedly that 'such
fautes escapeth some times, contrary as wel to the printers as
the authours mynde'.[4]

A more generous attitude to the printer is displayed in
William Bullein's preface to *The gouernement of healthe* [1558].
The author says that since

I have had no conference with others, nor longe tyme of pre-
meditation in studie...it can not be but that many things have
missed in the print, as in folio lii. the XVIII. line, reade sighe for

---

[1] *STC* 22228, sig. *viii*, and see *vi* for more criticism of 'how Prynters
mys'.
[2] See for example, *STC* 770, 3549, 16936, 24456, etc.
[3] *STC* 1299, sig. aii*. Cf. 10752, sig. *i*. *The conspiracie of Catiline* (1557)
where T. Paynell says that the former edition was 'here and there (thorough
unlearned correctors) somewhat mangled and corrupted'.
[4] *STC* 13757, sig. Aiv*. Hooper, in 1550, had written *STC* 13763, *An
ouersight and deliberacion vpon the prophete Jonas*, which had a long list of
errata on sig. 38*. These were corrected in a second edition of the same year.

sight, etc. At the next impression such amendes shalbe made, that both silable and sentence shal be diligently kept in trew order, to thy contentacion.[1]

Although in accordance with the growing practice, authors blame the 'naughty printer', it must be admitted that the printer was not so grossly indifferent to accuracy as some authors would have us believe. Many of them had an official corrector whose duty it was to read the proof and get it into an accurate state. Palsgrave, in his *Lesclarcissement*, speaks of 'my corrector'[2] as if in contradistinction to the printer's agent, while on the other hand we know that William Baldwin, a well-known literary figure, held an official position as 'corrector' for Edward Whitchurch.

A welcome picture of a corrector's activities is given by George Joye, a Protestant controversialist in exile, who had at one time been a close ally of Tyndale. Joye was commissioned by an Antwerp publisher to go over the text of Tyndale's *New Testament* and make any necessary corrections. This Joye did, so thoroughly as to call forth Tyndale's vigorous rebukes in the preface of his new edition of 1534. Tyndale there accused Joye of going beyond his duty as a corrector, animated 'by a lytle spyse of covetousnes and vayne glorie (two blynde gydes)'. To this Joye replied in *An apologye* (1535) which reads:

> The printer came to me agen and offred me .ii. stuuers and a halfe for the correcking of every sheet of the copye, which folden con-tayneth .xvi. leaves, and for thre stuuers which is .iiii. pense halpenny starling, I promised to do it. So that in all I had for my labour but .xiiii. shylyngis flemesshe which labour had not the goodnes of the deede and comon profyte and helpe to the readers compelled me more then the money, I wolde not have done yᵗ for .v. tymes so miche, the copy was so corrupt....[3]

---

[1] *STC* 4039, sig. S iv[r]. Bullein kept his word, see *STC* 4040.
[2] And see above, p. 219 n. 3, which speaks of 'unlearned correctors'.
[3] *STC* 14820, sig. C v[v].

The Antwerp printer evidently did not trust his own resources, and so got in a learned outside corrector to do the work, just as F. Regnault, the Paris printer, by mouth of Grafton and Coverdale petitioned Cromwell to be allowed to continue to sell books in England, 'so that hereafter he prynte no moo in the English tong, onlesse he have an English man that is lerned to be his corrector'.[1]

Most of the work of the corrector, of course, has left no trace. His business was to produce an accurate text, and the more successful he was the less we are aware of his existence. But occasionally we come across his work, most obviously in the lists of errata, or of 'Faultes escaped', which fill up the last leaf of many works. At times we are asked to overlook these 'fautes escaped in the printyng through overmoche haste',[2] or are told that

the errours escaped in printyng, though every diligent reader of him selfe may easely correct, yet in the behalfe of the unlearned sort, I have added the corrections of theim to the ende of the boke, where every man that listeth to loke may be satisfyed, both in the wordes and sentences of the faultes escaped.[3]

Another author bids us before reading his work to 'mende the fautes escaped wyth thy penne, begynnynge with the cyphers on the toppe of the pages...'.[4] Lastly, we may note the way in which Robert Record, in his *Castle of knowledge* (1556), throws the onus on the reader of seeing that all is correct before he begins to read. He writes:

Though faultes ofte times doo muche abounde,
When men doo leaste suche chaunce suspecte:

---

[1] See the full text above, p. 32. Cf. the correction of the 'Matthew Bible' (Antwerp, 1537) which was made by John Rogers, a disciple of Tyndale.
[2] *STC* 20116, sig. A ix^r. (1544); 7660, sig. A iii^v (1545); 19926, sig. A viii^r (1560).
[3] *STC* 12427, verso of title-page (1557); 7659, sig. A iii^v (1538).
[4] *STC* 26140, sig. *4^r (1555). Cf. *STC* 3288 [1520?], sig. C v^r where the reader is asked 'to correcte this boke with your penne or knyfe'.

> Yet good redresse maye soone be founde,
> If faultes bee spied and full detecte.
> But who that will in woorke proceede,
> And seeke not firste the faultes tamend,
> I promise him smalle gaine indeede,
> Thoughe truthe to seeke hee do pretend:
> Therefore amend if thou will speede
> These faultes, ere thou on me doo reade.[1]

Not all the care that authors and correctors took could ensure a perfectly accurate text, and subsequent editions frequently advertise the fact that they are 'corrected' or 'newly revised'. Much of this, no doubt, is only a publisher's flourish to attract custom for his new wares, but a comparison of the two editions usually shows that the printer has some right to state that the second or subsequent edition is 'newly and most trewly corrected', or 'newly revised, corrected and printed', or 'amended in many places'.[2] Sometimes the printer is more explicit, as the title-page of the second edition of *Wicklieffes Wicket* (1548) shows. The new edition claims to be 'faythfully overseene and corrected, after the originall and first copie, the lacke wherof was cause of innumerable and shamfull erroures in the other edicion [1546]. As shall easyly appeare to them that lyste to conferre the one wyth the other.'[3]

The function of an editor in preparing his copy for a reprint is laid down by Robert Copland in a verse at the end of de Worde's edition of *Guyscarde and Sygysmonde* (1532). Copland says to the book:

> And yf thou happe to reimpressyon,
> Desyre them the whiche shall be the cause
> Though they be yll, that no transgressyon

---

[1] *STC* 20796, sig. &vi^r. There follows 24 lines of faults, and in the 'preliminaries' on sig. aviii^r Record is forced to add six or seven 'faultes omitted out of the corrections'.

[2] See, for example, *STC* 6000, 6001 and 6002 Cranmer's *Defence...of the Sacrament* (1550).

[3] *STC* 25591^a. Cf. *STC* 23208, sig. Ai^r; 23966, sig. Ai^r.

By them nor theyrs be made in ony clause.
Correccyon, I agre; but there a pause.
Folowe your copy, and lette thamendynge alone
He may yll mende two tonges that can but one.[1]

'Follow your copy and leave emendations alone!'—excellent
advice; but, as Copland realized, not everyone was willing to
observe the narrow line between correcting and emending.

At times, such unwillingness was a virtue, for in the fierce
competition which existed among printers publishing rival
editions of well-known legal or scholastic works little heed was
oftentimes paid to accuracy. The irritation that this caused to
printers with higher standards is well illustrated by the 'letter
to the reader' written by Pynson and appended to his 1525
edition of *Lytylton tenures newly and moost truly correctyd
and amendyd*. Pynson had apparently been the only publisher
of the *Tenures* for some thirty years, and he did not relish the
intrusion of another (and as he held, inferior) printer on his
domain. So he prefaces his new edition with the following:

Greetings to his reader from Richard Pinson,
Printer to his Majesty the King.

Behold, Fair Reader, Littleton now meets you (if I mistake not)
in more chastened mood. I have taken care that he is published
from my press not only in a more correct form, but also in more
elegant type than (when) he escaped from the hands of Robert
Redman, but more properly Rudeman, because among a thousand
men you will not easily find one more unskilled. In fact, I wonder
why he can now call himself a printer, unless perchance the devil,
when he made a cobbler into a sea captain, also made him a printer.
Formerly the scoundrel professed himself a bookseller as skilled as
ever sprang forth from Utopia, well knowing that a thing can be
called a book when it merely has the appearance of being one and
little else. Yet the villain has dared to promise that by his skill he
can print truly and faithfully all the revered and holy laws of
England. If you will read Littleton (presuming on your care and

---

[1] Sig. Dii^v (Roxburghe Club facsimile, 1818).

diligence) you will see at once whether he is speaking falsehood or truth. Farewell.[1]

Once he had got his book into its final proof state the printer had to decide the two all-important questions—how many copies should he print and at what price should he sell the work. An experienced modern publisher once told me that if he could have solved these two questions accurately throughout his career he would now be a rich man, and certainly the problem confronting the sixteenth-century publisher was at least as difficult of solution as that of his twentieth-century successor, aided as the latter is by all the devices of modern sales organization. Pynson or Berthelet had to make the best guess they could, and unfortunately but few figures have survived to show what these guesses were. In the earliest days of printing on the Continent Dr Haebler has estimated that between four and five hundred copies would be a fair average for a book published between 1480-90.[2] Whether Caxton worked to such a figure we have no means of telling, but it is not unreasonable to think that in a comparatively poor country such as England he did not venture on editions of this size in some of his major works such as *The Golden Legend* or the *Morte Darthur*.

His immediate successors rapidly developed the custom of printing books in a smaller format, often consisting of a comparatively few pages only.[3] The risk they took was much reduced, and Dr Haebler's figure was probably frequently exceeded by them, as the few figures I have been able to collect will suggest. Before discussing these, however, it is necessary to emphasize the fact that religious manuals and the Scriptures fall into a class of their own, and were printed in

---

[1] *STC* 15726, sig. A i[v]. With this may be compared de Worde's milder rebuke of P. Treveris who printed Whittinton's *De heteroclitis nominibus* so badly that he ruined the sense, which is restored in de Worde's edition of 1533. *STC* 25477, sig. A i[v], and compare a similar complaint of de Worde in *STC* 25508.

[2] *Inkunabelkunde*, pp. 142-5, quoted by McKerrow, *op. cit.* p. 131.

[3] After 1500, for example, de Worde printed mainly in quarto form, and many of his successors seldom, if ever, launched out into folios.

much larger editions than other books.[1] To consider Tyndale's *New Testament* only. We find that an edition was printed at Cologne in 1525 consisting of 3000 volumes in octavo, while a similar number in quarto and octavo were printed at Worms the next year.[2] Two years later, Hans van Ruremond, a Dutchman, printed an edition of 1500 copies, of which he brought 500 into England, while about the same time an Antwerp printer sent 700 copies to F. Birckman, a London stationer, for sale.[3]

Early in the next decade these were all sold (presumably most of them in England), and the demand continuing, the Dutch printers wished to exploit it to the full. Tyndale was urged to revise his edition, but was so slow in doing this that an edition (said to be of 2000 copies) was printed from the old text and sold at once (1534). In the meantime George Joye was at work correcting Tyndale's text, and his version was published in August of the same year. To Joye's fears that the edition would never sell, his publishers replied that if Tyndale printed 2000 and they a like number, 'what is so little a number for all England?'[4]

Publication continued apace. We know of two editions in 1534, four in 1535, and five in 1536, and so the steady stream went on. By this time it was possible to print the Scriptures in England, and T. Godfray's folio edition of 1536 opened a new era, while in 1538 a new revision by Coverdale appeared. Unfortunately, we have no knowledge of the size of these editions, but there is no reason to think they were not substantial, and this view is supported by what we know of the publication of 'Matthew's version' of the Bible in 1537, where the publisher tells us that he has had 1500 copies printed,[5] and that he originally hoped to sell it for as much as fifteen shillings apiece.

[1] A. W. Pollard, *Records of the English Bible* (1911), p. 4.
[2] Duff, *Printers*, p. 223.   [3] Duff, *op. cit.* p. 218.
[4] Duff, *op. cit.* pp. 229–30.
[5] J. A. Kingdon, *Incidents in the Lives of T. Poyntz and R. Grafton* (1895), part ii, p. 29.

To turn from editions of the Bible to editions of ordinary works. Here, unfortunately, our information is scanty, but what there is, is reasonably consistent. A schedule attached to a lawsuit of Pynson's reveals that he printed at least 600 copies of five books, including *Dives and pauper* and the *Fall of princes*, and service-books such as *Festial*. He also printed 1000 copies of a book called *Jornalles*. This, Mr A. W. Pollard took to be the English for 'Diurnale'—one of the smaller service-books.[1] Again in 1499 he printed two octavo editions of the *Abbreviamentum statutorum*,[2] one of which was done for three members of the Inner Temple who took 409 copies. Whether this was the whole of the edition is not known—the fact that he published another edition the same day suggests that this was a special edition, limited by the needs of his clients, and that he also produced a trade edition at the same time.[3]

In 1519 Pynson entered into an agreement with William Horman, Vice-Provost of Eton, to print for him a book called *Vulgaria*, consisting of aphorisms and sentences in English and Latin, compiled by Horman for the use of his pupils. It made a substantial quarto of 650 pages, and Horman asked for an edition of 800 copies, which Pynson agreed not to reprint for five years, without permission.[4] Another contract made by Pynson concerned the printing of Palsgrave's *Lesclarcissement de la langue francoyse*, a folio of over 1000 pages. The final form of the indenture[5] is dated 18 January 1524, and contains in it a clause limiting the number of copies to be printed to 750. Pynson apparently printed only the first two parts of 118 pages. The third part was printed by John Hawkins, and finished on 18 July 1530.

---

[1] H. R. Plomer, 'Two Lawsuits of Richard Pynson', *The Library*, New Series, vol. x (1909), pp. 115-33.

[2] *STC* 9514, 9515.   [3] See above, p. 217.

[4] Pynson never reprinted, but de Worde did so in 1530.

[5] No less than three drafts are in existence. See *L. and P. Henry VIII*, vol. III, no. 3680; IV, no. 39. The third draft is in the hand of T. Cromwell, corrected by Palsgrave.

Both these books were in the nature of 'commissioned works' and belonged to the author, the printer being paid for his work and not allowed to sell copies on his own account. Pynson had six copies for presentation purposes, and so strict was Palsgrave's hold on the rest that we find a certain Stephen Vaughan, sometime of the diplomatic service, writing in desperation to his patron Cromwell, asking him to assist him to obtain a copy. He adds that he learns that Palsgrave has told Pynson to sell only to those he names, lest his profit as a teacher should be diminished, and that when he approached Palsgrave in London he refused to sell him a copy.[1]

A very different work, William Roy's *Rede me and be nott wrothe* [1528],[2] was printed at Strasburg by J. Schott as part of the campaign directed against Wolsey. In a letter to the Cardinal, written in October 1528, Hermann Rinck says on oath that Schott has admitted to the printing of a thousand copies of the work in a format of six sheets, and also to another edition of a thousand copies in nine sheets, both at the order of Roy and Tyndale.[3] Another controversial work—the *Nun's book*—we are told by Cranmer, was printed in an edition of 700 copies, Dr Boking taking 500, leaving the remainder to J. Skot the printer to sell.[4] No other figures for this period are known to me, and very few for a long while after, so that they may be worth quoting as a help to giving a general, if sketchy, picture. In 1576 Lambard's *Perambulation of Kent* was published in a quarto edition of 600 copies, while the dedication

[1] *L. and P. Henry VIII*, vol. IV, no. 5459.

[2] *STC* 21427. In a preface to the second edition of 1546 we are told, 'this boke was prynted in the Cardynalles tyme whiche wan he harde that it was done, caused a certayne man whome I coulde name if I lysted, to bye them all uppe, that they shulde not come abrode to uttre their moste wycked feates that he and all those of that pestylent secte ded than' (*STC* 21428, sig. Aiiʳ).

[3] *L. and P. Hen. VIII*, vol. IV, part ii, no. 4810.

[4] *Ibid.* vol VI, p. 648. Elizabeth Barton, the 'Nun of Kent', who declared herself to be a 'poor wench without learning' was used as a tool by Bocking, a monk of Christ Church, Canterbury, and others to defend the Catholic religion against the Protestants. She was executed in April 1534. No copy of the book appears to have survived.

to John Dee's *General and rare memorials pertayning to the perfecte arte of nauigation* the next year says that only 100 copies were printed of this folio work. Even the First Folio of Shakespeare (1623) is thought by some scholars to have been issued in an edition of 600 copies only.

It is true, of course, that by the latter half of the sixteenth century larger editions than these were allowed, for from 'A Copie of certen orders concerning printing', made by the Stationers' Company in 1588 we learn that

> no book is to be printed in numbers exceeding 1250 or 1500 in one impression except nonpareille and brevier,[1] and four impressions a year of the Grammar and four of the Accidence severally in quarto and octavo, and also all Prymers and Catechisms, and that every one of these and of all books in nonpareille and brevier do not exceed 2500 or 3000 copies at the most, except statutes and proclamations.[2]

In other words, the ordinary edition of books, except certain religious and educational ones, was limited to 1500 copies or less. This was in order to protect the workmen, and was made at a time when the demand for books was far greater than it had been say fifty years before. We shall not be far wrong in thinking that very special reasons were required to persuade a printer to print more than 600–700 copies of any ordinary work in the first seventy-five years of printing in England.

As to the rate at which the printing-house worked we are very inadequately informed. Caxton yields a little information, for he tells us that the *Cordiale*, a folio volume of 76 printed leaves (152 pages) was put to press on 3 February 1479, and was finished by the evening of 24 March—that is, seven weeks later. If we allow for Sundays and a few Saints' Days this would mean that Caxton's workmen composed four pages (one sheet) of the edition per day. The same rate was observed in the printing of *The myrrour of the worlde*, but other of

---

[1] I.e. Bibles, etc.
[2] E. Arber, *op. cit.* vol. II, p. 43. And see vol. II, p. 883, and vol. v, p. liii.

Caxton's productions appear to have come off the press much more slowly.

The only other record known to me in this period is supplied by the agreement, dated 1524, made between R. Pynson and John Palsgrave for the printing of *Lesclarcissement de la langue francoyse*. By this Pynson agreed to print a sheet on both sides (four folio pages) each day, and Palsgrave bound himself not to fail in sending the necessary copy.[1] Caxton and Pynson, therefore, seem to be agreed that a sheet a day was a possible output.[2]

To this we may add the interesting fact that in his investigation of the output of the Elizabethan printer, Edward Allde (1548–1628),[3] Dr R. B. McKerrow came to the conclusion that Alde also printed one sheet a day, and that there was 'a curious agreement' between this and the fact that three books of the seventeenth century were each known to have been printed at this rate. I therefore conclude that the ordinary printing-house of this period worked normally at the rate of one sheet a day.

When we turn from numbers to prices of books we are almost as much in the dark. A very few individual prices are known to us, some because they are stated in print on the volume itself; others because they are written in a contemporary hand on the title-page, or elsewhere; others that are mentioned as the price at which the book changed hands at the stationers, or as the value attached to the book in inventories of various kinds. The first group present no great difficulty of interpretation—all we have to regret is their comparative rarity. For example, we find printed on the title-page of Part III of *La Graunde Abbregement de le Ley* (J. Rastell, 1516) the words, 'The price of the whole boke (xl s.) which boke contayneth

---

[1] *L. and P. Henry VIII*, vol. III, no. 3680; vol. IV, no. 39.

[2] Between 14 and 23 January 1559, R. Tottel printed an account of the progress of Queen Elizabeth through the City. This was a work of five quarto sheets, so that if we allow for the time necessary to compile the account and for a Sunday, the rate here would also be somewhere about one sheet a day.

[3] *The Library*, Fourth Series, vol. X (1930), pp. 139 ff.

iii grete volumes'. The work is a folio of 798 leaves of con-tracted Law-French in a small type, and must have been a considerable tax on Rastell's printing-house.

Another work to bear its price clearly stated upon it was *A necessary doctrine and erudition for any Christen man*, printed by T. Berthelet in 1543. This work, known as 'the King's Book', was part of Henry's religious propaganda, and was issued in quarto and octavo format many times during that year. The quarto editions varied from 180 to 228 pages, and some of them bear the words: 'This boke bounde in paper bourdes or claspes, not to be solde aboue xvj d.',[1] while the octavo edition of 312 pages similarly bound was to be sold 'not aboue' twelve,[2] thirteen[3] or fourteen[4] pence. An edition was also printed by J. Mayler the same year, 'not to be solde aboue xij d.'.[5] These prices are a fair reflection of the current rates for the ordinary run of books.

Similarly, *The Book of Common Prayer* of 1549 onwards frequently bears in it the royal edict concerning its price, which runs as follows: 'No maner of persone shall sell the present Booke unbounde above the price of two shillynges and twopence. And bound in Forell for ii s. x d; and not above. And the same bounde in Shepes Lether for iii s. iii d., and not above. And the same bounde in paste or in boordes, in Calais Lether, not above the price of iiii s. the piece.'[6]

The price of Bibles was also controlled, and is sometimes stated, as in R. Jugge's quarto edition of the *New Testament* of 1552, where we find on the back of the title-page of some copies an authorization of the King's Council limiting the price of the book to 22 pence 'in paper and unbound', as a 'reasonable and convenient' one.[7] The octavo edition was to be sold for one shilling, and one in a smaller size (16mo) could be bought for ninepence.

[1] *STC* 5168, sig. e6ᵛ. The price of unbound stock was 12 d.
[2] *STC* 5173, sig. v4ʳ.
[3] *STC* 5172, sig. v4ʳ. The last 'i' of xiii d. is struck out by pen in the U.L.C. copy.   [4] *STC* 5171.   [5] *STC* 5175.
[6] *STC* 16268, sig. T6ᵛ.   [7] *STC* 2867, sig. A iᵛ.

Prices on title-pages or elsewhere in contemporary hands are of interest, but can only be used with caution. They may represent the price charged by the bookseller, or they may not. We have no means of telling, save in very rare instances where the price of the book in St Paul's Churchyard happens to be known. Such is the case with the *Paraphrases of Erasmus upon the New Testament*, published in two volumes, 1548–9. At the end of volume two of one copy is written p̄rm̄ huius libri. vi s., while we know from the 1548 Churchwarden's accounts of St Margaret's, Westminster, that they paid five shillings for the half-part of the *Paraphrases*.[1]

Our most extensive and valuable information, however, comes from booksellers' accounts and definite statements of various kinds concerning the cost of books. A few account-books of this period have survived: the first one of four pages only of about 1510; the second that of the Oxford bookseller, John Dorne, which contains 1851 entries of sales in 1520; the third a fragmentary document of 1535 (perhaps from de Worde's shop), and fourthly a few pages of John Day's ledger of 1557.

Of these Dorne's accounts are the most illuminating. Although a number of his entries are not very helpful, since they lump a number of items together, there are a large number of individual prices which are most useful. For example, we learn that the ruling price in Oxford at that time for broadsheets of ballads and the like was a halfpenny or a penny; that a single leaf of carols, or of popular lives of saints, or prognostications, or books on carving or husbandry all cost a penny. Similarly we can see the cost of many sorts of books from the rhyme of *Robin Hood* for 2d., or the romances of *Sir Eglamour*, or *Robert the Devil* for 3d. or 3½d., and so up to the massive volume of *The Golden Legend* for 3s. 4d. or 3s. 8d., or Lyndewode's *Constitutions* bound in leather for 6s. 8d.[2]

[1] T. H. Darlow and H. F. Moule, *Hist. Cat. of the printed editions of Holy Scripture* (1903), vol. I, pp. 37–8.
[2] F. Madan, 'The Day-book of John Dorne', *Oxford Historical Society, Collectanea*, vol. I (1885), pp. 71–178. See also H. Bradshaw's comments on this in his *Collected Papers* (1889), pp. 420–50.

As might have been expected at Oxford, the scholastic text-books of Stanbridge, Whittinton, Sulpitius and others were much in demand, and a study of the prices charged for such books shows that Dorne was selling them at the rate of two sheets (or gatherings) for a penny. Thus Stanbridge's *Parvula*, a quarto of 16 leaves in two sheets, cost a penny, as did his *Vulgaria*; and similarly Whittinton's *De Synonymis* or his *Declinationes* sold at the same rate.

Not only school-books but other books appear to have been valued at approximately this rate. An analysis of some 35 items of Dorne's list which can be identified with reasonable certainty, shows that 17 of them were sold at two sheets a penny, and 27 of them at rates varying from $1\frac{1}{2}$ to $2\frac{1}{2}$ sheets a penny.

The second account of most value is that of 1535. This gives us the prices of 170 items, of which the school-books and a number of other works are sold at prices which agree very well with those in Dorne's list. Unfortunately, a large number of items cannot be closely enough identified to enable us to know exactly what edition was being offered for sale. For instance, there is a copy of *Antibossicon* priced at fourpence, but it is uncertain whether it is the work written by W. Horman, or that of W. Lily. Both were published by R. Pynson in 1521, and since Lily's work contained 46 pages and that of Horman 120, it is probable that it was a copy of Lily that was sold.[1]

The other two fragments of account-books of about 1510[2] and 1557[3] add a little additional information, but do not alter the general picture, nor do the two book-bills of Katherine Parr, dated 1544 and 1548.[4]

A different, but valuable source of information, is to be

---

[1] W. A. Jackson, 'A London bookseller's ledger of 1535', *The Colophon*, New Series, vol. I (1936), pp. 498–509.

[2] E. G. Duff, 'A Bookseller's Accounts, *circa* 1510', *The Library*, New Series, vol. VIII (1907), pp. 256–66.

[3] Egerton MS. 2974, fos. 67, 68.

[4] F. Rose-Troup, 'Two Book Bills of K. Parr', *The Library*, Third Series, vol. II (1911), pp. 40–8.

found in the schedule of 1510 attached to a suit brought by Richard Pynson against a certain John Russhe 'of the cittie of London', who appears to have bought books in bulk so that he might 'sende them unto the countre to sell'.[1] He defaulted in his payments to Pynson, and in justification of his claim, Pynson set out the names, prices and numbers supplied of a dozen or so volumes, many of which can be exactly identified. There were five folio volumes, viz. *The Canterbury Tales* (1490); Aesop's *Fables* [1500?]; Bartholomew's *De proprietatibus rerum* (1495); *Dives and pauper* (1493); and Boccaccio's *The falle of princis*, translated by Lydgate (1494). The prices of each of these 'redy bounde the pece' are given, and so it is possible to estimate the average number of leaves (or sheets) supplied for a penny. Here again, as we found from Dorne's accounts, the purchaser would get a little over two sheets for a penny, and if we remember that this was for a bound volume, and allow a little for the cost of binding, we arrive at the figure of two to three sheets a penny. Similarly, three quarto volumes provide us with the same figure, so that we may feel fairly assured that we have a reasonably accurate yardstick by which to estimate the price of any early sixteenth-century book.

Lastly, some information can be obtained from inventories such as that made of his library in 1556 by Sir William More.[2] Sir William gives the titles of many books, English and foreign, and attaches a price to most of them. This is not necessarily the price he paid for them and may be only his valuation at that date. Many of them, however, appear to be priced at the current market rate, so that the Bible is valued at ten shillings and the New Testament at two; while Chaucer's *Works* are entered at five shillings, as are Fabyan's *Chronicles*. At the other extreme, entries like Barclay's *Fifth Eclogue*, or *A book of medicine for horses* seem properly valued at a penny. There-

[1] H. R. Plomer, 'Two Lawsuits of Richard Pynson', *The Library*, New Series, vol. x (1909), pp. 115–33.

[2] J. Evans, 'Extracts from the Private Account Book of Sir W. More', *Archaeologia*, vol. xxxvi (1855), pp. 284–92.

fore, while Sir William's figures are not so trustworthy as those of Dorne and others, they may be taken as reflecting fairly the prices of his day.[1]

Once the book was printed off it was put on sale by the printer, either in unbound quires (sheets, quaterni or fascicules), or in bound volumes. Undoubtedly a great deal of trade was done in unbound stock, as may be seen from John Dorne's day-book, and from other accounts quoted above. In the first place, a great many works consisted of a few quires only, and were hardly worth binding, and were better kept to bind with others of similar size, until there were enough to make a reasonably sized book. Secondly, this allowed of works dealing with the same subject being kept together in a convenient form, as in a volume now in the University Library, Cambridge. Here, in a contemporary binding, 'John Crowcheman, Mercer of London', as he describes himself on the title-page of the first item, has had bound together four highly controversial religious tracts.[2]

Many of the printers were binders also, or employed binders to work for them. T. Berthelet, for example, employed binders capable of turning out work of the highest quality, and his account of work done for Henry VIII speaks of volumes 'gorgeously bound', or 'in white leather, gorgeously gilted on the leather', or bound 'in crimson satin'.[3] Less expensive bindings were more common, and boards, parchment and leather were generally employed, the latter often being stamped with geometrical and floral patterns.

So far we have considered the problems arising from the production of a book as if they concerned one person only, and in general so they did. The book was printed by *A.B.* and was to be purchased at his press or at his shop. But this was

[1] For a fuller treatment of this subject, see my article 'Notes on English Retail Book-prices, 1490–1560', in *The Library*, Fifth Series, vol. v (1950), pp. 172–8.

[2] U.L.C. Syn. 8.54.168, containing *STC* 21428, 1291², 11842ᵃ and 10430.

[3] Arber's Transcript, vol. II, pp. 50–60. Berthelet's claims to be considered a binder are conclusively demolished by Hobson, *Bindings in Cambridge Libraries* (1929), pp. 80–1.

not the only possibility. It would appear that there was far more interrelation between the printers than has sometimes been thought, and modern study of types, woodcuts, printer's ornaments and borders reveals this. We constantly find books being printed by one printer for another, either as a routine matter of business, or at times perhaps to help a colleague out of a temporary difficulty. At one moment *A* is found printing a book for *B*, and then a year or so later, the process is reversed, or *B* is printing for *C*, and so it goes on.

The printing of books for individual stationers who had no presses of their own was a practice which began soon after Caxton's death, and lasted throughout the period. As early as 1494 the important grammar of John of Garland—the *Synonyma*—was printed at Paris by Wolfgang Hopyl, 'to be sold by Nicholas Lecomte, at the sign of St Nicholas, in Paul's churchyard', and this was followed by other works printed at Paris, Rouen and even at Venice. While the number of presses at work in England was small it was understandable that such should be the case, and well on into the next half century books continued to be printed abroad for English booksellers.

As their resources developed, the English printers began to usurp this trade, for a number of booksellers preferred to have their books printed for them, and did not engage actively in printing themselves. The best example is Walter Lynne, who had a shop in St Paul's Churchyard, 'next the great school', where he sold many books printed for him between 1547 and 1550. He describes himself as 'one that spendeth all hys tyme in the settynge forth of bokes in the Englysshe tounge', and his publications came from the presses of at least four printers. Another stationer, John Gough, had most of his books printed for him by J. Nicholson or John Mayler, the latter printing at least ten different works for him in three years.

On the other hand some printers appear to have confined themselves to printing for others and to have taken little part in selling their wares. Nicholas Hill, for example, printed for no less than sixteen printers and booksellers, and William Copland did the same for ten.[1]

The interconnexion between many of the printers is also shown by their habit of sharing the cost of producing an edition. For instance the success of W. Thynne's edition of Chaucer's *Works* (T. Godfray, 1532) led to its being reprinted in 1542 by R. Grafton for two others—W. Bonham and J. Reynes. The market still remaining unsatisfied, it was reprinted about 1545 by four printers, each taking a certain number of copies, and placing his own colophon upon them[2] although the copies were otherwise identical. Another large work, the first collected edition of *The workes of Sir T. More* (1557), was printed 'at the costes of J. Cawod, J. Waly and R. Tottell'. N. Hill's edition of the *Returna Brevium* (1546) we noted was done for three stationers, each having his own name in the colophon as the printer. Similarly his 1551 edition of the Bible was for a syndicate of three, as was Hilsey's *Primer* (1539), while a large number of books were published as a joint venture by two printers or stationers.[3]

Co-operation and joint ventures notwithstanding, the printers were, and had been, in eager competition with one another since the early rivalries of de Worde and Pynson.[4] As the number of printers grew so did the competition between them. Each printer, therefore, did what he could to extol the peculiar virtues of his edition. Title-pages not only claim that the work is 'newly corrected', or 'enlarged', but that it is 'necessary and needful for every person to look in', or 'very pleasant and profitable to read for all manner of persons, especially gentlemen'. A new work proudly displays itself as 'never before printed', or 'truly translated after the verity of the Hebrew and Greek texts'. People are invited to buy

[1] Others who printed little for themselves were J. Herford and R. Kele.

[2] Cf. *STC* 645–8, Anglerius, Petrus Martyr, *The Decades of the newe worlde* (1555), published by four well-known printers.

[3] See above for *The Royal Book* (p. 16). Another early example is *STC* 13176, *The grete herball* (1526) some copies having the device of P. Treveris, and others that of L. Andrewe. [4] See above, p. 194.

a book telling of the feats of Hannibal and Scipio by a printer's flourish which reads:

> Who so ever desireth for to rede
> Marciall prowesse, feactes of chivalrie,
> That maie hym profite at tyme of nede,
> Lette hym in hande take this historie, etc.[1]

In short, printers then as now, were not slow in drawing attention to their wares, but they went further, perhaps, than their successors in crying them up at the expense of those of their rivals. We have already seen the very vigorous way in which Pynson dealt with Redman (or more properly Rudeman) for trespassing on his domain,[2] while Redman was outspoken about the printing of the Year Books by Pynson and others, whereby they were 'greatly defaced and emblemished'.[3] Many other examples could be cited. They generally have some truth in them, but the differences are often exaggerated to provoke a sale for the new edition.

It will be remembered how John Mychel of Canterbury pleaded with his fellow-printers to suffer him 'quietlye to enjoye the benefite of these myne owne labours, and to have the advantage of myne owne invencion' in the compilation of his *Breviat Cronicle*, and how unavailing was his plea.[4] The lack of copyright left the work at the mercy of any who cared to reproduce it, and few briskly selling books have but a single imprint upon them. The lengths to which this could go is set out in Thomas Languet's indignant preface to his second edition of 'Cooper's Chronicle' (1560). This work he had first published in 1549, and in the meanwhile had been collecting materials for a second edition. He writes:

> I had gathered longe sens (gentle reader) dyvers profytable thinges out of moste commendable hystories, thynkynge when tyme served to adde them to this my chronicle, but upon certayne occasions I deferred the matter untill this last yeare. At that tyme entendyng to goe forward with my purpose, I understoode by

---

[1] *STC* 5718, sig. a i[v].
[2] See above, p. 223.
[3] See above, p. 78.
[4] See above, p. 132.

reporte that certaine persons for lukers sake, contrarie to honestie, had caused my chronicle to be prynted without my knowlage, alterynge in my dooynge what they lysted, and annexyng an other mans addicions unto my woorke. Wherfore I, not purposynge to leave of that I entended, overlooked theyr edicion. Wherein as I saw some thynges of myne lefte out, and many thynges of others annexed, so dyd I finde almost five hundred fautes and errours eyther of the prynter, or els of hym that undertooke the correction; yea and many of them in those thynges that are in this woorke chiefly to be regarded. I can not therfore doe other wyse but greatly blame their unhonest dealynge, and openly protest that the edicion of this Chronicle set foorth by Marshe and Seres in the yere of Christe, 1559 is none of myne, but the attempte of certayne persons utterly unlearned. This, gentle reader, I thought good to advertise the, leste the fautes by other mens lewdnesse committed, should be fathered upon me, to my reproch and sclaunder.[1]

The time was evidently ripe for stricter control, and shortly before Languet wrote these words the Stationers' Company had received a new Charter, and a new and more disciplined regime was at hand. Here we may leave our early printers. The incorporation of the Stationers' Company in the early summer of 1557 saw them a growing and prosperous body of men with three-quarters of a century behind them in which the foundations of their trade had been laid. Typographically their works are lacking in distinction for the most part; but, as we have seen, their services to their countrymen were worthy of praise. Most of them were nothing more than ordinary business men whose trade it was to provide the public with printed matter, just as their fellows provided them with clothes or food. They had no great ideals, but they went about their job with enterprise and a lively concern to enlist all those whom they thought could help them by patronage, scholarship or knowledge. In so doing they put before their countrymen, both in quality and quantity, a variety of wares which made Englishmen, as never before, 'the heirs of the ages'.

[1] *STC* 15218, ai^v. The work referred to is *An epitome of cronicles; to the reigne of Quene Elizabeth by R. Crowley* (1559), *STC* 15221.

HANDLIST OF PUBLICATIONS BY WYNKYN DE WORDE, 1492-1535

The following is an attempt to bring together a list of publications by de Worde, whether still in existence or not. It accepts the attribution made by earlier biographers, cataloguers and others, although it is not always possible to check their statements, and it is probable that a number of 'ghosts' have thus been given a further fugitive existence. On the whole it has seemed better to adopt this, rather than the more severe policy of the *STC* (where seeing is believing) on the ground that the source of the information is always given in the last column of the list, so that the purist may at once omit the item from his consideration. I owe a special debt of gratitude to Miss E. Pafort of the Pierpont Morgan Library, New York, who, in addition to the valuable information contained in her article 'A group of Early Tudor School-books' (*Library*, Fourth Series, vol. XXVI (1946), pp. 227–61), also most kindly sent me a copy of her own list of de Worde's publications. Mr F. S. Ferguson also gave me the benefit of his unrivalled knowledge of these early books. With their aid it has been possible to add nearly two hundred and fifty titles to those already given in the *STC*. They may be distinguished by the figures, 1, 2, 3 etc. added to the *STC* number, viz. 1131.1.

Symbols used for Libraries and other owners of Books registered

BAMB.	Bamborough Castle.
BO.	Boston Public Library.
BRIT.	Britwell Library.
C.	Cambridge University Library.
C².	Trinity College, Cambridge.

C3.	Emmanuel College, Cambridge.
C4.	King's College, Cambridge.
C5.	St John's College, Cambridge.
C6.	Pepysian Library, Magdalene College, Cambridge.
C7.	Corpus Christi College, Cambridge.
C8.	Jesus College, Cambridge.
C15.	Pembroke College, Cambridge.
C19.	Peterhouse, Cambridge.
CH.	Chapin Library, Williamstown, Va.
CL.	J. L. Clawson.
COLUMBIA	Columbia University Library, N.Y.
D.	Trinity College, Dublin.
D2.	Marsh Library, Dublin.
DEV.	*Catalogue of the Library of the Duke of Devonshire*, 4 vols. (1879).
DIBDIN	F. T. Dibdin, *Typographical Antiquities*, vol. II. (1812).
DUFF	E. G. Duff, *Hand-Lists of English Printers, 1501–1556*, vol. I (1895).
DUR.	Durham Cathedral.
DUR3.	Cosin Library, Durham.
E.	Advocates' Library, Edinburgh (National Library of Scotland).
FOLG.	Folger Library, Washington, D.C.
G.	Hunterian Museum, Glasgow.
HAIGH	Haigh Hall (Crawford Library).
HD.	Harvard University Library.
HEARNE	*Bibliotheca Hearneiana*, ed. B. Botfield (1848).
HEBER	*Catalogues of the Library of R. Heber*, 16 parts (1834–7).
HERBERT	W. H. Herbert, *Typographical Antiquities*, vol. I (1785).
HN.	Huntington Library, California.
HUTH	*Catalogue of the printed books...collected by Henry Huth*, 5 vols. (1880).
JOHNSON	J. Johnson, *Typographia* (1824).

L.	British Museum, London.
L².	Lambeth Palace, London.
L²².	Lincoln's Inn Library, London.
LINC.	Lincoln Cathedral.
M.	John Rylands Library, Manchester.
MARL.	Marlborough College.
MELBOURNE	A. B. Foxcroft, *A Catalogue of English books and fragments from 1477 to 1535* (1933).
MICHIGAN	Michigan University Library, Mich.
NY.	New York Public Library.
O.	Bodleian Library, Oxford.
O³.	Christ Church, Oxford.
O⁵.	Corpus Christi College, Oxford.
O⁸.	St John's College, Oxford.
O¹⁰.	Exeter College, Oxford.
O¹¹.	Merton College, Oxford.
O¹².	Magdalen College, Oxford.
O¹⁴.	New College, Oxford.
P.	Peterborough Cathedral.
PARIS	Bibliothèque Nationale, Paris.
PFOR.	C. H. Pforzheimer.
PML.	Pierpont Morgan Library, New York.
Q.	Bernard Quaritch, Ltd., New Bond Street, London.
ROB.	W. H. Robinson, Ltd., Pall Mall, London.
ROX.	*Roxburghe Library*, ed. W. C. Hazlitt (1868–73).
RAWLINSON	*A catalogue of...the collection made by T. Rawlinson*, 16 parts (1721–34).
SAL.	Salisbury Cathedral.
SHR.	Shrewsbury School.
SOTHEBY	Sotheby & Co. Ltd., Bond Street, London.
ST.	Stonyhurst College.
WASH.	Library of Congress, Washington, D.C.
WOLLATON.	Wollaton Hall Library.
Y.	Yale University.
YK.	York Minster.

STC number	Author or Subject heading	Short title of work	Format	Date	Libraries containing copie
78	Abingdon	Jest of the mylner of Abington	4°	n.d.	PML.
167.1	Æsop	Fables, trs. W. Caxton	F°	[1500?]	L.
169	do.	Fabule...cum commento	4°	1503	L., O.
170	do.	do.	4°	1516	M.
171	do.	Aesopi Phrygis et vita et fabellæ	8°	1535	O.
253	Alanus	Parabola Alani cū cometo	4°	23 Aug. 1508	O.
254	do.	Alanus de parabolis	4°	1510	L., O.
254.1	do.	do.	4°	26 Oct. 1513	O⁸.
254.2	do.	do.	4°	1517	JOHNSON, no. 1
254.3	do.	do.	4°	1523	DIBDIN, Bibliographical Deca merone, III, 25
254.4	do.	do.	4°	1 Aug. 1525	L.
254.5	do.	do.	4°	n.d.	J. B. INGLIS s 1871, no. 147
258.1	Albertus Magnus	[The secrets]	8°	n.d.	C¹⁵. (imp.)
270.1	do.	Questiones de modis significandi	4°	29 Apr. 1510	NORWICH CITY LIBRARY
271	do.	do.	4°	[1515]	L., C.
272	do.	Modi significādi	4°	16 Mar. 1515	O.
278	Alcock, J. Bp.	Mons perfeccionis, the hyll of perfeccoñ	4°	22 Sept. 1496	BAMB.; HN.
279	do.	Mons perfectionis	4°	23 May 1497	L., C., E., M.
281	do.	do.	4°	27 May 1501	C., LINC., P.;
281.1	do.	do.	4°	1511	Harleian Cat. 6940
283	do.	[Sermon for a boy bishop] In die Innocencium...	4°	[1498]	O⁵., C⁸., HN.
282	do.	do.	4°	[1499]	L., ST.
284	do.	[Sermon on Luke viii] Sermo...Qui habet...	4°	[1497]	M.
285	do.	do.	4°	[1497]	P. (wants lea

242

TC mber	Author or Subject heading	Short title of work	Format	Date	Libraries containing copies
286	Alcock, J. *Bp.*	[Spousage of a virgin to Christ] Desponsacio uirginis xpristo	4°	[1496?]	C.
287	do.	do.	4°	[1497?]	O.
319	Alexander grammaticus	[Doctrinale] Textus Alexandri	4°	1503	LINC.; FOLG.
18	do.	do.	—	[1514–15?]	O.
87	Almanack	Almanack for XII. yere	16°	1508	L., O.; MICHIGAN
89	do.	Almacke (*sic*) for XV. yeres	8°	[1522]	L.
91	do.	[Almanack for – years]	8°	[1534?]	L. (1 leaf only)
56	Anne [Bullen]	The noble tryumphaunt coronation	4°	[1533]	L.
70	Antichrist	The byrthe and lyte of Antechryst	4°	[1520?]	C.
8.1	Apollonius	King Appolyn of Thyre	4°	28 Feb. 1510	DEV.; HN.
37	Ars	Ars moriendi	4°	[1497]	M.
38	do.	do.	4°	1506	C., M., BAMB.
2	Art	The craft to liue well and to die well	F°	21 Jan. 1505	C. (imp.)
3	do.	The arte or crafte to...dye well	4°	[1506]	L.
2	Arthur, *King*	Le morte Darthur	F°	25 Mar. 1498	O., M.
3	do.	do.	F°	18 Nov. 1529	L. (imp.)
5	Austin, *Saint*	The myrrour of the chyrche	4°	1521	L., L²., C.
5	do.	do.	4°	1527	L.
0.1	Barchly, J.	Regulae informationis	—	1506	L². (frag.)
4	Barclay, A.	Egloges	4°	[c. 1515]	HN.
	do.	Fyfte Eglog	4°	[1518?]	L.; HN.
	Baron, S.	Sermones	8°	[c. 1510]	O., C.; FOLG.
	Bartholomeus Anglicus	De proprietatibus rerum	4°	[1495]	L., O., C.; HN., PML., FOLG.
1	do.	do.	4°	1507	HERBERT, I., 145

STC number	Author or Subject heading	Short title of work	Format	Date	Libraries containing copie.
1743.1	Becon, T.	The pomander of prayer	4°	1532	M.
1912	Bernard, *Saint*	The golden epistle	4°	23 Nov. 1530	O¹⁰.; FOLG., PM¹
1913	do.	do.	4°	[1532?]	L.; PML.
1916	do.	Medytacōns of saynt Bernarde	4°	9 Mar. 1496	O.
1917	do.	do.	4°	9 Mar. [1499]	L., C.; HD.
1918	do.	do.	4°	19 Sept. 1525	C.
1966	Bernardinus of Siena, *Saint*	The chirche of the evill men and women	4°	22 Aug. 1511	O., C.; HN. (Pa printed?)
1978	Betson, T.	Treatyse to dyspose men to be vertuously occupyed	4°	[1500]	C., BAMB.; FOL
1987	Bevis	[Sir Bevis of Hampton]	4°	[1500]	O. (2 leaves)
1987.1	do.	do.	4°	[after 1528]	C. (frag.)
3258.1	Bonaventura, *Saint*	Alphabetum religiosorum	4°	1532	O¹⁰.
3273	do.	Paruum bonum quod alias Incendium amoris...	4°	1511	O.
3261	do.	Speculum uitae Christi	F°	1494	C⁴., L²., M. (bc imp.), Holkh: Hall
3265	do.	do.	4°	[before Mar. 1509]	O.
3264	do.	do.	4°	4 Mar. 1517	L., O. (both in FOLG.
3266	do.	do.	4°	7 Sept. 1525	L., L²., G.; HN
3267	do.	do.	4°	8 Feb. 1530	O., C⁵., M.; BO
3278	Bonde, W.	The pylgrimage of perfection	F°	28 Feb. 1531	L., C., M.; FO: HD.
3288	Book	Boke of a ghoostly fader	4°	8 Mar. 1528	C., C⁵.
3289	do.	Boke of keruynge	4°	1508	C.
3290	do.	do.	4°	1513	L.
3295	do.	Boke of Comforte	4°	[1505?]	C., M.; PML.

STC number	Author or Subject heading	Short title of work	Format	Date	Libraries containing copies
304	Book	[The book of Courtesy]	4°	[1492]	O. (1 leaf)
309	do.	[The book of Hawking, &c.]	F°	1496	L., O., C⁶., M.; HN., HD., PML.
309.1	do.	do.	4°	1532	DIBDIN, *Bib. Decam.* III, 254
317	do.	The boke of huntynge	4°	[1518-21]	O. (frag.)
318	do.	Treatise of hunting	4°	[1530?]	C. (lacks title)
547	Brant, S.	The shyppe of fooles	4°	6 July 1509	PARIS, WASH.
547.1	do.	do.	4°	20 June 1517	L., O.
547.2	do.	do.	4°	1527	DEV.
500	Brendan, *Saint*	Lyfe of Saynt Brandon	4°	[1520?]	L.
585.1	Bushe, P.	Exposycyon of miserere mei Deus	4°	1501	HERBERT, I, 137
585.2	do.	do.	4°	1525	HERBERT, I, 186
50	Calais	The . . . tryumphe at Caleys and Bulleyn	4°	[1532]	L.
51	do.	do.	4°	[1532]	L.
92	Canutus	Treatyse agaynst pestelēce	4°	[1510]	C.
92.1	do.	do.	4°	[1510?]	HN.
51	Capgrave, J.	[Nova legenda Anglie]	F°	27 Feb. 1516	L., O., C²., M.; HN., FOLG., WASH.
51.1	do.	do.	F°	1521	DEV., SOTHEBY, 20 Nov. 1923
5.1	Carminum	De carminum generibus	4°	Feb. 1525	DIBDIN, II, no. 353
8	Carta	Carta feodi . . .	4°	[1506?]	L. O., M.; HN. HD.
9	do.	do.	4°	[1507?]	L., M.; HD., HN.
9.1	do.	do.	4°	[1506]	L., L²²., C., M.
9.2	do.	do.	4°	[n.d.]	C.; HN.
9.3	do.	do.	4°	[n.d.]	D.
9.4	do.	do.	4°	[n.d.]	HN.

STC number	Author or Subject heading	Short title of work	Format	Date	Libraries containing copies
4815	Catharine of Siena, *Saint*	The Orchard of Syon	F°	28 Sept. 1519	L., O., C.; FOLG. NY.
4840	Cato, Dionysius	Catho pro pueris	4°	1513	FOLG.
4840.1	do.	Liber Cathonis	4°	15 Aug. 1508	Q.
4840.2	do.	do.	4°	22 Sept. 1512	C²., ROB., Cat. no. 77
4841	do.	do.	4°	20 Dec. 1514	L.
4842	do.	do.	8°	1532	L.
5065	Chastising	Chastysing of goddes chyldern	F°	[c. 1492]	L., C⁸., G.; FOL HN., PML.
5092	Chaucer, G.	Assemble of fowles	4°	24 Jan. 1530	HN.
5085	do.	The Caunterbury Tales	F°	1498	L., C.; PML., FO
5095	do.	Troylus and Cresyde	4°	1517	L.; HN.
5136	Child	The wyse chylde of thre yere olde	4°	[1520?]	L.
5162	Christian man	[Christiani hominis institutum]	4°	[1510?]	L.
5204	Christmas	Christmasse carolles	4°	1521	O. (last leaf o▪
5277.1	Cicero	Tullyes offyces	8°	1533	DUFF, I, 20
5278	do.	do.	8°	30 Sept. 1534	L., O., C.; HN. FOLG., PML.
5456	Cock Lorrel	Cocke Lorelles boke	4°	[1518]	L.
5543.3	Colet, J.	Catechism	8°	1534	DUFF, I, 20
5572	Cologne	The thre Kynges of Coleyn	4°	[1496]	O.; HN.
5573	do.	do.	4°	[after July 1499]	L., E.
5574	do.	do.	4°	1511	C. (imp.)
5575	do.	do.	4°	1526	PML.
5575.1	do.	do.	4°	1530	DIBDIN, II, no▪
5605	Communication	Cōmunycacyon bytwene God and man	4°	[1534?]	L., C. (imp.)
5608.1	Complaint	Complaint of the lover of Christ	4°	—	BRIT.
5609	do.	Complaynt of the soule	4°	[1510?]	L., C⁷.
5610	do.	do.	4°	1532	O.

STC number	Author or Subject heading	Short title of work	Format	Date	Libraries containing copies
5643	Contemplation	The contemplation of sinners	4°	10 July 1499	L., O⁵., C., M.
5728	Copland, R.	**Complaynt of them** that ben to late maryed	4°	[1535?]	L.; HN.
5729	do.	Complaynt of them that be to soone maryed	4°	[1535?]	HN.
5759	Cordiale	[Cordiale sive de quatuor novissimis]	4°	[before 1501]	O., M., DUR.; FOLG.
5953	Craft	Crafte of graffynge & plantynge of trees	4°	[c. 1520]	L. (imp.)
6034	Creature	The dyenge creature	4°	1507	M.; FOLG.
6035	do.	The deyenge creature	4°	1514	L., C.
6035.1	do.	do.	4°	[1531–4]	O.; Y.
126	Cura	Cura clericalis	8°	1532	HN., PML.
456.1	Declensions	Declensions of nouns	4°	[1518?]	C. (4 leaves)
470	Degore, Sir	Syr Degore	4°	[1515?]	PML.
572.1	Demands	The demaūdes joyous	4°	1509	C.
573	do.	do.	4°	1511	C.
784.1	Despauter, J.	De accentibus	—	Feb. 1526	L.
830	Dictes	The dyctes and sayenges of the phylosophers	4°	1528	L., O., C.; HN., FOLG.
833	Dietary	The dyetary of ghostly helthe	4°	20 Nov. 1520	C.; HN.
836	do.	do.	4°	6 Aug. 1527	FOLG. (lacks sheet B)
895	Dionysius, Carthusianus	The mirroure of golde...	4°	29 Mar. 1522	L., C.
897	do.	do.	4°	30 May 1526	L., L².
915	Disputation	The dysputacyon or cōplaynt of the herte...	4°	[1510?]	HN.
931	Doctrinal	The doctrynalle of dethe	4°	[1498]	M.; HN.
932	do.	do.	4°	1532	L.

247

STC number	Author or Subject heading	Short title of work	Format	Date	Libraries containing copies
7009	Donatus, A.	Accedence	4°	[1495]	O., C⁸.
7010	do.	do.	4°	[1499]	O., C⁶.; HN. (imp
7016	do.	Donatus minor cum Remigo	4°	[1495?]	O.
7014.1	do.	Donatus minor cū Remigo	4°	[1503–4]	O.
7015	do.	do.	4°	[1517]	L., M.
7500	Edward the Confessor	The lyfe of saynt Edwarde cōfessour	4°	1523	L.
7541	Eglamoure	[Sir Eglamoure]	4°	[1500]	C. (1 leaf)
7571	Elias	Helyas Knight of the Swan	4°	6 Feb. 1512	L. (1 leaf), C. (frag.); C. H. McCORMICK
7571.1	do.	do.	4°	[1525?]	C.
7706	England	Modus tenend' Curia Baron	4°	[1508?]	L., O.
7727.1	do.	Modus tenendi unum Hundredum	4°	[1520?]	M.
9349	do.	Statutes [1 H. VII]	F°	n.d.	C⁴.
9350	do.	Statutes [7 H. VII]	F°	n.d.	C⁴.
9351.1	do.	Statutes Anno VII° (XI.XII.XIX) Henrici vii	F°	1508	PML., HD.
9352	do.	Anno XI. Henrici vii	F°	1496	C⁴.
9353	do.	Anr. ed. Henrici vii	F°	1496	M.
9354	do.	Anr. ed. Henrici vii	F°	1496	L., G.; HD.
9354.1	do.	Anno XII. Henrici vii	F°	[1502?]	C⁴.
9357.1	do.	Anno XIX. Henrici vii	F°	[1505?]	DIBDIN, II, no.
9357.2	do.	do.	F°	1506	DIBDIN, II, no.
9357.3	do.	Statutes [1–19]. Henrici vii	4°	1508	RAWLINSON, Part xvi (1732 no. 2358
9996	do.	Chronicles of England [St Albans Chronicle]	F°	1497	L., O., C. (imp M.; FOLG., PM
9997	do.	do.	F°	1502	L., O., D².; PM

STC number	Author or Subject heading	Short title of work	Format	Date	Libraries containing copies
9985	England	Cronycles of Englande	F°	1515	L., M.; HN.
9985.1	do.	do.	F°	1519	HERBERT, I, 161
?001	do.	Cronycle of Englonde [St Albans Chron.]	F°	1520	O. (imp.), C⁴. SHIRBURN CASTLE; CH.
?002	do.	Cronicles of Englonde [St Albans Chron.]	F°	9 Apr. 1528	L., G., LONGLEAT; HN., WASH., Y.
?012	do.	A lytell shorte Cronycle	4°	25 June 1530	C.
?466.1	Erasmus	Book of good maners for chyldren	16°	1522	DUFF, I, 14
?467	do.	do.	8°	10 Sept. 1532	L.; HN.
?467.1	do.	do.	8°	20 Jan. 1534	HN.
?50.1	do.	De copia valorum	12°	1528	DIBDIN, II, no. 330
?50.2	do.	[Colloquia]	4°	Id. Aug. 1519	MAITTAIRE, Ind. I, 373
?50.3	do.	do.	4°	Sept. 1520	M.
50.4	do.	do.	4°	1522	STAFFORD CASTLE (1556), see DIBDIN, Bibl. Decam. III, 253
?0.5	do.	do.	4°	1525	DIBDIN, II, no. 327
?0.6	do.	do.	4°	1535	DIBDIN, II, no. 328
?8.1	do.	[Enchiridion]		1501	HN.
?9	do.	do.	8°	15 Nov. 1533	L., O.; HN., FOLG.
?o	do.	do.	8°	12 Feb. 1534	L., O., C⁴.; HN., FOLG.
?7.1	do.	Libellus de constructione octo partium orationis	12°	1531	V. HAEGHEN, Bibliotheca Erasmiana (1893)
?0.1	do.	Treatise upon the Pater Noster	4°	1524	DIBDIN, II, no. 329
?3	Example	The example of euyll tongues	4°	[1525?]	L., DEV.
??	Exornatorium	Exoneratorium curatorum	4°	[1518?]	L., G.
??	do.	do.	4°	[c. 1522]	L., C⁷.

STC number	Author or Subject heading	Short title of work	Format	Date	Libraries containing copies
10685	Fantasy	Fantasy of the passyon of the Fox	4°	16 Feb. 1530	C.
10839	Feylde, T.	Controversy between a lover and a Jaye	4°	[1522?]	HN.
10839.1	do.	do.	4°	n.d.	BRIT., DEV.
10902	Fisher, J. *Card.*	Fruytfull saynges of Dauyd [on the Seven Penit. Psalms]	4°	16 June 1508	L., C.; HN., FOL PML.
10903	do.	do.	4°	12 June 1509	L., C.; HN., FOL PML.
10903ᵃ	do.	do.	4°	12 June [1515?]	C⁶., Q.; BO.
10904	do.	do.	4°	12 June [1518?]	L., O.
10906	do.	do.	4°	13 June 1525	L.; NY.
10906.1	do.	do.	4°	1527	W. MASKELL s 1854, no. 388
10907	do.	do.	4°	13 Aug. 1529	L.; HN.
10891	do.	A mornynge remembraūce	4°	[1509]	L., O., C.; HN FOLG., PML.
10893	do.	[Sermon against Martin Luther]	4°	[1521?]	L., C7.
10894	do.	do.	4°	[1521?]	C., BRIT.; HN. FOLG.
10895	do.	do.	4°	[1528?]	L.
10900	do.	[A sermon on Henry VII]	4°	1509	L., O., M.; HN
10901	do.	do.	4°	[1509]	L.; HN., FOLC
11024	Fitzjames, R. *Bp.*	Sermo die lune in ebdomada Pasche	4°	[1495?]	L., O., C.
23875.1	Flower	Floure of the Commaundementes of God	4°	1505	LONGLEAT
23876	do.	do.	4°	14 Sept. 1510	L., O., C., M.
23877	do.	do.	4°	8 Oct. 1521	L., O., C., M. FOLG., PML.
15345	Four	Four leaues of the true-loue	4°	[1510]	L.; HN.
1008	do.	Four sons of Aymon	F°	8 May 1504	C. (frag.); H (imp.)

STC number	Author or Subject heading	Short title of work	Format	Date	Libraries containing copies
1361.1	Frederick	Frederyke of Jennen	4°	[1518–]	O. (2 leaves only)
4522	Friar	Frere and the boye	4°	[1510?]	C.
1407	Fruit	Fruyte of redempcyon	4°	21 May 1530	L.
2435.1	Galfredus Anglicus	Promptoriũ paruulorum...	—	n.d.	C.
2435.2	do.	do.	4°	1509	DUFF, I, 8
2436	do.	do.	4°	17 Jan. 1511	L.
2437	do.	do.	4°	26 May 1512	HN., FOLG.
2438	do.	do.	4°	5 Sept. 1516	L., O., C.; HN.
2438.1	do.	do.	4°	1518	DUFF, I, 11
2438.2	do.	do.	4°	1519	O.
2438.3	do.	do.	4°	1522	DUFF, I, 14
2439	do.	do.	4°	1528	L.
2602	Garland, J.	[Equivoca]	4°	1499	L.
2603	do.	do.	4°	1502	O.
2605	do.	do.	4°	13 Dec. 1505	C.; FOLG.
2608ᵃ	do.	do.	4°	1510	DULWICH, HEBER, part ii, no. 2236
2608	do.	do.	4°	16 Aug. 1514	C. (frag.), D., Q.
2608.1	do.	do.	4°	4 Apr. 1517	Q.
2610	do.	Synonyma	4°	12 Mar. 1500	L.
2613	do.	do.	4°	1502	O.; UNIV. OF CINCINNATI
2614	do.	do.	4°	20 Nov. 1505	C.; FOLG.
2615	do.	do.	4°	1509	L., O.
2615.1	do.	do.	4°	11 Feb. 1510	DULWICH; NY.
2616	do.	do.	4°	29 July 1514	D., Q.
2616ᵃ	do.	do.	4°	20 Feb. 1517	Q.
2617	do.	do.	4°	1518	L.
2621	Generides	Generides	4°	[1504–5?]	C². (3 leaves); HN. (4 leaves)
2622.1	Gesta	Gesta Romanorum	4°	[1517?]	C⁵.
2646	Goodwyn, C.	Chaũce of the dolorous louer	4°	8 Mar. [1520?]	BRIT.

STC number	Author or Subject heading	Short title of work	Format	Date	Libraries containing copies
12091	Gospels	Gospelles of dystaues	4°	[1510?]	L., O. (frag.); HI
12139	Governal	Gouernall of helthe	4°	[1510?]	C.
12352	Gregory I	Lyfe of S. Gregorys mother	4°	1515	C. (frag.)
12381	Gringoire, P.	The castell of laboure	4°	1506	L., C.
12381.1	do.	do.	4°	[1510?]	L.
12412.1	Gryphus, P.	Oratio	4°	22 Nov. 1506	O³.
12472	Guido de Monte Rocherii	Manipulus curatorum	8°	22 April 1502	L., O., G.
12472.1	do.	do.	—	1506	DIBDIN, II, no. 1
12475	do.	do.	—	13 Feb. 1509	L.
12475.1	do.	do.		1511	HERBERT, I, 15
12508.1	Guistard	Guystarde and Sygysmonde	4°	1532	C., DEV., ROX.
12541	Guy	[Guy of Warwick]	—	[1500]	O. (1 leaf)
12942.1	Hawes, S.	The Comfort of Lovers	4°	[1511?]	L.
12943	do.	The cōuercyon of swerers	4°	1509	L.; HN. (imp.)
12945	do.	The example of virtue	4°	[1509?]	C. (frag.), C⁶.
12946	do.	do.	4°	[1520?]	C. (1 leaf)
12947	do.	do.	4°	20 Apr. 1530	HN., PFOR.
12948	do.	The pastime of pleasure	4°	11 Jan. 1509	C. (frag.), HAⱼ HOUSE (imp.)
12949	do.	do.	4°	3 Dec. 1517	PML.
12953	do.	Joyfull medytacyon on the coronacyon of Hen. VIII	4°	[1509]	C.; HN.
13069.1	Hegendorphinus	Dialogus	—	June 1532	DUNN (frag.)
13075	Henry VII	[Elegy on the death of Henry VII]	F°	[1509]	O.
13439	Higden, R.	Polychronicon	F°	13 Apr. 1495	L., C., E., M.; FOLG., PML.

252

STC umber	Author or Subject heading	Short title of work	Format	Date	Libraries containing copies
9996	Higden, R.	Polychronicon (Description of Britain)	F°	1498	L., C.; PML., FOLG.
9997	do.	do.	F°	2 May 1502	L., O., D².; FOLG., BO.
9985	do.	do.	F°	1515	L., M.; HN., FOLG., PML.
001	do.	do.	F°	1520	O. (imp.); CH.
002	do.	do.	F°	9 April 1528	L., LONGLEAT; HN., WASH., Y.
604	Holt, J.	Lac puerorum	4°	[1507–8]	L.; MICHIGAN
609	Holy Ghost	The abbaye of the holy Ghost	4°	[1496]	L., C., BAMB.
610	do.	do.	4°	[1500]	E.; FOLG.
610.1	do.	do.	4°	1531	MAITTAIRE, *Ind.*, I, 22
686	Honorius	Lucydarye	4°	[1522–24]	L.; FOLG.
809	Horman, W.	Introductorium lingue latine	4°	[1495]	C⁶.
810	do.	do.	4°	[1499]	O.
12	do.	Vulgaria	4°	1530	L.; FOLG.
27.1	Horse	The proprytees and medycynes for hors	4°	[1500?]	HN.
29	Hortus	Ortus vocabulorum	F°	1500	L., O., C⁴., M.; HN.
29.1	do.	do.	4°	1508	HERBERT, I, 147
30.1	do.	do.	4°	1 May 1509	L. (Bagford Fragments)
31	do.	do.	8°	12 Aug. 1511	L.; WASH.
32	do.	do.	4°	15 Feb. 1514	L.; HN.
33	do.	do.	4°	28 July 1516	O.; HD.
34	do.	do.	4°	22 Oct. 1518	O., M.
6	do.	do.	4°	1 Apr. 1528	L., C.
7	do.	do.	4°	1532	L.
5	Hugo *de Sancto Victore*	Exposycyon of S. Augustyne's rule...	4°	1525	O.

STC number	Author or Subject heading	Short title of work	Format	Date	Libraries containing copies
13998.1	Huon of Bordeaux	Huon of Bourdeaux	4°	[c. 1534]	HAIGH
14039	Hyckescorner	Hyckescorner	4°	[1515–16?]	L.
14042	Hylton, W.	[Scala perfectionis]	F°	1494	L., C., M.; FOLG. HN., PML.
14043.1	do.	do.		3 Jan. 1519	OSCOTT COLLEGE
14044	do.	do.	4°	31 Mar. 1525	L.
14045	do.	do.	4°	27 May 1533	L., C.; HN., FOLC
14077.1	Indulgence	Church of Our Lady & Saynt George. Southworke	Bs.	[c. 1520]	M².; FOLG.
14081	Information	Informacōn for pylgrymes vnto the holy londe	4°	[1498?]	E.
14081.1	do.	do.	4°	1504	W. CLARKE, Rep Bibl. p. 417
14082	do.	do.	4°	16 May 1515	PML.
14083	do.	do.	4°	26 July 1524	C⁵. (wants title)
14097	Innocent VIII	Bull	s. sh.	1494	L²., C⁵ (lower h only)
14098	do.	do.	F°	1495	L., O., C.
14102	do.	Indulgence	4°	[1498]	L., O., M; PML., NY.
14109	Interlocution	Interlocucyon betwyxt man and woman	4°	[1528?]	L.; MICHIGAN
14111	Interlude	Thenterlude of Youth	4°	[1530–35]	L². (frag.)
14128	Ipomydon	Ipomydon	4°	[c. 1522]	L. (3 leaves)
5733	do.	[The life of Ipomydon]	4°	[c. 1530–31]	PML.
14280.1	Isumbras, Sir	[Isumbras]	4°	[1530?]	Q., Cat. 1930, no. 914
14280.2	do.	do.	4°	[1530?]	do.
14323	Jacob	Thystory of Jacoby and his twelve sones	4°	[1510?]	L., O. (frag.)
14507	Jerome, Saint	Vitas patrum	F°	1495	L., O., C., M.; FOLG., PML.
14508	do.	Lyf of saint Jerom	4°	[1500?]	L.

STC number	Author or Subject heading	Short title of work	Format	Date	Libraries containing copies
518	Jerusalem	The dystruccyon of Jherusalem by Vaspazyan & Tytus	4°	[1509–16]	L.
519	do.	do.	4°	28 Jan. 1528	PML.
540.2	Jesus Christ	Christ cross me spede		n.d.	BRIT.
546	Jesus Christ	The shedynge of the blood of...Jhesu Cryste	4°	[before 1500]	HN.
558	do.	The passyon of our lorde	4°	6 Oct. 1521	O., C.
559	do.	do.	4°	1532	L. (wants 2 leaves)
72	do.	The VII shedynges of the blode of Jhesus cryste	4°	1509	C., BAMB.
48	John of Arras	[Melusine]	F°	[1510?]	O. (frag.)
49	John of Capistrano	[Capistranus]	4°	[1510?]	L., O.
50	do.	do.	4°	[1530?]	L., O.
56	Joseph, of Arimathea	A treatyse...of Joseph of Arimathy	4°	[1510?]	L., C.
8.1	Jousts	Justes of the moneth of Maye & June	—	[1507]	C6.
63	Justices	The boke of Justyces of peas	4°	1506	HN., MICHIGAN
4	do.	do.	4°	1510	L., O.; HN. (imp.)
4.1	do.	do.	4°	1515	HN.
4.2	do.	do.	4°	1520	F. PERKINS' sale, 1889, no. 230(1)
4	Kempe, M.	Treatyse of contemplacyon	4°	[1501]	C.; HN.
4	Kur'ān	A lytell treatyse... called Alcaron	4°	[1515?]	L.; HN.
8	La Sale, A. de	The fyftene joyes of maryage	4°	[c. 1509]	O. (2 leaves)
8.1	do.	do.	4°	1509	PML., FOLG. (wants last 6 leaves)

STC number	Author or Subject heading	Short title of work	Format	Date	Libraries containing co
15345	Leaves	The.IIII.leues of the trueloue	4°	[1530?]	L.; HN.
15376	Le Fèvre, R.	The Recuyles...of Troye	F°	1502	C⁶. (wants 4 leaves)
15377	do.	do.	F°	[1503]	L. (imp.), C⁴. PML.
15397	Le Grand, J.	A lytell boke called good maners	4°	[1500?]	C.
15398	do.	do.	4°	10 Dec. 1507	L.; HN., FOLC PML.
15399	do.	do.	4°	[1515?]	O.
15473.1	Leo X	[Indulgence in favour of...St Thomas of Acres]	—	[1515?]	O.
15576	Libellus	Libellus sophistarum ad vsum Cantibrigiensium	4°	7 Sept. 1510	C., C⁵.
15577	do.	Libellus sophistarum ad vsum Oxoniensium	4°	12 Aug. 1512	O.
15578	do.	do.	4°	[1515?]	L.
15578.1	do.	Libellus sophistarum ad vsum Cantabrigiensium	4°	[1523?]	O.
15579	do.	do.	4°	4 June 1524	L²., O.
15579.1	do.	Libellus sophistarum ad vsum Oxoniensium	4°	16 July 1530	L².
15601.1	Lily, W.	De octo orationis partium constructione	8°	Feb. 1531	M.
15602	do.	do.	8°	1533	L.
15608	do.	De generibus nominum	8°	1533	L.
15609.1	do.	Rudimenta parvula	—	n.d.	O.
15805.1	Liturgies	Breviary	F°	1506	J. E. Hodgk (frag.), DUFI 17

TC nber	Author or Subject heading	Short title of work	Format	Date	Libraries containing copies
;o6	Liturgies	Breviary	8°	11 Kal. Julii, 1507	O.
o8	do.	do.	4°	11 Kal. Jan. 1509	O., C5.
;63.1	do.	Graduale	F°	17 Kal. Jan. 1527	JOHNSON, no. 282
75	do.	Hours	4°	[1494]	L. (leaves 1–6), L²., O. (wants 11 leaves), C. (imp.)
76	do.	do.	4°	[1494]	L. (87 leaves only)
78	do.	do.	8°	[1494]	O5. (Y 1–4, 6 only)
8	do.	do.	8°	1502	O.
9	do.	do.	4°	31 July 1503	L.
8	do.	do.	8°	[1508]	C. (4 leaves)
o.1	do.	do.	4°	1510	JOHNSON, no. 77
4	do.	do.	4°	1513	L. (imp.)
9	do.	do.	12°	24 July 1514	C.
2	do.	do.	4°	1519	L. (wants A 1, A 8)
3.1	do.	do.	12°	1522	JOHNSON, no. 78
4	do.	do.	4°	20 Nov. 1523	L., SAL.
5	do.	do.	12°	[1523?]	C3.
7	do.	do.	4°	[1526?]	C. (imp.)
;	do.	do.	4°	[1526]	L². (imp.), C., SAL.
4	do.	Hymns and Sequences	4°	6 Feb., 17 Mar. [1500]	O10. (wants leaves 1–6); C6. (wants leaves 26, 27)
.1	do.	do.	4°	7 Oct., 29 Dec. 1502	Nantwich Church, Cheshire; PML. (wants leaves 49, 56)
	do.	do.	—	30 June 1508 (part 1 only dated)	L. (wants leaves 55, 56 of part 2)
	do.	do.	4°	6 July, 26 Aug. 1509	O. (Hymns only); HN., FOLG.

STC number	Author or Subject heading	Short title of work	Format	Date	Libraries containing copie
16124	Liturgies	Hymns and Sequences	4°	10 Jan., 8 May 1512	Naworth Castl FOLG., HN. (Sequences on
16125	do.	do.	4°	12 June, 8 July 1514	L., C². (Sequen only), D².
16126	do.	do.	4°	8 June, 14 June 1515	L. (Hymns onl O⁸., D².; FOLG (Sequences onl HN. (Hymns only)
16128	do.	do.	4°	1517	L.
16131.1	do.	do.	4°	[c. 1525]	C.
16131.2	do.	do.	4°	1527	Q. (Hymns o
16131.1	do.	do.	F°	1530	YK. (Sequenc only)
16160	do.	Manuale ad vsum Ebor	8°	4 Id. Feb. 1509	L. (imp.), O., HN.
16169	do.	Missale	F°	2 Jan. 1497	HN.
16172	do.	do.	F°	20 Dec. 1498	L. (imp.), C., M.
16182.2	do.	do.	F°	20 Apr. 1508	O⁵. (imp.)
16189	do.	do.	F°	6 Id. May 1511	C⁸.
16231	do.	Ordinale	4°	23 Feb. 1504	O.
16231.1	do.	do.	4°	21 June 1507	C. WORDSWO Tracts of C. Maydestone,
16254	do.	Psalter	8°	20 May 1499	M.
16255	do.	do.	4°	12 Apr. 1503	L. (wants si A I–B I), D².
16256	do.	do.	16°	20 May 1504	C. (wants n leaves)
16855.1	Love	Love and complayntes betwene Mars and Venus	4°	n.d.	ROXBURGHE 1812, no. 3
16891	Lucian, of Samosata	Complures Luciani	8°	27 June 1528	L.

STC number	Author or Subject heading	Short title of work	Format	Date	Libraries containing copies
05	Lydgate, J.	[The assembly of the gods]	F°	[1498]	L. (wants leaf 16); HN. (frag.), PML.
06	do.	do.	4°	[n.d.]	C.
07	do.	do.	4°	[1500?]	L.; HN. (frag.), MINNESOTA LAW LIB.
11	do.	The chorle and the byrde	4°	[1500?]	DEV.
12	do.	do.	—	[1510?]	C.
14.1	do.	Complaint of the Black Knight	4°	n.d.	DEV.
16	do.	Courte of Sapyence	4°	1510	L.
16.1	do.	do.	4°	1520	ALLEN sale
0	do.	The horse, the sheep and the ghoos	4°	[1499?]	C.
1	do.	do.	4°	[1500?]	DEV.
2	do.	do.	4°	[1500]	PML.
5	do.	The puerbes of Lydgate	4°	[1510?]	C.; CL., PML.
7	do.	do.	4°	[1525?]	L.; HN.
	do.	The storye of Thebes	4°	[1495?]	L. (wants leaf 88)
.1	do.	The temple of glas	4°	[1495?]	L., C. (wants leaves 25–28), DEV.; HN., Y.
	do.	do.	4°	[1500]	E.
.1	do.	do.	4°	n.d.	E.E.T.S. Extra Series, LX, xlvi
	do.	The vertue of ye masse	4°	[1520?]	L². (imp.), C.
	Lyndewode, W.	Constitutiones prouinciales	8°	31 May 1496	L., O. (wants 7 leaves), C., M.; HN. (two copies with variants)
	do.	do.	8°	15 April 1499	L²., O., M.; FOLG.
	do.	do.	8°	1508	L.
	do.	do.	8°	1517	C.; HN.
	do.	do.	8°	17 July 1526	HD.
	do.	do.	8°	28 Nov. 1529	L.; FOLG., HD., Y.

STC number	Author or Subject heading	Short title of work	Format	Date	Libraries containing copi
17241	Mancinus, Dominicus	Upon the foure cardynale vertues	4°	[1520?]	L., O.
17247	Mandeville, Sir J.	[Travels]	4°	1499	C., ST.
17249	do.	do.	4°	1503	O. (imp.)
17248	do.	do.	4°	[1510?]	O. (2 leaves)
17498	Martin, St Abp. of Braga	De quattuor virtutibus	4°	1516	L., O.; PFOR.
17499	do.	do.	4°	1523	O.
17499.1	do.	do.	4°	1525	DIBDIN, I I, no.
17499.2	do.	do.	4°	1529	ROYAL LIB. COPENHAGEN
17532	Martyrology	The martirloge	4°	15 Feb. 1526	L., O., CII., D² HN.
17537	Mary, B.V.	Lamentacyon of our Lady	4°	[1510?]	C.
17539	do.	Myracles of oure blessyd Lady	4°	[1496]	G.
17540	do.	do.	4°	1514	L.
17540.1	do.	do.	4°	1525	JOHNSON, no
17541	do.	do.	4°	1530	FOLG.
17568	Mary Magdalen	Complaynte of the lover of Cryst	4°	[1520?]	FOLG.
17723	Maydeston, C.	Directorium sacerdotum	4°	1495	L., C. (imp.)
17726	do.	do.	4°	[1499]	C. (wants pa last leaf)
17728.1	do.	do.	4°	1504	O.
17806	Melton, W. de	Sermo exhortatorius Cancellarii Ebor	4°	[before 1509]	L., P.
17841	Merlin	The byrth and prophecye of Marlyn	4°	1510	PML.
17841.1	do.	do.	F°	1529	L. (Bagford frags.), LIN (frags.)
17962	Mirk, J.	Liber festiualis and Quatuor sermones	4°	1493–4	L., O., C².; (all imp.)

TC mber	Author or Subject heading	Short title of work	Format	Date	Libraries containing copies
)65	Mirk, J.	Liber festiualis and Quatuor sermones	4°	1496	L. (pt. i, imp.), o., M.
)67	do.	do.	4°	1499	L. (imp.), M. (pt. 1, imp.); Y.
•71	do.	do.	4°	11 May 1508	C. (imp.), C³.; Y.
•71.1	do.	do.	4°	1 Aug. 1511	O⁴., M.
•72	do.	do.	4°	5 May 1515	O. (imp.), YK.
•72.1	do.	do.	4°	5 May 1519	HN.
74	do.	do.	4°	5 Nov. 1528	L., O.; Y.
•75	do.	do.	4°	23 Oct. 1532	O., C².
79.1	Mirror	Mirror of consolation	4°	1511	L., O¹⁰. C.; Y.
o5.1	Mosellanus, P.	Paedologia	4°	June 1532	HAZLITT, Collections, III, Suppl. I, 71
)2.1	Murmellius, J.	Composita verborum	4°	1520	P.
)2.2	do.	do.	4°	[c. 1521–22]	PML. (imp.)
)3	do.	do.	4°	1529	O.
•75	Nevill, W.	The castell of pleasure	4°	1518	HN.
₂8	Nicholas, Saint	Saynt Nycholas of Tollentyne	4°	[1525?]	L.
;6	Nicodemus	Nychodemus gospell	4°	23 Mar. 1509	O., C.
•7	do.	do.	4°	1511	L.; PML.
•7.1	do.	do.	4°	20 Feb. 1512	O. (imp.)
•8	do.	do.	4°	10 Mar. 1518	L.
o	do.	do.	4°	12 Apr. 1532	C.
₈	Oliver of Castile	Olyver of Castylle	4°	1518	PML. (lacks leaf 1)
₈	Ordinary	Ordynarye...of crysten men	4°	1502	L. (imp.), O. (frag.), C.; FOLG., PML.
)	do.	do.	4°	1506	L., O., C.; HN., FOLG.; PML.
₂.1	Os	Os, facies, mentum	4°	1508	HEBER, II, no. 2453 (4 leaves only)

STC number	Author or Subject heading	Short title of work	Format	Date	Libraries containing co|
18873	Os	Os, facies, mentum	4°	[1511–12?]	L. (3 leaves or
18874	do.	do.	4°	1512	FOLG.
18875	do.	do.	4°	1518	L.
18934	Ovid	Flores...de arte amandi	4°	1513	L., YK.; HN.
19119	Pain	The payne and sorowe of euyll maryage	4°	[1509?]	HN.
19207ª	Paris	Parys and...Vyenne	4°	[1510?]	O. (frag.)
19213	Parker, H.	Dives & pauper	F°	3 Dec. 1496	L., O., C., D., PML., NY.
19305	Parliament	Parlyament of deuylles	4°	1509	C.; HN.
	Parvula. See Stanbridge, J.				
19478	Patten, W. Bp.	[Indulgence]	16°	n.d.	L². (imp.)
19596	Penitents	The rule of the... Penytents	4°	1509	BAMB.
19767.1	Perottus, N.	Grammatica	4°	15 Nov. 1512	HN.
19795	Peter of Luxemburg	The next way to heuen	4°	[1510?]	L., LINC.; HN
19898	Pico della Mirandola	Lyfe of J. Picus Erle of Myrandula	4°	[1510?]	L.; HN., PML. WASH.
20034	Ploughman	How the plowman lerned his pater-noster	4°	[before 1517]	C.
20079	Poeniteas	Peniteas cito libellus	4°	[1514?]	L.
20080	do.	do.	4°	[1515?]	FOLG.
20081	do.	do.	4°	[1520?]	L.
20107	Ponthus	History of King Ponthus	4°	[1501?]	O. (frag.)
20108	do.	do.	4°	1511	O. (wants fi two leaves)
20412	Profits	The XII profytes of trybulacyon	4°	[1499]	BAMB., M.
20413	do.	do.	4°	28 May 1530	L., O.; HN.,
20414	Prognostication	Prognostication for 1498	4°	[1497]	O. (2 leaves
20417	do.	do.	4°	26 Dec. 1523	C. (frags.)

STC number	Author or Subject heading	Short title of work	Format	Date	Libraries containing copies
435.1	Promptorium	Promptorium paruulorum	4°	1 Dec. 1509	L. (Bagford frags.)
436	do.	do.	4°	17 Jan. 1510	L., C. (wants last 4 leaves)
437	do.	do.	4°	26 May 1512	HN., FOLG.
438	do.	do.	4°	5 Sept. 1516	L., O., C., M.; HN., FOLG.
438.1	do.	do.	4°	1518	JOHNSON, no. 148
438.2	do.	do.	4°	1522	DUFF, I, 14
439	do.	do.	4°	13 May 1528	L.
602.1	Ragman	Ragman's roll		n.d.	HAZLITT, Collections, I, 350
378	Remigius	Dominus que pars	4°	[1500]	O.
382	Remorse	The remors of conscyence	4°	[c. 1500?]	L.
383	do.	do.	4°	[after 1532]	C. (wants sheet b)
394.1	Retorna	Returna Brevium	4°	1519	M.; HN.
421.1	Reynard	Reynard the fox	4°	[1525]	C. (2 leaves only)
007	Richard I	Rycharde cuer de Lyon	8°	1509	O., M.
008	do.	do.	4°	1528	L., O.; PML.
070	Robert, the Devil	Robert the deuyll	4°	[1502?]	C. (wants 1st leaf)
071	do.	do.	4°	[1517?]	L.
71.1	do.	do.	—	n.d.	O. (frag.)
087	Robin Hood	Geste of Robyn hode	4°	[1500]	O. (2 leaves only)
089	do.	do.	4°	[1505?]	C.
090	do.	do.	4°	[1510?]	O. (4 leaves only) [? J. Notary]
59	Rolle, R.	Contemplacyons	4°	1506	L., BAMB., M.
60	do.	do.	4°	[1525]	O., C. (imp.); HN., CL., FOLG.
60.1	do.	Devoute Medytacyons	4°	1503	DENT sale, Part 2, 1827, no. 257
60.2	do.	do.	4°	4 Feb. 1508	L.
60.3	do.	do.	4°	4 Feb. 1517	BRYDGES, Cens. Lit. I, 20

STC number	Author or Subject heading	Short title of work	Format	Date	Libraries containing copie
21262	Rolle, R.	Remedy ayenst... temptacyons	4°	1508	L.
21262.1	do.	do.	4°	1517	DUFF, I, 11
21263	do.	do.	4°	21 Jan. 1519	L.; FOLG. (imp
21286.1	Romans	Gesta romanorum	4°	[n.d.]	C5.
21298	Rome	Ye VII wyse Maysters of rome	4°	[1520?]	L. (imp.)
21318.1	Rosary	Rosary of Our Saviour, Jesus	4°	1530	DIBDIN, II, no. :
21334	Rote	The Rote...of consolacyon	4°	[1496]	DUR. (wants leaves 48–64)
21335	do.	do.	4°	[after 10 July 1499]	C6.; CL.
21335.1	do.	do.	4°	1509	C6.
21336	do.	do.	4°	1511	L., C.
21337	do.	do.	4°	23 Mar. 1530	C., C2.; PML.
21430	Royal Book	The booke named the royall	4°	[1507]	L., O.; FOLG.,
21473	do.	do.	8°	7 Oct. 1525	C2.; HN.
21472	Ryckes, J.	The ymage of loue	8°	[1532?]	O.
21798	Savonarola, G.	Expositio...in psalmum In te domine speraui	4°	[n.d.]	O.; FOLG.
21827	Schottenius, H.	Instructio prima puerorum	8°	1533	O.
22409	Shepherd's Kalendar	The Kalender of shepeherdes	F°	8 Dec. 1508	O12.
22409.1	do.	do.	—	1511	SHIRBURN CA:
22411	do.	do.	—	24 Jan. 1528	O. (wants titl and col.); HN
22557	Simon	The fruyte of redempcyon	4°	1514	L., C.
22558	do.	do.	4°	1517	C., M.
22559	do.	do.	4°	21 May 1530	L.
22560	do.	do.	4°	1532	L.
22580	Sirectus, A.	Formalities	4°	[1513?]	L., O14. (frag.
22597	Skelton, J.	The Bowge of Court	4°	[n.d.]	E.

STC number	Author or Subject heading	Short title of work	Format	Date	Libraries containing copies
22978	Spagnuoli, B.	Bucolica	4°	May 1523	HN.
22979	do.	do.	4°	1526	O.
23013	Spare	Spare your good	4°	[1518–19]	O. (frag.)
23111.1	Squire	The squire of low degree	—	[c. 1520]	HN. (frag.)
23140.1	Stanbridge, J.	Accidence	4°	[c. 1505]	C4.
3140.2	do.	do.	4°	[c. 1510]	C.
3140.3	do.	do.	4°	1519	HN.
3142	do.	do.	4°	[1520?]	L. (imp.), O. (2 edns.)
3147.2	do.	[Accidentia]	4°	1523	HEARNE, p. 4
3148	do.	do.	4°	[1525?]	Q.
3148.1	do.	do.	4°	[1526–29]	O.
3148.2	do.	do.	4°	[1529]	L., O., MARL. (imp.)
3150	do.	do.	4°	[1530?]	L.
3151.1	do.	do.	4°	20 Feb. 1534	C5.
3152	do.	do.	4°	1534	L.; MINNESOTA
3153.1	do.	The longe accydence	4°	1513	C5.
3154	do.	do.	4°	[1517]	L.
3155.1	do.	[Gradus comparationum] Sum es fui	4°	[c. 1504–09]	C4.; COLUMBIA
3159	do.	do.	4°	[c. 1510?]	O., C2.
3157	do.	do.	4°	[c. 1516–17]	L., C4.
3159.1	do.	do.	4°	[c. 1518–19]	O.
3159.2	do.	do.	4°	[c. 1519–20]	M.; HN.
59.3	do.	do.	4°	[c. 1520]	PML.
59.4	do.	do.	4°	1523	HEARNE, p. 4
59.5	do.	do.	4°	[c. 1523–25]	MARL.
59.6	do.	do.	4°	18 July 1526	M.
60	do.	do.	4°	6 Nov. 1527	O.; CH., COLUMBIA
60.1	do.	do.	4°	[1526–28]	M.
61	do.	do.	4°	1530	C2.; FOLG.
63	do.	do.	4°	1532	Q., MARL. (frag.)

STC number	Author or Subject heading	Short title of work	Format	Date	Libraries containing co
23164	Stanbridge, J.	Long parvula	4°	1509	O.
19440	do.	Parvula	4°	[c. 1495–96]	O.
19439	do.	do.	4°	[1497]	L., C.
19439.1	do.	do.	4°	[before 4 Dec. 1499]	HN. (frag.)
19439.2	do.	do.	4°	[1499–1500]	HN. (frag.)
19441	do.	do.	4°	[c. 1501–03]	C.
23171	do.	do.	4°	[1507]	O., HN.
19442.1	do.	do.	—	1508	DUFF, I, 7
23164.1	do.	do.	—	[1510–11]	O.
23164.2	do.	do.	—	[after 1510]	C⁴.
23164.3	do.	do.	—	[c. 1511]	CH. [Not 231
23167	do.	do.	—	[c. 1512]	L.
23167.1	do.	do.	—	[c. 1513]	PML.
23166	do.	do.	—	[c. 1513–14]	O., Q.
23166.1	do.	do.	—	[c. 1516–17]	HN. [Not 23
23167.1	do.	do.	—	Mar. 1520	PML.
23168	do.	do.	—	1521	L., MARL. (la title)
23168.1	do.	do.	—	1523	HEARNE, p.
23169	do.	do.	—	1526	O., C.
23173	do.	do.	4°	1528	L. (lacks title
23174	do.	do.	4°	1529	O.
23174.2	do.	do.	4°	1530	C⁴.
23177.1	do.	Vocabula	4°	1500	JOHNSON, nc
23177.2	do.	do.	4°	1501	JOHNSON, nc
23177.3	do.	do.	4°	1507	JOHNSON, nc
23177.4	do.	do.	4°	[c. 1508]	C.
23178	do.	do.	4°	1510	L., O., C¹⁹; F
23179.1	do.	do.	4°	1514	C⁴.
23185.1	do.	do.	4°	[1520?]	HN.
23181.1	do.	do.	4°	1521	MARL.
23181.2	do.	do.	4°	1523	HEARNE, p.
23182	do.	do.	4°	16 Feb. 1525	O.

STC number	Author or Subject heading	Short title of work	Format	Date	Libraries containing copies
23182.1	Stanbridge, J.	Vocabula	4°	1529	Q.
23182.2	do.	do.	4°	1530	JOHNSON, no. 46
23183	do.	do.	4°	17 Nov. 1531	O.
23183.1	do.	do.	4°	17 Aug. 1532	JOHNSON, no. 47
23183.2	do.	do.	4°	6 Jan. 1534	C5.
23185	do.	do.	4°	[n.d.]	O.; FOLG., HN.
23194	do.	Vulgaria	4°	[c. 1509?]	C. (frag.)
23194.1	do.	do.	4°	[1509?]	SOTHEBY, 9 July 1918
23195.1	do.	do.	4°	[c. 1514–15]	MARL. (wants A 1)
23195.2	do.	do.	4°	1515	M.
23196	do.	do.	4°	1516	M.
23196.1	do.	do.	4°	[1518?]	C4.; MICHIGAN
23196.2	do.	do.	4°	1519	HN.
23198	do.	do.	4°	[1520?]	L. (imp.), O.; HN., PML., MELBOURNE
23198.1	do.	do.	4°	[c. 1521]	FOLG. (not 23198)
23198.2	do.	do.	4°	1523	HEARNE, p. 4
23198.3	do.	do.	4°	[1526–28?]	O.; WASH.
23197	do.	do.	4°	[1528?]	L. (lacks title);
23244	Stella	Stella clericorum	8°	20 Oct. 1531	C. (lacks title); PML.
23427	Sulpitius, J.	Opus insigne grammaticum	4°	4 Dec. 1499	O., C.
23427.1	do.	do.	4°	19 Dec. 1504	SHR. (lacks title)
23428	do.	Stans puer ad mensam	4°	[after 8 June] 1515	L.
23428ᵃ	do.	do.	4°	1516	M.
23429	do.	do.	4°	1518	L., C4.
23429ᵈ	do.	do.	4°	Prid. Kal. Nov. 1524	Q. (Britwell copy)
23430	do.	do.	4°	[1510]	C.
23435ᵃ	Surdit	Surdit, King of Ireland	4°	[1525?]	O. (2 leaves only)

STC number	Author or Subject heading	Short title of work	Format	Date	Libraries containing copies
23551.1	Benno	Lyf of Hyldebrande ...and Henry IV	8°	1533	RAWLINSON, pt. xv (1729), no. 1990
23552	Swinnerton, T.	A mustre of scismatyke bysshoppes..	4°	20 Mar. 1534	L., O.
23876	Ten Commandments	The floure of the commaundementes...	F°	14 Sept. 1510	L., O., C., C⁴., C⁵. M.; HN.
23877	do.	do.	F°	8 Oct. 1521	L., O., C., M.; HN FOLG.
23908	Terence	Vulgaria	8°	3 Aug. 1529	C. (frag.)
23941	Theodulus	Liber theodoli cum commento	4°	28 Apr. 1509	L.
23943	do.	do.	4°	10 Mar. 1515	L., O., C.
23954.1	Thomas à Kempis	Imitatio Christi	4°	1502	JOHNSON, no. 7
23955.1	do.	do.	4°	[1510?]	C.
23956	do.	do.	4°	[1519?]	L., C., M.; FOLG
23958.1	do.	do.	4°	[1519?]	C. (Bk. iv only)
23959	do.	do.	4°	[1520?]	C.
23960	do.	do.	4°	[1528?]	L. (imp.); HN.
24092.1	Titus	Tytus and Gesyppus	4°	[n.d.]	DEV.
13075	Torent	Sir Torrant of Portugal	4°	[not before 1509]	O. (frag.)
24154	Tower	The Toure melodyous	4°	[1515?]	O. (frag.); HN.
24224	Treatise	How every man... ought to fast	4°	[1500]	C⁶.
24225	do.	do.	4°	1532	Oᴵᴵ., M.
24234	do.	This treatise is of loue	F°	[1493]	C., C²., M.; HN. PML.
24240	do.	Treatyse of a galaunt	4°	[1510?]	L. (first and la leaf only); HN (4 leaves), FO
24240.1	do.	do.	4°	[1515?]	MELBOURNE
24241	do.	do.	4°	[1520?]	L.
24242	do.	do.	4°	[1522?]	L. [J. Skot fo W. de Word

STC number	Author or Subject heading	Short title of work	Format	Date	Libraries containing copies
24243	Treatise	Treatyse of fysshynge with an angle	4°	[c. 1532–34]	HN., PML.
24302	Tryamour	Sir Tryamour	4°	[n.d.]	C. (2 leaves only)
24540.1	Ursula	The lyf of saynt Ursula	4°	[n.d.]	DEV.
24571.1	Valentine	Valentine and Orson	—	[1502?]	DEV. (frag.)
24766	Vineis, R. de	The lyf of saint Katherin of Senis	F°	[1493?]	L., C.; HN., FOLG.
24766.1	do.	do.	F°	[n.d.]	DEV.; HN. (frag.)
24812.1	Virgil	Bucolica	4°	8 Apr. 1512	RAWLINSON, Part xv (1729), no. 888
24813	do.	do.	4°	1512	L. (imp.)
24814	do.	do.	4°	22 Nov. 1514	O., M., Ham House
24814.1	do.	do.	4°	4 Dec. 1516	DIBDIN, II, no.236
24814.2	do.	do.	4°	22 Aug. 1522	The Bookworm, I, 12; PRINCETON
24815	do.	do.	4°	12 Mar. 1529	O. (imp.), Q. (imp.)
24815.1	do.	do.	4°	7 June 1533	DIBDIN, II, no. 237
24866	Vocabulary	A lytell treatyse for to lerne Englysshe & Frensshe	4°	[1497]	L.
24875	Voragine, J. de	The Golden Legend	F°	20 May 1493	L. (imp.), O., M.; FOLG., HN., PML.
24876	do.	do.	F°	8 Jan. 1498	L. (imp.), O. (imp.), C. (imp.), M.; PML (imp.)
24877.1	do.	do.	4°	1507	L². [with imprint of R. Pynson]
24878	do.	do.	4°	[1510?]	L., C². (imp.)
24879	do.	do.	F°	15 Feb. 1512	L., C., C³., M.
24879.1	do.	do.	F°	30 Feb. 1521	HN., FOLG.
24880	do.	do.	F°	27 Aug. 1527	L., O., C., M.; HN., FOLG.
24944	Wakefield, R.	Oratio de laudibus trium linguarum	4°	1524	L., O., C., M.; HD.

STC number	Author or Subject heading	Short title of work	Format	Date	Libraries containing copies
24946	Wakefield, R.	Syntagma de hebreorum	4°	[1530?]	L., O., C.
25007	Walter of Henley	Boke of husbandry	4°	[c. 1506?]	C.
25008	Walter, W.	The Spectacle of Louers	4°	[before 1511]	O. (2 leaves), DEV.; HN.
25417	Whitforde, R.	Exposicyon of saynt Augustynes rule	4°	28 Nov. 1525	O., C⁴., Cᴵᴵ, ST.
25419	do.	do.	4°	1527	FOLG. (imp.)
25422	do.	A werke for housholders	4°	2 May 1530	O.; HN.
25423	do.	do.	4°	2 May 1533	L.; FOLG.
25443.1	Whittinton, R.	Antylycon in defensionem R.W.	4°	5 Jan. 1521	DEV.
25443.2	do.	[Declinationes nominum]	4°	8 May 1515	Lord Robartes (frag.)
25444	do.	do.	4°	[1515?]	C².; HN.
25444.1	do.	do.	4°	[1515?]	HN.
25444.2	do.	do.	4°	2 Aug. 1516	DIBDIN, II, no. 24
25445	do.	do.	4°	1517	L., O., C⁴.; HN.
25446	do.	do.	4°	1519	L., O.; WASH.
25447	do.	do.	4°	[1520?]	L.; HN.
25448	do.	do.	4°	1521	L., E.; HN., HD.
25449	do.	do.	4°	1523	L.; CH.
25450.1	do.	do.	4°	1524	HN.
25452	do.	do.	4°	1525	L.
25453	do.	do.	4°	1525	L., O. (2 issues)
25454	do.	do.	4°	1527	O.; HN.
25455	do.	do.	4°	[1529]	C.
25456	do.	do.	4°	1529	O., Cᴵ⁹., Q.
25457.1	do.	do.	4°	1531	SOTHEBY, 14 July, 1916, no 470.
25458	do.	do.	4°	1533	M.

STC umber	Author or Subject heading	Short title of work	Format	Date	Libraries containing copies
5459.1	Whittinton, R.	De heteroclitis nominibus	4°	[1515?]	C².
5459.2	do.	do.	4°	[1515]	HN.
5459.4	do.	do.	4°	[c. 1517–18]	O.
5461	do.	do.	4°	7 Id. 1519	O., C⁴., MARL.; PML.
5463	do.	do.	4°	[c. 1519–20]	O., C.; HN.
5462	do.	do.	4°	1520	L., O.
5464	do.	do.	4°	1521	O., C⁴., Q.; HN.
5464.1	do.	do.	4°	Prid. Kal. Aug. 1522	P., YK.
5466	do.	do.	4°	Id. Feb. 1523	O., M.; HN.
5466.1	do.	do.	4°	Kal. Feb. 1524	MYERS & CO., Cat. 277 (1930); CH.
5467	do.	do.	4°	19 Dec. 1524	L., O.
5468	do.	do.	4°	Prid. Kal. Aug. 1525	C.; HN.
5469	do.	do.	4°	Id. Jul. 1526	L., P. (imp.)
5470	do.	do.	4°	Id. Maii 1527	L., O.
5471.1	do.	do.	4°	Id. Julii 1527	DIBDIN, II, no. 283
5472	do.	do.	4°	20 May 1529	M.; HN.
5476	do.	do.	4°	Mar. 1531	Q.
5476.1	do.	do.	4°	10 Nov. 1531	Christie sale of 18 June 1925
5477	do.	do.	4°	1533	L., M.; FOLG., HN.
5479	do.	[De nominum generibus]	4°	[c. 1510–11]	L.
5496.1	do.	do.	4°	[c. 1513–14]	HN.
5496.2	do.	do.	4°	1516	O., M.
5496	do.	do.	4°	[1515–17?]	O.; HN.
5496.3	do.	do.	4°	[1515–17?]	C².
5496.4	do.	do.	4°	[1519?]	O.
5479.1	do.	do.	4°	Kal. Nov. 1519	Robson & Co. (1912)
5479.2	do.	do.	4°	1520	HD.

271

STC number	Author or Subject heading	Short title of work	Format	Date	Libraries containing copies
25480.1	Whittinton, R.	[De nominum generibus]	4°	Kal. Feb. 1521	O.; PML.
25481	do.	do.	4°	Id. Junii 1521	M., Q.
25482	do.	do.	4°	Prid. Id. Oct. 1521	L.
25483	do.	do.	4°	Prid. Non. Feb. 1522	L., MARL., SHR.
25483.1	do.	do.	4°	1522	HERBERT, I, 164
25484	do.	do.	4°	Prid. Kal. Sept. 1522	Q.
25484.1	do.	do.	4°	Prid. Non. Sept. 1522	CH.
25485.1	do.	do.	4°	Kal. Mar. 1524	HN.
25486	do.	do.	4°	19 Dec. 1524	L.
25487	do.	do.	4°	8 Kal. May 1525	O.; HN.
25488	do.	do.	4°	3 Kal. Sept. 1526	O.
25488.1	do.	do.	4°	3 Kal. Sept. 1526	C.
25489	do.	do.	4°	Prid. Non. Mar. 1527	O., P.
25490	do.	do.	4°	Prid. Kal. July 1528	O.; COLUMBIA
25491	do.	do.	4°	29 May 1529	L., O.
25491.1	do.	do.	4°	Prid. Kal. June 1529	HN.
25493.1	do.	do.	4°	6 Aug. 1533	HN.
25494	do.	do.	4°	16 Oct. 1534	L.
25497	do.	De octo partibus orationis	4°	[1515?]	L.
25497.1	do.	do.	4°	[1515?]	O., C².
25498.1	do.	do.	4°	[1516–19]	HN.
25498.2	do.	do.	4°	[1516–19]	HN.
25499	do.	do.	4°	8 Id. Apr. 1519	L., O., C.; FOI

TC nber	Author or Subject heading	Short title of work	Format	Date	Libraries containing copies
oo	Whittinton, R.	[De syllabarum quantitatibus]	4°	Id. Julii 1521	L., MARL., Q., FOLG.
oi	do.	do.	4°	13 Apr. 1522	Q.
o3	do.	do.	4°	Dec. 1523	L., O.; HN., COLUMBIA
o4	do	do.	4°	Jan. 1525	O.
o4ᵃ	do.	do.	4°	[1525?]	O.
o5	do.	do.	4°	19 Feb. 1527	O., C^{19}.; HN.
o6	do.	do.	4°	Prid. Kal. Jn. 1529	L.
o6.1	do.	do.	4°	1530	JOHNSON, no. 223
o8	do.	do.	4°	3 Sept. 1533	L.; HN.
o8.1	do.	do.	4°	1533	HN.
o9.1	do.	do.	4°	12 Aug. 1513	HN.
ᵗ5	do.	do.	4°	[c. 1515]	O.
ᵗo	do.	do.	4°	1516	O.; HD.?
ᵗ1.1	do.	do.	4°	10 Aug. 1517	C^2. (imp.), Q.
2	do.	do.	4°	7 Id. Mar. 1519	L., O.; HN., CALIFORNIA (pt ii)
2.1	do.	do.	4°	Kal. Nov. 1519	L., O.
3	do.	do.	4°	1519	L. (part i)
4	do.	do.	4°	1519	L.; HN.
5	do.	do.	4°	1521	O., Q.; CH.
5ᵃ	do.	do.	4°	1521	L., C., P., MARL. (part ii)., SHR.
3	do.	do.	4°	[1521?]	O. (lacks C4-6)
5.2	do.	do.	4°	1522	HN.
8	do.	do.	4°	1524	L., O., C^{19}.; HN.
4	do.	do.	4°	[1524?]	O.
	do.	do.	4°	[1525?]	CH., MELBOURNE
	do.	do.	4°	1526	O. (part ii), WOLLATON
.1	do.	do.	4°	1527	HAZLITT, Coll. II, 643
	do.	do.	4°	1528	L., O., M.; HN.

STC number	Author or Subject heading	Short title of work	Format	Date	Libraries containing copi
25526	Whittinton, R.	[De synonymis]	4°	[1515?]	HN.
25526.1	do.	do.	4°	[1515–16]	HN. (imp.), Annmary Bro Memorial
25540	do.	do.	4°	[c. 1516]	O.
25527	do.	do.	4°	9 Kal. Aug. 1517	L.; HN. (frag.
25527.1	do.	do.	4°	1517	C².
25538	do.	do.	4°	[1517–18?]	O.
25528	do.	do.	4°	9 Kal. Feb. 1519	O., SH.; PML.
25539	do.	do.	4°	[1520?]	O.
25530	do.	do.	4°	1521	L., MARL.
25531	do.	do.	4°	1522	P., Q. (2 cop
25533	do.	do.	4°	Aug. 1523	L., C., C¹⁹; CH
25534	do.	do.	4°	Feb. 1525	L.; HN., CH.
25535	do.	do.	4°	Feb. 1527	L., O.; FOLG.
25535.1	do.	do.	4°	4 Feb. 1529	BRIT. (imp.); DUFF, I. 19
25536	do.	do.	4°	Mar. 1529	O., C.; CH., I (imp.)
25537	do.	do.	4°	1533	O. (imp.)
25540.2	do.	[Epigrammata]	4°	10 Kal. Maii, 1519	C⁴., DEV., ET HN.
25541	do.	[Syntaxis]	4°	3 Sept. 1512	O.; HN.
25543	do.	do.	4°	1517	L., O., C⁵.
25545	do.	do.	4°	1518	O., C².; HN.
25546	do.	do.	4°	1519	O., C.
25547	do.	do.	4°	Id. Mar. 1520	L.
25547.1	do.	do.	4°	Id. Oct. 1521	MARL.
25548	do.	do.	4°	Nov. 1521	O.
25550	do.	do.	4°	13 Jan. 1524	Q; HN.
25551	do.	do.	4°	13 Nov. 1524	L., O., C.; H COLUMBIA
25552	do.	do.	4°	13 Apr. 1525	L.; HN.
25553	do.	do.	4°	1526	O.

STC number	Author or Subject heading	Short title of work	Format	Date	Libraries containing copies
25553.1	Whittinton, R.	[Syntaxis]	4°	Prid. Non. Mar. 1527	O., C¹⁹.
25554	do.	do.	4°	Prid. Kal. Nov. 1527	L., O.
25556	do.	do.	4°	Id. Nov. 1529	L., O.
25556.1	do.	do.	4°	1532	Christie: sale of 18 June 1925 (lot 787)
25557	do.	do.	4°	1533	L., O., M.
5557.1	do.	do.	4°	1534	RAWLINSON (1727), no. 1785
5558	do.	De verborum praeterita	4°	1521	L. (imp.), MARL., SHR.
5559	do.	do.	4°	1521	L., Q.
5559.1	do.	do.	4°	1521	O.
5560	do.	do.	4°	1522	P., Q.; CH.
5562	do.	do.	4°	1524	L., O., M.; HN.
5562.1	do.	do.	4°	[1524]	HN.
5563	do.	do.	4°	1525	O.; HN.
5564	do.	do.	4°	13 Sept. 1526	O. (imp.), C., C¹⁹
5564.1	do.	do.	4°	Id. Mai 1527	P.; MELBOURNE
5564.2	do.	do.	4°	4 May 1528	HN.
565	do.	do.	4°	Kal. Sept. 1529	L., O.
565.1	do.	do.	4°	1530	WOLLATON
567	do.	do.	4°	[1533]	L.
571	do.	Vulgaria	4°	1520	M., Q.; HN.
571.1	do.	do.	4°	Non. Mart. 1520	C5.
572	do.	do.	4°	1521	L., O., MARL., SHR.
572.1	do.	do.	4°	1522	Q.
573	do.	do.	4°	1523	HEARNE, p. 5, Q.; HN.
74	do.	do.	4°	1524	O., C¹⁹., Q.
76	do.	do.	4°	1525	L., O.; CH., HN.

STC number	Author or Subject heading	Short title of work	Format	Date	Libraries containing copies
25577	Whittinton, R.	Vulgaria	4°	1526	C.
25578	do.	do.	4°	1527	L.; HN.
25580	do.	do.	4°	[1527–29]	O. (lacks H₈)
25579	do.	do.	4°	[1533]	O.
25580.1	do.	do.	4°	1534	Christie; sale of 8 June 1925 (lot 717)
25982	World	Mundus & Infans	4°	17 July 1522	D.

TRIAL LIST OF TRANSLATIONS INTO ENGLISH PRINTED BETWEEN 1475-1560

The list which follows is the first attempt, so far as I am aware, to collect in one place the translations, and where possible the names of the translators, of works printed in this period. It is often difficult, if not impossible, to tell whether a work is a translation or not, and further investigation is necessary to clear up many points. In the meantime, this list may serve as a useful guide for those interested in this important aspect of Tudor literature.

STC number	Author or Subject heading	Short title of work	Date	Translator
19	A.B.C.	The BAC booke in latyn and in Englysshe	[1538]	—
175	Aesop	Historyes and fables of Esope	1484	W. Caxton
178	do.	Fables in Englysshe with all his lyfe	[1550?]	—
191	Africa	Description of the countrey of Aphrique	1554	W. Prat
193	Agapetus	The preceptes teachyng a prynce...his duetie	[1532?]	T. Paynell
201	Agrippa, H. C.	The commendation of matrimony	1540	D. Clapham
203	do.	Of the nobilitie of woman kynde	1542	D. Clapham
256	Alban, *Saint*	Lyfe of Seint Albon... and also...of Saint Amphabel...	1534	J. Lydgate
259	Albertus Magnus	Secretes of the vertues of herbes	[1549]	W. Copland
260	do.	The boke of secretes	[n.d.]	—

STC number	Author or Subject heading	Short title of work	Date	Translator
292	Alesius, A.	Of the auctorite of the word of god	[1537?]	E. Allen?
293	Alessio	The secretes of Alexis... Part I	1558	W. Warde
300	do.	The secretes of Alexis... Part II	1560	W. Warde
321	Alexander	[Romance of King Alexander]	[1550?]	—

Almanacks, Kalendars and Prognostications

—	Laet, J.	[A prognostication]	[n.b. 1492]	—
406.1	Adrian	The prostication (*sic*) of Master Adrian for 1520	[*c*. 1520]	—
20414	Prognostications	[Prognostication for 1498]	[1497]	—
20415	do.	[Prognostication]	[1500?]	—
504	Red, W.	Almanach Ephemerides in anno...M.d.xix...	[1507]	—
15121	Laet, G.	The pronosticaciõ of maister Jasper of the yere M.CCCCC.XVI	1516	N. Longwater
15122	Laet, G.	Prognostication for M.CCCCC.XVI	1517	—
15123	Laet, G.	Prenostica...	1518	—
151.1	Adrian	Prognitication...for MDXX	[1520?]	—
15124	Laet, G.	Prenosticatio...for M.D.XX	1520	—
15125	do.	The pronostication of maister J. Laet...	1520	—
20417	Prognostications	[A Prognostication]	1523	—
20418	do.	[A Prognostication]	1523	—
15126	Laet, G.	A prognosticacyon for M.V.C. & XXIIII	[1524]	—
13522	Hippocrates	Prognosticacion drawen out of Ipocras...	[1530?]	—
15127.1	Laet, G.	Almanack and Pronostication of...M.CCCCC.XXX	1530	—
15128	do.	Pronosticum pro anno domini M.CCCCC.XXX	1530	—
23951	Thibault, J.	Pronosticacyon. The yere M.CCCCC.XXX	[1530]	—

STC umber	Author or Subject heading	Short title of work	Date	Translator
952	Thibault, J.	Pronostycacyon of the yere M.CCCC.XXXIII	[1533]	—
129	Laet, G., the younger	The prognosticacion for the yere M.D.XXXIIJ	[1533]	—
30	do.	[A prognostication]	[1534]	—
43	Brunsfelsius, O.	A very true pronosticaciō... for 1536	[1536]	J. Ryckes
18.1	—	A faythfull & true Pronosticacion vpō the yeare M.CCCC.XXXVI	1536	M. Coverdale
15	Erra Pater	The pronostycacyon for euer	[1536?]	—
30.1	Laet, G., the younger	Almynack and pronostication of	1537	—
16	Erra Pater	Pronostication for euer	[1538?]	—
19	Prognostications	[A Prognostication]	[c. 1539?]	—
20	do.	[A Prognostication]	[c. 1539?]	—
17	Erra Pater	The pronostycacion for euer	[1540?]	—
73	Laet, G., the younger	Almanacke and Prognostication for M.CCCC.XLI	1541	—
31	do.	Pronosticacion of the yere M.vᶜxli	[1541]	—
21	Prognostications	[A Prognostication]	[1541?]	—
8	Erra Pater	The pronostycacyon of Erra Pater	[1542?]	—
72	Laet, G., the younger	An Almanacke and Pronosticacion of M.CCCC.XLIII	[1543]	—
5	do.	An Almanack and Pronosticacion of 1543	[n.d.]	—
2	Prognostications	A mery pronosticacion for the yere a thousande fyve hundreth fortye & foure	[1544]	—
2	Laet, G., the younger	Pronosticacion for the yere M.vᶜxliiii	[1544]	—
6	do.	An Almanack and Pronosticacion	1544	—
9	Scute, C.	A pronostication for the yere 1544...	[1544]	—

STC number	Author or Subject heading	Short title of work	Date	Translator
523	Walter, M. and H. Ry.	An Almanacke and Pronosticacon for 1544	1544	M. Coverdale
3842	Brothyel, M.	A Pronostyacyon anno 1545	1545	—
477	Laet, G., *the younger*	An Almanacke and Pronostication for MDXLV	1545	—
477.1	do.	An Almanacke and Pronostication for MDXLVI	1546	—
11646	Gasser, A. P.	A prognostication for this yere m.dxlvi	[1546]	—
477	Laet, G., *the younger*	An Almanacke & pronostication...M.D.XL.VI	1546	—
21779.1	Sauvage, J.	An Almanack and Prognostication	1547	—
21779.2	do.	An Almanack and Prognostication	1548	—
470	Laet, A.	An almanack and prognostication for MCCCCC.XLVIII	1548	—
20423	Prognostications	A faythfull and true pronostication vpon the yere 1548	[1548?]	M. Coverdale?
20424	do.	A faythful and true pronostication vpon the yere M.CCCCC.XLIX	[1548?]	M. Coverdale
21780	Sauvage, J.	A prognostication for the yere MCCCCCL	1550	W. Harrys
464	Huring, S.	An Almanack and Prognostication for M.CCCCC.DLI	1551	—
462	Hubrigh, J.	[An Almanacke and Prognostication for 1553?]	[1553?]	—
486.1	Motulind, A. de	A ryght excellente treatise of Astronomie	1554	F. van Brunswike
487	do.	An almanacke and prognosticacion for 1555	[1554]	—
11801.1	Gesner, J.	[An Almanacke and Prognostication]	[1555?]	—
492	Nostradamus, M.	An Almanacke for 1559	1559	—
18695	do.	The Prognosticacion for 1559	1559	—

STC number	Author or Subject heading	Short title of work	Date	Translator
546	Amant	Lamant mal Traite de sa mye	[1543]	J. Clere
547.1	Ambrose, *Saint*	A deuout prayer of Saint Ambrose...	1555	T. Paynell
564	Anabaptists	Wōderfull worckes of the Rebaptisers of Mūster in Westuaell	[s.n.]	—
645	Anglerius, P. M.	The Decades of the newe world	1555	R. Eden
675	Antidotarius	The antidotharius...	[1530?]	—
708.1	Apollonius	King Appolyn of Thyre	1510	R. Copland
754	Aristotle	The ethiques...	1547	J. Wilkinson
768	do. [*Supposititious works*]	De cursione lune	[1530?]	—
769	do.	The nature of the dayes in the weke	[1535?]	—
770	do.	The secrete of secretes	1528	R. Copland
777	Arnaldus de Villanova	The defence of age...	[1540]	J. Drummond
785	Arsanes	Orations...agaynst Philip	[1560?]	T. Norton?
786	Ars	Ars moriendi...	[1491]	W. Caxton
789	Art	The arte & crafte to knowe well to dye	1490	W. Caxton
791	do.	The Art of good lywying & good deying	1503	—
792	do.	The craft to liue well and to die well	1505	A. Chertsey
793	do.	The arte or crafte to lyue well and to dye well	[1506]	—
801	Arthur, *King*	Le morte Darthur	1485	Sir T. Malory
807	Arthur of Little Britain	Arthur of lytell Brytayne	[1555?]	J. Bourchier
822	Artopoeus, P.	The diuisyon of the places of the lawe and of the gospell	1548	W. Lynne?
862	Assault	The assaute and cōquest of heuen	1529	T. Paynell

STC number	Author or Subject heading	Short title of work	Date	Translator
908	Augsburg Confession	The confessyon of the fayth of the Germaynes...	1536	R. Taverner
919	Augustine, *Saint*	Certein places gathered out of S. Austens boke intituled, De essentia diuinitatis	1548	H. Bodius
25417	do.	The exposicyon of saynt Augustynes rule, after saynt Hugh [of S. Victor]	1525	R. Whitforde
920	do.	The predestination of saints	1550	N. Lesse
921	do.	Of perseueraunce unto thende: The predestination of saintes	[1556?]	J. Scory
923	do.	Twelve sermons	n.d.	T. Paynell
84	do.	The twelfe steppes of abuses	1550	N. Lesse
955	do.	A woorke concernyng adulterous mariages	1550	W. Conway
965	Austin, *Saint*	The myrrour of the chyrche	1521	R. Copland
987	Avila, Luis de	The commentaries...which treateth of the wars in Germany	1555	J. Wilkinson
1007	Aymon	The four sons of Aymon	1489	W. Caxton
1180	Bacon, R.	Of the beste waters artyfycialles	[1530?]	—
1253	Baldwin, W.	A treatise of morall phylosophie...	1547	W. Baldwin
5293	Banatusius Magnomontanus	[Two declarations made by Scipio and Flaminius.] With (Cicero, De Senectute)	1481	J. Tiptoft?
1375	Barbara, *Saint*	The lyf of Saynt Barbara	1518	—
1384	Barclay, A.	The Egloges	[c. 1515]	A. Barclay
1386	do.	The maner of dauncing of base daunces	1521	R. Copland
1536	Bartholomaeus, Anglicus	De proprietatibus rerum	[1495]	J. Trevisa
1542.1	Basil, *Saint*, the Great	Exhortation to hys younge kynsemen to the studie of Scripture	1557	W. Barker

TC nber	Author or Subject heading	Short title of work	Date	Translator
42.2	Basil, *Saint*, the Great	Letter to Gregory of Nazianzus showing that... certain godly men used the life monastical	[n.d.]	R. Sherry
44	Basle	The answere that the preachers of the gospel at Basile made	[1548]	G. Bancroft
4	Beard, R.	Alphabetum primum Beeardi	[n.d.]	W. Copland
6	Beauty	The Beaute of women	[1525?]	—
5	Benedict, *Saint*	The rule of saynte Benet	1491	W. Caxton?
9	do.	The rule of seynt Benet	[1516?]	J. Fox
8	Bernard, *Saint*	A moche fruytefull treatyse of well liuynge	[1545?]	T. Paynell
1	do.	The golden epistle	[1530?]	R. Whitforde
2	do.	do.	1530	—
5	do.	Medytacōns of saynt Bernarde	1496	'A devout student of Cambridge'
4	do.	The Pype or Tonne of the lyfe of perfection	1532	R. Whitforde
2	Bernard	A brief or short monicyon... of the cure and care of a housholde...(i.e. A werke for housholders)	1530	R. Whitforde
3	Bernardinus of Siena, *Saint*	The chirche of the euill men and women	1511	H. Watson
	Betson, T.	A...treatyse to dyspose men to be vertuously occupyed	[1500]	T. Betson
	Bible	Biblia the bible that is the holy scrypture	1535	M. Coverdale
	do.	The byble which is all the holy scripture	1537	'T. Matthew'
	do.	The most sacred bible newly recognised by R. Taverner	1539	[Revision by R.T. of No. 2066]
	do.	The Byble in Englyshe [1st Great Bible]	1539	[Revision by M. Coverdale of no. 2066]
	do.	The byble that is to say all the holy scripture	1549	[Revision by R.T. of no. 2066]

STC number	Author or Subject heading	Short title of work	Date	Translator
2093	Bible	The bible and holy scriptures conteyned in the olde and newe testament	1560	W. Whittingh A. Gilby and T. Sampson
2350	Bible, Pentateuch	The fyrst boke of Moses called Genesis. (The seconde —the fifth boke)	1530	W. Tyndale
2368	Bible, Psalms, Latin and English	The Psalter both in Latyne and Englyshe	1540	—
2369.1	Bible, Psalms, English Prose Versions	Psalmes of the passion (part of Horae ad usum Sarum. Paris)	1498	—
2370	do.	The psalter of Dauid in Englishe. (Text of M. Bucer)	1530	—
2372	do.	Dauids psalter diligently trāslated	1534	G. Joye
2373	do.	The psalter...wher unto are added other deuoute praiers...	[1540?]	—
2374	do.	The psalter...whereunto is annexed certayne godly collettes	[1542?]	See no. 2370
20478	do.	Deuout psalmes and colletes...	1547	—
2375	do.	The psalter...the letany and other deuout prayers	1548	M. Coverda
2385	do.	The psalter poynted	1566	—
2419	Bible, Psalms, English Metrical Versions	Certayne psalms...drawen into Englishe metre [19 psalms]	[n.b. 1547]	T. Sternhol
2420	do.	Certayne psalms...drawen into English metre [37 psalms by Sternhold and 7 by Hopkins]	1549	T. Sternhol J. Hopkins
2426	do.	Certayne psalms...drawen into Englishe metre [37 by Sternhold and 14 by others]	[1553]	T. Sternhol
2725	do.	The psalter of Dauid newely translated...	1549	R. Crowley
2726	do.	Certayne psalmes called the vii penitentiall psalmes...	1549	Sir T. Wya

TC mber	Author or Subject heading	Short title of work	Date	Translator
27	Bible, *Psalms, English Metrical Versions*	Certayne psalmes drawen into Englishe...meter...	1550	W. Hunnis
28	do.	Certayne psalmes...drawen into Englyshe metre...	1553	F. Seager
48.1	Bible, *Anonymous commentary*	Paraphrasis on the Psalms of Dauid	1535	—
48	do.	An epitome of the psalmes...	1539	R. Taverner
52	Bible, *The Books of Solomon*	The proverbes of Solomon (Here foloweth the boke... called Ecclesiastes)	[1532?]	—
3	do.	The prouerbes of Salomon	[1541?]	Gt. Bible version
4	do.	The bokes of Salomon	[1544?]	J. Hall?
0	do.	Certayne chapters of the prouerbes of Salomon drawen into metre	[1550?]	T. Sternhold
8	do.	The canticles or balades of Salomon, phraselyke declared in Englysh metres	1549	W. Baldwin
7	Bible, *Prophets*	The prophete Isaye	1531	G. Joye
8	do.	Jeremy the prophete (Lamentations), The Songe of Moses	1534	G. Joye
4.1	do.	The exposicion of Dauid... gathered out of P. Melancton and G. Joye	1545	—
3	do.	The prophete Jonas...	[1531?]	W. Tyndale
4	Bible, *Proverbs*	Certayn chapters of the Prouerbs, etc. translated into metre	1550	J. Hall
1	Bible, *Apocrypha*	The volume of the bokes called Apocripha	1549	—
2	do.	An epistle of the prophete Hieremie	[bef. 1540]	—
	Bible, *Maccabees*	The third boke of the Machabees...	1550	W. Lynne
	Bible, *New Testament, Latin and English*	The newe testament in Englyshe and Latyn...	1538	W. Tyndale
	do.	The newe testament both Latine and Englyshe...	1538	M. Coverdale

STC number	Author or Subject heading	Short title of work	Date	Translator
2823	Bible, *New Testament, English*	[The new testament]	1525	W. Tyndale ar W. Roye
2825	do.	The new testament...	1534	W. Tyndale ar G. Joye
2836	do.	The new testament...	1538	M. Coverdale
2871	do.	The newe testament...	1557	W. Whittingh
2872	do.	The newe testament...	[1561?]	W. Tyndale revised by R. Jugge
2972	Bible, *Gospels*	The pystles and gospels...	[n.d.]	—
2976	do.	The epystles and gospels...	1550	—
2979	do.	The pistels & gospels...	[n.d.]	—
2984	Bible, *Acts*	The actes of the apostles... in metre	1553	C. Tye
21038	Bible, *Ephesians*	A commentary in Englyshe vpon Sayncte Paules epystle to the Ephesyans	[1540]	L. Ridley
21039	Bible, *Colossians*	An exposicion in Englishe vpon the epistle to the Colossians	1548	L. Ridley
2987	Bible, *James*	An exposicyon vpon a pece of Saint James epistle	1536	—
21042	Bible, *Jude*	An exposition in the epistell of Jude	1538	L. Ridley
21040	Bible, *Philippians*	An exposytion in Englyshe vpon the epistyll to the Philippiãs	[1550?]	L. Ridley
2996	Bible, *Selections*	Certain praiers and godlye meditacions	[1550?]	—
3015	Bible, *Appendix*	A briefe and compendiouse table...	1550	W. Lynne
3017	do.	A bryefe summe of the whole byble	[1548]	A. Scoloker
3036	do.	The summe of the holye scripture...	1529	S. Fish
3045	do.	The images of the old testament...	1549	—
2854	do.	The first (second) tome or volume of the paraphrase of Erasmus on the N.T.	1548–9	N. Udall, M. Coverda and E. Aller
3047	Bibliander, T.	A godly consultation...	1542	—

286

STC number	Author or Subject heading	Short title of work	Date	Translator
13148	Blair, J.	[Acts and deeds of Wallace]	[1508?]	Henry the Minstrel
3124	Blanchardine	[Blanchardine and Eglantine]	1489	W. Caxton
3158	Blundeville, G., see Grisone, F.			
3175	Boccaccio, G.	The falle of princis	1494	J. Lydgate
3183	do.	History of Galesus, Cymon and Iphigenia	[1560?]	T.C.
3186	Boccus	Kyng Boccus & Sydracke	[1530?]	Hugo of Campeden
3188	do.	Certayne questions of Kynge Bocthus...	[1535?]	—
3197	Boemus, J.	The fardle of facions...	1555	W. Waterman
3199	Boethius, A.M.T.S.	Boecius de consolacione philosophie	[1478?]	G. Chaucer
3200	do.	The boke of comfort called... de consolatione philosophiæ	1525	J. Walton
3201	do.	The boke called the comforte of philosophye	1556	G. Colvile
3203	Boethius, H.	The hystory and croniklis of Scotland	[1540]	J. Bellenden
3412	Bonaventura, Saint	Alphabetum religiosorum	1531	R. Whitforde
259	do.	[Speculum uitæ Christi.]	[1486]	N. Love
264	do.	do.	1517	J. Morton
277	Bonde, W.	The Pylgrimage of perfection (and The Rosary of our Saviour...)	1526	W. Bonde
305	Book	[The Book of Divers Ghostly Matters] i.e. The Seven Poyntes of trewe loue...The xii. proffites of tribulacyon... The rule of saynte Benet	1491	W. Caxton
308	do.	[The Book of Hawking, Hunting, &c.]	1486	Dame J. Berners
325	do.	The boke of Noblenes	[1550?]	J. Larke
326	do.	The book of the order of chivalry, see Lull, R.		
327	do.	A new boke of Presidentes...	1543	T. Phaer?
350.1	do.	The booke of pretty conceits	[1520?]	—

287

STC number	Author or Subject heading	Short title of work	Date	Translator
3357	Book	The boke of Wysdome	1532	J. Larke
3359	do.	In this boke is conteyned the Articles of oure fayth. The x. commaundementis. The vii. works of mercy. The vii. dedely synnes. The vii. pryncypall vertues. The vii sacramentis of holy Chirche	[1520?]	—
3379	Borde, A.	A dyetary of helth...	[1542?]	A. Borde
3545	Brant, S.	The Shyp of folys	1509	A. Barclay
3547	do.	The shyppe of fooles	1509	H. Watson
3600	Brendan, *Saint*	The lyfe of Saynt Brandon	[1520?]	—
3603	Brentius, J.	A very fruitful exposicion vpon the syxte chapter of saynte John	1550	R. Sherry
14638	do.	The vertue of Christes resurrection (with A sermon ...of pacience)	1550	T. Sampson
23959	Bridget, *Saint*	Four revelations of Saynt Birget. (With the folowyng of Christ, etc.)	[1521?]	—
4602	do.	The lyfe of seynt Birgette	1516	J. Capgrave
3943	Brunsfelsius, O., *see* Prognostications, p. 279			
3943.1	do.	Prayers of the Byble	[1535]	—
3962	Bucer, M.	A briefe examination of a certaine declaration	[1559?]	—
3963	do.	The gratulation of M. Martin Bucer unto the Churche of Englande	[1549]	Sir T. Hoby
3965	do.	A Treatise, how...Christian mens almose ought to be distributed	[1557?]	—
14717	Bugenhagen, J.	The Christen sermon made at the buryall of...Luther	[1546?]	J. Bale
4021	do.	A compendious letter...	1536	—
4045	Bullinger, H.	The christen state of matrimonye	1541	M. Coverdale
4054	do.	Commentary vpon the seconde epistle to the Thessalonians	1538	—

288

STC number	Author or Subject heading	Short title of work	Date	Translator
1059	Bullinger, H.	An holsom antidotus against the Anabaptistes	1548	J. Veron
1068	do.	Dialogue between yᵉ seditious libertin and the true christian	1551	J. Veron
1069	do.	A...defence of the baptisme of children	1551	J. Veron
1071	do.	The olde faythe...	1547	M. Coverdale
246	do.	A sermon of the true confessinge of Christe (with A treatise of the cohabitacyon of the faithfull with the vnfaithfull)	1555	—
79	do.	A treatise...concernynge magistrates...Also concernyng the affayres of warre	1549	W. Lynne
80	do.	Two epystles (by H. B. and J. Calvin)	1548	—
93	Buonaccorsso de Pistoja	The Declamation of Noblesse (with Tully of Old Age)	1481	J. Tiptoft
85.1	Bushe, P.	The exposycyon of Miserere mei Deus	1501	P. Bush
89.1	Bustard, A.	The Cessyons of Parlyament...	[n.d.]	A. Bustard
5	Cabasilas, N.	A briefe treatise, conteynynge a...declaration of the Popes usurped primacy	1560	T. Gressop
7	Caesar, J.	Iulius Cesars commentaryes	1530	W. Rastell
9.1	Calvin, J.	The catechisme	1550	W. Huycke
2	do.	Certain homilies conteining profitable admonition for this time...	1553	R. Horne
7	do.	An epistle both of godly consolacion and also of aduertisement...	1550	Edward, duke of Somerset
4	do.	The epistle declaring that Christ is the end of the lawe	1557	—
5	do.	Two epistles (by J. C. and H. Bullinger)	1548	—

STC number	Author or Subject heading	Short title of work	Date	Translator
4410	Calvin, J.	A...treatyse concernynge the sacrament (with The order that the Church in Denmarke doth use)	[1549?]	M. Coverdale
4435	do.	The mynde of M. J. Caluyne, what a faithfull man...ought to do	1548	R.G.
4436	do.	Of the life or conuersation of a christen man	[1549]	T. Broke
4450	do.	Sermons vpon the Songe that Ezechias made...(with A meditation of a penitent Sinner)	1560	A. Lock?
4463	do.	A short instruction agaynst the pestiferous errours of Anabaptistes	1549	—
4468	do.	Whether christian faith maye be kepte secret in the heart...	1553	—
4468.1	do.	Whether it be lawfull for a chrysten man to...be partaker of the masse... without offending God...	1548	—
4589	Canutus	A litil boke...for the pestilence	[c. 1486]	—
4592	do.	A treatyse agaynst pestelēce	[c. 1510]	—
4594	Caorsin, G.	The siege of Rhodes	[c. 1482]	J. Kay
4602	Capgrave, J.	[Nova Legenda Anglie] (with The lyfe of seynt Birgette, and A deuoute boke (W. Hilton)	1516	John of Tynemouth and J. Capgrave
4626	Carion, J.	The thre bokes of Cronicles	1550	W. Lynne
4720	Cary, W.	An Herball	1525	—
4807	Catechismus	[A short Catechism...]	1553	J. Poynet
4815	Catharine of Siena, *Saint*	The orchard of Syon	1519	D. James
4817	do.	The life of...Saincte Katheryne	[1550?]	—
	See also Vineis, R. de			
4850	Cato, D.	[Cato's Disticha]	[1477?]	B. Burgh
4854	do.	Preceptes of Cato the Sage...	1553	R. Burrant

STC number	Author or Subject heading	Short title of work	Date	Translator
391	Cebes	The table of Cebes the philosopher	[c. 1530]	Sir F. Poyntz
312	Celius, M.	An excellent admonicion and resolucion (with The Temporysour)	1555	R.P.
920	Cessolis, J. de	[The game and playe of the chesse]	[1476?]	W. Caxton
913	Charles I, Emperor	Charlemagne (Charles the Great)	1485	W. Caxton
914	Charles V, Emperor	The answere of Carolus... concerninge a generall councell at Trident	[1543?]	—
916	do.	The ordynaūces that the emperour caused to be red to the estates	[1532?]	—
918	do.	The tryumphant vyctory... agaynst the turkes	[1532]	R. Copland
57	Chartier, A.	[The Curial]	[1484]	W. Caxton
38	do.	[La bele dame sauns mercy]	[1526]	Sir R. Roos
55	Chastising	The Chastysing of goddes Chyldren	[c. 1492]	—
58	Chaucer, G.	The workes...(containing The Romaunt of the Rose, Boethius)	1532	G. Chaucer
58	do.	The letter of Dydo to Eneas. (Part of The boke of Fame... with dyuers other...workes)	[1526?]	—
6	Child	The wyse chylde of thre yere old	[1520?]	—
1	Christian Shoemaker	A goodly dysputacion betwene a Christen shoemaker and a popyshe parson	1548	A. Scoloker
8	Christians	The Ordynarye of Crystyanyte or of crysten men	1502	A. Chertsey
0	do.	The ordenarye for all faythfull Chrystiās	1548	A. Scoloker
	Christine de Pisan, see Du Castel, C.			
0	Chrysostom, Saint, John	[Homily iii.] Of Detraction (with Dyvers holy instrucyons...)	1541	R. Whitforde

STC number	Author or Subject heading	Short title of work	Date	Translator
14637	Chrysostom, Saint John	An homilie vpon that saying of S. Paul. . . With a discourse vpon Job and Abraham	1544	T. Chaloner
14638	do.	A sermon of pacience (with an Homilie by J. Brentius)	1550	T. Sampson
14639	do.	A sermon that no man is hurted but of hym selfe	1542	T. Lupset
14642	do.	A treatise cōcerning the restitucion of a synner	1553	—
822	do.	⌊Two orations of praying] with (The diuisyon of the places of the lawe. . .)	1548	W. Lynne
22428	Cicero, M. T.	[Ad Herennium libri quatuor] as part of (A treatise of schemes and tropes)	1550	R. Sherry
5293	do.	De Amicicia	1481	J. Tiptoft
5276	do.	The booke of freendeship	1550	J. Harrington
5278	do.	The thre bookes of Tullyes Offyces	1534	R. Whittinton
5280	do.	[Three bookes of duties]	1553	N. Grimald
5292	do.	Tullius de Senectute	[1535?]	R. Whittinton
5293	do.	Tulle of olde age	1481	J. Tiptoft
22429	do.	The oration. . . to Caesar of Marcus Marcellus (with A treatise of the figures of grammer and rhetorike)	1555	R. Sherry
5313	do.	The Paradox of M. T. Cicero	1540	R. Whittinton
5408	Clerke, J.	Opusculum plane diuinum de mortuorum resurrectione. . .	1545	J. Clerke
5468	Cocles, B.	Epitomye of the whole art of phisiognomie	[1556]	T. Hill
5550	Colet, J.	The sermon. . . made to the conuocation at Paulis	[1530?]	T. Lupsett
5550.1	do.	The VII Petitions	[n.d.]	—
5572	Cologne	The thre kynges of Coleyn	[1496]	—
5579	Colonne, G. delle	The hystorye. . . of Troye	1513	J. Lydgate

STC number	Author or Subject heading	Short title of work	Date	Translator
5580	Colonne, G. delle	The auncient historie...of the warres	1555	J. Lydgate
5581	do.	The faythfull and true storye of the destruction of Troye	1553	T. Paynell
605.1	Comparation	Comparation of a Virgin and a Martyr	1537	T. Paynell
608	Complaint	A complaynt of a dolorous louer	[1536?]	—
609	do.	Complaynt of the soule	[1510?]	—
631	Connaissance	A lyttell treatyse cleped La conusaunce damours	[n.d.]	—
636.1	Consolation	A consolation for troubled consciences (part of Prayers of the Byble)	[1535]	—
641	Constantine I, Emperor	A treatyse of the donation gyuen...vnto Syluester, pope of Rhome...	[1534]	B. Picern
643	Contemplation	The contemplation of sinners	1499	—
718	Cope, Sir A.	The historie of...Anniball and Scipio	1544	Sir A. Cope
758	Cordiale	[The 'Cordiale sive de quatuor novissimis']	1479	A. Woodville, Lord Rivers
806	Corvinus, A.	A postill or collection of moste godly doctrine vpon euery gospell through the yeare	1550	—
889	Coverdale, M.	The defence of a certayne poore christen man	1545	M. Coverdale
92	do.	Goostly psalmes and spirituall songes	[1539?]	M. Coverdale
99	do.	A very excellent and swete exposition upon the two and twentye Psalme of David	1537	M. Coverdale
3	Cranmer, T.	Cathechismus	1548	W. Lynne
6	do.	A confutatiō of vnwrittē verities...	[1558]	E.P.
6	Cromer, M.	A notable example of God's vengeance...	[1560?]	—

STC number	Author or Subject heading	Short title of work	Date	Translator
6142	Curtius Rufus, Q.	The historie of Quintus Curcius...	1553	J. Brende
6152	Cyprian, *Saint*	Certein workes...(A sermon touching mortalitie...A boke conteining an exhortation to martyrdome...Epistle unto the people of Thibaris)	1556	J. Scory
6156	do.	A sermon made on the Lordes prayer	1539	T. Paynell
6157	do.	A...sermon...of mortalitie of man	1534	Sir T. Elyot
	Dares, *see* Colonne, G. delle			
6451	Deceit	The deceyte of women	[1560?]	L. Andrewe?
6470	Degore, Sir	Syr Degore	[1515?]	—
6473	Deguileville, G. de	The pylgremage of the sowle	1483	J. Lydgate
6551.1	Delgasto	A joyfull new tidynges of the goodly victory that was sent to the Emperour	[c. 1542]	J. Mayles
4410	Denmark	The order that the churche in Denmarke doth use (with A treatyse concernynge the sacrament)	[1549?]	M. Coverdale
3043	Derendel, P.	The true...purtreatures of the woll bible	1553	—
	Dictes or sayengis, *see* Tignonville, G. de			
	Dietary, *see* Borde, A.			
6837	Difference	The dyfference of astronomy	[1535?]	—
14652	Diocles	An epistle of Diocles unto Kyng Antigonus. (In The treasuri of helth)	[1550?]	H. Lloyd
	Dictes and sayenges, *see* Tignonville, G. de			
	Dietary, *see* Borde, A.			
6894	Dionysius, Carthusianus	The lyf of prestes	[1533?]	—
6895	do.	The mirroure of golde...	1522	Margaret, Countess of Richmond
6931	Doctrinal	The doctrynalle of dethe	[1498]	—

STC number	Author or Subject heading	Short title of work	Date	Translator
6931.1	Doctrinal	The doctrinal of sapyence	1489	W. Caxton
7269	Du Castel, C.	The book of fayttes of armes & of chyvalrye	[1489]	W. Caxton
7270	do.	The body of polycye	1521	—
7271	do.	The Cyte of Ladyes	1521	B. Anslay
7272	do.	The C. hystoryes of Troye	[1540?]	R. Wyer
5068	do.	[The letter of Cupid], part of Chaucer's *Works*	1532	T. Hoccleve
7273	do.	The morale prouerbes of Cristyne	[1478]	W. Caxton
7363	Du Ploiche, P.	A treatise...(of the catechisme; of the letanie, etc.)	[1553]	P. Du Ploiche
7499.1	Edward, *Saint*	A prayer ayenst thonder and tempeste shewed by an angel to seynt edward (part of Horae ad usum Sarum. Paris)	1498	––
7541	Eglamoure, Sir	[Sir Eglamoure]	[1500]	—
7571	Elias	Helyas Knight of the Swan	1512	R. Copland
4766	Elizabeth, *Saint*	Revelations of Saynt Elizabeth...(with The lyf of saint Katherin of Senis)	[1493?]	—
7630	Elyot, Sir T.	The bankette of sapience	1539	Sir T. Elyot
7677	Emanuel, King of Portugal	Of the new landes...	[1520?]	—
7714	England, *Local Courts*	The maner of kepynge a courte baron	[1540?]	—
9176	England, *Public Documents*	The promisse of matrimonie	[1475]	—
9176	do.	The lettre of annuelle port...	[1485?]	—
9272	England, *Statutes*	The boke of magna carta...	1534	G. Ferrers
9518	do.	An abridgment of the statutes	1527	J. Rastell
9521	do.	The grete abbregement of the statutys...	[1531?]	J. Rastell
10084	England, Church of	A treatise cōcernynge diuers of the constitucyons provynciall and legantines	[1535?]	—

STC number	Author or Subject heading	Short title of work	Date	Translator
10429	Epinus, J.	A very fruitful and godly exposition upō the xv. psalme	[1550?]	N. Lesse
10432	Epistle	A moste pythye...epistell to anymate all trew Christians...	1556	R. Pownoll
10435	Erasmus, Saint	The lyfe of Saynt Erasmus	1520	—
10436	Erasmus, D.	Prouerbes or adagies...	1539	R. Taverner
10443	do.	Apopthegmes...	1542	N. Udall
10445	do.	[Apothegmata. Selections.] Flores aliquot sententiarum...	1540	R. Taverner
10449	do.	Bellum Erasmi	1533(–4)	—
10450	do.	The censure and iudgement of Erasmus	[1550?]	N. Lesse
10454	do.	A dialoge or communication of two persons	[1540?]	—
10455	do.	A mery dialogue, declaringe the propertyes of shrowde shrewes, and honest wyues	1557	—
10459	do.	Two dyaloges	[1550]	E. Becke
10460	do.	A very pleasaunt and fruitful diologe called the epicure	1545	—
22428	do.	That chyldren oughte to be taught and brought up gently in vertue and learnynge...	[1550]	—
10464	do.	A comfortable exhortation agaynst the chaunces of death	1553	—
10466	do.	The Complaint of peace	1559	T. Paynell
10467	do.	A lytell booke of good maners for chyldren	1532	R. Whittinton
10470.1	do.	A declaration in the prayse of Physyke	[n.d.]	—
10471	do.	De contemptu mundi	1533	T. Paynell
22428	do.	[De duplici copia verborum ac rerum] (part of A treatise of schemes & tropes)	1550	R. Sherry
10474	do.	De immensa dei misericordia	[1526?]	G. Hervet
10477	do.	A deuout treatise vpon the pater noster...	[1526?]	M. Roper

STC number	Author or Subject heading	Short title of work	Date	Translator
2477.1	Erasmus, D.	Dicta sapientum. The sayenges of the wyse men of Grece...	[n.d.]	—
2479	do.	Enchiridion...the manuell of the christen knyght	1533	W. Tyndale?
2488	do.	A shorte recapitulacion...of Erasmus Enchiridion	1545	M. Coverdale
2489	do.	An Epysteil...cōcernyng the forbedinge of eatynge of flesshe	[1530?]	M. Coverdale
2490	do.	An Epistle concernynge the veryte of the Sacrament of Christes body	[1535?]	—
2491	do.	The Epistle sente vnto Conradus Pelicanus	1554	—
2492	do.	A ryght frutefull epystle in laude and prayse of matrymony	[1530?]	R. Taverner
2493	do.	An exhortation to the diligent studye of scripture with 'An exposition on the seventh chapter of the first epistle to the Corinthians'	1529	W. Roy?
2495	do.	An exposicyon of the xv. psalme	1537	—
2497.2	do.	An introduction of the eyght partes of speche...	1542	—
2498	do.	A lytle treatise of the maner and forme of confession	[1535?]	W. Marshall?
2500	do.	The praise of folie	1549	Sir T. Chaloner
2503	do.	The paraphrase of Erasmus upon yᵉ Epistle of Paule unto Titus	[1535?]	L. Cox
2504	do.	A playne...exposytion of the commune crede...	[1533]	—
2505	do.	Preparation to deathe...	1538	—
2507	do.	A Scorneful image...	[n.d.]	—
2508	do.	A Sermon [on the marriage at Cana]	[1532?]	—
2509	do.	[A Sermon of the chylde Jesus]	[1540?]	—

297

STC number	Author or Subject heading	Short title of work	Date	Translator
10510	Erasmus, D.	A Treatise perswadynge a man patientlye to suffre the deth of his frende	[1532]	—
10532	Esquillus, P.	Wonderfull news of the death of Paule the III	[1552]	W.B.
10563	Eulenspiegel, T.	[Howe Howleglas served a taylor, etc.]	[1510?]	—
10564	do.	A merye jest of a man that was called Howleglas	[1528?]	—
20917	Evesham	A mervelous revelacion... by Sent Nycholas to a monke of Evyshamme	[1485]	—
10608	Example	The example of euyll tongues	[1500?]	—
10751	Felicius, C.	The conspiracie of Lucius Catiline	1541	T. Paynell
10808	Ferdinand I, Emperor	The supplicacion...made unto King Ferdinandus...	[1543?]	M. Coverdale
10831	Ferrarius, J.	A woorke...touchynge the good orderynge of a common weale	1559	W. Bavande
21449	Finé, O.	The rules...touchinge the use of the common almanackes	[1558]	H. Baker
10888	Fisher, J., Cardinal	A godlie treatisse declaryng the benefites of prayer	[1560]	—
10969	Fitzherbert, Sir A.	The newe boke of Justices of the peas	1538	Sir A. Fitzher
11092	Flores, J. de	Histoire de Aurelio et Isabelle...	1556	—
11211	Fountain	The foūtayne or well of lyfe	[1532?]	—
11220	Fox, E.	The true dyfferens betwen ye regall power and the ecclesiasticall power	[1548]	Henry, Lord Stafford
11313	Francis of Assisi, Saint	The Alcaron of the barefote friers...	1550	E. Alberus
11361	Frederick, of Jennen	Frederyke of Jennen	1518	—
11392	Frith, J.	The preparacyon to the crosse...	[1530?]	R. Tracy
11396–7	Froissart, J.	[The chronicles]	1523–5	J. Bourchier

STC number	Author or Subject heading	Short title of work	Date	Translator
1402	Frontinus, S. J.	The strategemes...of warre	1539	Sir R. Morison
1470	Fullonius, G.	The comedye of Acolastus	1540	J. Palsgrave
1499	G., J.	The myrrour or lokinge glasse of lyfe	[1532?]	J. Gough
2468	Galen, C.	The fourth boke of the Terapentyke...(part of The questyonary of cyrurgyens, by G. de Cauliaco)	[1542]	R. Copland
2551	Garcie, P.	The rutter of the sea...	[1555?]	R. Copland
2585	Gardiner, S.	De vera obedientia: an oration	1553	M. Wood
2590	do.	A detection of the deuils sophistrie...	1546	S. Gardiner
708	Gelli, G. B.	Circes	1557	H. Iden
716	Gemini, T.	Compendiosa totius anatomie delineatio	1553	N. Udall
721	Generides	The history of...Generides	[1504–5?]	—
723	Geneva	[The confession of our faith]	[1556]	—
745.1	George, Saint	The lyf of saynt George	[c. 1515]	A. Barclay
973	Gerson, J.	Behoveful teaching and remedy...to come out of sin...(part of Prymer of Salisbury use)	1531	—
800	Gesner, C.	The treasure of Euonymus...	[1559]	P. Morwyng
	Gesta Romanorum, see Romans			
809	Gherit, van der Goude	The interpretacyon of the Masse	1532	—
899	Giovio, P.	A shorte treatise vpon the Turkes chronicles	1546	P. Ashton
01	Giulio, de Milano	The xliiii sermon, touchyng the Lordes supper	[n.d.]	—
03	do.	Of the Christian sabboth	1552	T. Langley
	Godefrey of Boloyne, see Heraclius			
31	Godfridus	The boke of knowledge... apperteynynge to astronomye	[1530?]	—

STC number	Author of Subject heading	Short title of work	Date	Translator
11966	Goes, D. à.	The legacye...of prester John unto Emanuell, Kynge of Portyngale	1533	J. More
11967	Goeurot, J.	The Regiment of life	1544	T. Phaer
	Golden Legend, see Voragine, J. de			
12091	Gospels	The gospelles of dystaues	[1510?]	H. Watson?
12104	Gosynhill, E.	The vertuous scholehous of vngracious women	[1550?]	W. Lynne
12138	Governal	The Gouernayle of helthe...	[1489]	W. Caxton
12140	Governance	The Governaunce of Kynges...	1511	—
12348.1	Gregory I, Saint	A devout prayer to the trinite made by saynt Gregory (part of Horae ad usum Sarum, Paris)	1495	—
12352	do.	Lyfe of Saynt Gregorys mother	1515	—
12365	Gribaldi, M.	A notable and maruailous epistle	1550	E. Aglionby
12379	Gringore, P.	[The castle of labour]	[c. 1503]	A. Barclay
5728	do.	The complaynte of them that ben to late maryed	[1535?]	R. Copland
5729	do.	A complaynt of them that be to soone maryed	[1535?]	R. Copland
12387	Grisone, F.	The arte of ryding, and breakinge greate horses	[1560?]	T. Blundeville
12427	Guevara, A. de	The diall of princes	1557	T. North
12431	do.	A dispraise of the life of a courtier	1548	Sir F. Bryan
12436	do.	The golden boke of Marcus Aurelius	1535	J. Bourchier
12468	Guido, de Cauliaco	The questyonary of cyrurgyens	[1542]	R. Copland
12477	Guido, of Alet	The Ghost of Guy	[1492]	—
12508.1	Guistard	Guystard and Sygysmonde	1532	W. Walter
12540	Guy, Earl of Warwick	[The history of Guy of Warwick]	[n.d.]	—
12732	Hamilton, P.	Dyuers frutful gatheriges of scrypture...	[1532?]	J. Frith

Harris, W., see Market

STC number	Author or Subject heading	Short title of work	Date	Translator
3021	Hegendorff, C.	Domestycal or housholde sermons	1548	H. Reginald
3022	do.	The seconde parte...	1549	H. Reginald
3081	Henry VIII, King	An epistle to the Emperours maiestie...	1538	—
086	do.	A copy of the letters, wherin Kyng Henry the eyght made answere vnto a certayn letter of Martyn Luther	1526	—
175	Heraclius, Emperor	Godefrey of Boloyne	1481	W. Caxton
176	Herbal	The grete herball	1526	—
	Herbals, see Cary, W.			
208	Herman V., Archbishop	A brefe and playne declaratyon of the dewty of maried folkes	[1553?]	H. Dekyn
210	do.	The right institutiō of baptisme	1548	R. Ryce
213	do.	A simple and religious consultation	1547	—
21	Herodian	The history of Herodian	[1550?]	N. Smyth
56	Hetoum, Prince	A lytell cronycle	[1520?]	A. Barclay?
34	Hieronymus, von Braunschweig	The noble experyence of the vertuous handywarke of surgeri	1525	—
35	do.	The vertuose boke of distyllatyon	1527	L. Andrewe
38	Higden, R.	Polychronicon	1482	J. Trevisa
	Hippocrates, see Almanacks, Kalendars and Prognostications			
2	Holy Roman Empire	Actes of the disputaciō in the Cowncell...at Regenspurg	1542	M. Coverdale
6	Honorius, Augustodunensis	The lucydarye	[1508?]	A. Chertsey
	Horologium Sapientiæ, see The Book of Divers Ghostly Matters			
8.1	Huon of Bordeaux	Huon of Bourdeaux	[c. 1534]	J. Bourchier
6	Hurlestone, R.	Newes from Rome concerning the papisticall Masse	[1550?]	R. Hurlestone

STC number	Author or Subject heading	Short title of work	Date	Translator
14024	Hutten, U. von	De morbo gallico	1533	T. Paynell
14071.1	Image	The Image of Love	1525	J. Gough
14075	Indagine, J. ab	Briefe introductions vnto the art of chiromancy	1558	F. Withers
14081	Information	Informacōn for pylgrymes vnto the holy londe	[1498?]	—
14104	Institution	The institucion of a gentleman	1555	N. Grimald?
14128	Ipomydon	[Ipomydon]	[c. 1522]	—
5733	do.	[The life of Ipomydon]	[c. 1530]	—
14270	Isidore, Saint	The gathered counsailes of saynct Isodorie	1534	—
25420	do.	An instruction to avoyde and eschewe vices (with Dyvers holy instructions...)	1541	R. Whitforde
14276	Isocrates	The godly advertisement of Isocrates...	1557	J. Bury
14277	do.	The doctrinal of princes	[n.b. 1534]	Sir T. Elyot
14281	Isumbras, Sir	[The history of sir Isenbras]	[1530?]	—
14287	Italy and France	The determinations of the moste famous Universities of Italy and Fraunce	1531	T. Cranmer?
15882	Jerome, Saint	An anthem with a colet of Saynt Jherom. Saynt Jheromes psaulter (both part of Horae. Paris)	1495	—
14503	do.	An exposicyon upon the li. psalme	1538	—
14505	do.	[Four tokens of Judgement]	[1530?]	J. Dousbrugh
14507	do.	Vitas patrum	1495	W. Caxton
14508	do.	The lyf of saint Ierom	[1500?]	—
14518	Jerusalem	The dystruccyon of Jherusalem by Vaspazyan and Tytus	[1509–16]	—
14553	Jesus Christ	The myrrour or glasse of Christes passion	1534	J. Fewterer
14553.1	do.	The new notborune mayd...	[1525]	—

STC mber	Author or Subject heading	Short title of work	Date	Translator
58	Jesus Christ	The passyon of our lorde	1521	A. Chertsey
71	do.	Rosary of our Sauyour Iesu...	[1520?]	—
76	do.	The true beliefe in Christ and his sacramentes	1550	W. Roy
20	Joannes, Campensis	A paraphrasis vpon all the psalms	1539	—
	John, Prester, see Emanuel, King			
48	John of Arras	[Melusine]	[1510?]	—
49	John of Capistrano, Saint	[Capistranus]	[1510?]	—
52	John XXI, Pope	The treasuri of helth	[1550?]	H. Lloyd
17	Jonas, J.	The true hystorye of the departynge of M. Luther with (An oracyon...of P. Melanchton, and The Christen sermon...by J. [Bugenhagen])	[1546?]	J. Bale
9.1	Jordanus de Quedlinburg	Jordans medytacyons...in Englysshe	[n.d.]	—
5	Joseph, ben Gorion	A compendious history of the Jewes commune weale	1558	P. Morwyng
6	Joseph, of Arimathea	A treatyse...of Joseph of Arimathy	[1510?]	—
7	do.	The lyfe of Joseph of Armathia	1520	—
4	Judgment	The judgemēt of all vrynes	[1540?]	—
9	do.	The trew judgemēt...vppon the Sacrament	[1548?]	—
5	Judicial	The iudycyall of vryns	[1527?]	—
	Julius II, Pope	The dyalogue bytwene Jullius the seconde, and saynt Peter. [By P. F. Andrelinus or G. Balbi]	1535	—
	Knights of Saint John	The begynnynge...of the knyghtes hospytallers of saynt Iohan baptyst of Ierusalem	1524	—
	Kur'ān	A lytell treatyse...called Alcaron	[1515?]	—

303

STC number	Author or Subject heading	Short title of work	Date	Translator
7668	Laertius, D.	Of the knowledeg whiche maketh a wise man	1533	Sir T. Elyot
15178	Lambert, F.	The minde and judgement of maister F. Lambert of the wyll of man	[1548]	N. Lesse
15179	do.	The summe of christianitie	1536	T. Revel
15187	Lamwell, Sir	The treatyse of Syr Lamwell	[n.d.]	—
15258	La Sale, A. de	The fyftene joyes of maryage	1509	R. Copland
15263	Lasco, J. à	Compendium doctrinae de vera Dei et Christi ecclesia	1551	—
15286	Latimer, H.	The sermon...made to the clergie...translated out of latyne	1537	—
15296	La Tour Landry, G. de	[The knyght of the toure]	[1484]	W. Caxton
15375	Le Fèvre, R.	The recuyell of the historyes of Troye	[1475?]	W. Caxton
15383	do.	[The history of Jason]	[1477]	W. Caxton
15385	Legate, R.	A briefe catechisme and dialogue between the husbande and his wyfe	1545	R. Legate
	Legenda Aurea, see Voragine, J. de			
15394	Legrand, J.	The book of good maners	1487	W. Caxton
15453	La Maire, J.	The abbreuyacyon of all generall councellys	1539	J. Gough
15531	Leuwis, D. de	The lyfe of prestes	[n.d.]	—
15605	Lily, W.	An introduction of the eyght partes of speche	1542–3	W. Lily
15693	Lippomano, L.	A copye of a verye fyne and wytty letter	1556	M. Throckme-
15707	Litany	The golden letany in Englysshe	1531	—
15760	Littleton, Sir T.	Lytylton tenures in Englysshe	[1525?]	J. Rastell
15969	Liturgies, Hours	(The maner to lyve well)	1531	R. Copland
15986	do.	A prymer in Englyshe...	[1535?]	—
15988	do.	A goodly prymer in englyshe	1535	--
15989	do.	A goodly prymer in Englysshe...	[1535?]	G. Joye

STC number	Author or Subject heading	Short title of work	Date	Translator
;988.1	Liturgies, *Hours*	A primer in Englysshe...	[1535?]	G. Love
;992	do.	This prymer of Salysbery vse, both in Englyshe and in Laten	1536	—
;993	do.	Thys prymer in Englishe and in Laten...is newly trāslated after the Laten texte	1536	—
;997	do.	This prymer in Englyshe and in Laten...	[1537?]	—
;998	do.	A goodly prymer in Englysshe, newely corrected	[1537?]	—
;999	do.	The prymer with the pystles and gospels in Englysshe	[1537?]	—
)00	do.	The primer in English for children...	[1537?]	—
•09	do.	The manual of prayers, or the prymer in Englysh & Laten...	1539	J. Hilsey
14	do.	The primer in Englishe wyth the A.B.C. for children...	[1539?]'	—
16	do.	A primer or boke of prayers...	1540	—
•25	do.	The Prymer in Englyshe and Latyn...	1542	—
;o	Liturgies, *Geneva*	The forme of common praiers vsed in the churches of Geneua. The mynstracion of the sacramentes...The vysitacion of the sycke: And the Cathechisme of Geneva	1550	T. Broke
3.1	Livius, T.	The historie of...Anniball and Scipio...	1544	A. Cope
.4	Lord's Prayer	[The pater noster in English] in Hore beatissime virginis Marie	1523	—
•6	do.	A metricall declaration of the vii petitions of the pater noster	[n.d.]	--
.4	Lucian, of Samosata	A dialogue betwene Lucian and Diogenes	[n.d.]	Sir T. Elyot
;	do.	[Necromantia;] A dialog of the poet Lucyan	[1530?]	J. Rastell?

STC number	Author or Subject heading	Short title of work	Date	Translator
16898	Lucretia, of Siena	The goodli history of the Ladye Lucres	[1550?]	—
3326	Lull, R.	[The book of the order of Chivalry]	[1484]	W. Caxton
16962	Luther, M.	A boke...agaynst the newe idole, and old deuyll	1534	—
16963	do.	A boke of the discrypcyon of the images of a verye chrysten bysshop	[1536?]	—
16964	do.	The chiefe and pryncypall Articles of the Christen faythe (with The Confessyon of the faythe of Doctor M. L.; Of the ryght olde Catholyke Churche; The thre symboles of the Christen faythe; A singular and fruteful maner of prayeng...)	1548	W. Lynne?
16980	do.	A faythfull admonycion of a certen trewe pastor	1554	E. Pamphilus
16982	do.	A frutefull and godly exposition of the Kyngdom of Christ (with A sermon... oute of the eyght Psalm)	1548	W. Lynne
16983	do	A frutfull sermon: made of the angelles	[1560?]	J. Fox
16984	do.	The last wil and last confession of Martyn Luthers faith	1543	W. Lynne?
16988	do.	A Propre treatyse of good workes	[1535?]	—
16992	do.	A ryght notable sermon vppon the twenteth chapter of Johan	1548	R. Argentine
17626	do.	A sermon...of the greate blasphemy agaynst God which the Papystes daylie do use	[1548]	—
16982	do.	A sermon...oute of the eyght Psalm	1548	W. Lynne
16994.1	do.	A supputation of the years	1550	—

TC mber	Author or Subject heading	Short title of work	Date	Translator
99	Luther, M.	A very excellent & swete exposition vpon the xxii psalme	1537	M. Coverdale
26	Lydgate, J.	The proverbs...upon the fall of prynces. [Taken from Boccaccio]	[1510?]	J. Lydgate
—	do.	Stans puer ad mensam, *see* Sulpitius, J.	—	—
3	Lyndewode, W.	Constitutiones prouincialles..	1534	—
5	Lynne, W.	The beginning and endynge of all popery...	[1548?]	W. Lynne
7	Maccabre, *Dance*	The daunce of Machabree (with The falles of princes)	1554	J. Lydgate
2	Macer, Æ.	Macers herbal practysyd by Doctor Lynacro	[1530?]	—
3	do.	A newe herball of Macer	[1535?]	—
0	Mainardi, A.	An anatomi, that is to say a parting in peeces of the Mass	1556	—
1	Mancinus, D.	The englysshe of Mancyne upon the foure cardynale vertues...	[1520?]	—
2	do.	The myrrour of good maners	[1523?]	A. Barclay
5	Mandeville, Sir J.	[The voyages and Travels of Sir J. Mandeville]	[1496]	—
4	Marcort, A.	A declaration of the masse...	1547	—
0	Margaret of Angoulême	A godly medytacyon of the christen sowle...	1548	Elizabeth, d. of Henry VIII
;	Margaret, *St.*	[The life of St. Margaret]	[1493]	—
0	Market	The market or fayre of vsurers...	1550	W. Harris
.1	Marshall, W.	The maner of subvention of poore people	[1532?]	W. Marshall
0	Martin, *St.*, *Abp.* of Braga	The rule of an honest lyfe, with (The Encheridyon of a spyrytuall lyfe)	[1538?]	—
	do.	The Forme and rule of honest lyuynge	1546	R. Whittinton
	do.	The Myrrour or glasse of maners	1547	R. Whittinton

STC number	Author or Subject heading	Short title of work	Date	Translator
17532	Martyrology	The martiloge in englysshe...	1526	R. Whitford
17535	Mary, the Blessed Virgin	The compassyon of our lady	1522	—
17536	do.	An exposicion upon...the Magnificat	1538	M. Coverdale
17537	do.	The lamentacyon of our Lady	[1510?]	—
17539	do.	The myracles of oure blessyd Lady	[1496]	—
17542	do.	The Myrroure of oure Lady...	1530	T. Gascoigne?
17542.1	do.	Our ladyes Chambre, or Parler	[n.d.]	—
17544	do.	The Rosarye of our lady in englysshe	[1510?]	—
17557	Mary, of Nimeguen	A lyttell story of...Mary of Nēmegen	[1518?]	L. Andrewe?
17568	Mary Magdalen, Saint	Complaynte of the louer of Cryst saynt Mary Magdaleyn	[1520?]	—
17626	Mass	The dysclosyng of...yᵉ popysh masse, with a sermon annexed of Martin Luther	[1548?]	—
17630	do.	The vpcheringe of the messe	[1547]	—
17773	Meditation	An excellent and right learned meditacion	1554	—
17776	Meditations	Godly meditacions verye necessarie to bee sayde of all Christen men	[1550?]	—
17788	Melanchthon, P.	A ciuile nosgay	[1550?]	J. Goodale
17788.1	do.	Apologie of Melanchon who defendeth the aforesaid Confessyon of the Germaynes	[1536?]	R. Taverner
17789	do.	The epistle of P. Melancton made vnto Kynge Henry the eyght...	1547	J. Crespin?
14823	do.	The exposicion of Daniel...	1545	G. Joye
17791	do.	A godlye treatyse of prayer	[1553?]	J. Bradford
17788.2	do.	The confession of fayth delyvered to...Charles V by the lordes of Germany	[n.d.]	—

STC number	Author or Subject heading	Short title of work	Date	Translator
792	Melanchthon, P.	The iustification of man by faith only	1548	N. Lesse
793	do.	A newe work cōcerning both partes of the Sacrament to be receyued of the lay peple	1543	E. Allen
717	do.	An oracyon...at the buryall of Martyne Luther	[1546?]	J. Bale
)80	do.	A praier...against the pope...	1554	—
?98	do.	A very godly defense, defending the mariage of preistes	[1541]	L. Beuchame
?99	do.	A waying and considering of the interim	1548	J. Rogers
:17	Menandrinus, M.	The defence of peace	1535	W. Marshall
'21	Menewe, G.	A confutacion of that popishe and antichristian doctryne whiche mainteinith yᵉ ministracyon of the sacrament vnder one kind...	[1555?]	—
22	do.	A plaine subversyon of all the argumentes for the maintenaunce of auricular confession...	[1555?]	—
'64	Micron, M.	A short and faythful instruction for symple christianes...	[1560?]	T.C.
32	Mirror	A myrrour or glasse for them that be syke	[1536?]	J. Gough?
;2	Montpellier	The practyse of cyrurgyons of Mountpyller...	[1540?]	—
:2.1	do.	Thre practyses nowe vsed at Mountpyller by monsyre Emery	[n.d.]	—
_4	Montulmo, A. di	A ryghte excellente treatise of astronomie	[1554]	F. van Brunswick
_4	More, Sir T.	Utopia	1551	R. Robinson
8	Mosellanus, P.	[Tables of schemes and tropes] (part of A treatise of schemes & tropes)	1550	R. Sherry

STC number	Author or Subject heading	Short title of work	Date	Translator
18214	Moulton, T.	The myrrour or Glasse of Helth...	[1539?]	T. Moulton
18244	Muenster, S.	Treatyse of the newe India...	1553	R. Eden
13210	Musculus, W.	A godly treatyse of matrimonye (part of The right institucion of baptisme)	1550	R. Ryce
18310	do.	Of the lawful and vnlawful vsurie amõgest christians	[1556]	T.L.
18312	do.	The temporysour...	1555	R.P.
18403	Natura Brevium	Natura brevium newly corrected in Englisshe	1532	—
18528	Nicholas, Saint	Saynt Nycholas of Tollentyne	[1525?]	—
18565	Nicodemus	The treatys of Nychodemus gospell	1507	—
18694	Nostradamus, M.	An excellent treatise...	1559	—
18764	Ochino, B.	Sermons	1548	R. Argentine
18766	do.	Certayne sermons	[1550?]	R. Argentine & A. Cooke
18767	do.	Fouretene sermons concernyng the predestinacion and eleccion of God	[1550?]	A. Cooke
18770	do.	A tragoedie or dialoge of the uniuste primacie of the Bishop of Rome	1549	J. Ponet
12511	Ockham, William of	A dialogue betwene a knight and a clerke	[1531?]	J. Trevisa
18779	Octavian, Emperor	Octauyan, the Emperoure of Rome	[1558?]	—
18787	Œcolampadius, J.	A sarmon to yong men and maydens	[1548?]	J. Fox
18808	Oliver, of Castile	[Oliver of Castille]	1518	H. Watson
—	Order	The order of chivalry, see Lull, R.		
18841	do.	The order of matrimony	[1548]	A. Scoloker
18849	Original	The original and sprynge of all sectes...	1537	—
18877	Osiander, A.	The coniectures of the ende of the worlde	1548	G. Joye

STC number	Author or Subject heading	Short title of work	Date	Translator
18878	Osiander, A.	How and whither a christen man ought to flye the horrible plage of the pestilence	1537	M. Coverdale
18934	Ovidus Naso, P.	The flores of Ovide de arte amandi...	1513	—
18970	do.	The fable of Ovid treting of Narcissus	1560	T. Howell
19119	Pain	The payne and sorowe of euyll maryage	[1509?]	—
19148	Palingenius, M.	The first thre bokes of the zodyake of lyfe	1560	B. Googe
19206	Paris, le chevalier	[Paris and Vienne]	1485	W. Caxton
19211	Parker, H.	Exposition and declaration of the psalme Deus ultionum dominus	1539	H. Parker
19305	Parliament	The parlyament of deuylles	1509	—
	Paul III, *Pope. See* Esquillus, P.			
19494	Paynell, T.	The piththy and moost notable sayinges of al Scripture	1550	T. Paynell
19525	Pedersen, C.	The richt way to the kingdome of heuine...	1533	J. Gau
19795	Peter, of Luxemburg, *St.*	The next way to heuen	[1510?]	—
19811	Petrarch, F.	The tryumphes of F. Petracke [*c.* 1553?] with (Vyrgyll in his epigrames of Cupide and Dronkenesse)		H. Parker
19812	Petronilla	[Petronilla]	[n.d.]	J. Lydgate
19848	Philippson, J.	A famouse cronicle of oure time [i.e. Sleidanes Commentaries]	1560	J. Daus
19898	Pico della Mirandola, G. F.	The lyfe of J. Picus...	[1510?]	Sir T. More
6157	do.	The rules of a Christian lyfe	1534	Sir T. Elyot
19902	Pierius, J.	A treatise...'pro sacerdotum barbis'	1533	—
19918	Pilgrimage	Book of the pylgrymage of man	[1525?]	—

STC number	Author or Subject heading	Short title of work	Date	Translator
19926	Pilkington, J.	Aggeus the prophete. . .	1560	—
	Pius II, *Pope, see* Lucretia, of Siena			
20034	Ploughman	How the plowman lerned his pater noster	[n.d.]	—
20052	Plutarch	Howe one may take profite of his enmyes	[1533?]	Sir T. Elyot?
20057	do.	The education or bringinge up of children	[1535?]	Sir T. Elyot
20058.1	do.	Quyete of Mynde	[1528]	Sir T. Wyatt
20061	do.	The gouernaūce of good helthe, Erasmus beynge interpretoure	[1530?]	
20062	do.	The preceptes of Plutarch for the preseruation of good healthe	1543	J. Hales
20064	do.	Three morall treatises	1558	T. Blundeville
20073	do.	Practica Plutarche. . .	[1530?]	—
20087	Pole, R., Cardinal	The seditious oration of Cardinal Pole	[1560]	F. Wythers
20107	Ponthus	[The noble history of King Ponthus]	[1501?]	H. Watson
20116	Porcia, J. di	Preceptes of warre	1544	P. Betham
20120	Porteous	Porteous of noblenes	1508	A. Cadiou
20195	Prayers	[Fifteen Oes]	[1491]	—
20196	do.	The xv. Oos in Englysshe with other prayers	1529	—
20200	do.	Praiers of holi Fathers	[1540?]	—
20398.1	Proclus, D.	Sphaera	[n.d.]	T. Linacre
20399	do.	The descripcion of the sphere	[1550]	W. Salisbury
20412	Profits	The xii. profytes of trybulacyon	[1499]	W. Caxton
20480	Ptolemy, C.	The compost of Ptholomeus	[1532?]	R. Copland
4854	Publilius Syrus	Wyse saiynges. . .of Puplius (*sic*) corrected and interpreted by D. Erasmus	1553	R. Burrant
	Pylgremage of the sowle, *see* Deguileville, G. de			
20524	Pythagoras	A brefe and plesaunte worke of Pictagoras	[1560?]	—

STC number	Author or Subject heading	Short title of work	Date	Translator
3507	Radegunde, Saint	The lyfe of saynt Radegunde	[1521?]	H. Bradshaw
0701	Rastell, J.	[Exposiciones terminorum legum Anglorum]	[1525?]	J. Rastell
0749	Ratramnus	The boke of Barthram... intreatinge of the bodye and bloude of Christ	1548	Sir H. Lynde
0795	Reckoning	The iust reckenyng of the whole nomber of the yeares, from the beginnyng of the worlde	1547	A. Scoloker
840	Regius, U.	A cōparison betwene the olde learnynge & the newe	1537	W. Turner
843	do.	A declaration of the twelve articles of the christen faythe	1548	W. Lynne
982	do.	A godly sermon...upon the ix. Chapter of Mathewe, (with A frutefull... exposition of the kyngdom of God)	1548	W. Lynne
847	do.	An instruccyon of christen fayth howe to be bolde vpon the promyse of God	[1550?]	J. Fox
849	do.	A lytle treatise after the maner of an epystle	1548	W. Lynne?
82	Remorse	The remors of conscyence	[1500?]	—
19	Reynard the Fox	Reynart the foxe	[1481]	W. Caxton
65	Rivius, J.	A treatise against the foolishnesse of men...	[1550?]	J. Banks
70	Robert, the Devil	The lyf of Robert the deuyll	[1502?]	—
	Robert of Shrewsbury, see The lyfe of saynt Winefryde			
3	Roesslin, E.	The byrth of mankynde	1540	R. Jonas
	Romaunt de la Rose, see Chaucer, Works, 1532			
6.1	Romans	Gesta Romanorum	1517	—
7	do.	The hystorye of Gesta Romanorum	1557	—
7	Rome	[Seven wise masters of Rome]	[1493]	—
8	do.	The sum of the actes and decrees made by dyuerse bysshops of rome	[1539?]	—

STC number	Author or Subject heading	Short title of work	Date	Translator
21318	Rosary	The mystik sweet rosary of the faythful soule	1533	—
21318.1	do.	The Rosary (part of Horae ad usum Sarum. Paris)	1530	—
21334	Rote	The Rote or myrour of consolacyon & conforte	[1496]	—
21427	Roy, W.	Rede me and be nott wrothe	[1528]	W. Roy
21429	Royal Book	[The Royal Book]	[1486]	W. Caxton
21431	Roye, G. de	The doctrinal of sapyence	1489	W. Caxton
21472	Ryckes, J.	The ymage of loue	[1532?]	J. Gough
21561	Saint German, C.	A dyaloge...betwyxt a doctoure of dyuynyte and a student in the lawes of Englande	[1530]	—
21596	Salerno	Schola Salernitana. Regimen Sanitatis Salerni...	1528	T. Paynell
21626	Sallustus Crispus, C.	The warre...agaynst Iugurth	[1520?]	A. Barclay
21629	Salomon, the Jew	A wounderfull prophecie...	1543	—
21740	San Pedro, D. de	The castell of love	[1540?]	J. Bourchier
21753	Sarcerius, E.	Common places of scripture...	1538	R. Taverner
15986	Savonarola, G.	An exposicyon upon the LI psalme...(part of Prayers of the Byble)	[1535]	—
15986	do.	A meditacyon upon the psalme of In te domine speravi (part of Prayers of the Byble)	[1535]	—
21807	Scarperia	Heuy newes of an horryble earthquake in Scharbaria	[1542]	—
22153	Seeing	The seynge of uryns	1525	—
22216	Seneca, L. A.	De remediis fortuitorum. Dialogus inter sensum et rationem	1547	R. Whittinton
22226	do.	Thyestes	1560	J. Heywood
22227	do.	Troas	1559	J. Heywood

STC number	Author or Subject heading	Short title of work	Date	Translator
22238	Sermon	A sermon declaringe how vue ar iustified by faith	[1549?]	E.T.
3305	Seven Points	The Seuen Poyntes of trewe love	1491	W. Caxton?
7664	Severus, A.	The image of gouernance	1541	Sir T. Elyot
22367	Shape	[The wonderful shape and natures of man]	[1527?]	L. Andrewe
22407	Shepherds' Kalendar	The kalendayr of the shyppars	1503	A. Barclay?
22408	do.	The Kalender of shepherdes	1506	—
22409	do.	The kalender of shepeherdes	1508	R. Copland
22899	Solomon, King	The sayinges or prouerbes...	[1530?]	—
2905	do.	The dyalogus...betwxt Salomon and Marcolphus	[1492]	—
2992	Spagnuoli, B.	A lamentable complaynte of Baptista Mātuanus	[1560?]	J. Bale
3004	Spangenberg, J.	The sum of diuinitie...	1548	R. Hutten
3407	Sturmius, J.	The epistle...sent to the Cardynalles and Prelates	1538	Sir R. Morison
7030	Sulpitius, J.	Stans puer ad mensam	[n.d.]	J. Lydgate
3552	Swinnerton, T.	A mustre of scismatyke bysshoppes of Rome	1534	J. Roberts
3553	Switzerland	The confescion of the fayth of the Sweserlādes	[1548]	G. Ussher
3574.1	Sylvester, B.	The cure & governaunce of a housholde	[n.d.]	—
3710	Taverner, R.	An epitome of the psalmes...	1539	R. Taverner
711	do.	The Garden of Wysdom	1539	R. Taverner
713	do.	The second booke of the Garden of Wysedome	1539	R. Taverner
935	Ten Commandments	[The Ten Commandments] part of Hore beate Marie	1523?	—
876	do.	The floure of the commaundementes of god	1510	A. Chertsey
884ᵃ	Tenures	The tenours and fourme of indentures	[1541?]	—
394	Terentius, P.	Terens in englysh	[1520?]	J. Rastell?
399	do.	Floures for Latine spekynge	1533	N. Udall

STC number	Author or Subject heading	Short title of work	Date	Translator
23904	Terentius, P.	Vulgaria quedam abs Terencio in Anglicā linguam traducta	[1483]	J. Anwykyll
23916	Tertullian, Q.	The seconde booke of Tertullian. [Ad uxorem]	1550	J. Hooper
	Thibault, J., see Almanacks, Kalendars and Prognostications			
23954	Thomas, à Becket, Saint	The lyfe of the blessed martyr Saynte Thomas	[1520?]	A. Barclay?
23955	Thomas, à Kempis	The Imytacion and followynge...of Criste	1503, 04	W. Atkinson and Margaret, Countess of Richmond
23961	do.	do.	[1531?]	R. Whitford
23962	do.	The fourth boke of the folowynge of Chryste	[1532?]	—
24056	Thucydides	The hystory...	1550	T. Nicolls
6826	Tignonville, G. de	The dictes or sayengis of the philosophres	1477	A. Woodville
24112	Tommai, P.	The art of memory	1548	R. Copland
24133	Torent, of Portyngale	[Torente of Portyngale]	[1509?]	—
24217	Treatise	A frutefull treatis of baptyme and the Lordis souper...	1541	—
24218	do.	A goodly treatise of faith, hope and charite	1537	—
24219	do.	A godleye and learned treatise wherin is proued the true justificacion of a christian manne	[1555?]	—
24222	do.	A lytel treatyse of the xv. tokens	[1505?]	J. van Doesborc
24222.1	do.	A lytell necessarye treatyse... of the estate of the Comonalte...	[n.d.]	—
24223	do.	The knight of Curtsey and the lady of Faguell	[n.d.]	—
24224	do.	How every man & woman ought to fast on ye Wednesday	[1500]	—
24226	do.	A moche profitable treatise against the pestilence	[1534?]	T. Paynell

STC number	Author or Subject heading	Short title of work	Date	Translator
24228	Treatise	A newe treatyse deuyded in thre parties	[1550?]	T. Paynell
24234	do.	[This treatyse is of loue...]	[1493]	—
24238	do.	A treatise declaryng...that pyctures...are in no wise to be suffred in churches	[1535]	—
24250	do.	A treatyse to teche a mā to dye and not to feare dethe	[1538?]	—
24266	Trent	Newes concernynge the general coūcell holden at Trydent	[1549]	J. Hollybush (H. van Ruremonde)
24267	Trental	This trental is wryten in latyn, frenche and in englysshe	[1515?]	—
21308.1	Triades	The Triades or Trinites of Rome	[n.d.]	—
4302	Tryamour	Sir Tryamour	[n.d.]	—
4318	Tunstall, C.	Certaine godly and deuout prayers	1558	T. Paynell
3305	Twelve Profits	The XII. profits of tribulation	1491	W. Caxton
4462	Tyndale, W.	A pathway to the holy scripture	[153-]	W. Tyndale
4514	Ulric, Saint	An epistle of moche learnīg	[1537?]	Edmund Hatfield
4540.1	Ursula	The lyf of saynt Ursula	[n.d.]	Edmund Hatfield
4571.1	Valentine	Valentine and Orson	[1502?]	H. Watson
4591	Valuation	The valuacyō of golde and sylver	[1520?]	L. Andrewe
4595	Vasseus, J.	The iugemēt of vrynes	1553	H. Lloyd
4654	Vergilius, P.	An abridgement of... P. Vergile	1546	T. Langley
4665	Vermigli, P. M.	A discourse concerning the Sacrament of the Lordes supper...	[1550?]	N. Udall
4666	do.	An epistle unto the Duke of Somerset	1550	T. Norton
246	do.	A treatise of the cohabitacyon of the faithfull with the vnfaithfull	1555	—

317

STC number	Author or Subject heading	Short title of work	Date	Translator
24676	Veron, J.	Certayne litel treaties...	1548	—
24679	do.	The.V.abhominable blasphemies cōteined in the masse	1548	—
24682	do.	The godly saiyngs of the old auncient fathers...	1550	J. Veron
24720	Vigo, J. de	The most excellent workes of chirurgerye...	1543	B. Traheron
24724	do.	[The health of the body of man]	[1535?]	—
24747	Vincent of Lerins, *Saint*	A boke writtē by one Vincētius Lerinensis	1554	—
24748	do.	The golden treatise	[1559?]	A.P.
24754	do.	The waie home to Christ	1554	J. Proctor
24762	Vincentius, Bellovacensis	The myrrour of the worlde	[1481]	W. Caxton
24766	Vineis, R. de	[The lyf of saint Katherin of Senis]	[1493?]	—
24781	Viret, P.	A notable collection of places of the sacred scriptures	1548	A. Scoloker
24784	do.	A verie familiare exposition of the Apostles Crede	[1548]	P. Viret
24796	Virgilius Maro, P.	Eneydos	[1490?]	W. Caxton
24797	do.	The XIII bukes of Eneados	1553	G. Douglas
24798	do.	Certain bokes of Virgiles Æneis	1557	Henry, Earl of Surrey
24799	do.	The seuen first bookes of the Eneidos	1558	T. Phaer
24799.1	do.	The fourth boke of Virgill...	[1548?]	Henry, Earl of Surrey
24828	do.	The lyfe of Virgilius...	1518?	—
24847	Vives, J. L.	An introduction to wysedome	1540	Sir R. Morison
24855	do.	The office and duetie of an husband	[1553?]	T. Paynell
24856	do.	The instruction of a christen woman	[1529?]	R. Hyde
24865	Vocabulary	Vocabulary in French and English	[1480]	—

STC umber	Author or Subject heading	Short title of work	Date	Translator
873	Voragine, J. de	Legenda aurea	[1483]	W. Caxton
894	Vyllagon, Sir N.	A lamentable and piteous treatise...	1542	—
	Wallace, see Blair, J.			
007	Walter of Henley	Boke of husbandry	[c. 1510?]	R. Grosseteste?
009	Walther, R.	Antichrist	1556	J. Olde
127	Watt, J. von	Ye olde god & the newe	1534	W. Turner
506	Werburge, Saint	The holy lyfe...of saynt Werburge	1521	H. Bradshaw
249	Werdmueller, O.	The hope of the faythful	[1554?]	M. Coverdale
251	do.	How a Christen mā ought to behaue himselfe	[c. 1553]	M. Coverdale
255	do.	A spyrytuall and moost precyouse pearle	1550	M. Coverdale
20	Whitforde, R.	Dyuers holy instrucyons...	1541	R. Whitford
53	Winifred, Saint	The lyfe of saynt Wenefryde	[1485]	W. Caxton
66	Xenophon	The discipline, schole and education of Cyrus	[1560?]	W. Barker
69	do.	Treatise of householde	1532	G. Hervet
19	Ypres	The forme and maner of subuētion for pore people practysed in Hypres	1535	W. Marshall
35	Zwingli, U.	A briefe rehersal of the death of Christ	[1560?]	—
36	do.	Certeyne preceptes	1548	R. Argentine
36.1	do.	The detection of ye blasphemies for errours...	1548	T. Dorset
38	do.	The rekening...of the faith of H. Zwingly	1543	—
40	do.	The accompt, rekenynge... of the faith of H. Zwinglius	1555	T. Cotsforde
1	do.	A short pathwaye...	1550	J. Veron
2	do.	The ymage of bothe pastoures	1550	J. Veron

BIBLIOGRAPHY

Acts of the Privy Council of England, see DASENT, J. R.

ADAMSON, J. W. '*The Illiterate Anglo-Saxon' and other Essays* (Cambridge, 1946).

AMES, J. *Typographical Antiquities: being an historical account of Printing in England* (1749). *See also* DIBDIN, HERBERT.

ARBER, E. *A transcript of the Registers of the Company of Stationers of London: 1554–1640.* 5 vols. (Birmingham, 1875–94).

BAUMER, F. LE VAN. *The Early Tudor Theory of Kingship* (New Haven, 1940).

BLADES, W. *The biography and typography of William Caxton.* 1877; revised 1882.

BOSANQUET, E. F. *English Printed Almanacks and Prognostications: A Bibliographical History to the year 1600.* The Bibliographical Society (Oxford, 1917).

BOSANQUET, E. F. 'Corrigenda and Addenda.' *The Library*, Fourth Series, VIII, (1928), pp. 456–77.

BRADSHAW, H. *Collected papers* (Cambridge, 1889).

BRITISH MUSEUM. *Catalogue of books in the library of the British Museum printed in England, Scotland, and Ireland, and of books in English printed abroad, to the year 1640.* 3 vols. (1884).

CAXTON, WILLIAM, *see* CROTCH, W. J. B.

CONLEY, C. H. *The First English Translators of the Classics* (New Haven, 1927).

COWLEY, J. D. *A Bibliography of Abridgments, Digests, Dictionaries and Indexes of English law...to 1880.* Selden Society (1932).

CROTCH, W. J. B. *The Prologues and Epilogues of William Caxton.* Early English Text Society. Original Series, 176 (1928).

DARLOW, T. H. & MOULE, H. F. *Historical Catalogue of the printed editions of Holy Scripture.* 4 vols. (1903–11).

DIBDIN, T. F. *Typographical Antiquities. Begun by Joseph Ames, augmented by William Herbert.* 4 vols. (1810–19). *See also* AMES, J. & HERBERT, W.

DIBDIN, T. F. *Typographical Antiquities. Begun by Joseph Ames, augmented by William Herbert.* 4 vols. (1810–19). *See also* AMES, HERBERT.

DUFF, E. GORDON. *A Century of the English Book Trade...from the issue of the first dated book in 1457 to the incorporation of the Company of Stationers in 1557* (1905).

DUFF, E. GORDON. *The English Provincial Printers, Stationers and Bookbinders to 1557* (Cambridge, 1912).

DUFF, E. GORDON, *Fifteenth Century English Books*, The Bibliographical Society (Oxford, 1917).

DUFF, E. GORDON. *The printers, stationers and book binders of Westminster and London from 1476 to 1535* (Cambridge, 1906).

BIBLIOGRAPHY

EVANS, J. 'Extracts from the Private Account-Book of Sir W. More.' *Archaeologia*, vol. XXXVI (1855), pp. 284–92.

FOXE, J. *Actes and Monuments* (The book of martyrs), ed. J. Pratt. 8 vols. (1877).

GRAY, G. J. *The earlier Cambridge stationers and bookbinders and the first Cambridge printer*. The Bibliographical Society (Oxford, 1904).

GREG, W. W. *A Bibliography of the English Printed Drama to the Restoration*. The Bibliographical Society. Vol. I (Oxford, 1939).

Hand-lists of English Printers, 1501–56. Parts I–IV, ed. by E. GORDON DUFF et al. The Bibliographical Society (1895–1913).

HERBERT, W. *Typographical Antiquities. Begun by Joseph Ames*. 3 vols. 1785–90. See also AMES, J. & DIBDIN, T. F.

HODNETT, E. *English Woodcuts, 1480–1535*. 2 vols. The Bibliographical Society (Oxford, 1935).

ISAAC, F. S. *English and Scottish Printing Types, 1535–58* (Oxford, 1932).

KINGDON, J. A. *Incidents in the lives of T. Poyntz and R. Grafton* (1895).

KINGDOM, J. A. *Incidents in the lives of T. Poyns and R. Grafton* (1895).

KINGSFORD, C. L. *Prejudice and Promise in Fifteenth Century England* (Oxford, 1925).

LAMBLEY, K. *The teaching and cultivation of the French language in England during Tudor and Stuart times* (Manchester, 1920).

LATHROP, H. B. *Translations from the Classics into English from Caxton to Chapman, 1477–1620* (Madison, 1933).

Letters and Papers of Henry VIII, ed. J. S. BREWER & J. GAIRDNER. 21 vols. in 34 (1862–1910).

McKERROW, R. B. *An Introduction to Bibliography* (Oxford, 1927).

McKERROW, R. B. *Printers' and Publishers' Devices in England and Scotland, 1485–1640*. The Bibliographical Society (Oxford, 1913).

McKERROW, R. B. & FERGUSON, F. S. *Title-Page Borders used in England and Scotland, 1485–1640*. The Bibliographical Society (Oxford, 1932). For additional material, see *The Library*, Fourth Series, XVII (1936), pp. 264–311.

MADAN, F. 'The Day-book of John Dorne'. Oxford Historical Society, *Collectanea*, I (Oxford, 1885).

MAITLAND, S. R. *Early Printed Books...at Lambeth* (1843).

MOULE, H. F., see DARLOW, T. H.

PALMER, H. R. *List of English editions and translations of Greek and Latin classics printed before 1641*. The Bibliographical Society (Oxford, 1911).

PLOMER, H. R. *Robert Wyer, Printer and Bookseller*. The Bibliographical Society (1897).

PLOMER, H. R. *Wynkyn de Worde and his Contemporaries...to 1535* (1925).

POLLARD, A. W. *Records of the English Bible* (Oxford, 1911).

POLLARD, A. W. & REDGRAVE, G. R. et al. *A Short-title Catalogue of Books printed in England, Scotland, & Ireland and of English Books printed Abroad, 1475–1640*. The Bibliographical Society (Oxford, 1926; reprinted 1946).

REED, A. W. *Early Tudor Drama* (1926).

SAYLE, C. E. *Early English printed books in the University Library, Cambridge.* 4 vols. (Cambridge, 1900–7).

SHAABER, M. A. *Some forerunners of the newspaper in England, 1476–1622* (Philadelphia, 1929).

Short-title Catalogue, see POLLARD, A. W.

SIMPSON, P. *Proof-Reading in the Sixteenth, Seventeenth and Eighteenth Centuries* (Oxford, 1935).

STEELE, R. *A Bibliography of Royal Tudor and Stuart Proclamations, 1485–1714.* Bibliotheca Lindesiana. 2 vols. (Oxford, 1910).

WORMAN, E. J. *Alien members of the book-trade during the Tudor period.* The Bibliographical Society (Oxford, 1906).

ZEEVELD, W. G. *Foundations of Tudor Policy* (Harvard, 1948).

GENERAL INDEX

ABC, 22, 24, 26, 39
Abell, Thomas, 139
Actors, Peter, printer, 'stationer to the King', 23, 38
Adamson, J. W., 'Literacy in England in the Fifteenth and Sixteenth Centuries', quoted, 19, 20
Ad imprimendum solum, 36, 36 n. 3
Aeschylus, 157
Aix-la-Chapelle, John of, 23
Alcock, John, Bp., 47
Alexander de Villa Dei, 86
Allde, Edward, printer, 229
Almanacks, printed, 120, 273-80
Anatomy, works on, 108
Andrewe, Laurence, printer and translator, 99, 165
Anslay, Brian, translator, 41, 61
Antwerp, printing at, 34, 35, 74, 121, 165, 185, 210, 220
Anwykyll, John, 86
'Appolonius of Tyre', 162, 191
Aragon, Queen Catherine of, 137
Arber, E., *A transcript of the Registers of the Company of Stationers of London, 1545–1640*, 228
Aristotle, supposititious works of, 117
Arithmetic, books on, 113, 114, 115
Arnold, de Villa Nova, 103 n. 4
Arnold, Richard, 126
'Arnold's Chronicle', xiii, 121, 126
Arthur, Prince of Wales, 137
Arundel, Henry Fitzalan, 12th earl of, 59
Ascham, Anthony, 118
Ashton, Peter, translator, 136, 175
Astronomy, books on, 110, 116–18, 205
Atkinson, William, translator, 164
Audley, Sir Thomas, 174

Authors
  ecclesiastical, 3
  economic security of, 3
  mock-modesty of, 55
  part-time, 6

Baldwin, William, printer, 48, 220
Bale, John, Bp., 34 n. 3, 36, 50, 150, 217, 219
Ballads, 150, 151, 194
'Bankes' Herbal', 98, 98 n. 3, 100
Bankes, John, 61, 171
Bankes, Richard, printer, 103, 195, 210, 218
Barclay, Alexander, translator, xiv, 45, 94, 132, 148, 169, 192, 218
  Fifth Eclogue, price of, 233
Barnes, Robert, 36
Barnwell Fair, 24
Bartholomew the Englishman, 11, 110, 116, 183, 216 n. 2
  De proprietatibus rerum, 11
Barton, Elizabeth, 'the Maid of Kent', 227
Batman, Stephen, Bp., 110
Beauchamp, Edward, Earl of Hertford, 48
Becon, Thomas, 36, 47, 48, 72, 136 n. 2
Berners, Lord (John Bourchier), 132
Berthelet, Thomas, 'printer to the King', 34, 38, 41, 81, 84, 103, 110, 111, 129, 139, 140, 141, 153, 164, 165, 180, 196, 199, 200, 204, 211, 224, 230, 234
Betham, Peter, translator, 174
Bible, 26, 32, 35, 75
  'Great Bible', 35
  'Matthew's Bible', 34, 221 n. 1, 225
  New Testament, 26, 34, 75
  price of, 230, 233

Birckman, Francis, stationer, 225
Blundeville, Thomas, 112
Bocking, Edward, 227
Bodrugan, Nicholas, 144
Boethius, 157
Bokenham, Osbern, 3, 8
Boleyn, Anne, 138
Bonde, William, 57
Bone, Gavin, 199 n. 1
Bonham, William, stationer, 147, 236
Book of Common Prayer, The, 208, 230
    price of, 230
Book-fairs at Barnwell, 24; at Frankfort, 23
Books
    colophons, 209–11; careless, 211; false, 209–10
    composition, speed of, 207–8
    copy, difficulties over, 201–7
    demand for, 54–64, 192, 194
    distribution of, 20
    editions, errors in, 221–2; new, 77–8, 222; size of, 224–8
    educational, 85–97
    'fill-ups' in, 208–9
    foreign printed, 84, 85, 193
    format of, 20, 224
    heretical, 33–6
    historical, 123–34
    importation of, 31, 32, 65, 182, 184
    legal, 76–85
    market for, 41
    medical, 97–109
    as 'New-Year gifts', 48, 49
    output of, 29, 194
    polemical, 71
    'preliminaries' of, 211
    prices of, 229–34
    prohibited, 36, 37, 74
    proof-sheets of, 215–16
    as propaganda, 70–4, 141, 193
    religious, 65–76, 155–6
    survival of, 20, 182–3
    title-pages of, 211–14
    variety of, 65–151
    woodcuts in, 215

Booksellers
    agents of, 23, 24
    provincial, 21, 30
    talks with, an encouragement to translators, 42–3, 59
    warned against sale of heretical books, 33, 37
Book-trade
    aliens and, 30–2
    regulation of, 30–9
Borde, Andrew, 104, 118, 120, 205
Bosanquet, E. F., *English Printed Almanacks and Prognostications,* 118 n 7, 119
Bourman, Nicholas, printer, 114, 145
Bradford, John, 209
Brandt, Sebastian, *Shyppe of Fooles,* 43, 148, 161, 192, 218
Brende, John, translator, 60, 134, 168
Britton, John, Bp., 85, 201
Broadsides, 135
Bruges, printing at, 11, 12'
Brut, The, 9, 125, 126, 128
Bryce, Hugh, 16
Bühler, Curt, 216
Bullein, William, 219
Bullinger, Heinrich, 166
Burgundy, Margaret, Duchess of, 10

Caesar, Julius, *Commentaryes,* 127, 157
Calvin, John, works of, translated, 57 n. 2, 169
Cambridge, 85
    Barnwell Fair, 24
    booksellers at, 23
    Corpus Christi College, 2
    printing at, 21, 23 n. 2, 108
Canterbury, printing at, 21, 131–2, 237
Canutus, Bp., 97
Capgrave, John, 3, 74
Carion, John, xiii, 63
Carmelianus, Petrus, 137
Carols, 26
Catechism, The, 39
Catiline, Lucius, 133

INDEX OF PASSAGES

The following is a list of books from which passages have been quoted in extenso.